JOSHUA

BERIT OLAM
Studies in Hebrew Narrative & Poetry

Joshua

L. Daniel Hawk

David W. Cotter, O.S.B.
Editor

Jerome T. Walsh
Chris Franke
Associate Editors

A Michael Glazier Book
THE LITURGICAL PRESS
Collegeville, Minnesota

www.litpress.org

A Michael Glazier Book published by The Liturgical Press

Cover design by Ann Blattner

1	2	3	4	5	6	7	8

Library of Congress Cataloging-in-Publication Data

Hawk, L. Daniel (Lewis Daniel), 1955–
   Joshua / L. Daniel Hawk.
      p.   cm. — (Berit Olam)
   "A Michael Glazier book."
   Includes bibliographical references and index.
   ISBN 0-8146-5042-2 (alk. paper)
      1. Bible. O.T. Joshua—Criticism, interpretation, etc.   I. Title.
II. Series.

BS1295.2.H35   2000
222'.206—dc21

                                                                    00-040555

To my parents, Lewis and Barbara Hawk
from whom I learned both faith and tolerance

CONTENTS

Charts

ACKNOWLEDGMENTS

My reading of Joshua owes much to the influence of two mentors whose teaching, by word and example, has shaped the way I read the biblical text. I wish to begin this work, therefore, by acknowledging, with gratitude, my long-standing indebtedness to them. During my seminary experience, Dr. Robert Lyon challenged me to consider how profoundly issues of power and violence are addressed by Scripture and expressed through interpretation. At the doctoral level, my dissertation on Joshua was written under the direction of Dr. David M. Gunn, who gave unselfishly of his time and ideas and whose insights and questions opened up a way of reading that introduced me to new possibilities for understanding Scripture and its relevance for our world. With the passage of time, I appreciate even more fully the extent to which their encouragement and commitment have enriched my personal and scholarly development.

In a more immediate sense, I wish to thank Dr. Fred Finks and the trustees and administration of Ashland Theological Seminary and Ashland University for granting me the sabbatical leave during which most of this book was written, and for a generous financial grant that allowed me, along with my family, to spend the summer of 1999 at Tyndale House, Cambridge. My thanks extend as well to the staff at Tyndale House, who made our stay both enjoyable and profitable, and especially to Dr. David Instone Brewer, who helped me negotiate some particularly thorny technology problems. I am also grateful to Dr. David Cotter, who provided stimulating feedback and valuable encouragement during the process of writing. Finally, I wish to express my appreciation to my wife Linda, and my sons Daniel and Andrew, for their patience at those times when I seemed preoccupied with matters other than family.

L. Daniel Hawk
December 28, 1999

INTRODUCTION

Joshua is a book about boundaries. It opens with an announcement that signals the end of an era (the death of Moses), a description of the borders that define the Promised Land, and a command to cross a geographical boundary (the Jordan) into a new and fulfilling life with God (1:1-5). The subsequent narrative devotes a great deal of attention to crossing this boundary (3:1–4:24) and later, when the nation has succeeded in subduing the kings of Canaan, an even greater block of text presents an elaborate description of the boundaries which delineate tribal lands (13:1–21:45). As the story nears its conclusion a squabble about the boundary-status of the Jordan threatens to divide the people of God (22:1-34). Corresponding to these geographical boundaries are others which circumscribe behavior and separate Israel from other peoples. Strict obedience to the law of Moses, also introduced in the book's opening, situates both disposition and action within narrow parameters that prohibit turning either "to the right hand or to the left" (1:7). Throughout the story the narrator meticulously documents Israel's obedient faithfulness to God, Joshua, and the law of Moses by recording its prompt execution of command and corroborates it with comments that Joshua and the nation remain faithful to obligations to live within the sphere of divine commandments (8:35; 11:15; 22:1-6). Separation from other nations, emphatically prescribed by the law of Moses (e.g. Deut 7:1-6), finds vigorous expression in the extermination of entire populations and is punctuated by the stern admonitions of Joshua (23:12-16). The impulse to fix and maintain these boundaries drives the story from start to conclusion, interweaving themes of land, behavior, and ethnicity into an intricate tapestry.

The prominence of boundaries as a narrative motif indicates that there is much more at work in this book than triumphal assertions of Israelite supremacy or validations of ancestral claims. Boundaries define and demarcate. They include and exclude. In essence, they function to differentiate what is inside from what is outside, rendering distinctive what is enclosed. As a metaphor they reveal a fundamental concern with issues of identity. What makes Israel unique? What differentiates it from all other nations? And how is a distinctive identity constructed and maintained? The various sets of boundaries elaborated in Joshua— those circumscribing land, behavior, and ethnicity—differentiate Israel from all other nations and offer an ostensible framework for constructing a sense of Israelite identity. Through the medium of narrative, the book depicts Israel as a nation that inhabits the land God promised to its ancestors, fulfills the commands of God given through Moses, and preserves ethnic integrity by avoiding contact with surrounding peoples and their gods.

The narrative itself relates a story that antagonizes modern sensibilities. Joshua may establish a sense of national identity, but seems to do so by linking this project with the attempted annihilation of native populations and the occupation of their land. More troubling still, it repeatedly implicates God in the wholesale slaughter of the indigenous inhabitants of the land. In this book, God takes the side of the invaders and fights for them as they struggle to take the land and exterminate those who populate it. The program is expressed through a simple scheme: God gives the land to the Israelites in faithfulness to promises made to their ancestors and ensures their success by directing and participating in their battles. God also insists that Israel will fulfill its destiny only to the extent that it eliminates non-Israelites from the land. The establishment of national identity is thus associated with a program of violence against other peoples, one that is sanctioned and sanctified by divine edict. What are contemporary readers to make of such a book? How can readers in an age saturated with ethnic violence find meaning in a story that seems to endorse brutality against others?

I want to suggest that Joshua holds a particular relevance for the contemporary reader precisely because it addresses issues that haunt the present age. Sadly, an air of the familiar hangs uneasily about these ancient stories of ethnic violence and religious fervor. Israel's campaign to drive out and exterminate the peoples of Canaan resounds in more recent stories of dispossession, colonization, and ethnic cleansing. The contents of the book therefore confront readers, and particularly readers of faith, with deeply disturbing questions, and perhaps for this reason Joshua has generally been neglected as a resource for theological reflection. Giving a place to Joshua, especially within those religious communities that accord it canonical status, may be a dangerous enterprise given the complicity of religious institutions with the violent exertion of power, both in the past and the present. The stories of conquest and occupation can all too easily be taken as paradigms for the legitimation of similar operations by those who believe that God is with them.

Yet something extraordinary happens in Joshua. Reports of failures to acquire cities and lands challenge the triumphal descriptions of conquests. The incorporation of native peoples into the larger Israelite community counters reports of mass slaughter. Tribes and clans spill over geographical boundaries. And stories of transgression and internal conflict counter the assertions of Israel's uniform obedience to God. Boundaries of territory, race, and practice are indeed strongly drawn at the surface of the narrative but are constantly subverted. By the time the book reaches its conclusion, other peoples still inhabit vast tracts of the promised land, some with concessions that allow them to remain permanently. There have been lapses in and modifications to the Mosaic torah. And encounters with pious Canaanites and rebellious Israelites have collapsed the notion that Israel is somehow different than or superior to the surrounding nations.

The book's focus on themes of land, religion, and ethnic separation, and the conflicted presentation of these themes, reveals a struggle to comprehend the meaning of Israel's past, particularly as it addresses the nation's self-understanding as the people of God. Joshua is concerned not only with preserving stories about Israel's occupation of the land, but also, in a more profound sense, with coming to terms with those stories. Somewhere within the course of a complex compositional history, stories, lists, and other materials were drawn together to present a sophisticated reflection on Israel's identity as a people. While scholars have discussed this process of composition at length, with general agreement that Joshua is fundamentally concerned with establishing a sense of national identity, relatively little attention has been devoted to the way the book constructs identity. The themes which configure Joshua, namely obedience to the commandments of Moses, possession of Canaan, and the extermination of the peoples of the land, express markers universally associated with the construction of national identity: religious practice, claims to land, and ethnic separation. How these themes are played out, and to what end, will constitute the focus of this reading. In essence, I will be concerned with two questions: 1) How does Joshua construct an identity for the people of God? and 2) What does Joshua hold to be the essential mark(s) of Israelite identity? Or, to put it another way, what distinguishes "Israel" from all other peoples?[1]

---

[1] The capacity of narrative to construct identity is beginning to receive attention within the scholarly community, and Joshua figures prominently in many of these

Making Sense

Narratives provide a common medium for articulating a sense of identity. Human beings generally tell stories to make sense of the world. By uniting and organizing disparate events and experiences we invest life with order and coherence and thus deny the nagging possibility that existence has a random and uncontrollable character. Driven by an innate impulse to find order in experience, we attribute significance to events by relating them to others and locating them within personal narratives which assure us that reality is indeed ordered and manageable, that life does in fact "make sense." We infuse our narratives with our own unique perspectives, values, and aspirations and rely on them to unite our past with our present and future. Constructing a coherent sense of the past is vital for negotiating a future that always confronts us with an element of uncertainty. Patterns discerned in past events provide paradigms that inform expectations and plans. Narratives thus provide comprehensive frameworks within which to fit all that life throws at us, and for this reason the construction and maintenance of a coherent personal narrative is essential for mental well-being.[2] When we can fit all the pieces together and establish relevant connections between events we speak of "having it all together." Conversely, when life ex-

---

discussions. One of the first and most significant of these is R. Polzin, *Moses and the Deuteronomist: A Literary Study of the Deuteronomistic History* (New York: Seabury, 1980). Polzin made the important observation that the book is driven by a deeper agenda than is apparent on the surface of the text (that is, the issue of interpreting Deuteronomy). In addition to Polzin's work, I have found the following works to be useful resources: T. J. Mullen, Jr., *Narrative History and Ethnic Boundaries: The Deuteronomistic Historian and the Creation of Israelite National Identity* (Atlanta: Scholars, 1993); L. L. Thompson, "The Jordan Crossing: Ṣidqôt Yahweh and World Building," *JBL* 100 (1981) 343–58; D. S. Jobling, "'The Jordan a Boundary': Transjordan in Israel's Ideological Geography," *The Sense of Biblical Narrative II*, JSOTSup 39 (Sheffield: JSOT, 1986), and L. Rowlett, "Inclusion, Exclusion, and Marginality in the Book of Joshua," *JSOT* 55 (1992) 15–23. The issue of ethnic difference, both in the text and in its subsequent interpretation are treated by D. M. Gunn, "Colonialism and the Vagaries of Scripture: Te Kooti in Canaan (A Story of Bible and Dispossession in Aotearoa/New Zealand)," *God in the Fray: A Tribute to Walter Brueggemann*, ed. Tod Linafelt and Timothy K. Beal (Minneapolis: Fortress, 1998) 127–42 and R. A. Warrior, "A Native American Perspective: Canaanites, Cowboys, and Indians," *Voices from the Margin: Interpreting the Bible in the Third World*, ed. R. S. Sugirtharajah, 2nd ed. (Maryknoll, N.Y.: Orbis, 1995) 277–85.

[2] See, for example, D. Spence, *Narrative Truth and Historical Truth: Meaning and Interpretation in Psychoanalysis* (New York: Norton, 1982).

ceeds our narrative constructs and we have a difficult time discerning connections and patterns, we may say that "life is falling apart."

In order to understand the structuring operations of narrative, it is useful to make a distinction between narrative and story. Put simply, we may think of story as the raw material of narrative. Story can be conceived as an ideal or abstract which assumes a particular form when it is narrated. In this sense, the story behind the biblical text of Joshua can be told in any number of ways and through a variety of media. My youngest son has a children's Bible that relates the story of the "battle of Jericho" in different and simpler terms than the biblical text, and the narratives recorded on the pages of these books differ from an animated version on videotape or the retelling of the story in sermonic form. Yet despite these differences in media and presentation, essentially the same story can be recognized in each.[3] There are even different "biblical" narratives of the battle of Jericho. The presentation of the same event (Joshua 6) in the Masoretic text differs markedly from that articulated by various renditions of the Septuagint. (The latter seems to derive from an early translation of the book into Greek, no longer extant, which is conventionally referred to as the Old Greek version.)[4] On another level, every English translation of Joshua 6 tells the story in different terms, and each therefore constitutes a distinct narration of the common story.

Because human beings perceive events with a consciousness of their location in time, narratives utilize time as a means of organizing, explaining, and evaluating experience. The construction of a narrative therefore involves a whole complex of decisions: where to start, where to end, what to include, how to present events, and how to connect them. These decisions are often unconscious and arbitrary. I can illustrate

---

[3] The distinction between *story* and *narrative* is overly simplistic and not without considerable complications. (For example, if one narrative rendering of a *story* omits or encapsulates an event that another emphasizes, are they both really telling the same story?) Nevertheless, I have found the distinction useful for heuristic purposes and thus retain it here. For more precise discussions of terminology and concepts, see S. Chatman, *Story and Discourse* (Ithaca, N.Y.: Cornell University, 1978); G. Genette, *Narrative Discourse* (Ithaca, N.Y.: Cornell University, 1980); and S. Rimmon-Kenan, *Narrative Fiction: Contemporary Poetics* (London: Methuen, 1983).

[4] The significant variations between the ancient Hebrew and Greek versions of the book have generated considerable discussion. A number of essays by A. G. Auld provide a good starting point for further study; *Joshua Retold: Synoptic Perspectives*, OTS (Edinburgh: T&T Clark, 1998) 7–57. R. D. Nelson also offers thorough descriptions and analyses of these differences throughout his commentary on Joshua; *Joshua*, OTL (Louisville: Westminster John Knox, 1997).

the process through an interchange that takes place frequently in my household. At the dinner table my wife Linda and I ask each other about our respective "days." I usually describe "my day" with a one word evaluation: good, bad, busy, etc. Elaboration then leads to the construction of a narrative in which I recount the events of the day in a manner that confirms and explains my evaluation. It might have been a "good" day because some singularly wonderful thing happened to me, or it might have been a "bad" day because I perceived a particular accumulation of things that seemed to go wrong. My perception of the day may in fact have very little to do with the events themselves, but rather with whether I got enough sleep the night before or enjoyed a good breakfast, or with the relative level of overall stress in my life or with the state of my relationships with those I love. Nevertheless, my perception of the day as a whole (as arbitrary as it may be) impacts a whole series of decisions that I make as I tell Linda about "my day" (a day distinguished from all other days I've experienced and from the "days" everyone else has experienced at the same time). As I engage in an overview of my day, I may include, omit, expand, or abbreviate events as I construct a framework which enables me to make sense of what I've experienced.

In a more deliberate and comprehensive fashion, something like this structuring operation underlies written narratives. Narratives both construct and persuade. They tell stories from a particular point of view and construct a sense of the world which encodes values, perspectives, and ideologies. And they seek to impress readers with the truthfulness of their constructions and of the beliefs which they express. To do so narratives employ an array of devices which link and configure the events of the story into a comprehensive whole. These devices suggest meanings that can be appreciated more profoundly as the reader follows the story from beginning to end.[5]

The book of Joshua employs a number of configuring devices. Some are common in modern literature, while others, although common in the Hebrew Bible, are not familiar to the contemporary reader. Repetition of vocabulary, grammatical structures, events, or images unites diverse events and signals their common import. For example, the repetition of the phrase "be strong and courageous" in the opening speech of the book implies that the zeal that is to characterize the pos-

---

[5] My own understanding of narrative has been influenced particularly by S. Crites, "The Narrative Quality of Experience," *JAAR* 39 (1971) 291–311; reprinted in *Why Narrative? Readings in Narrative Theology* (Grand Rapids: Eerdmans, 1989) and Paul Ricoeur, *Time and Narrative,* trans. Kathleen McLaughlin and David Pellauer, 3 vols. (Chicago: University of Chicago, 1984–8).

session of the promised land ought also to characterize the strict observance of the commands of Moses (1:6, 7, 9). The repetitive language which relates the capture of cities in the south of Canaan (10:28-38) renders a sense of continuity and emphatically communicates Joshua's unbridled success in subjugating the kings of Canaan. On a broader scale, a structural pattern which narrates the execution of a command by appropriating the language of the command itself occurs at many points throughout the book to signal Israel's obedience (e.g. 3:6; 4:1-9; 5:2-3; 6:3-14; 11:6-9). Repetition of figures within the narrative may constitute a leitmotif that points to deeper thematic significance. For example, the recurring images of stones, as monuments (4:1-9, 19-24; 24:25-27), altars (8:30-35; 22:10-12, 26-29), and grave cairns (7:26; 8:29; 10:27) implies a permanence that breaks through the time-boundedness of the story to emphasize the continuing significance of the associated event. Repetition can also be undertaken through more complex structures which render events in symmetrical patterns. Chiasm introduces a pattern and then reverses it, as in the tongue-twister "she slit the sheet; the sheet she slit." As in this example, the pattern and reversal may be articulated at the grammatical level and exhibit a simple structure. More elaborate chiasms link ends to the middle in order to emphasize the significance of the parts within the whole. Such a chiasm configures the tense interchange between an Israelite delegation from Canaan and the tribes which have settled in the Transjordan (22:10-34), illuminating the nature of the conflict and the means of its resolution. Repeated terms or constructions may also function as a frame or inclusio which encloses a particular event or utterance, providing a backdrop for appreciating the significance of the intervening material. A case in point is "the burning anger of the LORD" which encloses the story of Achan's transgression (7:1, 26), providing a frame within which the reader may understand the connection between the failed assault at Ai and Achan's theft. References to Shechem occur only at the beginning and end of the covenant ceremony which marks the final episode of the book, furnishing a scenic background rich with associations (24:1, 25). And references to the deaths of Israel's leaders frame the entire book, beginning with the death of Moses (1:1-2) and ending with the deaths of Joshua and Eleazar (24:29-30, 33). In a final variation on the use of patterned repetition, segments of Joshua employ a paratactic structure. Parataxis involves the alternation of parallel stories or texts, with little or no explicit connection made between them. The scheme suggests connections, but these remain implicit and thus engage the reader in the construction of meaning. The structure can be detected in 14:6–15:63, where brief narratives associated with Caleb alternate with the description of Judah's lands and cities, and more broadly in 2:1-24; 6:1–10:15, where anecdotes of individual encounters with Canaan alternate with battle narratives that report Israel's victories over the peoples of Canaan.

Joshua also makes heavy use of allusion to imbue events with a particular thematic texture. Allusion exploits the Hebrew Bible's intertextual dimension and involves telling a story in a way that evokes connections to another story or text. By implicitly recalling other stories or texts, through the appropriation of common language, structure, or figures, the narrator can invest an event with subtle yet powerful overtones. The story of Rahab and the spies (2:1-24), for example, appropriates the structure and vocabulary of the story of Sodom and Gomorrah (Gen 19:1-29). Through this allusion, the narrator injects an air of impropriety into the story, and by reversing character roles, skillfully transforms themes of deliverance and identity. The subsequent conquest of Jericho (6:1-27) contains allusions to legislation for the Jubilee Year (Lev 25:8-55), raising questions about ownership and transference of property. In a similar manner, the story of Achan's transgression alludes at many points to the Deuteronomic laws concerning apostasy (Deut 13:6-18), thus hinting that the story is a paradigm for issues of greater communal import than the theft of dedicated plunder.

The most distinctive feature of the book, however, is its employment of discontinuity. Abrupt shifts and contradictory assertions create an overall sense of uncertainty and openness. This often takes the form of temporal and geographical discontinuity, particularly during the pivotal episode in which Israel crosses the Jordan into the land promised to its ancestors (3:1–4:24). Although rendered elaborately, the account is anything but straightforward, doubling back and forth across the Jordan and abruptly recapitulating what has already been reported. In a related sense, contradictory reports and information give conflicting information about matters essential to the story. The narrator reports that Joshua took the entire land and gave it as an inheritance to Israel (11:21-23) and even provides a catalogue of defeated kings (12:9-24). Yet immediately following this catalogue the reader discovers that vast areas remain outside Israelite control (13:1-7). The descriptions of the tribal allotments to Judah and the Joseph tribes pointedly include reports that the tribes were not able to dispossess many of the indigenous inhabitants (15:63; 16:10; 17:14-18). However, the section concludes with the report that the LORD gave Israel the entire land and that none of Israel's enemies withstood them (21:43-45). On yet another level, the book employs a discontinuity of perspective, most notably through conflicting references to "the other side" of the Jordan. At times, the "other side" refers to the Transjordan (1:14, 15; 2:10; 7:7; 9:10; 12:1, 7; 13:8, 27, 32; 14:3; 17:5; 18:7; 20:8; 22:4, 7, 10) but at others it refers to the land west of the Jordan (5:1; 9:1; 22:7).

Shaping Characters

Joshua does not present the reader with well-developed characters. Only the title character and the LORD appear consistently throughout the narrative, and even then they do so only to serve the development of the plot. The two are introduced in tandem at the beginning of the book, where their words lay out the themes of the narrative and inaugurate the story. Joshua's name, "the LORD rescues," underscores a central motif of the book, that Israel's victories against the peoples of the land are accomplished only with the help of God. Yet it also has a slightly ironic quality. The verbal component of the name generally refers to help or deliverance from trouble and is frequently associated with divine aid or salvation, both as entreaty (1 Chr 16:35; Pss 3:7 [MT 8]; 12:1 [MT 2]; 106:47) and affirmation (Exod 14:30; Judg 2:18; 1 Sam 14:23; 2 Kgs 19:34; Ezek 34:22). The whole tenor of Joshua, however, suggests that Israel is not in grave peril. Indeed, if anyone in this book is in need of rescue, it is not Israel but the peoples of the land (as the stories of Rahab and the Gibeonites pointedly illustrate), for the LORD is with Israel to ensure their victory.[6]

Joshua himself represents a mediating presence between God and the nation. He relays divine directives and promises to the people (1:10-11; 3:9-13; 6:6, 16-17) and leads them so that these may be fulfilled (5:2-3; 7:14-18; 8:1-9, 27). He does the same with the commands of Moses (1:7-9), as the narrator explicitly notes (8:35; 11:15, 20, 23), and reiterates Moses' warnings to the nation's leaders as the story draws to its close (23:1-16). After the kings have been subdued, he oversees the allotment of lands to the tribes (13:1-7) and exhorts those who are slow to occupy them (18:1-10). On the other hand, Joshua intercedes on behalf of the nation (7:6-9) and, in his exemplary execution of the Mosaic commandments, represents the national ideal. Joshua serves as a model

---

[6] In contrast to the frequent repetition of the verb *yāšāʿ* ("save") throughout the book (within the name Joshua), the verb itself occurs only twice, both times on the lips of those of ambivalent status. The Gibeonites call on Joshua to save them from the coalition of kings arrayed against them (10:6), and the eastern tribes (accused of rebellion by "the Israelites") employ it to signify the power their kindred have in either precipitating or dissipating a internecine conflict (22:22). The former case illustrates the sense that Israel faces no real peril from the military might of the kings. When, in this case, the kings do arise as aggressors, they direct their fury toward one of the other peoples of the land and not Israel. Joshua then attacks the kings who have attacked Gibeon. Later, when the kings finally gather against Israel (11:4), Joshua again goes on the offensive, reinforced by divine promises (11:7), and prevails with apparent ease.

of the zeal called for by the Mosaic program for the possession of the land, epitomizing this zeal by personally killing enemy kings while repeating the exhortations the LORD initially directed to him (10:22-26). Throughout the book, Joshua is closely identified both with the LORD and with the people. Joshua's victories are at the same time both Israel's victories and the LORD's victories, so that it is enough simply to mention that Joshua took cities or subdued the land (10:28-42; 11:16-23). The final, climactic episode of the book explicitly articulates his mediating role in the narrative as he leads the nation in a ceremony of covenant-making (24:1-28). Here he both speaks God's words (vv. 2-13) and stands against the assembled nation (vv. 19-20). Yet he also models the response which all Israel is being called to make by declaring his choice to serve the LORD (vv. 14-15).

The LORD is the other dominant character of the book and is identified by this title in the NRSV and many other English translations. The title in fact translates the divine name YHWH and follows an ancient practice whereby the title stands as a substitute. (YHWH is not vocalized in the Hebrew Bible. Thus only the consonants are given here.) Since the Hebrew text renders God with this name, rather than by the substituted title, I will retain it from now on when referring to the character, except when quoting the NRSV. The narrative ostensibly aligns YHWH with conventionally patriarchal concerns (e.g. possession, organization, and legitimation of land, warfare, structures of authority) and national aspirations. YHWH initiates and directs most of the action in the book, beginning with an opening exhortation (1:2-9) and proceeding with continued involvement in Israel's affairs, either directly (through commands relayed through Joshua) or indirectly (through the commands of Moses, rituals of allotment, or recapitulations of YHWH's acts on behalf of Israel). Above all, YHWH is portrayed as one who gives. YHWH is the God who gives the land to Israel (1:2, 3, 6, 11; 2:9; 5:6; 9:24; 21:43; 23:13, 15, 16), gives Israel victory over its adversaries (6:2, 16; 8:7, 18; 10:8, 12; 11:6, 8), and assigns each tribe its place in the land.[7] The stories of Israel's victories over the kings of the land demonstrate YHWH's supremacy in the land and confirm that YHWH is not only faithful to the promises made to Israel's ancestors but also has the power to fulfill them. In another sense, these stories also reinforce the theme that the nation must act in complete accord with YHWH. YHWH's presence ensures that Israel will achieve the fulfillment of its

---

[7] The reference to the tent of meeting (18:1) and to Eleazar (19:51) indicate YHWH's involvement in the division of the land, which is carried out through the use of lots.

objectives (a point illustrated, in the negative, by Achan's transgression and the disastrous defeat at Ai [7:1-26]). Repeated language and structures emphasize that Israel exists as a people (and will continue to exist) only because of divine initiative and participation in its national life. Loyalty to YHWH brings success, identity, and coherence; disloyalty brings failure, disaster, and disintegration.

The remaining characters in Joshua exist more as types and metaphors. Priests appear at the intersection of geographical and temporal boundaries. They are most prominent in the story of the Jordan crossing, where they lead Israel to the Jordan and station themselves within it while the nation crosses (3:14–4:18). Afterward they lead the nation in a series of ritual processions around Jericho, as Israel prepares to engage in its first conflict with the powers of Canaan, and signal victory with trumpet blasts (6:1-16). After the victory at Ai they stand between the peoples assembled on Mounts Ebal and Gerizim. Eleazar the priest oversees the transition from conquest to occupation by joining Joshua in the division of the land (14:1; 19:51; 21:1). Later, his son Phinehas mediates a dispute between the tribes west and east of the Jordan, involving an altar constructed between them in the environs of the Jordan (22:13, 30-32). Throughout the book, then, priests represent a mediating and transforming presence and, in their role as bearers of the ark, the presence of God among the people.

The kings of Canaan, prominent in the first section of the book, represent the powers which Israel must overcome in order to possess the land. Their appearance at many points in the narrative illustrates how easily YHWH, Joshua, and Israel, when acting in concert, prevail against even the most intimidating obstacles. They are introduced through surrogates (the kings' men) when Israelites first enter the land (2:2-7) and are the vehicles through which the narrator builds tension and suspense. The kings become an increasingly powerful and aggressive threat as Israel takes the cities of the land. They lose heart when Israel crosses the Jordan (5:1) but gather to fight against Israel after Jericho and Ai fall (9:1). Assuming the role of aggressors, they direct their fury at Gibeon rather than Israel (10:1-5), finally confronting Israel in a massive show of force at the waters of Merom (11:1-9). Kings and their cities are linked by the rhetoric of the narrative and by the fates they share. (The king of Ai, for example, is buried under a heap of rubble, resembling the state of his ruined city [8:29].)[8] The execution of kings decisively demonstrates Israel's victory over the powers of Canaan

---

[8] References to "the city and its king" occur at many points in the first section of the book (8:1-2; 10:28, 29, 36, 39; 11:12).

(8:29; 10:22-27; 11:12), and the catalogue of kings and cities confirms
the assertions of comprehensive victory which conclude the accounts
of battles, presenting an impressive listing of defeated cities and kings.

The book offers a strikingly conflicted depiction of Israel. On the
corporate level we read of a nation united by its obedience to YHWH
and Joshua. All Israel crosses the Jordan at the direction of Joshua
(3:17), and the males who have crossed undergo circumcision in response to Joshua's command (5:2-7). The nation as a whole faithfully
follows Joshua's decrees in battle and achieves great victories as a result (6:1-25; 8:18-29; 10:6-15, 42-43; 11:10-14). All Israel assembles at
Mounts Ebal and Gerizim in obedience to the commands of Moses
(8:30-35) early in the book and comes together at roughly the same site
at the end to affirm its devotion to YHWH (24:1-28). However, stories
which narrow the scope and present Israel on a smaller scale, in terms
of individuals or groups, present us with a much different picture. Israelite spies agree to a pact with a Canaanite prostitute in order to
save their lives, even though such a pact is expressly forbidden by
Moses (2:8-14; cf. Deut 7:1-5). Pedigreed Achan steals and hides what
has been devoted to YHWH, bringing disaster upon the entire nation and
eventually upon himself and his family (7:1-26). Disguised Gibeonites
easily dupe Israelite leaders into making a forbidden covenant (9:14-
15). The tribe of Joseph complains of the chariots of iron which the
Canaanites possess (17:14-18). And the tribes which settle in Canaan
determine to make war against their kindred across the Jordan because the latter have constructed an altar at the Jordan (22:10-12). The
negative image of Israel presented by these vignettes counters that
presented by the united, obedient, and victorious Israel in the corporate sense.

A final set of characters comprises a diverse assortment of individuals and groups. All are united by two characteristics: an ambivalent
status and an energetic determination to secure a place in the land.
Rahab, the prostitute of Jericho, praises YHWH and wangles an agreement that spares her and her family from the fate suffered by the rest of
the inhabitants of the city (2:1-24). Though a Canaanite, she "has lived
in Israel ever since" (6:25). Likewise, Gibeonite emissaries concoct a
plan to ensure their survival and trick the Israelites into exempting
them from the fury of Israel (9:1-26). They too live among Israel "to
this day," at the center of Israel's communal life (9:27). Corresponding
to these outsiders who live "within Israel" are various Israelite insiders
of ambiguous status. Caleb, a chieftain of the tribe of Judah but of uncertain pedigree (a "Kenizzite"), vigorously demands cities occupied
by gigantic inhabitants of the land, even though he is well over eighty
(14:6-15). His daughter Achsah, along with the daughters of Zelophe-

had, confront us with examples of women who ask for and receive legitimate claims to land within a patriarchal system that parcels property out to males (15:13-19; 17:3-6). The Levites also seek and receive land, even though they, apart from all other tribes, cannot seek land as an "inheritance" (21:1-3, 41-42). Finally, there are the tribes of Reuben, Gad, and half-Manasseh who, though connected to the rest of the nation by bonds of kinship, choose to live on the other side of the Jordan. These tribes speak for all Israel in declaring their zeal for the commands of Moses (1:16-18), and Joshua later commends them for their faithfulness (22:1-5). Taken as a group, these characters stand at the center of most of the stories in Joshua, offering yet another indication of the book's fundamental preoccupation with issues of identity.

Author and Narrator

Joshua displays evidence of having undergone a complex process of composition. Study of the book has revealed that it comprises a collection of materials deriving from diverse settings and time periods. The shape and contents of these source materials, and the process by which they were edited and configured into the book we now have, raise an assortment of questions for which there are few clear answers.[9] For this reason, it is difficult to speak in terms of an "author" when we read Joshua in its canonical form. The concept of a "narrator" will serve better for our purposes. We may think of a narrator simply as one who tells the story and offers a perspective for comprehending its meaning in part and whole.[10] The narrator of Joshua is unspecified and retains a distance from the events of the story. Even so, we can make a few observations about the narrator's interests and strategies. The narrator generally relates events in a straightforward fashion and as a rule restricts commentary to summary remarks. These summaries reveal a propensity for hyperbole, particularly in assessing Israel's

---

[9] For more information on the book's compositional history, see the introductions of the commentaries by R. D. Nelson, *Joshua*, and R. S. Hess, *Joshua*, OTL (Downers Grove: InterVarsity, 1996), as well as A. D. H. Mayes, *The Story of Israel between Settlement and Exile* (London: SCM, 1983) 40–57 and A. G. Auld, *Joshua, Moses and the Land* (Edinburgh: T & T Clark, 1980) and Auld, *Joshua Retold*.

[10] On narrators in the Hebrew Bible, see D. M. Gunn and D. N. Fewell, *Narrative in the Hebrew Bible*, OBS (Oxford: Oxford University, 1993) 52–63 and, more broadly, Meir Sternberg, *The Poetics of Biblical Narrative* (Bloomington: Indiana University, 1985).

success in taking and occupying the land.[11] Thus we read that Joshua defeated and captured the entire land (10:40-43; 11:16-23) and that YHWH gave all the land promised to Israel's ancestors (21:43-45). We are informed of Joshua's obedience in similarly expansive terms (8:34-35; 11:15). These summations, however, clash with stories the narrator relates and with reports of failures (e.g. 15:63; 16:10; 17:14-18; 19:47). By pitting commentary against narration, the narrator constructs a series of contesting polarities: obedience/disobedience, success/failure, completion/openness, insider/outsider, ideal/real.

The narrator generates a sense of tension between these polarities by juxtaposing various texts and building suspense within individual accounts. A common technique for the latter entails supplying the reader with information not available to characters in the story. The reader thus knows what the king's men at Rahab's door do not, that the spies they seek are hidden on the roof of the house (2:4a). Likewise, the reader knows the identity of the disguised emissaries from Gibeon who parlay with Joshua and the elders (9:3-15). And the reader also knows that the wrath of YHWH has been kindled against Israel when a contingent attacks Ai (7:1). Conversely, the narrator may build suspense by withholding information. A case in point is the construction of an altar at the Jordan (22:10-12). We are not immediately told why the eastern tribes construct the altar, even though they precipitate a crisis by doing so. The narrator leaves it to the eastern tribes themselves to offer a rationale, but this occurs later in the story as the tribes attempt to defuse the conflict (22:22-29). Through the skillful interplay of perspectives—within, around, and outside texts—the narrator thus draws the reader into the narrative and creates a sense of tension and uncertainty.

Joshua and Deuteronomy

The narrator configures the story of Israel's acquisition of the land with the unique perspective of Deuteronomy in mind. In other words, Deuteronomy constitutes a sort of narrative lens through which the reader may understand the story Joshua tells. The book begins by making implicit connections to Deuteronomy. The speeches of YHWH, Joshua, and the eastern tribes articulate Deuteronomy's distinctive vocabulary,

---

[11] The use of hyperbole in reporting military campaigns has been documented by L. K. Younger, *Ancient Conquest Accounts: A Study of Ancient Near Eastern and Biblical History Writing,* (Sheffield: JSOT, 1990) 190–2, 241–9.

reiterate essential Deuteronomic themes, and appropriate specific Deuteronomic texts (Deut 3:18-20; 7:24; 11:24-25; 17:18-20; 31:6-8, 23). The very fact that Joshua begins with speech, rather than exposition, forges a powerful subliminal link to Deuteronomy, a book which essentially constitutes a speech delivered to Israel as it prepares to enter the land. By evoking Deuteronomy at the beginning, the narrator offers a point of view through which the reader may apprehend the meaning of the subsequent story and the significance of the events within it.

Deuteronomic themes and vocabulary infuse the rest of the narrative, giving it form and coherence. Direct links are forged by Joshua's address to Israel's leaders (23:1-16), which comprises an amalgam of Deuteronomic texts after the fashion of the initial speeches (Deut 7:1-5; 11:16-28), and by the ceremony at Mts. Ebal and Gerizim (8:30-35) in fulfillment of a Mosaic decree (Deut 27:1-14). For the most part, however, Deuteronomic texts are brought into Joshua by way of allusion. Rahab praises YHWH in Deuteronomic language (2:11b; cf. Deut 4:39). The levitical priests bear the ark of the covenant, in strict compliance to Deut 10:8. The identification and execution of Achan recalls the Deuteronomic prescriptions for identifying and executing apostates (Deut 13:6-18). Other allusions to Deut 1:19–3:11 emphasize the rebellious character of Achan's transgression and illuminate its consequences. The Gibeonites cite the Deuteronomic legislation for the conduct of war in their attempt to trick Joshua and the Israelite leaders (Deut 20:10-18), intensifying the tension between what Moses decreed and what Israel is about to do. In addition, their words, appearance, and role within Israel echo the covenant words of Deut 29:1-15. Finally, the summaries of conquest and occupation (10:40-42; 11:15; 11:16-23; 21:43-45) employ Deuteronomic vocabulary and phrasing (the narrator, in essence, speaking in the language of Deuteronomy).

At a higher level, the Deuteronomic account of the campaigns against Sihon and Og (Deut 2:24–3:11) establishes a prototype for reporting the campaigns in Canaan. The accounts of the campaigns at Ai (8:1-29) and the waters of Merom (11:1-15), and to a lesser extent those against Jericho (6:1-25) and the cities of the south (10:28-39), follow the structure and language of the Deuteronomic report. In addition, the narrator of Joshua summarizes all the campaigns of Canaan in terms strongly reminiscent of Deuteronomy's summary of the Transjordanian campaigns, even to the point of including a reference to an ancient race (11:16-23; cf. Deut 3:8-11).

On an even broader scale, the structure of Joshua as a whole corresponds to that which gives shape to Deuteronomy's overview of the acquisition of the land in the Transjordan (2:24–4:43). Both Deuteronomy and Joshua begin with the command to cross a prominent geographical boundary (the Arnon in Deuteronomy, the Jordan in Joshua) and relate campaigns against the kings of the land (Josh 1:1–12:24; cf. Deut 2:24–3:11). After summaries of the conquests, Joshua then follows Deuteronomy in reporting the allocation of conquered lands to the tribes who will inhabit them (Josh 13:1–21:45; cf. Deut 3:12-17). As in Deuteronomy, Joshua then uses the ambivalent situation of Reuben, Gad, and half-Manasseh as a vehicle for raising the difficult issue of the Transjordan and those remaining there (Josh 22:1-34; cf. Deut 3:21-29). In Deuteronomy, Moses stays in the Transjordan, while Joshua crosses over to occupy Canaan. In Joshua, the two and one-half tribes stay in the Transjordan, while the others occupy Canaan. Both texts also remind their readers of troubling issues associated with rebellion and divine anger.[12] From here, the two accounts move to exhortations by the respective national leaders (Deut 4:1-40; Josh 23:1–24:28). Moses' speech, predicated on the prior review of Israel's recent experience, articulates a number of themes. It begins with strident admonitions to keep commandments which he has given (vv. 1, 2, 5, 6, 9, 14) and sets these within the obligation Israel undertook when it made the covenant at Horeb (vv. 10-14). Moses then addresses the opposite issue and warns Israel in the strongest terms against idolatry, punctuating his words with predictions that YHWH will expel the nation for this offense (vv. 15-31). He ends by calling Israel to acknowledge its unique experience with YHWH (vv. 32-36), emphasizing in particular the conviction that YHWH has chosen Israel and has given it the land (vv. 37-38). Moses then concludes by calling the nation to devote itself exclusively to YHWH (v. 39), so that it may remain in the land (v. 40). Joshua, in turn, confronts the assembled nation in similar terms. In his "farewell address" (Josh 23:1-16) he exhorts Israel to obedience to the Mosaic torah and devotion to YHWH (vv. 6-11). Like Moses, he then warns his listeners not to turn aside to other gods (vv. 12-13), underscoring his warnings with predictions of expulsion from the land (vv. 13-16). In the final scene, Joshua recapitulates Israel's experience with YHWH in a way that emphasizes YHWH's initiative and choosing (24:2-13) and then calls Israel to exclusive devotion to YHWH (vv. 14-16). Both accounts thus utilize narrative material to bring the reader to a place of decision.[13]

---

[12] The Deuteronomic text recalls an incident at Meribah (Num 20:1-13), during which Israel acted rebelliously (v. 10) and YHWH decreed that Moses would not be allowed to enter the promised land. The reference to Peor in both Deuteronomy (3:29) and Joshua (22:17) makes another intriguing connection between the texts. Peor was the site of an egregious act of national apostasy (Num 25:1-18).

[13] The Deuteronomic account actually ends with a report that Moses designated three cities east of the Jordan as cities of refuge for homicides, whereas

Finally, Joshua incorporates the basic themes of Deuteronomy. Devotion to YHWH, expressed positively through obedience to the commands of Moses and negatively by not turning aside to other gods, constitutes the central concern of Deuteronomy (e.g. 6:4-15; 8:11-20; 11:1-28; 30:15-20). YHWH has chosen Israel and has done marvelous things on its behalf. Israel in turn must offer itself wholeheartedly to YHWH alone (6:4-5; 7:1-11; 10:12-22). YHWH demonstrates faithfulness to Israel in the most profound sense through the promised gift of the land and fights for Israel so that the ancestral promise may be realized (4:36-38; 6:3; 7:17-24; 9:4-5; 12:1). However, YHWH also declares that Israel will experience the blessings of the land only to the extent that it clings to YHWH and holds to the commandments given through Moses. Adherence to the commandments will bring a rich life in the land, but turning aside will threaten the loss of all that YHWH has given (7:12-16; 11:26-28; 28:1-45; 30:15-20). Because enjoyment of life in the land is predicated on Israel's steadfast commitment to YHWH and the commandments, Moses urges Israel to keep its distance from those who would draw it away from YHWH. Although Deuteronomy's rhetoric presents Israel as a nation on the offensive, its preoccupation with the temptations of Canaan intimate a community under siege, one that guards the walls with unceasing vigilance to prevent the incursion of hostile powers.[14] The peoples of the land represent the greatest threat in this regard and, to eliminate the threat, extreme measures are directed against them. Deuteronomy emphatically calls for the annihilation of the land's indigenous populations and repeatedly warns that they will lead the nation to destruction if allowed to survive (6:14-15; 7:1-5, 25-26; 12:1-3; 20:16-18; 29:17-21 [MT 16-20]; 31:16-21). The power of the peoples points to the fragility of Israel's internal boundaries. The inhabitants of the land must be wiped out without a trace, for if any vestige remains the nation will remain in jeopardy.

The Deuteronomic themes of devotion, obedience to the commandments, occupation of the land, and extermination of indigenous peoples shape the story of Joshua and bring us back to our starting point.

Joshua concludes with reports of burials. In Joshua, the list of cities of refuge is included within the apportionment of lands (20:1-9).

[14] In a trenchant essay on the topic, Louis Stulman writes of Deuteronomy's "ethos of encroachment" as it is expressed through the book's law code. He observes that Deuteronomy perceives itself to be under threat from foreigners and argues that the book undertakes a program to ensure and clarify the integrity of its internal boundaries; "Encroachment in Deuteronomy: An Analysis of the Social World of the D Code," *JBL* 109 (1990) 613–32.

Joshua's use of these configuring motifs reveals that it shares the same concerns and apprehensions. What Deuteronomy expresses through paranesis and law, Joshua expresses through narrative. Both texts work together to construct an identity for Israel which clarifies and bolsters the nation's internal boundaries.

The Construction of Identity

Picking up from our earlier discussion, we may perceive parallels between the purposes and programs of the narratives which individuals tell and those which communities tell. On the social level as well, narratives construct a sense of the world that renders coherence and meaning to the group's existence. As constructs, narratives thus express the values, perceptions, and ideologies of the communities which produce them. Decoding the narratives, through attention to metaphors and structures, offers insight into their rhetorical agendas, particularly as these reveal a sense of self-understanding in relationship to others and the world.

The formation of identity involves the construction of dichotomies. Defining who and what one is also presupposes who and what one is not. Ascribing features to the group, positively and negatively, provides a mechanism for distinguishing the group from others and establishing the parameters for determining membership within it. Since questions of inclusion and exclusion are fundamental to the task of establishing and maintaining identity, communities may project onto "others" those characteristics which it perceives in opposition to its own. In the process of constructing its own identity, therefore, a community constructs the identity of "others" in a way that confirms its uniqueness and establishes its boundaries. Since these ascriptions are constructions, they often clash with lived experience, since interaction with "others" inevitably challenges the community's stereotypes. "Near others," those in close proximity (e.g. in geographical, racial, or social terms), represent particularly strong challenges, since high levels of interaction suggest more points of similarity than of difference. In order to assert its identity, then, a group must radically dichotomize (and therefore distance itself from) these "near others," projecting on them, in the strongest terms, those attributes that oppose those which it ascribes to itself.[15]

---

[15] The classic description of social organization through ascription is the introductory essay in F. Barth, *Ethnic Groups and Boundaries* (Boston: Little, Brown and Co.,

Both Deuteronomy and Joshua present Israel as an integer. The language of totality and wholeness saturates the phraseology of both books. Israel acts as one people, bound by covenant to one God, obedient to the entire law with a whole heart, worshiping at one sanctuary.[16] Much of Deuteronomy is engaged, in one way or another, with articulating and enforcing this essential integrity. "All Israel" constitutes the subject of address at a number of points (1:1; 5:1; 11:6), and the various elements of Israelite society are explicitly integrated at the covenant ceremony on the plains of Moab (29:10-12). Israel must devote itself to the One God and to no others (5:6-7; 6:4, 14), being careful to perform "all the commandments" (5:26 [MT 29]; 11:8, 22; 19:9; 27:1) and "all the words of the law" (17:19; 28:58; 31:12) and to do so with all its "heart and life" (4:29; 6:5; 13:3 [MT 4]; 10:12; 26:16; 30:10).[17] Israel the land, like Israel the people, must be homogeneous. As a corollary, the peoples of the land must therefore be eliminated so that no non-Israelite presence remains in the land (7:1-5, 24; 12:2-4; 20:17-18).[18]

Joshua follows Deuteronomy's emphasis on homogeneity and totality. Here as well, the narrator presents Israel as a unit. References to "all Israel" (1:2; 3:1; 5:5; 8:15, 21; 10:29; 24:1) and "the entire congregation" (9:18; 18:1; 22:18) reiterate national unanimity. When acting as a unit, in direct obedience to Joshua, the nation succeeds in taking "all the land" (10:40; 11:16, 23) and defeating "all the kings" (10:42; 11:12). YHWH also acts comprehensively, giving all the land promised to the ancestors, giving all Israel's enemies into its hands, and bringing every divine promise to pass (21:43-45). Moreover, both Israel and Joshua act in accordance with YHWH's decrees and Moses's commandments, reinforcing

---

1969). Also helpful are M. Nash, *Ethnicity and Nationalism* (London: Pluto, 1993), A. D. Smith, *The Ethnic Origins of Nations* (Oxford: Blackwell, 1986); R. L. Cohn, "Before Israel: The Canaanites as Other in Biblical Tradition," *The Other in Jewish Thought and History* ed. L. J. Silberstein and R. L. Cohn (New York: New York University, 1994) 74–90, and J. Z. Smith, "What a Difference a Difference Makes," *To See Ourselves as Others See Us*, ed. J. Neusner and E. S. Frerichs (Chico: Scholars Press, 1985).

[16] This theme is expressed throughout Deuteronomy by the ubiquitous repetition of the Hebrew term *kôl* ("all, entire").

[17] M. Weinfeld offers a more complete listing of these phrases, with explanation; *Deuteronomy and the Deuteronomic School* (Oxford: Oxford University, 1972) 332–41. Also see G. J. Wenham, "The Deuteronomic Theology of the Book of Joshua," JBL 90 (1971) 140–8.

[18] The Hebrew verb *yāraš* expresses the connection between the two operations. With reference to the land, it signifies occupation of territory (expressed by its connection to the verb *yāšab;* 11:31; 17:14; 19:1; 26:1). With reference to people, however, it signifies conquest of the inhabitants (9:1, 3; 7:17; 11:23; 12:29).

the identification of the people with its leader and its God (Josh 1:7-9, 16-18; 8:30-31; 11:15; 22:2-3).

Conversely, the peoples of Canaan are characterized by their plurality and heterogeneity. In contrast to unified Israel, the peoples of the land are signified in plural terms: "the Hittites, the Girgashites, the Amorites, the Canaanites, the Perizzites, the Hivites, and the Jebusites" (Deut 7:1; cf. 20:17; Josh 3:10; 9:1; 11:3; 12:8; 24:11). Instead of one leader under the direction of one God, they have many kings (Josh 5:1; 8:2; 9:1; 10:1-5; 11:1-18; 24:12) and worship many gods (Deut 6:14; 7:4, 16; 12:29-31; 31:16; Josh 23:7, 12-13; 24:15) in diverse ways at many sites throughout the land (Deut 7:25-26; 12:2-4, 29-31; 29:17-18 [MT 16-17]). From the Deuteronomic perspective, then, oneness signifies Israel, while plurality signifies the others who live in the land. A fracture of Israel's distinctive unity therefore threatens the disintegration of the nation. Embracing the plural and diverse, whether theologically or socially, erases the community's integrity, making it indistinguishable from the other peoples of the land. Instead of being one, Israel becomes one of many. To emphasize the point, Moses repeatedly links ethnic intermingling (that is, a turn to social plurality) with apostasy (a turn to theological plurality):

> Make no covenant with them and show them no mercy. Do not inter-marry with them, giving your daughters to their sons or taking their daughters for your sons, for that would turn away your children from following me, to serve other gods. Then the anger of the LORD would be kindled against you and he would destroy you quickly (Deut 7:2b-4).

The import of this admonition should not be missed. Breaking social boundaries goes hand in hand with breaking theological boundaries. Intermarriage with the peoples creates a pluralistic society and leads to a pluralistic theology. And should this happen the nation will suffer the same fate as the diverse inhabitants of the land (8:19). The severity of the threat posed by Canaanite plurality can be appreciated by the extreme measures instituted to counteract it. Israelites who follow the Canaanite way receive the same punishment suffered by the peoples of the land. They too are eliminated, enabling Israel to "purge" the heterogenous from its midst and thus preserve the integrity of the community and its internal boundaries. Whether inside or outside, the heterogenous must be destroyed.

This basic dichotomy shapes the themes of territorial possession, adherence to divine ordinances, and ethnic separation which configure Joshua. Taking the entire land, obeying all the commandments, and exterminating all the peoples of the land are inextricably connected as Israel seeks the realization of divine promises and national aspirations. The reports of battles in particular offer a forceful demonstration of the scheme. When Israel carefully obeys YHWH it prevails over kings and cities. However, many aspects of the book subvert these assertions and thus prohibit the reader from viewing ethnic purity, correct practice, or possession of land as essential marks of Israelite identity. Joshua concludes with the peoples of the land among the people of God, (6:25; 9:26-27), vast tracts of land outside of Israelite control (13:2-6; 15:63; 16:10; 17:12-18), the gods of the land among YHWH's people (24:14, 15, 23), grim portents of apostasy (23:14-16), and Joshua's declaration that Israel cannot serve YHWH (24:19). And even so, Israel remains the people of God! As a whole, Joshua thus has the remarkable effect of illustrating the relative character of a national identity founded on territorial claims, kinship bonds, or proper religious practices. The essence of Israelite identity, we learn in the final, climactic episode, is rather YHWH's exclusive choosing of Israel and Israel's exclusive choosing of YHWH (cf. 24:2-15). In the end, we discover that Israel is a people defined by decisions, in the reciprocal choosing of YHWH and the nation.[19]

Changing Stories

Memory has a plastic quality that allows it to be reshaped and fitted into new mental molds. The passage of time brings new experiences, perceptions, and challenges that may significantly alter what and how one remembers. The greater the distance from the event, the

---

[19] There is considerable debate concerning when Joshua took on the essential shape of the Masoretic Text, but most students of the book would place this event during the Josianic reform (cf. 2 Kgs 22:1–23:27), the exile, or the post-exilic era. It is important to note that, in each of these periods, Israel was faced with the challenge of rethinking its identity as a people. Josiah's reform took place as Assyrian power waned in Syria and Palestine, leading to an attempt to recover territory that had belonged to the northern tribes and to destroy rival sanctuaries. The period suggests a number of those factors that A. D. Smith associates with ethnic formation, e.g. nostalgia, organized religion, inter-state warfare: *(Ethnic Origins)* 32–41. On the other hand, the dislocation of the Jews from their land would have also precipitated profound questions of identity as the community sought to preserve its identity in exile. Biblical texts deriving from the post-exilic era also manifest a struggle to define Israel, with some texts asserting a construction of identity along the lines of race or adherence to the Mosaic torah (Ezra 9:1–10:44; Neh 8:1-18; 10:38-39; 13:1-3) and others emphasizing devotion to YHWH (Isa 56:1-8).

more opportunities there are to perceive new significance in individual and communal stories. New contexts and issues shape a sense of what memories "mean." The book of Joshua bears witness to the plasticity of memory. At one level, the book constitutes an amalgam of materials, drawn from diverse contexts, all of which are allowed to speak with their own voices. Joshua does little to mute the triumphalism and brutality of Israel's memories of conquest or to complete piecemeal remembrances of lands and boundaries. Yet something quite profound is accomplished in the way these memories are connected and presented. The whole of Joshua conveys a very different message than the pieces within it. With a perspective enhanced by the passage of time and meditation on life with YHWH, the book reflects a richer understanding of what it means to be the people of God. In its final form (and I use this term advisedly), Joshua establishes a sense of identity which demonstrates (negatively) that Israel cannot be defined, in a fundamental sense, by land, religious observance, or racial affinity, but (positively) that its identity, at the core, must be understood in light of chosenness and choosing.

Joshua does not deny a place to those voices which assert the importance of national aspirations, claims to land, or religious beliefs and practices. But it illustrates, through the power of narrative, that none are, nor should be, definitive marks of what it means to be the people of God. By placing ideologies of land, ethnic separation, and religious practice at the forefront, and allowing them full expression, Joshua confronts the reader with their powerful influence on the people of God. But by refusing them unequivocal expression, the book reveals them to be derivative and relative. In an age such as ours, in which ideologies of religion, race, and territory have given rise to countless expressions of horrific violence, Joshua should be required reading, especially for those who perceive a continuity between the story Joshua relates and their own story. Joshua should be studied, not shunned, precisely because it holds the mirror up to all who regard themselves as the people of God. The reflection may both repel and inspire. But until it is confronted forthrightly the divine promise will remain elusive.

Chapter One
RIGHTS OF PASSAGE
Joshua 1:1-18

Narratives typically begin with an exposition that constructs a story world, initiates the plot, and presents a perspective by which the reader may understand and connect the events which will follow. The exposition introduces one or more of the main characters, as well as the themes that will connect the events and convey their significance. Joshua begins with four speeches which introduce Israel's God (vv. 2-9), Israel's new leader (vv. 11, 13-15) and representatives of the nation (vv. 16-18). Each speech is a carefully crafted unit which evokes the words of Moses by incorporating Deuteronomic themes and texts. Voicing the distinctive concerns and cadences of Deuteronomy, the speakers convey the crucial importance of integrity by speaking in terms of wholes and units (signified by the Hebrew word *kôl*): "*all* the people" (v. 2), "*every* place" (v. 3), "*all* the land"(v. 4), "*all* the days" (v. 5), "*all* the law" (v. 7), "*everywhere* you go" (vv. 7, 9), "*all* that is written" (v. 8), "*all* the warriors" (v. 14), "*all* you have commanded" (vv. 16, 18), "*everywhere* you send us" (v. 16), "as we obeyed Moses in *all* things" (v. 17), "*whoever* rebels" (v. 18). Taken together, the speeches implicitly communicate a unanimity between God, Joshua, and the nation and reiterate Deuteronomy's insistence that integrity is at heart of all that Israel is and does.

The narrator thus signals that the events which follow should be read and understood in light of Deuteronomy. Through various allusions to the words of Moses (in form, vocabulary, and theme) the reader is reminded that Joshua does not stand in isolation but is to be read within the context of the much larger story that extends back to the early chapters of Genesis. The reader who has been tracking that larger story knows that the consummation of long-anticipated promises

1

is at hand. YHWH's command that Israel prepare to enter the land (v.2) does more than set events in motion. It infuses the story with an electric expectancy. Possession of the land represents the fulfillment of a hope conveyed by ancestral promises (Gen 12:1-7; 13:14-18; 15:17-21) and, in a more profound sense, represents a place for wandering humanity to live once again in communion with its Creator (cf. Gen 3:24). The reader also knows that there are yet obstacles and perils that threaten fulfillment, namely the peoples of the land, whose might and technology are formidable (Num 13:31-33; Deut 9:1-2).

Although we may be tempted to view the peoples of the land as the greatest impediment to the fulfillment of the promises, the narrator utilizes the opening speeches to suggest otherwise. The speeches focus on the causal relationship between the divine gift of the land, obedience to the commands of Moses, and Israel's success in taking the land. Forms of the verb *nātan* ("give") appear eight times within the speeches, beginning with YHWH's self-designation as the one who gives the land (v. 2).[1] YHWH begins the story with announcements of gifts and promises (vv. 2b-6) and then informs Joshua of the response necessary to actualize the promises (vv. 7-9), namely, the strict and zealous observance of the commandments of Moses. The pattern is repeated when Joshua addresses the Reubenites, Gadites, and the half-tribe of Manasseh. Joshua reiterates the divine promise of land which YHWH made through Moses (v. 13) and then stipulates what the tribes are to do (vv. 12-15). In both cases, the speakers declare that successful settlement of the land is contingent on obedience to the commands of Moses (vv. 7c, 8c, 15b). The linking of divine gift, obedient response, and victory in the land suggests that the Canaanites will not pose a significant threat to Israel. YHWH claims both the right and the power to deliver the land to Israel and promises to bring complete victory over the peoples (vv. 2b-4). The *real* obstacle to fulfillment is therefore not the formidable resolve of the Canaanites but a potential lack of resolve on the part of Joshua and Israel. The imperative verbal forms which dominate the speeches stress that success also depends on Israel's determination to obey YHWH as it enters the land. Will the nation be faithful in carrying out the full measure of the Mosaic commandment? Will Israel complete the conquest of the land? Will it fail to obey the words of Moses and so forfeit the land altogether?

By opening the story with these themes, the narrator continues the hortatory thrust of Deuteronomy and reminds the reader of the conditional, and thus open, character of the divine promises. The initial speeches not only introduce the goal and program of the story but also

---

[1] The participial form of the verb is employed here.

reveal how it will reach a satisfactory conclusion. YHWH has given Israel the land. It is there for the taking. But gaining possession of the gift will depend on Israel's determination to be wholeheartedly obedient to the Deuteronomic program for success: a unified nation, led by one leader, loyal to one God, in possession of the entire land.

The Shadow of Moses: 1:1-2a

Joshua begins with the announcement of an end; that is, the death of Moses. The report of Moses' death recalls the final episode of Deuteronomy and forges yet another link between the two books. In a broader sense, it also indicates the continuity between Joshua and all that has gone before and signals a major transition in Israel's story. The epochal significance of Moses' death is underscored by repetition. YHWH begins the address to Joshua by repeating the report in essentially the same terms as the narrator. Aside from YHWH, Moses has been the central figure in the formation of Israel as a people, the divinely-chosen leader by whom Israel has been guided, defined, and constituted. Moses has performed YHWH's mighty acts. Moses, and only Moses, has delivered YHWH's words of promise, assurance, life, and purpose (cf. Num 12:1-9). Through the mediation of Moses Israel has been brought into covenantal relationship with YHWH (Exod 19:1–24:18). Through his intercession YHWH sustained the people in the desert (Exod 15:22–17:7) and relented from making an end to them (Exod 32:11-14; Num 11:1-3; 14:13-25). Through Moses Israel's festivals have been established and explained and its laws promulgated. Moses has established the contours of Israel's religious system and of its essential social configuration. In sum, Moses has been at the center of all of the formative events and critical junctures which have shaped Israel into a people. And so, as the book of Joshua begins, Israel is at the same time YHWH's people and Moses' people.

Moses stands at the center of Israel's transformation from a captive people on the eve of deliverance (Exod 3:7-12) to a wandering nation on the eve of settlement. Israel in Egypt has no coherence, no hope, and no experience of YHWH's mighty power. Israel on the plains of Moab, however, is a unified people, bound by covenant to YHWH, and impelled by the divine promise given to its ancestors. The pivotal figure in this transition, Moses embodies the contrary elements of this national transformation within his own character. Born into the tribe of Levi and Israel's divinely-appointed leader, he nonetheless is reared at the heart of Egyptian society and can be easily mistaken for an Egyptian. Having guided Israel to the banks of the Jordan he dies and is buried on Mount Nebo, forever outside the land promised to Israel yet still within the sphere of Israelite settlement.

Since Moses has been forbidden to enter the land (Num 20:12; Deut 31:1) and thus cannot lead Israel across the Jordan, his death marks the beginning of a new era, in which Israel will enter a new life as a settled people. It is clear from the outset, however, that Moses will continue to exert considerable influence on the nation even though he is no longer physically present. He will remain present, indirectly but no less potently, through his words and his designated successor, Joshua. Even as this new era begins, Moses remains the dominant figure in the narrative. His name is mentioned ten times within the chapter, compared to four occurrences of Joshua's name. The four speeches are little more than a reiteration of Moses' words, first by YHWH, then by Joshua, and finally by the tribes who have chosen to settle the Transjordanian acquisitions. The definition of the land (vv. 3-4) repeats the Mosaic description of the land in Deut 11:24-25. The promise that YHWH will be with Joshua (v. 5b), YHWH's charge to Joshua (v. 6b), and the repeated exhortation to "be strong and courageous" all echo Moses' words to Israel and Joshua on the occasion of the latter's commissioning to succeed Moses (Deut 31:6-8, 23). In addition, the divine assurance that no one will be able to stand against Joshua (v. 5a) repeats that given to Israel in Deut 7:24. YHWH's command that Joshua meditate on "this book of the law" alludes to Moses' rule for Israelite kings (Deut 17:18-20). And the latter interchange with the Transjordanian tribes (vv. 12-18) actualizes a decision rendered by Moses with reference to the eastern tribes (Num 32:1-32; Deut 3:18-20).

The narrator employs a number of devices to link Joshua to Moses and to signal a smooth succession of leadership. The title "Moses' assistant" recalls other situations in which Joshua has been so named (Exod 24:13; 33:11; Num 11:28), reminding the reader of Joshua's close association during those events in which Moses exercised his leadership: at the giving of the tablets at Sinai (Exod 24:12-14), on those occasions when Moses would speak with YHWH "face to face" at the tent of meeting (Exod 33:7-11), and when the spirit of YHWH descended on the elders of Israel (Num 11:16-30). As with Moses, YHWH now speaks directly with Joshua and grants him the assurance that he will be with him as he was with his predecessor. Joshua therefore functions as the medium of divine guidance and exhortation, and the eastern tribes, later speaking for the whole of Israel, promise to obey him as they had obeyed Moses (vv. 16-18).[2]

---

[2] On the topic of continuity, see A. D. H. Mayes, *The Story of Israel between Settlement and Exile* (London: SCM, 1983) 43–7. Mayes remarks, "what Deuteronomy sets

The narrator also carefully separates the two men and implies Joshua's continuing subordination to Moses. In contrast to the title ascribed to Joshua, Moses is repeatedly designated "the servant of YHWH," first by the narrator and then by YHWH himself. Most recently ascribed to Moses at the report of his death (Deut 34:5), the title is repeated three more times in the opening speeches (vv. 7, 13, 15) and recurs throughout the book.[3] The epithet, in contrast to Joshua's, suggests a three-tiered chain of command which is later confirmed when YHWH endorses Moses' words and requires the new leader to observe them diligently (vv. 7-8). Moses may be dead, but the strongly Mosaic cast of this first chapter intimates that his presence will remain with Israel, both through his words and through the person of his successor. A strong sense of continuity is thus rendered between what has gone before and what will now transpire. At the same time, however, Moses' death will mean the transformation of Israel—from a community propelled by the energy of an original, unitary vision to a people now motivated by essentially conservative impulses ("be careful to act in accordance to all the law that my servant Moses commanded you"). The transformation begs a question. How will Israel bring the Mosaic vision to completion in the face of new historical realities? Through the text Moses still exercises his authority, still makes the divine will known, and still informs Israel in the decisions it must make. He will continue to speak, but the public proclamation of his words is now, as it will be ever after, simply a reiteration of what he has already said. Yet there will be new situations, unforeseen or unaddressed by those words. And Moses himself will not be available to provide answers. Only the "book of the law" will be there, and the grid that it supplies will not always fit the decisions that must be made. Moses' words, frozen in space and time in the form of a written text, will continue to shape, inspire, and guide Israel, but they will be no substitute for his person. Moses will now lead by proxy, through his assistant Joshua, who will faithfully carry out the tasks assigned to him, leading the nation into the land with its promise of life and fulfillment. Joshua however will be no Moses.

---

forth as words of Moses to Israel or to Joshua is in Joshua 1 set forth as words of God: this exalts not only the authority of the word of Moses but also the role of the narrator as Moses' successor" (43). Here he follows R. Polzin's argument that Joshua 1 establishes the authority of the Deuteronomistic narrator as well as Moses, thus initiating a hermeneutical meditation on the word of God; see also R. Polzin, *Moses and the Deuteronomist* (New York: Seabury, 1980) 73–80.

[3] Each of subsequent instances reinforces Mosaic authority by referring to his commands (8:31, 33; 11:12, 15; 22:5) or his role in taking land (12:6; 13:8 14:7; 18:7; 22:2, 4).

Be Strong and Courageous! 1:2-9

The opening speech consists of a series of exhortations which YHWH
delivers to Joshua. These exhortations introduce the major themes of
the book—the possession of the land (vv. 2-6) and obedience to the
torah of Moses (vv. 7-9)—and render them in the distinctive language
of Deuteronomy. The speech comprises a chain of quotations drawn
from key Deuteronomic texts. In an odd reversal of roles, YHWH becomes Moses' mouthpiece, reiterating Moses' words for a new time
and context. YHWH's words and Moses' words thus blend into one, ele-
vating Moses' words and confirming the authority of his commands.[4]

THE GIFT OF THE LAND

Israel begins its first journey without Moses by crossing a boundary.
YHWH initiates the action by issuing a command to Joshua, reviewing
divine attributes and promises, and then returning to the language of
command. The first segment of the speech thus encloses promises (vv.
3-5) within commands (vv. 2, 6), implicitly enforcing the connection between divine initiative and human response. The commands display a
parallel structure. Each begins emphatically, with two imperatives
("Now arise! Cross this Jordan!" v. 2; "Be strong and courageous!" v. 6),[5]
and together they remind Joshua of his commission: to lead the people
across the Jordan (v. 2) and to put them in possession of the land (v. 6).
Each then concludes with an affirmation that YHWH has given the land.

The intervening material combines a number of Deuteronomic
promises. YHWH's promise to grant "every place that the sole of your
foot will tread upon," along with the description of the land's extent
(vv. 3-4), repeats Deut 11:24-25a. In Deuteronomy the text is enclosed
by admonitions that underscore the essential connection between obedience and success. Before the delivering the promise, Moses places
conditions on its fulfillment (Deut 11:22-23):

> If you will diligently observe this entire commandment that I am com-
> manding you, loving the LORD your God, walking in all his ways, and

---

[4] Polzin (*Moses*, 73–80). R. D. Nelson asserts that YHWH's speech introduces the
main themes of the book: crossing of the Jordan (v. 2), conquest of the land (vv. 3-6,
9), allotment of the land (v. 6), and obedience to the law (vv. 7-8); *Joshua*, OTL
(Louisville: Westminster John Knox, 1997) 30.

[5] NRSV "Now proceed to cross the Jordan" does not capture the force of the Masoretic text.

holding fast to him, then the LORD will drive out all these nations before you, and you will dispossess nations larger and mightier than yourselves.

These conditions are echoed in the admonition which follows (Deut 11:26):

> See, I am setting before you today a blessing and a curse; the blessing, if you obey the commandments of the LORD your God that I am commanding you today; and the curse, if you do not obey the commandments of the LORD your God, but turn from the way that I am commanding you today to follow other gods that you have not known.

The Deuteronomic text articulates the tension between gift and response; the land across the Jordan will become "Israel" to the extent that YHWH defines it and the people walk it. It therefore contains an implicit charge to actualize what YHWH has declared; the land which Israel should "tread upon" ought to constitute the whole of the land which YHWH has decreed for it.

In Joshua, YHWH reiterates these words of Moses and envelops them with exhortations to cross and gain the inheritance. Repetition of the promise recalls the Deuteronomic context and confronts the reader immediately with the tension between the programmatic and the peripatetic. The tension is underscored by a small modification of the Deuteronomic text. Whereas Moses had declared that "every place on which you set foot *shall be yours*," YHWH now declares, "Every place on which the sole of your foot will tread upon *I have given to you, as I promised to Moses*."[6] The modification reminds the reader that the land is the gift of YHWH and the fulfillment of a divine promise, accentuating the vital relationship between what YHWH promises and (through the exhortations to cross and take possession) what Israel must do.

The description of the land (v. 4) delineates a vast area (touching both the "great" river and the "great" sea) but is curiously vague. The Great Sea in the west and the river Euphrates constitute definite points of reference, but what is meant by the phrase "from the wilderness and the Lebanon?" Both terms denote geographical regions rather than natural boundaries, with the reference to the wilderness being particularly indistinct. Which "wilderness" is meant?[7] The Masoretic text uses

---

[6] The NRSV translates the common phrase differently in Deut 11:24 and Josh 1:3, even though they are identical in the MT. Josh 1:3 is the more literal of the two translations: "every place that the sole of your foot will tread upon."

[7] Many areas in Canaan and the surrounding areas are denoted by the Hebrew word *midbār*, here translated "wilderness." The term may specify any arid region,

a "from . . . to" formula *(min . . . wĕ'ad)* commonly employed to signify the extent of territory by marking its extremities (Exod 23:31; Esther 1:1). Following this cue, the NRSV seeks to resolve the ambiguity by
linking the phrase "as far as the great river" with "the Lebanon," so
that both signify the northernmost limits of Israel's promised possession. By extension, then, "the wilderness" must signify the opposite
extremity, perhaps the Judean wilderness or the Negev. The Masoretic
text, however, is much more problematic, especially if the "from . . .
to" formula is presumed, for it reads literally *"from* the wilderness and
this Lebanon *to* the great river, the River Euphrates." Following the
formula, the syntax here seems to associate the wilderness and the
Lebanon over against the Euphrates.[8] While we should not make too
much of conjunctions and particles, the fact remains that the construction of the Masoretic text injects a sense of uncertainty into the very
important matter of defining the boundaries of the land. In any case,
the indefinite nature of the land's description again focuses attention
on the issue of Israelite resolve. Lacking any clearly-defined boundaries, the extent of the land will be defined by those places which Israel
actually traverses.

As in the previous verse, there is also an addition to the Deuteronomic text. The phrase "all the land of the Hittites" is inserted after the
reference to the Euphrates River, adding a distinctively political cast to
the description of the land. The Hittites ruled a vast empire that extended into northern Syria until it collapsed around 1200 B.C.E. The
Bible attests to the presence of Hittites throughout Syria and Palestine
(Gen. 24:3-4; 27:46; 1 Sam 26:6; 2 Sam 11:3), and it is not clear whether
the phrase here refers to the region of erstwhile Hittite hegemony in
Syria or to the larger territory specified by the rest of the verse. The

---

large or small, and most often occurs in conjunction with a qualifying noun when
used as a territorial designation (e.g. "the wilderness of Beersheba" [Gen 21:14];
"the wilderness of Moab" [Deut 2:8]; "the wilderness of Zin" [Num 13:21], "the
wilderness of Shur" [Exod 15:22]). It occurs alone in texts which correspond to the
present one (Gen 15:18; Exod 23:31), where it seems more explicitly to demarcate
the southern boundary of the land. Noting its varied uses within Joshua, R. S. Hess
concludes that it constitutes a general description of the area west of the Jordan and
to the south; *Joshua,* TOTC (Downers Grove: InterVarsity, 1996) 70. For a concise
discussion of the boundaries of the promised land, see T. Butler, *Joshua,* WBC
(Waco: Word, 1983) 11.

[8] The problem may have arisen due to a scribal omission; another "from" *(min)*
precedes "the wilderness" in Deut 11:24. Or it may simply be a variation of the
Deuteronomic text.

note, however, does more than clarify geography. The insertion of the phrase within the land promise reminds both Israel and the reader that the land is already inhabited. Israel, like the other nations to whom YHWH has given territory (Deut 2:1-25), will have to have to take possession of the territory from someone else. Rather than settling an uninhabited area, which will offer no opposition, Israel will have to overcome opponents if it is to acquire the land.

Because the Israelites will face powerful inhabitants determined to resist them, assurances of victory and divine presence follow the delineation of the land (v. 5). Both are based on Deuteronomic texts and carry militaristic connotations. The first, "no one shall be able to stand against you," continues the quotation from Deut 11:25 (see also Deut 7:24) and ensures the outcome of Israel's confrontations with the people of Canaan (although the added phrase "all the days of your life" hints that the process of taking the land will not be accomplished quickly). The second recalls Moses' charge to Joshua (Deut 31:8) and alludes to the reason that victories can be so confidently predicted: "as I was with Moses, so I will be with you; I will not fail you or forsake you." Here expressed in both positive and negative terms, the promise of divine presence expresses an essential affirmation of Israel's ideology of warfare: YHWH accompanies the armies of Israel and fights its battles.[9] The declaration of divine presence prefaces the Deuteronomic instructions for making war (Deut 20:1-14) and functions in many instances to inspire faith in YHWH in the face of superior enemy forces or difficult situations (Exod 3:12; Judg 6:11-16). Although usually a straightforward pronouncement, the assurance here links Joshua with Moses, once again confirming the line of succession and recalling Moses' own exhortation (Deut 3:21):

> Your own eyes have seen everything that the Lord your God has done to these two kings; so the Lord will do to all the kingdoms into which you are about to cross. Do not fear them, for it is the Lord your God who fights for you.

Deuteronomy identifies Moses above all as a leader through whom YHWH accomplished mighty deeds and displays of power (Deut. 34:10-12). YHWH implies that similar acts will be performed by Joshua as Israel moves from the desert to the land.

---

[9] For a thorough discussion of the phrase and its use in war oracles and in other contexts throughout the Hebrew Bible, see R. Rowlett, *Joshua and the Rhetoric of Violence*, JSOTSup 226 (Sheffield: Sheffield Academic Press, 1996) 121–69.

OBEDIENCE TO THE LAW

The second part of YHWH's speech also begins and ends with imperatives, in this case parallel commands to "be strong and courageous" (vv. 7a, 9a). The exhortations not only enclose others which
enjoin obedience to the book of the law but also constitute a catch
phrase which links this section with the previous one (cf. v. 6a). Through
this device, the speech joins the possession of the land with the observance of the Mosaic torah. As in the previous section, the double imperatives enclose material that deals with boundaries, but in this case the
boundaries circumscribe behavior rather than territory.

The exhortation to "be strong and courageous" (MT *ḥăzaq weʾĕmaṣ*)
is a stock phrase commonly associated with conflict or peril (Josh
10:25; 2 Sam 10:9-13; 1 Kgs 2:2; 1 Chr 19:13; 28:20; 2 Chr 32:7). Its use as
an exhortation for taking the land is therefore not unexpected, especially since Moses admonished both Joshua and the nation with the
same words (Deut 31:6, 7, 17; cf. Deut 3:28). However, its reorientation
toward adherence to the Mosaic torah is striking. The unexpected application of the phrase as a connecting device suggests that the two
tasks are inseparable. The same militant resolve that must attend Israel's conquest of the land must also characterize Joshua's strict observance of the words of Moses.[10] Failure of will in pursuit of either
task will compromise the rich life the nation seeks across the Jordan.

The commands to obedience (vv. 7-8) correspond to the highly-
charged nature of the exhortations, moving from negative to positive
in a chiastic pattern:

A Be strong and courageous, being careful to act in accordance
    with all the law that my servant Moses commanded you
    (v. 7a-b)

B Do not turn from it to the right hand or to the left, so that
    you may be successful wherever you go (v. 7c)

C This book of the law shall not depart out of your mouth
    (v. 8a)

C' You shall meditate on it day and night (v. 8b)

---

[10] The Hebrew language distinguishes between second person singular and
plural pronouns. The address in vv. 7-9 employs singular pronouns, indicating that
the subject of address is not Israel but Joshua. The speech, with its exhortations and
charges, is thus directed to Israel's leader first, making his resolve essential to completion of the task.

B' so that you may be careful to act in accordance with all that is written in it. For then you shall make your way prosperous, and then you shall be successful (v. 8c-d)

A' I hereby command you: Be strong and courageous; do not be frightened or dismayed, for the LORD your God is with you wherever you go (v. 9)

The structure of the section begins with parallel exhortations which link obedience (A) with divine promise (A') and then moves, from each end, to constructions which assert the fundamental connection between obedience and success, first in the negative ("do not turn" [B]) and later in positive ("you shall be careful to act in accordance" [B']).[11] At the center of the symmetry stand commands, expressed first in the negative and then in the positive, to keep the book of the law at the center of attention (C, C'). As a whole, the symmetry thus underscores the conviction that realization of divine promises will be achieved only through scrupulous observance of the divine commandments given through Moses.

The expression of obedience, in both positive and negative terms, echoes the language of Deuteronomy, especially as it addresses Israel's contact with the people of Canaan. Consider, for example, Deut 7:2-6, which surrounds negative commands with positive ones:

Positive   And when the Lord your God gives them over to you and you defeat them, then you must utterly destroy them (v. 2a).

Negative   Make no covenant with them and show them no mercy. Do not intermarry with them, giving your daughters to their sons or taking their daughters for your sons, for that would turn away your children from following me, to serve other gods. Then the anger of the LORD would be kindled against you and he would destroy you quickly (vv. 2b-5).

Positive   But this is how you must deal with them: break down their altars, smash their pillars, hew down their sacred poles, and burn their idols with fire (v. 6).

Expression of the same principles, in both positive and negative forms, alerts the reader to the comprehensive quality of obedient response that will be required of Joshua (and by extension, Israel). Israel must *do*

---

[11] The verbs in the second element (B') are not expressed in the imperative mode but are introduced by a particle (*lĕmaʿan*, "so that") which emphasizes that the ability to obey the law derives necessarily from keeping the law at the center of one's life.

certain things (that is, annihilate the peoples of Canaan and their religious paraphernalia) and *not do* others (that is, have any form of contact with the peoples).

The commands themselves leave little room for innovation or error.
The emphatic "be careful to act in accordance with," a common Deuteronomic expression (Deut 6:3, 15; 8:1; 11:32; 12:1; 31:12; 32:46), brackets
commands that employ verbs which signify comprehensive observance of the torah in thought, word and deed. The admonition that Joshua
must not "turn from it, neither to the right nor to the left" evokes the
notion of the Mosaic torah as a way of life that one "walks" (Deut 5:32-
33; cf. 17:8-13, 18-20; 8:6; 26:17) and which must be followed without
modification or deviation. The related charge that he must "meditate
on it day and night" places the book of the torah at the center of all reflection and decision-making.

The phrase "book of the law," occurs in Deuteronomy with reference to itself (25:61) and alludes once more to Joshua's commissioning
(31:24, 26)[12]. At that time, we are told, Moses wrote "the words of this
law" and ordered the Levites to put it next to the ark of the covenant as
a witness against Israel. The phrase thus intimates an implicit role for
the Mosaic torah: the law will testify to the people's future apostasy.
Predictions of Israelite disobedience and divine anger overshadow the
entire episode of Joshua's investiture (Deut 31:1-29), and allusions to
the event in the present text thus inject an element of uncertainty into
the admonitions to obedience. During Joshua's commissioning YHWH
informs Moses that he "knows what they are inclined to do, even now,
before I have brought them into the land that I promised them on
oath" (v. 21b). In addition, Moses confronts Israel, declaring that "I
know how rebellious and stubborn you are. If you already have been
so rebellious toward the Lord while I am still alive among you, how
much more after my death!" (v. 27). Between the ominous predictions
of YHWH (vv. 16-22) and Moses (vv. 24-29) stands the commissioning of
Joshua, punctuated by an exhortation to be strong and courageous and
a promise of divine presence (v. 23).[13] The many allusions to this episode, with its pessimistic assessment of Israelite fidelity and resolve,
thus jangle with the emphatic admonitions to adhere strictly to the
words of Moses. YHWH now demands complete obedience, yet has declared that Israel is incapable of such. How will rigorous obedience be

---

[12] The phrase also occurs in 2 Kgs 22:8, 11 in conjunction with the scroll found in
the temple during Josiah's reform. Here as well, Deuteronomy seems the likely referent.

[13] NRSV renders "be strong and bold" here, but the Hebrew terms are the same as
in Josh 1:6, 7, 9.

assessed when the people encounter situations not addressed by the book of the law?

An undercurrent of pessimism thus stands behind the exhortations and assurances of YHWH's opening speech. YHWH's words associate Israel's resolve in taking the land with a commensurate zeal in observing the words of Moses, introducing the two main trajectories along which the tale will be told and punctuating each theme with promises and exhortations. Yet the words also hearken back to warnings that Israel will be unable or unwilling to fulfill its promise.

Get Ready! 1:10-11

Joshua responds to YHWH's exhortations by issuing commands to the officers of people, thus extending the chain of command. He charges them to relay his words throughout the camp, just as he has been admonished to repeat the words of Moses (v. 8). The initial imperative to pass through the camp (*ʿibrû*) echoes the first command issued to Joshua (*ʿăbōr*) and the message given to the officers, like the previous speech of YHWH, combines a reiteration of the divine gift of the land with a call to action. The MT reinforces the program of initiative and response through the use of two participles. The first marks Israel as "those who cross" (*ʿōbĕrîm*), while the second again denotes YHWH as "the one who gives" (*nōtēn;* cf. v. 2).[14] Furthermore, infinitival forms of the verb *yāraš* ("to take possession of"), signifying the goal of the undertaking, enclose the promise of the land ("*to take possession* of the land that the LORD your God gives you *to possess*"). The terse language and staccato commands of this speech express a decisive response to the commands of YHWH which initiate the plot. The exhortations addressed to Joshua seem to have had their intended effect, for the new leader immediately moves the people to action.

Remember the Word of Moses! 1:12-15

The narrative moves from speech to speech, with no intervening report that the officers carry out their charge. Joshua's concern now shifts to the tribes of Reuben and Gad and the half-tribe of Manasseh.

---

[14] NRSV: you "are to cross over," the land the LORD your God "gives" you.

Beginning again with an imperative, he calls the tribes to honor a commitment made in response to the gift of land in the Transjordan. The admonition to "remember the word that Moses the servant of the LORD commanded you" refers to a troublesome incident that raises the question of the people's fidelity (Num 32:1-42). The trouble derives from an incident wherein the Reubenites and Gadites asked Moses to grant them the Transjordanian lands recently conquered by the Israelites. Moses responded angrily to the request, equating it with Israel's response to the spies' report at Kadesh-Barnea, which above all symbolized the failure of Israelite resolve and faith. Implying a similar lack of resolve ("Shall your brothers go to war while you sit here?" v. 6) Moses accused this "brood of sinners" (v. 14) of turning away from following YHWH (v. 15) and warned that they would experience the fierce anger of YHWH, just as the previous generation had. The situation was diffused only when the tribes volunteered to accompany the rest of the people into Canaan and assist them in taking possession of the land. Moses agreed to the compromise and informed Joshua, Eleazar, and the tribal leaders of the decision (v. 28). The Reubenites and Gadites then promised to "cross over armed before the LORD into the land of Canaan" (v. 32).

Moses' version of this incident appears in Deut 3:12-22. Joshua draws heavily from this text, closely following Deut 3:18-20 as he speaks to the eastern tribes.[15] However, he makes a slight but significant change. The Deuteronomic text speaks of the gift of the Transjordanian land as if it were a completed act and decrees that the eastern tribes may return to it after they have helped their kindred to achieve their "rest" in the land YHWH is "giving" to them (Deut 3:18b, 20).[16]

> Although the Lord your God has given you this land to occupy, all your troops shall cross over armed as the vanguard of your Israelite kin. . . . When the LORD gives rest to your kindred, as to you, and they too have occupied the land that the LORD your God is giving them beyond the Jordan, then each of you may return to the property that I have given to you.

Joshua, however, addresses the eastern tribes as those who also have yet to realize their "rest" and speaks as if the "giving" of the land is yet to occur (v. 16). By introducing the concept of rest at this point, Joshua equates the situation of the eastern tribes with that of the nation as a

---

[15] Polzin (*Moses,* 77–9) observes that Joshua repeats the sequence of the Deuteronomic account, which attributes the gift of the land alternately to YHWH and Moses. In Deuteronomy, the Mosaic "I have given" is ambiguous. Joshua, however, removes the ambiguity by inserting "Moses" in place of the "I" of Deuteronomy.

[16] The perfect form of *nātan* ("he gave") is used here.

whole (v. 18) and defines the state of affairs that will signify the completion of the program. The notion of land as "rest" represents the end which Israel seeks, peaceful existence in possession of the land (Deut 12:10; 25:19). It will appear later in the book to signify the completion of the program and the fulfillment of YHWH's promise to the nation (Josh 21:42; 22:4; 23:1). Joshua here implies that the eastern tribes, despite their possession of the Transjordanian lands, have not yet achieved the promised end, and cannot achieve it apart from their participation in the struggles of the entire nation. His words stress the necessity for unity. All Israel still seeks the promised rest, and the entire nation lives within the tension of a land that YHWH has already given and will yet give. Rest and land are both accomplished fact and future promise. The land which has been given must also be taken. One part of the nation cannot rest until all find rest.

The talk of unity masks a fractured Israel. The fact that certain tribes have chosen to live across the Jordan points to a difference of perspective in what constitutes the promised land.[17] United only during the campaigns to wrest Canaan from its indigenous inhabitants, the nation will be divided thereafter by a rift that cuts deeper than the geographical barrier that divides it. The Jordan valley not only constitutes a boundary but also a defining symbol and a point of reference. Traversing it signifies Israel's entry into the full measure of life YHWH gives. Although they also will enjoy life with YHWH, the tribes of Reuben, Gad, and half-Manasseh, cross not to gain inheritances but to fulfill an obligation. They enter the land not to seek life but to make good on a promise to "help their kindred." Crossing the Jordan does not therefore mean the same thing for them. Their objectives, energy, and aspirations are directed toward returning to a homeland rather than acquiring one.

Throughout Joshua's speech, the "givenness" of the Transjordanian land constitutes a persistent refrain expressing the united-yet-separate status of the eastern tribes. As we have noted above, Joshua declares that YHWH will give them their land (vv. 13b, 15a), thus joining them to the rest of the nation as a people awaiting the completion of the ancestral promise. Yet Joshua also speaks of their possession as "the land that Moses gave you beyond the Jordan" (vv. 14a, 15b), and in this he reveals the distinctive experience and perspective of the easterners.

---

[17] The status of the Transjordan is highly ambivalent, as the alternation between "YHWH gave"and "Moses gave" illustrates. The issue is discussed thoroughly by M. Weinfeld, "The Extent of the Promised Land—the Status of Transjordan," *Das Land Israel in biblischer Zeit*, GTA 25, ed. G. Strecker, (Göttingen: Vandenhoeck & Ruprecht, 1983) 59–75.

Those who live in the Transjordan retain a unique affinity to Moses not shared by the other tribes. Like Moses, they remain outside the promised land. The victories won to gain their possessions were achieved under his leadership, and it was he who determined their tribal allotments. The rest of the nation will remember Joshua as the divinely-appointed leader who won victories and allotted tribal inheritances, but the easterners' experience cannot endow him with the same acclamation. Their allegiance to him derives from their promise to Moses, and Joshua will play an incidental part in their stories and traditions. They have claims to the Mosaic tradition that the rest of the nation does not share, yet they will be marked as outsiders, those who live on the other side (Hebrew *bě⁽ēber*) of the Jordan.

All This We Will Do! 1:16-18

Questions of allegiance come to the fore during transitions of leadership, and Joshua must determine whether these tribes, who have little to gain and much to lose by crossing the Jordan, will recognize his authority. He receives an immediate and emphatic response. The eastern tribes explicitly recognize the succession of leadership, declaring "just as we obeyed Moses in all things, so we will obey you" (v. 17). Their words echo the opening speech of YHWH. Like YHWH, they proclaim their loyalty to Joshua in both positive and negative terms, promising whole-hearted obedience to every command (v. 16) and death to those who disobey (v. 18a).[18] They also repeat the promise of divine presence ("Only may the LORD your God be with you, as he was with Moses," v. 17b, cf. v. 5b) and the divine exhortation to "be strong and courageous" (v. 18b). Both declarations begin, in MT, with the Hebrew particle *raq* (NRSV "only"), a term which usually stands between two assertions and normally signals an exception, restriction or limitation. After an affirmative statement, it usually signals a strong disjunction and draws particular attention to what follows. What, then, do the eastern tribes mean when they say "only?" Are they placing limitations or qualifications on their loyalty? Are they making their obedience contingent on

[18] The Hebrew phrase *yamreh ʾet-pîkā*, translated "rebels against your orders" in NRSV, signifies rebellion against a divine decree, whether the verb occurs in the *Qal* stem (Num 20:24; 27:14) or the *Hiphil* stem (Deut 1:26, 43; 9:23). In all these cases, the rebellion is directed against an explicit command from YHWH. The eastern tribes use the phrase with reference to Joshua, thus affirming the divine authority of the commands he will issue.

YHWH's presence with Joshua and Joshua's courage and resolve? Or do they merely use it for emphasis?

The second of the two uses ("only be strong and courageous") presents additional difficulties. The phrase functions as a concluding exhortation and parallels YHWH's exhortation that Joshua observe the Mosaic torah (v. 7). In that context it signals a shift from resolve in taking the land to resolve in obeying the Mosaic torah and introduces a summary statement which emphasizes the crucial importance of resolve in both enterprises (as if to say *"above all* or *the main thing is,* be strong and courageous," cf. Deut. 4:9). However, the phrase does not seem to have the same function here (v. 18c). In this instance, it does not clarify or convey the essence of what has preceded it; although directed at Joshua, the preceding words have been addressed to the people of Israel. It introduces a reaffirmation of the promise of divine presence with Joshua, but not in response to any words addressed to him. Instead, like its occurrence in v. 17, the particle juxtaposes an exhortation to *Joshua* with a promise of obedience made by the *eastern tribes.* In both cases, the tribes articulate the divine words to Joshua immediately after they have pledged their obedience, with *raq* making the linkage. The particle seems to signal a connection between YHWH's presence, Joshua's resolve, and the eastern tribes' obedience to Joshua. Whether implicitly or explicitly, the tribes thus hint that their assistance and loyalty, like YHWH's, will depend on this resolve. Both uses of *raq* intimate that the Transjordanians' promises of obedience are not without reservation and thus possess an element of contingency.[19]

The eastern tribes affirm the authority of Joshua as Israel's new leader and conclude the chapter with a small irony. They, rather than Joshua, have the words of YHWH on their lips as the nation prepares to enter the land, and they, not Israel's new leader, speak the exhortation conventionally employed to inspire troops in battle. It will not be the last time that "outsiders" repeat the words of YHWH.

[19] Nelson, *Joshua*, 35–6.

Chapter Two
WHO'S WHO IN THE PROMISED LAND?
Joshua 2:1–12:24

The transformation of Israel from a nomadic people to a landed nation takes place in two stages. First, Joshua leads Israel to great victories over the peoples of Canaan and decrees the annihilation of captured cities and populations. Then, with Canaanite power effectively broken, he divides and apportions the land to the tribes. Joshua 2–12 relates the first phase of the process and presents a united people who prevail over mighty kings and walled cities. The episodes in this section highlight the themes of divine initiative and obedient response. YHWH fights Israel's battles and stipulates the disposition of captives and plunder. The Israelites in turn defeat their enemies as they seek the counsel of YHWH and act in obedience to divine decrees and ordinances.

The stories and reports which comprise this section may be grouped into three categories: battle reports, anecdotes, and reports of ritual observance. Stories of battles are prominent and develop the theme of conquest which moves the plot along. The first three campaigns, waged against cities in the central highlands, receive elaborate treatment and may be read as paradigms for all the campaigns conducted in Canaan. The first and third reports relate great Israelite victories at Jericho (6:1-27) and Gibeon (10:1-15) and attribute the victories to the participation of YHWH. The middle reports (7:2-5; 8:1-29) tell of a defeat at Ai, followed by a victory accomplished when YHWH supplies Israel with a particular stratagem. The remaining reports consist of terse summaries which appropriate stock forms and vocabulary (10:28-42; 11:1-15, 16-23; 12:1-24).

Associated with the battles of Jericho, Ai and Gibeon are anecdotes which focus on individuals rather than peoples (2:1-24; 7:1, 6-26; 9:1-27).

Each of these stories concerns some form of forbidden contact with Canaan, and together they advance a more subtle plot that raises fundamental questions of national identity. The first and third stories tell how and why certain peoples of the land are incorporated into the Israelite community. Both Rahab and the Gibeonites give glory to YHWH and display qualities associated with Israel. Though condemned by the rhetoric of Moses, their stories present them as survivors who take up permanent residence within Israel. The second story explores the opposite issue. The main character here is an Israelite who keeps for himself what has been reserved for YHWH. Achan's story ends when the entire nation turns against him and his family and stones them to death. In sum, the anecdotes deal with the issue of who may be included and excluded from the Israelite community and offer a rationale for the process. In the stories of Rahab and the Gibeonites, outsiders survive and live within Israel. Conversely, the story of Achan presents an insider who is excluded from the community.

The third group of stories, which presents instances of ritual observance, signifies both the continuity and transformation of Israelite identity. Most of the texts occur in a cluster which separates the story of Rahab and the spies from the report of the fall of Jericho. The crossing of the Jordan, an event that inaugurates Israel's transformation from a nomadic to a settled people, receives extensive treatment (3:1–4:24). It is followed in turn by reports of mass circumcision and the celebration of Passover, both constitutive rites of Israelite identity (5:2-12). A lengthy and elaborate set of rituals precedes the fall of Jericho (6:1-21), while another ritual purges Israel of an offending party (7:13-18) and leads to the conquest of Ai. A final ritual involves a covenant renewal ceremony which takes place in obedience to the commands of Moses (8:30-35) and depicts a nation bound by covenant to YHWH and circumscribed by the Mosaic law.

The campaigns at Jericho, Ai, and Gibeon employ a paratactic sequence which relates and connects the disparate events within these story groups. Anecdotes of individual encounters precede battles between the peoples, with little or no explicit explanation for the sequence. The reader is left to decipher structural and thematic cues which signal larger and more comprehensive meanings. The themes introduced in Joshua 1—YHWH's faithfulness in bringing Israel into the land, the crucial role of obedience, and the impulse toward integrity and totality—unite the various stories in this section into a larger whole. Battles and encounters take place against the backdrop of Deuteronomy's assertion that obedience leads to blessing and integrity brings success. Following their introduction in the initial speeches, the materials present both positive and negative expressions of these themes.

YHWH participates actively in bringing Israel into possession of the promised land. Much of the action begins in response to divine commands, relayed through Joshua, whom YHWH exalts as leader and divine intermediary (3:7, 14; 10:14). Through Joshua, YHWH leads Israel across the Jordan (3:7-8), gives directions for marking the event with memorial stones (4:1-3), decrees circumcision (5:2), and outlines plans of attack (6:1-5; 8:1-2; 11:6). YHWH takes an even more prominent role in Israel's campaigns to take the cities of Canaan. YHWH initiates each of the major battles with the announcement that he has "handed over" cities, kings, and enemies (6:2; 8:18; 10:8, 30, 32; 11:6). In summaries of the campaigns, the narrator confirms YHWH's role by explicitly attributing Israel's victories to YHWH's involvement (10:42; 11:20). Conversely, YHWH refuses to accompany Israel at Ai, and Joshua accuses the deity of "handing over" Israel to its enemies for the purpose of its destruction (7:7).

The theme of Israel's obedience is advanced through a number of devices. Israel's attention to ritual obligations (e.g. circumcision, Passover, and the erection of the altar on Mount Ebal) reinforces the impression that the nation as a whole carefully performs those acts which unite it to YHWH. Prompt and scrupulous execution of divine commands, often relayed through Joshua, confirms that Israel acts at YHWH's direction. Throughout the early chapters of the book, the narrator indicates the close correspondence between command and response by utilizing similar language to report each (e.g. 3:6; 4:15-18; 5:2-3; 6:22-23). More explicit endorsements of Israel's obedience appear in the form of the narrator's commentary on events. Thus we read that "the Israelites did as Joshua commanded" (4:8) and that "as the LORD had commanded his servant Moses, so Moses commanded Joshua, and so Joshua did; he left nothing undone of all that the LORD commanded Moses" (11:15; cf. 8:35). However, this portrait of national obedience is countered by instances of disobedience at the individual level. The spies who reconnoiter Jericho and the Israelite leaders who treat with the Gibeonites both make pacts that explicitly violate the command of Moses (Deut 7:2; Exod 34:15). Achan's sin represents an even more serious infraction which implicates the entire nation (7:1). In response to his theft of devoted items, YHWH accuses the nation of theft, deceit, and transgression of the covenant (7:11).

The Deuteronomic concern for integrity and homogeneity is articulated primarily through the reports of Israel's victories. The defeat of Canaanite kings, the conquest of their cities, and the massacre of the populace constitute a refrain sounded repeatedly as Israel takes one city after another. The people of Jericho and Ai are put to the edge of the sword, "both men and women, young and old" (6:21b; cf. 8:26), Joshua leaves "no one remaining" of the cities in southern Canaan (10:28, 30, 36, 38; cf. 10:32, 35), and "no one left who breathed" remains from the city of Hazor and the towns allied with it (11:11). The macabre refrain echoes a final time as the narrator summarizes Israel's conquests and casts them as expressions of careful obedience to the commands of YHWH and Moses (11:16-20). Summaries of conquests extend the scope of total victory to the entire land (10:40; 11:16, 23), and a list of conquered kings and cities conveys the magnitude of Israel's success (12:7-24). Israel fights as a unit during the execution of these campaigns and acts in complete accord with Joshua. During the conquest, leader and nation seem to coalesce, so that Israel's victories become Joshua's (10:28-41; 11:7-15, 16-23). The phrases "all Israel" and "the entire nation" occur repeatedly during the Jordan crossing (3:1,7,17; 4:1,11,14), the ceremony of circumcision (5:4,8), and the covenant renewal on Mts. Ebal and Gerizim (8:33, 35), and affirm that the community remains intact during these crucial events. "All Israel" also participates in the campaigns to take the cities of Canaan, particularly those in the South (10:29, 31, 34, 36, 38). Yet here as well, stories at the individual level challenge the claims of total conquest and the depiction of a unified, homogenous nation. The story of Rahab concludes with the incorporation of Canaanites into the Israelite community, while the covenant with Gibeon results in the incorporation of a geographical as well as ethnic enclave. And Achan's story reveals the presence of disobedient Israelites who do not follow the commands of Joshua or YHWH.

The stories of crossing and conflict thus create a series of interrelated oppositions: community vs. individual, obedience vs. disobedience, success vs. failure, unity vs. diversity. The "ideal" Israel, marked at the corporate level by unity, victory, and obedience conflicts with a narrated reality, at the individual level, which tells of disobedience, defeat, and diversity. The narrative oscillates back and forth between the corporate and the individual as Israel moves from the plains of Moab to the conclusion of its wars against the peoples of the land. These oppositions come together, however, through two leitmotifs that span the campaign of conquest.

Collections of stone, in the form of monuments or piles of rocks or rubble, characterize the first of these leitmotifs. They represent a permanence and presence, unite past, present, and future, and join the world of the story with the reader's world. On the one hand, stones signify YHWH's presence with Israel and Israel's obedient response to YHWH's graciousness. The stones erected at Gilgal commemorate YHWH's mighty acts at the Jordan (4:7) and in the nation's past (4:21-23), but they also represent "a memorial forever," whose meaning shall be recounted whenever children ask about them (4:6, 21). The construction of the stone altar on Mount Ebal (8:31) and the copying of the Mosaic law on stones (8:32) fulfill a prior command of Moses (Deut 27:1-8), express the nation's fidelity to YHWH and also serve as a memorial for future generations. The heaps of rubble at Ai (8:28, 29) and the stones at Makkedah (10:27) celebrate great victories achieved by YHWH's power and Israel's faith. Yet stones can also memorialize disobedience, failure, exclusion, and death. Achan and his family die under a hail of stones, and the heap raised over them silently witnesses to Israelite disobedience and its consequences.

The second leitmotif consists of a series of etiological notes, most of which occur in connection to the stone monuments. The notes have the effect of establishing a continuity between the story world and the reader's world. Phrases such as "to this very day" and "ever since" point to the enduring significance of the events to which they refer.[1] The etiological note explaining the name "Gilgal" does so by marking the removal of "disgrace" by an act of covenantal fidelity (6:8-9). Etiological notes confirm the continuing relevance of the monuments which testify to the acts of YHWH and the obedience of Israel at the Jordan (4:9), Ai (7:28, 29) and Makkedah (10:27). Other notices point in the opposite direction. The disobedience of Achan, and Israel's ignominious defeat at Ai, are underscored by the comment that the heap of stones over Achan "remains to this day" and that the site of his death has been called the Valley of Achor (Trouble) "to this day." Etiological notes also draw attention to the continuing presence of the peoples of the land within Israel. Rahab and her family have "lived in Israel ever since" (6:25), while the Gibeonites continue to cut wood and carry water at the altar of YHWH "to this day" (9:27).

Opposing sets of themes unite diverse materials in Joshua 2–12. Expressed positively, the themes reflect Deuteronomy's concerns for obedience, success, and unity. Expressed negatively, they point to Israel's disobedience, failure and disintegration. These oppositions come together in the leitmotifs of stones and etiologies, which become important vehicles for reorienting the issues they represent to the reader's context.

Israel and the Peoples of the Land

The oppositions which configure the plot of Joshua 2–12 mask a more profound conflict, namely the struggle to establish and maintain

---

[1] Both these and similar phrases in the NRSV translate the Hebrew ʿad hayyôm hazzeh.

the internal boundaries that define the nation and hold it together. These internal boundaries are established, in an ideal form, through the book of Deuteronomy and are embraced by Israel as it assembles to renew the covenant on the plains of Moab (Deut 29:1ff). Israel is YHWH's "treasured possession" (Deut 7:6; 14:2; 26:18), a people formed by a unique experience of YHWH's saving acts and mighty deeds (Deut 4:32-40). Bound by covenant to this God, its communal life is circumscribed by a code of laws that addresses both individual behavior and social organization. These laws draw boundaries which define behavior characteristic of the nation. Those obeying the commandments of Moses experience the life promised by YHWH and live under divine blessing. Those who disobey are subject to exclusion and death. In addition, the laws constitute a barrier between the coherent Israelite nation and the multifarious peoples of the land. Against the integrity of Israel, the peoples of the land signify the opposing concept of plurality, the "many" in contrast to the Israelite "one." Their diversity marks them as "other than Israel" and, more significantly, as a threat to Israelite identity. This threat is so potent that Deuteronomy mandates their annihilation. In a sense, the peoples of Canaan threaten Israel much more by their *difference* than by their walled cities or iron chariots. Canaanite multiplicity threatens the distinctive unity of Israel, for if any vestige of Canaan is left within the land the nation may become ensnared into imitating its peoples (Deut 12:29-32). For Israel to dwell securely in the land, all that is different must be eliminated.[2]

The stories related in Joshua 2–12 relate Israel's encounter with difference. The Deuteronomic markers of Israelite unity and Canaanite plurality appear throughout this section as "all Israel," under the leadership of Joshua, defeats the various kings and peoples of Canaan. They are opposed by the stories of Rahab (2:1-24; 6:22-25), Achan (7:1-26), and the Gibeonites (9:1-27). While the battle reports depict Israel's stunning victories over the peoples of the land (and the destruction of their cities), the stories associated with them challenge notions of Israelite distinctiveness. The three story complexes work together to create a profoundly ambivalent perspective toward the peoples of the land. Is Israel truly a united nation which diligently observes all the commandments of Moses? Are the peoples of the land, by definition, ex-

---

[2] It is important to note that Joshua nowhere explains the extermination of the Canaanites in terms of their sinfulness or corruption. Even in Deuteronomy, where the explanation appears (9:4-5), its rhetorical use (to highlight that Israel does not deserve the land) diminishes its impact. Their extermination is more frequently explained as a measure against their power to draw Israel away from YHWH (Deut 7:1-5; 20:16-18; Josh 23:12-13).

cluded from the Israelite community? What precisely are the boundaries which distinguish Israel from Canaan, and how far do the boundaries extend?

A Common Plot

The stories of the campaigns against Jericho (2:1-24; 6:1-27), Ai (7:1–8:29), and Gibeon (9:1–10:15) display a symmetry of structure and theme that suggests we are to read them in light of common concerns; namely, the issue of inclusion in and exclusion from the Israelite community. The first and third stories (Rahab, the Gibeonites) preface reports of Israelite victories with accounts of Canaanites who are spared from the destruction inflicted on those around them. The middle story reverses the elements of the other stories by inserting the story of an excluded Israelite (Achan) between accounts of an Israelite defeat and victory at Ai. Common elements configure each of the stories, although in the case of the middle story each is inverted. Taken as a whole, these elements comprise a single plot which moves from concealment to uncovering, and from inclusion or exclusion to the opposite status. The stories focusing on the Canaanites follow the same basic plot:

CHART 1: OUTSIDERS INCLUDED:
THE COMMON PLOT OF THE RAHAB AND GIBEON STORIES

---

1. *Concealment:*	Israelites secretly enter Jericho (2:1) and are hidden by Rahab (2:4).
	Gibeonites disguise themselves, hiding their identity (9:3-6).
2. *Interrogation:*	The king's men interrogate Rahab concerning the spies (2:2-3).
	Israelite leaders interrogate the Gibeonites (9:7-8).
3. *Diversion:*	Rahab sends the king's men into the hills after the spies (2:4b-5, 7).
	Gibeonites invite Israelite leaders to sample their provisions (9:12-13).
4. *Doxology:*	Rahab acclaims YHWH's mighty acts at the Red Sea and Jordan (2:8-11).
	Gibeonites acclaim YHWH's mighty acts against Egyptians & Amorites (9:9-11).

5. *Petition:*	Rahab asks the spies to spare her family (2:12-13). Gibeonites ask Joshua to make a treaty with them (9:6).
6. *Response:*	The spies agree to a pact with Rahab (2:14). Joshua and the leaders make a covenant of peace with the Gibeonites (9:15).
7. *Qualification:*	The spies declare their innocence and qualify the pact (2:17-20). Rahab agrees (2:21). Israelites grumble and the leaders consign Gibeonites to menial labor (9:16-23). Gibeonites agree (9:24-26).
8. *Battle Report:*	Israel achieves victory through YHWH's active participation.

   A. YHWH assures Joshua of victory at Jericho (6:2).
      YHWH assures Joshua of victory at Gibeon (10:8).

   B. Victory achieved by miracle (walls fall) at Jericho (6:20).
      Victory achieved by miracle (stones, sun standing still) at Gibeon (10:11-14).

   C. Israel massacres the people of Jericho (6:21).
      Israel massacres the armies of the five kings (10:20).

9. *Etiological Note:*	Rahab "lives within Israel to the present day" (6:27). The Gibeonites "cut wood and carry water to the present day" (9:27).
10. *Curse:*	Joshua utters a curse on those who rebuild Jericho (6:26). Joshua declares the Gibeonites accursed (9:23).

The story of the conquest of Jericho begins when two Israelite spies enter Jericho and attempt to conceal their identities as they scout the land. (Later they themselves are hidden on a rooftop under stalks of flax.) Their presence in the city is somehow discovered, and the king dispatches a posse to the house of Rahab, where they have taken refuge. The king's men interrogate Rahab in an attempt to find the spies, but she successfully diverts them by suggesting that the spies may have already escaped and have headed for the hills. With the posse off on a fruitless search, Rahab returns to the spies and speaks to them. She begins by acclaiming the mighty deeds of YHWH and confessing YHWH's supremacy. Then she asks the spies to spare her life and the lives of her family when Israel enters the land. The spies quickly agree to her request, and she helps them escape through a window in the wall. Once outside, the spies disavow responsibility for the oath they have just sworn and make qualifications to the agreement; she must tie a crimson cord to the window and remain inside with her family while the Israelites destroy the city. Rahab agrees to the additional terms and the spies return to Joshua. The story breaks off at this point in order to relate the crossing of the entire nation and resumes when the Israelites prepare to take the city of Jericho. YHWH announces the relative helplessness of Jericho and its king (who have been given over to Israel's power) and calls for a series of ritual marches around the city. Victory is gained on the seventh day, when the walls of the city fall as the Israelites shout. The victors destroy the city and its inhabitants but, as promised, spare Rahab and her family. The narrator closes the account with a note that Rahab has lived within Israel ever since and with the report of Joshua's curse over the demolished city.

The campaign at Gibeon follows essentially the same sequence, although the "Petition" and "Diversion" components occur out of sequence for dramatic effect. The battle with the five kings at Gibeon is preceded by a story which parallels that of Rahab and the spies. In this case Gibeonite "travelers" seeking to save their city enter the Israelite camp at Gilgal. Like the Israelite spies at Jericho, they conceal their identities, although much more effectively. They disguise themselves with tattered clothing, worn-out baggage, and stale provisions, giving the impression that they have been traveling for a long period of time. Their disguise not only reinforces their claim that they have traveled from a distant land but also implicitly suggests an affinity with Israel; they, like the Israelites, have been traveling for a long time. Presenting themselves as emissaries of a distant country, they request that Joshua make a treaty with them. Joshua, however, questions them in an attempt to discover their identity. The Gibeonites successfully divert this line of questioning by first acclaiming the mighty acts of YHWH and then by inviting the Israelite leaders to investigate their provisions rather than their identities. The leaders agree to the treaty and confirm it by an oath. However, the Israelites learn their true identity three days later (the length of time the spies had spent in the hills; cf. 2:22), and this leads to dissension in the camp. Joshua and the leaders decide to uphold the oath, but qualify it by decreeing that the Gibeonites must become menial laborers. They summon the Gibeonites, curse them for their deceit, and deliver the new terms. In response, the Gibeonites explain the reason for their deceit and accede to the Israelite demands. The narrator then concludes the account by confirming that Israel did indeed spare the Gibeonites, who have remained within Israel ever since. The ensuing battle against the five kings at Gibeon then follows the basic structure of the Jericho report. Faced by the combined forces of five kings, the Gibeonites call on Joshua to save them. In response, the Israelites march in force from Gilgal, accompanied by YHWH's assurance that the kings have been given over to Joshua. Here as well spectacular events lead to Israelite victory. YHWH throws the armies of the kings into panic, throws huge stones on them as they flee, and stops the sun so that the Israelites may continue the annihilation of the enemy forces. The five kings flee into a cave at Makkedah, where they are trapped until victory is complete. Joshua then commands that the kings be brought before him, strikes them down, and hangs them on five trees to symbolize that they are accursed (cf. Deut 21:22-23). The narrator concludes with a note that the stones which mark the site of their burial in the cave remain to this very day.

The middle set of stories, which relates the campaign at Ai, follows the pattern of the surrounding accounts but inverts both the sequence and the particular components. Whereas the others open with episodes that result in the incorporation of Canaanites into Israel, this campaign opens with an Israelite defeat on the battlefield and tells the tale of an Israelite who shares the fate of the peoples of the land. Victory is also achieved in the opposite manner, not by a united force which cuts down those already thrown into panic by YHWH's might, but by a divided force through an ingenious strategy. As in the other accounts, this one opens with an act of concealment: Achan the Israelite has secretly taken some of the spoil of Jericho for himself. As a consequence, YHWH no longer accompanies the armies of Israel. Rather, YHWH's anger burns against them. Israel goes up against Ai, but not in response to divine initiative and with an assurance of victory uttered not by YHWH but by Israelite spies. This time the Israelites, not their adversaries, are routed.

Seeking to uncover the reason for the defeat, Joshua interrogates YHWH and, reversing the divine promise that the nations will be handed over to Israel, asks why YHWH has handed Israel over to the inhabitants of the land. YHWH responds with a series of accusations, including the charge that Israel has transgressed the covenant, and reveals that Achan has not been successful in concealing his theft from divine eyes. Then YHWH commands Joshua to assemble the nation so that the offender can be identified by the casting of lots. During the subsequent assembly the lot falls to Achan, and Joshua commands him to give glory to YHWH and to "make confession" to YHWH (in contrast to the unsolicited praises uttered by Rahab and the Gibeonites). Achan readily confesses and reveals the location of the hidden items, which are recovered and presented in plain view of the entire nation. Unlike Rahab he makes no plea for his life nor for the lives of his family. There is no agreement of deliverance and no negotiation. Instead, Joshua immediately seals his fate by putting a curse on him: "May YHWH bring trouble on you this very day" (7:25, AT). At this pronouncement, all Israel unites to stone Achan and his family to death. The heap of stones raised over them, the narrator reports, remains "to this day."

The narrative then moves from the rubble raised over Achan to the destruction of the town called "Ruin." The battle follows the form of the other reports and begins with the divine declaration that the king of Ai, with his city, people, and land, have been handed over to the Israelites. As at Jericho, YHWH gives detailed instructions about the conduct of battle, but in this case his instructions employ a bit of irony; YHWH instructs some of the warriors to conceal themselves in ambush behind the city while the others encamp in plain view of the people of Ai. When the battle is joined, however, YHWH does not participate, allowing the shock of ambush to provoke panic in the enemy. The result is the same as in the other instances; the Israelite troops massacre the entire populace, after which Joshua orders the burning of Ai and hangs its king on a tree. The story concludes with the narrator's note that the heap of stones over Ai and over the king's body remains "to this day."

The story of Achan stands in opposition to those of Rahab and the Gibeonites. Achan, a pedigreed Israelite (7:1) steps outside prescribed boundaries and receives the full measure of violence previously reserved for the inhabitants of the land. The heap of stones raised over Achan links him explicitly to the heaps over Ai and its king. Achan the Israelite is excluded from the community and suffers the fate of the people of Canaan, while his counterparts in the other stories survive and continue to live in the land.[3]

CHART 2: INSIDERS EXCLUDED:
THE PLOT OF ACHAN'S STORY

---

1. *Concealment:*   Achan the **Israelite** steals some of the booty of Jericho (7:1).

    Battle Report: Israel is **defeated**.
    A. **Israelite spies** give assurance of victory (7:2-4).
    C. Israel is **routed** (7:5).

2. *Interrogation:*   Joshua interrogates YHWH (7:6-9).

3. *Diversion:*   YHWH diverts the issue from defeat to transgression (7:10-12).

---

[3] See also L. D. Hawk, "The Problem with Pagans," *Reading Bible, Writing Bodies,* ed. T. K. Beal and D. M. Gunn (London: Routledge, 1997) 153–63 and L. Rowlett, "Inclusion, Exclusion, and Marginality in the Book of Joshua," *JSOT* 55 (1992) 15–23.

4. *Doxology:*   Achan is **admonished** to give glory to YHWH
                        (7:19).

5. *Petition:*   Achan incriminates himself and offers **no plea**
                        for deliverance (7:20-21).

6. *Response:*   Achan and his family are **condemned to death**
                        (7:24-25).

10. *Curse:*   Joshua curses Achan (7:24).

8. *Etiological Note:* Achan's **grave** remains "to this day" (7:26).

9. *Battle Report:*   Israel destroys Ai.
   A. YHWH promises victory (8:1-2b, 18).
   B. Victory achieved through **deceit** (8:2c-21).
   C. The Israelites burn Ai and massacre its populace (8:22-27).

8. *Etiological Notes:* Ai remains a pile of rubble "to the present day"
                        (8:28).
                        The heap of stones over the king's body remains
                        "to this day" (8:29).

An inversion of character traits corresponds to the inversion in plot elements. In the first and third stories, the Canaanite characters possess attributes often ascribed to Israel. Rahab displays energy and courage as she aggressively seeks life in the land and wrests from the Israelite spies a promise that she and her family will live in the land. Likewise, the Gibeonite emissaries exhibit resourcefulness and initiative in securing continued life in the land. In both cases, Canaanite characters drive the action of the plot. And even more significant, the only words of praise to YHWH in these stories are spoken by them and not the Israelites. In contrast, the Israelite characters in these stories appear passive, inept, and driven by less than lofty impulses. The Israelite spies can only react to Rahab's words and, although making a pact with anyone in the land is strictly forbidden by Moses, they agree to spare her in exchange for their own lives. In a similar fashion, Joshua and the Israelite leaders fail to seize the initiative when confronted with the Gibeonites' ploy, are easily duped by their transparent ruse, and seem eager to make a (forbidden) treaty without seeking guidance from YHWH. The inversion is complete as the campaign at Ai unfolds. Here Israelite hearts melt, Israelite troops panic, and the unity of the community works against itself as one of their number provokes divine anger against all.

The juxtaposition of anecdotes and battle reports raises the question of Israelite distinctiveness and evokes a reflection on Israelite identity. The battle reports present the interaction of Israel and Canaan as a conflict between peoples. They share a common focus on the mighty acts of YHWH, who delivers peoples and cities into Israel's hands, and on the necessity of a united response on the part of Israel. When all Israel follows the initiative of YHWH the result is victory and the elimination of Israel's adversaries. When Israel acts on its own accord or when some undertake an independent path (as in the case of Achan), YHWH opposes the people and the nation cannot accomplish its tasks. For their part, the peoples of the land represent obstacles that must be overcome and eliminated in the pursuit of national aspirations—nothing more and nothing less.

The anecdotes, however, counter this perspective by narrowing the focus to the level of individual interaction with Canaan. Here the plot revolves around questions of identity and inclusion in the Israelite community. Each begins with an element of deceit or concealment. (Suggesting, perhaps, that not everything is as it seems?) And in each case, the story is driven by the impulse to discover or reveal. The posse at Jericho seeks the Israelite spies hidden on the roof of a Canaanite prostitute's house. The Israelite leaders seek the identity of the offender at Ai and the identities of the wayfarers from Gibeon. All conclude with a transformation of identity; Rahab and the Gibeonites are incorporated "within Israel," while Achan and his family take on the semblance of the pulverized Canaanite cities and their kings. The transformations, however, are not complete. Rahab and the Gibeonites are "within Israel to this very day," but Rahab lives outside the camp and the Gibeonites are set apart to cut wood and carry water for Israel. They are thus both Israel and not-Israel. The same is true of Achan. Though he is cursed and excluded, marked by a heap that resembles those at Ai and over the graves of kings, Achan yet retains his Israelite genealogy. He is, also, both not-Israel and Israel.

The transformation of identities in these stories, along with the marginal status of the characters, reflects a deep ambivalence regarding the community's internal boundaries. The narrator utilizes symmetry and contrast to hold both Canaanites and Israelites up for scrutiny in a way that challenges the inflexible idealism of Deuteronomy. The stories of Rahab and the Gibeonites make a strong case for extending the boundaries to include those "not-Israelites" who acknowledge the supremacy of YHWH, and their marginal status within Israel "to this very day" calls on the reader to embrace the ambiguity they represent. On the other hand, Achan's story insists that expansion of the boundaries must not be mistaken for their dissolution. "Not-Israelites" may become part of Israel, but transit in the opposite direction will not be tolerated.

On a deeper level, these stories introduce us to Canaanites who possess the positive attributes prized by Israel, and Israelites who possess traits ascribed to Canaan. In the face-to-face encounters between Israel and Canaan, we meet Canaanites who look like Israelites and Israelites who look like Canaanites. Canaanites, the "near others" within the story, exhibit a striking resemblance to the Israelite invaders and vie with Israelites for the role of protagonist in their stories.[4] Their prominence and characteristics have the odd effect of prompting "us" to identify with "them." While we can easily identify with Israel's victories over kings and cities, we cannot so easily identify with Israelites against Rahab, the Gibeonites, and even Achan. Given the bewildering confusion of attributes, whose interests do we follow? Are we to perceive the sparing of Rahab and the Gibeonites and the execution of Achan positively or negatively? To answer these questions, we must reflect on a more profound one, namely, what *essentially* defines the people of God? Is it possession of land? The stories would suggest otherwise, for peoples of the land remain among Israel, on the margins and in the center and Israelite Achan receives a burial plot instead of an inheritance. Is it obedience to the commands of Moses? Evidently not, for Israelites display disregard for the explicit commands of Moses, make covenants with peoples of the land (cf. Deut 7:1-5) and take what is devoted to YHWH. Is it an ethic of separation from others? No, for Rahab and the Gibeonites live among Israel to this very day, and bonds of kinship cannot alone insure membership in the community (as with Achan).

Taken together, the stories demonstrate that neither possession of territory, obedience to the commands of Moses, nor protection of ethnic purity mark the definitive core of Israelite identity. Rather, they reveal that *choices* determine who will be included or excluded from the nation. Rahab and the Gibeonites, through their acclamations of YHWH's acts and glory, implicitly affirm a choice for YHWH and for inclusion among the people of God. By taking devoted plunder, Achan chooses to defy YHWH and the explicit boundaries which signify allegiance to God and the community. On the basis of these choices, Rahab and the Gibeonites live among Israel "to this very day," while Achan is excluded and condemned. The boundaries which configure Israel, these stories suggest, are not those of race, territory, or practice but of choices. To be sure, the battle reports assert the importance of possession, obedience, and separation, but these are denied ultimacy by the stories associated with the campaigns. Israel is a people constituted by choices. Though implicit at this point, this definitive attribute will con-

---

[4] On the problems that "near others" raise for community identity, see R. L. Cohn, "Before Israel: The Canaanites as Other in Biblical Tradition," *The Other in Jewish Thought and History: Constructions of Jewish Culture and Identity*, ed. Laurence J. Silberstein and Robert L. Cohn (New York: New York University, 1994) 74–90.

tinue to appear in subsequent material, until it is given explicit expression in the final chapters of the book.

Ritual Confirmation

The rituals performed by Israel reinforce the narrative's subtle assertion that Israelite identity is a matter of choices. Rituals in Joshua confirm both inclusion and exclusion in the Israelite community and, for those who participate, contribute to the formation of unity and integrity. The performance of communal rituals occurs at key points within the narrative, affirming Israelite distinctiveness and unity against the peoples of the land. The Jordan crossing asserts the transformation of Israel into a landed nation, even though some elements of the people will later cross the river to return to homes on the "other side." Circumcision and the celebration of the Passover recall the promise of the land to Abram (Gen 17:8) and Israel's deliverance from Egypt (Exod 12:1ff), shared memories and experiences that set the nation apart from all others. The ritualized processions around Jericho enforce the notion that Israel enjoys its life in the land only as it devotes itself to YHWH. On the other hand, a ritual at Ai unites the community in an act which excludes those who have chosen to seek their own fulfillment apart from the claims of YHWH.

Each of the rituals unifies the nation through acts which express identification with YHWH and participation in the life of YHWH's people. The covenant ceremony at Mts. Ebal and Gerizim (8:30-35) therefore constitutes the definitive statement of identity within this swirl of stories. Located strategically after the debacle at Ai, the ceremony affirms the centrality of choosing intimated by the stories of Rahab and Achan and prepares the reader for its forceful expression in the subsequent story of the Gibeonites. Located in the vicinity of Shechem, a city notably absent from the list of conquests, the ceremony subordinates obedience to the commands of Moses and ethnic purity to the declaration of decision. Those who assemble between the mounts are diverse, comprising "alien as well as citizen" (v. 33). Yet by participating in the recitation of blessings and curses, all are united by affirming decisions and consequences (cf. Deut 27:1–28:29). This explicit expression of identity also looks ahead to the last episode of the book, which constitutes an even more elaborate reflection on the core of Israelite identity (Josh 24:1-28).

Chapter Three
STRANGERS IN THE NIGHT
Joshua 2:1-24

The story of Rahab and the Israelite spies is arguably the most richly textured text in the book of Joshua. The narrator skillfully incorporates elements of humor, irony, and folklore to disarm and engage the reader. Allusions to a variety of biblical texts and motifs suggest that the characters and themes of the story are imbued with a metaphorical significance that transcends the events themselves. The story begins and ends as a spy story (2:1a, 23-24) and broadly parallels other stories in which hand-picked men reconnoiter land in preparation for an assault (Num 13:1-33; Deut 1:22-25; Josh 7:2; Judg 1:23-25; 18:2-11). Stock elements of hidden identity, the threat of discovery, and a narrow escape create a highly-charged atmosphere of suspense. The core of the story, however, pursues a different topic and employs different conventions; namely, the shrewd woman who prevails over men.[1] At its heart is a series of negotiations conducted between a Canaanite prostitute and Israelite invaders, both of whom are seeking to save their lives. Rahab herself typifies a character common in folklore: the prostitute who gets what she wants through trickery. In this role she resembles other biblical prostitutes (also outsiders): Delilah, who seduces Samson through the power of her words (Judg 16:4-22), and

---

[1] For more on these folkloric elements, see Y. Zakovitch, "Humor and Theology or the Successful Failure of Israelite Intelligence: A Literary-Folkloric Approach to Joshua 2," *Text and Tradition: The Hebrew Bible and Folklore,* ed. S. Niditch (Atlanta: Scholars, 1990) 75–98 and D. J. McCarthy, "The Theology of Leadership in Joshua 1–9," *Bib* 52 (1971) 165–75.

Tamar, who masquerades as a prostitute (Gen 38:1-30) in order to secure her place within Israel.[2] The plot of the story, which concerns
Rahab's concealment of the spies, echoes other biblical stories in which
women hide men from their pursuers and facilitate their escape (1 Sam
19:11-17; 2 Sam 17:15-20).[3]

As a whole, the story subtly evokes one of the most disconcerting
texts in the Bible, the destruction of Sodom and Gomorrah (Gen 19:1-
29). At first glance the two texts seem to have little in common beyond
their common subject, the deliverance of citizens of a doomed city
through the intervention of two visitors. Yet both are linked by a remarkable correspondence in structure, vocabulary, atmosphere, and
character. The two narratives follow a common sequence which comprises five episodes.

CHART 3: THE COMMON TALE OF TWO DOOMED CITIES

Episode 1: Two Strangers Enter the City

SODOM   JERICHO

1. Strangers enter Sodom,   1. Strangers enter Jericho and
   intending to sleep in the city   lodge with Rahab (v. 1b).
   plaza, but lodge with Lot
   (vv. 1-3).

Episode 2: The Strangers Are Sought

SODOM   JERICHO

1. Citizens demand the strangers   1. The king's men demand the
   be brought out (vv. 4-5).   strangers be brought out
                                          (vv. 2-3).

---

[2] The parallels between Tamar and Rahab are especially intriguing. Both are
Canaanites who succeed in securing a place within "Israel" and mark their success
with a crimson cord (Gen 38:28-30; Josh 2:18, 21). Rahab's story also resembles that
of Naaman (2 Kgs 5:1-19). On the latter see R. Goldenberg, *The Nations That Know
Thee Not* (New York: New York University, 1998) 16–8. For more on prostitutes,
trickery, and escape, see P. Bird, "The Harlot as Heroine: Narrative Art and Social
Presupposition in Three Old Testament Texts," *Semeia* 46 (1989) 119–39.

[3] Michal helps David escape from the king's men by letting him down through
the window, just as Rahab does with the spies. In the other instance, an anonymous
woman hides Ahimaaz and Jonathan, David's two spies in a well and covers the
place with grain, just as Rahab covers the Israelite spies with flax. In a twist on this
motif, Jael pretends to hide the fleeing Canaanite general Sisera but kills him as he
sleeps (Judg 4:17-22).

2. Lot offers his daughters, who "have not known men," in order to save his guests (vv. 6-8).

2. Rahab claims "not to know" in order to save her guests (v. 4).

3. The men are blinded and sent away (vv. 9-11).

3. The men are fooled and sent away (vv. 5-7).

Episode 3: Destruction Is Announced

SODOM

JERICHO

1. Visitors announce the destruction of Sodom.

1. Rahab anticipates the destruction of Jericho.

2. Lot is told to gather his family (vv. 12-14).

2. Rahab negotiates the deliverance of her family (vv. 8-14).

Episode 4: Protest and Escape

SODOM

JERICHO

1. Lot is told to flee to the hills (v. 15-17).

1. Rahab tells the spies to flee to the hills (v. 16).

2. Lot protests and requests shelter at Zoar (vv. 18-20)

2. The spies attempt to modify their agreement (vv. 17-20)

3. The angels agree to modify the command (vv. 21-22)

3. Rahab agrees to the modification (v. 21).

4. Lot arrives at Zoar (v. 23)

4. The spies return to Shittim (vv. 22-24).

Episode 5: Destruction and Deliverance

SODOM

JERICHO

1. Sodom & Gomorrah are destroyed (vv. 24-25).

1. Jericho is destroyed (vv. 15-21)

2. Lot and his family are spared— except for his wife (v. 26).

2. Rahab and her entire family are spared (vv. 22-25).

Each begins when two men enter a city marked for destruction and receive shelter in the house of one of the inhabitants. In the Genesis version, Lot meets two angels at the gate of the city and invites them to spend the night at his house. The angels initially refuse, declaring instead that they intend to spend the night in the town square, but then yield to Lot's urging and accompany him to his house (19:1-3). The opening episode in Joshua relates a similar encounter but in more succinct language (2:1b): "so they (the spies) went, and entered the house of a prostitute whose name was Rahab, and spent the night there." Although terse, the Hebrew rendering of the report makes a significant linkage; the name "Rahab" (Hebrew *rāḥāb*) derives from the same root as the word employed to denote the town square *(rāḥôb)* where the angels intend to spend the night.

The next episode takes place in the middle of the night when people of the city come looking for the men. The men of Sodom surround Lot's house and ask, "Where are the men who came to you tonight?" The query is followed by a demand: "Bring them out to us so that we may know them." In an attempt to protect his guests, Lot offers his daughters, "who have not known a man," to the mob. This ploy, however, proves unsuccessful, and when they try to push through the door the angels rescue Lot and blind the men, who are left groping for the door. The king's men arrive at Rahab's house and make the same demand: "Bring out the men who have come to you, who entered your house." Rahab replies that she does not "know" where the men had come from and does not "know" where they went. She then succeeds in protecting her guests by sending the men out through the city gate and off into the darkness.

The tension mounts in the third episode as the destruction of the city is announced and the terms of deliverance are pressed. The angels try to impress a reluctant Lot with the grave peril he faces, declaring that YHWH is about to destroy the place. With a sense of urgency they prod him to gather his family together so that they may be saved. Lot, however, proves unsuccessful in this task as well; his sons-in-law think he is joking. As the dawn breaks, the angels seize the still-hesitant Lot, along with his wife and daughters, and bring them outside the city with orders to flee into the surrounding hills. Lot, however, objects to going into the hills and asks instead to be allowed to flee to one of the nearby towns. The angels agree to the request, continuing all the while to insist that he make haste. At Jericho Rahab, rather than the visitors, expresses a sense of urgency as she alludes to the imminent destruction of the city and presses the spies to make a pact which will spare her life and the lives of her family. In this case, both hosts and guests are in peril, and Rahab forcefully wrests a promise of deliverance in return for helping the spies escape from the city. She then lowers them through her window in the city wall and tells them (as the angels did Lot) to flee into the surrounding hills. At this point the spies protest the oath they have just made and, like Lot, suggest a modification more to their liking. Rahab agrees and the spies go on their way.

Both stories conclude with the destruction of the city and the salvation of the host family. The destruction of Sodom occurs at the hand of YHWH, who obliterates the city (along with Gomorrah) with a rain of sulfur and fire. Lot's wife, however, turns back to view the cataclysm and turns into a pillar of salt, leaving Lot with only his two daughters. The end of Rahab's story is delayed by three chapters of intervening material which relate Israel's entry into the land. The delay builds suspense as Rahab's fate hangs in the balance. (Will the Israelites honor the agreement?) Finally, Jericho, like Sodom, is utterly destroyed, although this time through the hands of the Israelites rather than by divine conflagration. Before the city is put to the torch, Joshua orders the spies to go into Rahab's house and bring her out, along with "all who belong to her." Unlike Lot, therefore, Rahab escapes the destruction of the city with her entire family intact.

Corresponding roles match the symmetry of structure shared by the two stories: the Israelite spies parallel the angelic visitors to Sodom, and Rahab coincides with Lot. However the *traits* of the characters in the two stories are reversed. Rahab dictates the course of events and moves the action forward with the same urgency as the angels display at Sodom. Like the angels, she proclaims the deeds of YHWH and dispels the group of citizens who come seeking the visitors. The spies, on the other hand, exhibit traits reminiscent of Lot. They appear passive and powerless throughout their encounter with Rahab. At the mercy of their host, they agree to a pact which secures her survival but later protest and attempt to revise the agreement.

The biblical narrator thus tells the story of the spies in Jericho in a manner that draws strong, though subliminal, connections to the story of the destruction of Sodom.[4] By shaping this story along the lines of the other, the narrator accomplishes two things. First, the dark mood rendered by the association suggests that something is seriously wrong at Jericho. Second, the reversal of character traits confuses issues of guilt and punishment. Like the people of Sodom, the Canaanite inhabitants of Jericho are wicked (Deut 9:4-5) and therefore subject to extermination. Yet Rahab displays the heroic traits attributed to the angels in the Genesis story, while the spies display the fluctuation of Lot. And unlike Lot, who is saved simply because of his genetic relationship to Abraham (Gen 19:29), Rahab's deliverance from the carnage is attributed to an act of deliverance (Josh 6:17). This Canaanite prostitute acts,

[4] In its connection to the story of Sodom and Gomorrah, the story of Rahab and the spies alludes as well to the story of the outrage at Gibeah (Judg 19:1-31). The texts do not, however, display distinct parallels in structure and vocabulary. It appears that Rahab's story has been shaped explicitly along the lines of the Genesis text. For more on the parallels between the two stories, see L. D. Hawk, "Strange Houseguests: Rahab, Lot, and the Dynamics of Deliverance," *Reading Between Texts,* ed. D. N. Fewell (Louisville: Westminster John Knox, 1992) 89–97.

in short, like an angel of God and succeeds, like Sodom's visitors, in rescuing an entire family from death.

Visitors to the City: 2:1

The story of the first Israelites to enter the promised land begins when Joshua sends two spies to reconnoiter the land, and "especially Jericho." The narrator places the action at Shittim, a site notable for its association with apostasy. At Shittim the Israelite men began to consort with Moabite women, who led them into the worship of other gods, particularly the Baal of Peor (Num 25:1-5). The widespread and blatant flaunting of the Mosaic commandments against such practices precipitated a crisis which was averted only when Phinehas, the son of Eleazar the priest, impaled a couple in the act of coitus. The site therefore exemplifies the Mosaic warning about the danger represented by the women of the land: they will seduce Israel to worship other gods, which will lead to the pouring out of divine wrath on the nation (Deut 7:2-4; cf. Josh 23:12-13; Judg 3:6; 1 Kgs 11:1-8). The brief reference to the spies' starting point thus reminds the reader of the danger represented by Canaan and its women.

It is therefore surprising to read of the spies' response to Joshua's simple but direct orders. Instead of "going and viewing" they "go and enter the house of a prostitute." Immediately the hint of sexual impropriety (and thus of apostasy) evoked by the reference to Shittim gains force. The narrator heightens a sense of uneasiness by employing vague but suggestive language to refer to the spies' activity. The Hebrew verb translated "entered" *(bôʾ)* can also refer to a man "coming to" a woman for the purpose of sexual intercourse (Gen 6:4; 16:2; 30:3; 38:8-9; Deut 22:13; 1 Sam 12:24; 16:21; Ezek 23:44; Prov 6:29), a possible meaning certainly suggested in connection with the house of a prostitute. A similar ambiguity occurs in connection with the Hebrew verb *šākab*, which literally means "to lie down" (NRSV "spent the night"). To "lie with" (Hebrew *šākab ʾim/ʾet*) is a common idiom for sexual intercourse (Gen 34:7; 39:7, 10, 12; Exod 22:16; Num 5:13; Deut 22:23; 28:30; 2 Sam 12:11). The choice of this verb, rather than the less ambiguous *lûn/lîn* ("to lodge, spend the night"), especially when paired with the previous verb, is thus strongly suggestive.[5]

---

[5] It is sometimes argued that the verb *lûn/lîn* can also refer to sexual relations, and therefore the word choice here is not significant. However, the few cases which are advanced to make this case are themselves quite vague (Lev 14:47; 2 Kgs 4:11; 9:16) and do not necessarily refer to sexual relations.

A sense of uneasiness is also created by the emphatic manner by which the narrator introduces Rahab. The MT assigns her three names: "a woman, a prostitute, and her name was Rahab." As a woman of Canaan and a prostitute, Rahab personifies the temptation to apostatize. Prostitution occurs frequently in the Hebrew Bible as a metaphor for the violation of YHWH's covenant (Exod 34:14-16; Deut 31:16-18; Judg 2:17; Jer 3:1-10; Hos 3:3) and the prostitute (Hebrew *zônâ*) often symbolizes waywardness from the divine ordinances (Prov 5:1-6; 7:1-27; Ezek 16:15-52). She is, in essence, the quintessential Other, radically opposite the spies. The spies are Israelites; she is a Canaanite. The spies are male; she is female. The spies are hand-picked (and we may assume of elite status); she is a prostitute, living on the margins of a man's world. And she is all the more menacing because she has an identity of her own. While the spies remain anonymous and indistinct, she is introduced by name. The name "Rahab" is identical to the Hebrew adjective meaning "wide" or "spacious" and links her implicitly to the land; the adjective occurs within the larger narrative (Genesis through 2 Kings) only in connection with the land of Canaan, where it signifies its goodness and abundance (Exod 3:8; cf. Gen 34:21; Judg 18:10). The name "Rahab," coupled with the epithet "prostitute," reminds the reader that the goodness of the land itself may seduce Israel from covenantal obedience to YHWH (Deut 6:10-15; 8:11-20; 32:11-15). Prostitution (signifying apostasy) thus serves as a motif which links the departure of the spies from Shittim, where the Israelites "began to prostitute themselves" *(wayyāḥel hāʾām liznôt)* with the women of Moab (Num 25:1), to their arrival at Jericho, where they enter the house of a prostitute. The crossing of the Jordan, from Shittim to Jericho, may be viewed as a direct journey from one location to another, but in terms of Israel's story, the crossing insinuates a doubling back to a troublesome place.

The Visitors in Peril: 2:2-7

A note of failure follows the suggestions of impropriety. Immediately following the report of the spies' entrance into Jericho, the narrator discloses that they have been unable to escape detection (v.2). The disclosure comes in the form of direct speech; the king is informed (although we are not told by whom) that spies from Israel have entered the city in order "to search the land." The use of direct speech adds authority and specificity to the revelation, and the reader is left to ponder how such information could have been gained. How does the anonymous informant know that the spies are Israelites? And how does he or she know what their mission is? Although using a different verb ("searching" vs. "viewing"), the informant's words echo Joshua's instructions to the spies. Could the informant have discerned this mission from the spies' actions (which seem at variance with their orders)? Or have the spies been talking too freely? In any case, the king of Jericho responds quickly and like Joshua "sends" men out on a mission of discovery. The scene shifts rapidly to Rahab's house with the king's command that she "bring out the men who have come to you, who entered your house" (v. 3). The order corresponds roughly to the report the king has received and emphasizes the spies' "outsider" status; the verb *bô'* ("come," "enter") occurs three times within the brief communique. A rationale accompanies the command ("for they have come only to search out the whole land") and conveys both information and a veiled threat. From the king's perspective, Rahab may not know the identity of her guests, but now that she has been informed, she will be considered an accomplice if she does not produce them.

At this point, the narrator shifts abruptly to the spies, whom Rahab has hidden (v. 4a). The common verbal form utilized in the MT *(wattiqqaḥ)* creates confusion concerning the sequence of events, making it impossible to know whether Rahab hides the spies in response to the king's message or whether she has hidden them prior to the arrival of the messengers. The grammatical structure indicates a simple sequence of events: the king sends, Rahab hides, Rahab answers. But the statement could also refer to a prior action ("she had taken them") and thus constitute an aside that informs the reader of the whereabouts of the spies as Rahab speaks to the king's men. The shift and confusion build suspense while at the same time confirming that she has thrown in her lot with her visitors.[6] Now faced with the king's edict, Rahab is in peril. Will she give the spies up? The comment also reminds the reader that the spies have become secondary characters in the drama. Suddenly, we are witnessing the action through Rahab's eyes, and for the duration of the encounter she will occupy center stage, even though no one within the story has addressed her by name. The narrator simply refers to her as "the woman," thus accentuating her difference from the "men" whom she is hiding. The scene, therefore, has the effect of highlighting Rahab's difference while transforming her from enemy to protagonist.

---

[6] The verb *wattišpĕnô* (NRSV "and she hid them," MT "and she hid him") recalls another story in which a woman hides someone in danger. It also occurs with reference to Moses' mother, who "hides" the child for three months in order to keep him from being killed by Pharaoh's men (Exod 2:2).

Rahab shrewdly deflects the demands of the messengers. Rather than denying that the spies had come (a response which almost certainly would lead to a search), she affirms that they have indeed come to her house. Her ready agreement is a ploy which establishes her credibility by implying that she is on "their" side. She then tells the messengers that the spies have left, framing her report with claims that she did not know where they had come from or where they have gone. Her repeated claim that "I do not know" makes a subtle pun on her occupation; Rahab the prostitute, after all, does "know" men.[7] Rahab then responds to the king's command with imperatives of her own: "Quick! Go after them! You might catch up to them!" (v. 5b, AT). Her words are terse, forceful, and leave no room for reply. But before the reader learns whether they have been effective, the narrator suspends the action for a second time with another aside that reveals where the spies have been hidden, under stalks of flax on the top of her roof. Using a technique common in contemporary cinema, the narrator thus builds suspense by shifting back and forth between pursuer and prey.[8]

After disclosing the spies' hiding place to the reader, the narrator returns to Rahab and the king's men. Without a response, the men leave quickly in a vain attempt to capture their quarry but do not cross the Jordan. With their departure, the spies are safe for the moment, though the narrator pointedly reports that the city gate was shut behind the pursuers. The spies thus find themselves trapped, completely enclosed within a Canaanite city, with no apparent way out.

Life and Death Decisions: 2:8-14

The next episode begins, in the MT, with two phrases introduced by independent pronouns (v. 8), setting up a contrast between the Israelite spies, their pursuers, and Rahab (a sense not captured by the NRSV's rendering of the first phrase "before they went to sleep"). The first pronoun

---

[7] As with the verbs *bôʾ* ("come to") and *šākaḇ*, ("lie down") the verb *yādaʿ* also occurs idiomatically to refer to sexual intercourse (Gen 4:1, 17; 24:16; 38:26; Num 31:17, 18; Judg 19:22, 25).

[8] Where the NRSV employs the verb "hide" in both asides (vv. 4a, 6), the MT uses two different Hebrew verbs. The verb *ṣāpan* (v. 4) seems to convey the sense of a hiding place that cannot be discovered or discerned and is often used to signify thoughts or precepts (Job 10:13; Ps 119:11; Prov 2:1). In the second instance, however, the verb is *ṭāman*, which often occurs in connection with hiding for the purpose of deceit (Gen 35:4; Exod 2:12; Josh 7:21,22; Job 31:33; Jer 18:22).

(*ḥēmmâ*, "they") contrasts the passivity of the spies with the vigilance
of Jericho's king and the energetic pursuit of the king's men: "now *they*
had not yet lain down" (AT; MT *wĕhēmmâ erem yiškābûn*). Since entering
Jericho, the Israelites have been the object of actions directed for or
against them; the king's men have demanded them and Rahab has hidden them. The repetition of the verb which initially defines their action
(v. 1b) also reminds the reader of the manner by which they have executed their mission. The second pronoun (*hîʾ*, "she") grammatically
links the spies to Rahab and counters their passivity with her energy:
"and *she* went up to them on the roof" (AT). Rahab now controls the situation, and the spies will be able to do little more than react.

Rahab addresses the spies in the same way she has just spoken to
the king's men, with a declaration of "knowing" followed by a string
of imperatives. Having just told the king's men what she does not
know, Rahab now confesses to the Israelite spies what she does know:
YHWH has given the land to Israel and the people of the land are terrified (v. 9). Strangely, she speaks of "the dread of you." "Dread" (*ʾêymâ*)
is a feature of Israel's theology of holy war and denotes a condition
often associated with the fearsome manifestation of YHWH's power or
presence (Gen 15:12; Exod 15:16; Job 9:34; 13:21; Ps 88:15). To be sure,
YHWH has promised to send his dread upon the inhabitants of the land
so that they will turn their backs on the Israelites (Exod 23:27). But
Rahab speaks not of the dread of YHWH but the dread of "you" (the Israelites? the spies?), and the slight change of expression tinges her
words with irony. What, after all, does anyone have to fear from such
spies as these? True enough, their enemies have turned their backs on
them, but it is Rahab who put them to flight.

Curious as well are Rahab's allusions to Israel's hymnody and
creeds. Before recounting YHWH's mighty deeds, she cites a relevant
passage from the "Song of Moses."

Dread of you has fallen on us	All the inhabitants of Canaan
And all the inhabitants of the land	melted away.
melt in fear before you.	Terror and dread fell upon them.
Josh 2:9b	Exod 15:15c-16a

She then recites the mighty acts of YHWH and Israel (which she declares
to be the source of the people's dread) before reiterating her claim that
the people's "hearts melted" (v. 11a).[9] Most surprising of all, she follows

---

[9] Melting hearts constitute a stock element of Israel's holy war ideology (1 Sam
14:16; Isa 14:31; Jer 49:23; Eze 21:20). For more on the "holy war" vocabulary in
Rahab's speech, see T. Butler, *Joshua*, WBC (Waco: Word, 1983) 33–5 and D. J. Mc-
Carthy, "Some Holy War Vocabulary in Joshua 2," *CBQ* 33 (1971) 228–30.

this recital with the appropriate response, praise for Israel's God. Her confession is couched in the language of Deuteronomy:

The LORD your God is indeed God in heaven above and on earth below.	So acknowledge today and take to heart that the LORD is God in heaven above and on the earth beneath; there is no other.
Josh 2:11b	Deut 4:39 (cf. 1 Kgs 8:23)

The confession of Rahab serves a number of purposes. Within the context of the story, it reassures the spies that Rahab is sympathetic to their cause and prompts them to let their guard down. In addition, her words provide important confirmation of YHWH's presence with Israel; the peoples of the land have been thrown into panic. On the narrative level, the confession dresses Rahab in Israelite garb. She knows the songs Israel sings, can recount Israel's history, and acclaims Israel's God.[10]

After finishing her introductory remarks, Rahab gets to the point and shifts from declaration to imperative. Having invoked the name of YHWH through her praise, she now presses the spies to swear to a pact in YHWH's name. The pact comprises four parts, introduced by a preamble which establishes Rahab's act of mercy as the rationale for the pact ("since I have dealt kindly with you").[11] Her elaborate request is designed to secure deliverance for herself and her family and is presented with enough specificity to preclude loopholes. The four stipulations of the agreement are, in succession: 1) "you in turn will deal kindly with my family;" 2) "(you will) give me a sign of good faith;" 3) "you will spare my father and mother, my brothers and sisters, and all who belong to them;" and 4) "(you will) deliver our lives from death."[12] As a whole, Rahab's proposal suggests a solemn covenant between the two parties. She begins by calling the spies to ratify an agreement in the name of YHWH and then (in the MT) reviews her loyal act (*ḥesed*) on behalf of the spies. This demonstration of loyalty, she implies, calls for a response in kind from the spies, to be expressed in the form of specific services performed for her benefit. [13]

---

[10] Ironically, Rahab is the first character in the story to introduce the *ḥērem* ("Sihon and Og, whom you utterly destroyed *(heḥĕramtem)*"; v. 10c).

[11] The NRSV changes the sequence of the MT, placing the preamble before her command to swear the oath.

[12] In MT the four points are linked in sequence by a chain of four *vav reversive* verbal forms.

[13] The entire Rahab narrative contains many allusions to the vocabulary and components of covenant-making. The terms "kindness" *(ḥesed)*, "truth" *(ʾĕmet)*, and

Rahab's request presents the spies with a dilemma. The law of Moses, which they have been charged to obey, explicitly forbids agreements with any of the peoples of the land (Exod 23:32-33; Deut 7:2-5). Agreement to such a pact would therefore constitute a flagrant violation of divine decrees (Deut 20:16-18), threatening the outpouring of divine wrath on the entire nation. The Israelites may therefore be forced from the land before they have even taken possession of it. On the other hand, Rahab's words clearly indicate that she seeks a sort of *quid pro quo*. By reminding them of what she has done for them she has highlighted the spies' predicament; her "kindness" may quickly vanish if her request is not granted.

The spies opt for survival over obedience and immediately agree to the pact: "Our lives for yours!" (v. 14a). The precise sense of the MT is difficult to discern (literally, "our lives in place of yours for death") but nonetheless demonstrates that the spies understand the alternatives of life or death which Rahab has set before them. They then put the agreement in their own language: "If you do not tell this business of ours, then we will deal kindly and faithfully with you when the LORD gives us the land" (v. 14b). Their restatement specifically confirms the first two points of Rahab's request (concerning kindness and truth) and even contains a feeble attempt to match Rahab's confession through a reference to YHWH's gift of the land to Israel. Yet while Rahab has acclaimed the mighty things YHWH has already done, the spies place the promise in the future ("when the LORD gives us the land"; MT *wĕhāyâ bĕtēt-yhwh lānû ʾet-hāʾareṣ*), despite YHWH's pronouncement that the land has already been given (1:3). The spies' phrasing of the promise thus expresses a certain degree of openness and has the added effect of setting the spies apart from Rahab, whose utterance of the promise corresponds more closely to YHWH's (v. 9a). The spies' response jangles with the calls for wholehearted obedience to the commands of Moses with which the book begins. Having entered the land to prepare for its conquest, the two Israelite spies have themselves been ensnared by a woman of Canaan. In contrast to Rahab, there are no words of praise for YHWH on their lips and no acknowledgment of the majestic rule of YHWH. The only words they speak are those necessary to save their lives.

"know" (*yādaʿ*) occur with frequency in covenant documents. Furthermore, the sequence of the story evokes covenant-making: the recital of mighty deeds (vv. 9-11), detailing of stipulations (vv. 12-13, 18-20), taking of an oath (vv. 14, 17), sanctions against breaking the stipulations (vv. 18-20), a sign of the covenant (vv. 12, 18-21). See K. M. Campbell, "Rahab's Covenant," *VT* 22 (1972) 243–4.

Renegotiation: 2:15-21

With an agreement secured, Rahab facilitates the spies' escape by lowering them through a window. At this point the narrator breaks in to divulge the location of her house—in the city wall—and accentuates the location by repeating it, "her house was in the city wall and in the wall she was living" (AT; v. 15b). The information moves the plot along by reporting how the spies made their escape, but it also underscores the sense that the boundary between Israel and Canaan is porous. The city wall itself is a boundary, a meeting place between Israel and others and the site of transformations. When the spies come to Canaan they enter this in-between place. (Did they ever spy out any more of Jericho or the rest of the land?) And when they leave through a hole in the wall, we are prompted to contemplate the changes that have occurred in this space and the breach they have made in the law. What impact will the agreement have on Israel? How will it affect the nation's integrity and its devotion to YHWH, especially in light of the threatening presence Rahab represents? Rahab is a character who inhabits a boundary, radically non-Israel in ethnicity and occupation but distinctively Israelite in loyalties and behavior.

As the spies depart, Rahab continues to issue imperatives. She urges them to hide out in the nearby hill country for three days, at which time their pursuers will return to the city.[14] (How does she know when they will return?) Once outside the wall the spies regain a sense of confidence and attempt to seize the initiative for themselves. Having made the pact, they now qualify it with restrictive amendments. Yet even here they do not speak in the forceful language of imperatives but in the indicative mood. Their words convey an implicit protest, insinuating that the agreement was made under duress. The spies evidently realize the serious transgression represented by the oath they have just made, and they try weaken its force by attaching conditions by which it might be nullified. Their response (in the MT) takes the form of a chiasm which shifts responsibility for the pact from themselves to Rahab and her house:

---

[14] The "three days" here does not fit well with the three days referred to in Josh 1:10. However, the reference here serves a stylistic rather than chronological purpose. References to "three days" link this story to the events of Josh 1 and to the climactic event of the Jordan crossing (3:1).

On another note, the text does not tell us where the spies are when Rahab issues her directives. Are they on the ground or dangling from the end of her rope?

A "Innocent are we of this your oath which you made us swear" (v. 17b).

B "We are coming into the land. This thread of crimson cord you are to tie in the window from which you lowered us. And your father and mother and siblings and all your father's house you are to gather to yourself at the house" (v. 18).

C "And those who go out of the doors of your house, to the outside, their blood will be on their heads; we will be innocent" (v. 19a).

C' "But those who are with you in the house, their blood will be on our heads if any hand is against them" (v. 19b).

B' "If you divulge this business of ours" (v. 20a).

A' "We will be innocent of your oath which you made us swear" (v. 20b; AT).

The spies begin and end by disavowing liability for the pact; it is "*your* oath which *you* made us swear" (vv. 17b, 20b). They then shift responsibility for keeping the oath to Rahab and her family (vv. 18-20a), laying down additional terms that imply that the fulfillment of the pact depends on actions of Rahab herself (B, B') and her family (C, C'). The spies thus reconstitute the issue of culpability by placing the decision squarely within the context of obligations that Rahab and her house (as opposed to the spies) must exercise.

Throughout the speech the spies protest their innocence. In the MT the word *nāqî* (usually translated "innocent") is repeated three times: at the beginning (v. 17b, NRSV "released"), the middle (v. 19a, NRSV "innocent") and at the conclusion (v. 20b, NRSV "released"). Used with reference to an oath, the term signifies a release from obligation (Gen 24:21) and generally denotes a state of blamelessness (Exod 23:7; Job 4:7; Ps 15:5). However, it occurs frequently in connection with *dam* ("blood") to signify wrongful death ("innocent blood"). The response of the spies brings all these nuances into play. The first occurrence expresses a plain denial of blame, "we are innocent"[15] The second refers

[15] The grammatical construction of the MT, two consecutive nominal sentences followed by a verbal sentence, does not warrant NRSV's translation of vv. 17b-18a: "we will be released from this oath that you made us swear to you if we invade the land and you do not tie this crimson cord in the window through which you let us down." The direct object, followed by the verb, signals a disjunction between the

to the death of anyone who leaves Rahab's house when the Israelites have conquered the town and puts a twist on the notion of innocent blood. Will "innocent blood" be shed here? Significant in this respect is the fact that the spies hedge on the promise of deliverance. They do not promise categorically that Rahab and her family will be spared, only that if "a hand comes against" anyone in Rahab's house, the spies will take responsibility (v. 19b)! The final reference occurs after the spies have reiterated their version of the pact and provides for their release from obligation: "And if you divulge any of this business of ours, then we will be innocent of your oath which you made us swear" (v. 20, AT), i.e. released from obligation.

The spies' modifications address each stipulation of Rahab's original request. They give her a "sign," a piece of crimson cord, but tell her that she must tie it to the window of her house (v. 18a, cf. v. 12c). They also confirm those of Rahab's family who will be spared, but ensure their survival only insofar as she succeeds in gathering them all to her house (v. 18b, cf. v. 13a). Finally, they agree to spare their lives, but only if they remain in the house (v. 19, cf. v. 13b). Rahab was wise to be so specific in the terms of her oath, since the spies are already looking for a way out. The amendments, however, do not trouble Rahab, and she readily agrees. Then she sends the spies away and ties the cord in her window. The piece of cord will presumably signal the invading Israelites that her house is exempt from the ban, and its selection as the "sign" encodes a message that both parties will understand. The "crimson cord" constitutes a double pun in MT. The cord *(tiqwat)* marks the "hope" *(tiqwâ)* which the pact has given Rahab, while its crimson color *(haššānî)* beckons the two *(šnēy)* spies. On a deeper level, the reddish color at the window recalls the Israelite deliverance from death in Egypt (Exod 12:1-32). The instructions which the spies give to Rahab parallel those which YHWH gives to Israel in preparation for the first Passover (Exod 12:21-28). Like Israel in Egypt, Rahab is told to mark a portal with red (lamb's blood on the doorway in Egypt, the crimson cord at the window in Jericho), to gather her family within her home, and to keep them within the house when destruction comes. The instructions are followed, in Exodus, by the promise that the Israelites will be spared from the destroyer. The spies also follow directives with promises, although as we have noted, their pledge is not unequivocal.

---

verbal sentence and the nominal sentences which precede it. Following the syntax of the MT we read: "We are innocent of this your oath which you made us swear. Look, we are coming into the land. This thread of crimson cord you will tie in the window through which you have lowered us."

By including this information, the narrator discloses that Rahab and her family participate in one of the constitutive events in Israel's story. Rahab's family will experience its own Passover, and later generations will (but for a change of particulars) be able to recite the story of national deliverance with the rest of the people. The incorporation of Rahab into Israel is now virtually complete.

Mission Accomplished? 2:22-24

The narrator concludes the account by relating the spies' journey back to the Israelite camp. The summary of their return corresponds to Rahab's instructions, indicating that the spies did exactly as they were told:[16]

"Go toward the hill country . . . Hide yourselves there three days, until the pursuers have returned; then afterward you may go your way."(v. 16)	"They departed and went into the hill country and stayed there three days, until the pursers returned." (v. 22)

The spies' descent from the hills caps a series of descents. In the earlier stages of the story, the plot had involved a "going up" (vv. 6, 8), and the climactic encounter had taken place on top of Rahab's roof. From that high place the spies and the plot now descend, first from the window in the city wall (v. 15) and now from the hill country to the Jordan (v. 23).[17]

The subsequent narrative downplays the spies' return, summarizing their report to Joshua with the laconic statement that they "came to Joshua son of Nun and told him all that had happened to them."[18] The episode then closes with words that, in any other situation, would stir the heart, "truly the LORD has given all the land into our hands; moreover all the inhabitants of the land melt in fear before us." The reader

---

[16] The text reflects the ironic nature of the spies' response to Rahab the Canaanite in contrast to Joshua the Israelite leader. They obey her precisely, while their obedience to Joshua's orders was only approximate.

[17] The name "Jordan" probably also derives from the verbal root (*yrd*) that means "to descend."

[18] The MT contains a pun. The participle translated "happened" (*hammōṣᵉʾôt*) derives from the same verb which reports that the pursuers could not "find" (*māṣāʾû*) the spies. It appears that successful escape has been the main topic of the report!

will recognize these as the words of Rahab (v. 9). Now safely back among their own people, the spies speak with boldness and confidence, and we may assume that their words are taken as such by Joshua. But the reader has viewed both the spies and the land from a different perspective. There is a danger in the land, a fact which the spies do not articulate. Hidden, ensnared, and outsmarted by a Canaanite prostitute, they ironically parrot her words. In a sense, Rahab, not the spies, offers the report to Joshua and gives the assurance of the divine promise that signals the beginning of the campaign to take Canaan.

Chapter Four
CHANGING STATE
Joshua 3:1–4:24

Along with the crossing of the Red Sea, the crossing of the Jordan represents one of the pivotal events in Israel's story. By passing through the former waters, the Israelites leave a settled existence enslaved to others and become a wandering nation sustained and led by the God who has promised deliverance. The latter crossing effects a similar transformation. The nation now leaves a nomadic life and begins a settled existence as the dominant population in the land which YHWH has promised. Within the context of the larger narrative, passages through water thus frame Israel's desert odyssey toward nationhood. Deliverance at the Red Sea inaugurates an "in-between" time, during which Israelite society is configured through covenant, law, ritual, and experience. Crossing the Jordan promises the completion of this period of national formation. Possession of the land not only represents the fulfillment of YHWH's promises but also signifies permanence, stability, and well-being. The Red Sea and the Jordan constitute geographical boundaries which take Israel into and out of the desert but also signify the beginning and end of Israel's constitution as a coherent people. They are therefore linked conceptually within the text, both through allusion (Rahab's deliverance) and by the narrator's explicit commentary (4:23-24).[1]

---

[1] The language of the narrative exhibits a marked liturgical quality that enhances the symbolic ramifications of the crossing. This is discussed in detail by L. L. Thompson, "The Jordan Crossing: Ṣidqôt Yahweh and World Building," *JBL* 100 (1981) 343–58.

The story of the crossing from Shittim (3:1) to Gilgal (4:19) can be summarized in simple terms. At the direction of Joshua the priests carry the ark of the covenant into the Jordan, and as they enter YHWH cuts off the waters. The entire nation then crosses, while the priests and ark remain in the middle of the riverbed. In the process, twelve stones are removed from the Jordan and carried onto the west bank. After the nation crosses, the priests bring the ark out of the riverbed and the water of the Jordan flows again. The Israelites set up the stones at the site (which is named "Gilgal") and encamp there. The *narration* of the event, however, produces a profound sense of dislocation. We might expect a straightforward and decisive report of this crucial event, but instead the narrator weaves a complex narrative that jumbles chronology, geography, and point of view. By means of repetitions, internal inconsistencies, and interruptions, the narrator renders a confusing account which can be made to cohere only with great difficulty. Nowhere else in Joshua does the narrative lapse into such disarray.

The narrative creates confusion through an awkward and disjointed style that provides few explicit links between events and often shifts the focus abruptly. A number of statements seem out of place. Joshua's command to select twelve men from the tribes (3:12) interrupts his exhortation to follow the ark of the covenant across the Jordan and makes little sense in its context, since Joshua does not say what the twelve men are to do. The command reappears, however, in 4:2, this time followed by a charge to take stones from the Jordan. In a similar vein, Joshua's command that the priests take up the ark of the covenant (3:6) is followed by a report that they did so. Yet immediately following, Joshua tells the people that the ark is about to pass before them (3:11). Later, when the people leave their tents to cross the Jordan, the narrator reports that the priests bearing the ark went before them. A report that the priests and ark crossed over before the people (4:11) interrupts an account of the nation's crossing (4:10, 12-13). At a later point, however, the priests are still in the Jordan, and Joshua commands them to come out (4:15-18). The location of the priests within the Jordan itself adds to the sense of discontinuity. Joshua commands the priests to come to the edge of the Jordan and stand still (3:8). They do this, and the waters stop flowing as Joshua had predicted (3:15). Yet at 3:17 we find the priests in the middle of the Jordan, where they remain until they come out (4:18).

Second, the narrative confuses and repeats the sequence of events. Joshua had earlier commanded the officers of Israel to pass through the camp to announce that the crossing of the Jordan would take place in three days (1:11). Using similar language, the narrator now reports that the officers go through the camp "at the end of three days" (3:2). The report seems to occur, however, after the spies have returned from their three-day journey into Canaan (2:22) and after Israel has left Shittim (3:1). How long has Israel been "preparing," three days or six days?[2] Temporal confusion is also generated by a sudden doubling back in the narrative after Israel crosses the Jordan. Except for the intrusions noted above, the Jordan crossing proceeds in a relatively straightforward fashion from 3:1 through 4:8; the priests dip their feet in the Jordan and the waters stop flowing (3:14-17), the entire nation crosses (3:17–4:1), and chosen men from each tribe remove stones from the Jordan and take them to the Israelite camp (4:2-8). Yet in 4:10 we find the priests still in the middle of the Jordan. The narrator then relates Israel's crossing again, this time adding that the people crossed "in haste," led by the eastern tribes (vv. 11-13). When the priests finally leave the Jordan (v. 18), the narrator returns to the matter of the twelve stones and offers an additional explanation for their installation (vv. 21-24; cf. vv. 6-7).

Third, the narrative contains a number of digressions and asides that disrupt the flow of action. As the priests and people approach the Jordan, the narrator interrupts briefly to inform the reader that the Jordan overflows all its banks throughout the time of harvest (3:15a). The aside not only takes the reader out of the story for the moment but also emphasizes the reader's distance from the action of the story. The narrator seems to presume that the reader does not live in the land and must therefore be informed about the Jordan flooding so that the magnitude of the miracle can be appreciated. Another such break occurs at 4:9, where the narrator reports that Joshua set up twelve stones in the middle of the Jordan (in contrast to those taken *out* of the Jordan and installed at Gilgal) and that "they are there to this day." A third instance occurs when the narrator interrupts the retelling of the Jordan crossing to inform the reader that YHWH exalted Joshua in the sight of Israel and that the people held him in awe all the days of his life (4:14). As in the previous instances, the statement transcends the narrative moment, this time through a proleptic comment that encompasses the entire period of the conquest.

Finally, the narrative oscillates between four intersecting themes, investing the Jordan crossing with multiple meanings. The account concentrates, at various points, on the unanimity and obedience of the people (3:1-6, 3:10–4:1, 10-13, 15-18), the sacral status of the priests and the ark (3:6, 12-17; 4:7, 9, 10-13, 15-18), the exaltation of Joshua (3:7-9; 4:14), and YHWH's miraculous stoppage of the Jordan (4:2-8, 19-24).

---

[2] The confusion is compounded by the fact that still another day must be added to the sequence. Shortly after this notice, Joshua commands the people to "sanctify themselves" in preparation for crossing the Jordan on the *next* day.

Rather than offering the reader a single perspective from which to apprehend the significance of the events, the narrator presents four.

The Jordan crossing portrays the nation's unity and obedience by depicting Israel as a unified people. References to "all Israel" (3:1, 7, 17; 4:14) and "the entire nation" (3:16; 4:1, 11) render the nation in holistic terms, and the crossing of the eastern tribes, ahead of all the rest, confirms that the crossing is experienced by all the people. Similarly, Israel's prompt and complete compliance with Joshua's commands is reported at many junctures, affirming the people's unanimous obedience to YHWH (3:6; 4:8, 18). The narrator explicitly notes Israel's obedience by remarking that the priests stood in the middle of the Jordan "until everything was finished that the LORD commanded Joshua to tell the people, according to all that Moses had commanded Joshua" (4:10).

The narrative confirms the sacral status and power of the priests and ark by placing them at the center of the action. Joshua sets the priests and ark apart by decreeing a distance of approximately two miles between them and the rest of the people (3:4). The priests who carry the ark take the lead in the procession to the Jordan (3:3) and pass in front of the people at key points in the text (3:6, 11, 14; 4:11).[3] When the priests dip their feet into the Jordan YHWH cuts off the water (3:15; 4:7a), and when they exit the riverbed the waters flow again (4:18). During the crossing itself, the priests stand prominently in the middle of the Jordan, remaining there until the entire nation passes through (3:17; 4:9, 10). The role of the priests in the text therefore conveys important information regarding their role and status within Israel. Priests "know the way" (3:4) across boundaries, and the nation is to follow their lead. They are separate from the rest of the people and alone may handle what is holy. Priests facilitate transit across boundaries by entering boundary regions, and once there they oversee the passages which transform the nation. The actions of priests are powerful and efficacious. They act at the command of YHWH, who endows their actions with extraordinary power.[4]

Three short texts advance the notion that the Jordan crossing elevates the status of Joshua as a leader of Mosaic stature (cf. 1:5b, 17b). The first does so authoritatively through the speech of YHWH, who begins not with instructions for the crossing but with an announcement

---

[3] The Hebrew preposition *lipnēy* ("before, in front of, in the presence of") appears in each of these verses as a constant marker of the prominence of the priests and ark.

[4] For more information on the role of priests in setting, maintaining, and crossing boundaries, see R. D. Nelson, *Raising Up a Faithful Priest* (Louisville: Westminster John Knox, 1993) 17–38.

that Joshua will be exalted "in the sight of all Israel, so that they may know that I will be with you as I was with Moses" (3:7b). YHWH next affirms Joshua's priority over the priests by declaring that "you are the one who shall command the priests" (v. 8). Following these divine endorsements, Joshua implicitly equates his words with those of YHWH by saying, "Draw near and hear the words of the LORD your God" (v. 9). Later in the text the narrator corroborates this exchange by linking the commands of Joshua with the commands of Moses (4:10b) and by reporting that YHWH indeed exalted Joshua in the sight of Israel (4:14).

The removal and installation of stones constitutes a significant subplot and offers a fourth perspective on the meaning of the crossing. The action is related through two passages that exalt YHWH rather than Joshua (4:2-8, 20-24). In each case, Joshua directs that stones taken from the Jordan be erected as memorials of YHWH's miraculous stoppage of the water. The passage focuses, however, on Joshua's explanation of the meaning of the stones (and thus of the event itself). The stones will serve as a sign to future generations (v. 6), whose questions about them will elicit a recital of YHWH's mighty work at the Jordan. The first explanation looks to the future, with Joshua declaring that the stones will be "a memorial forever" (v. 7c), and focuses on the act as demonstration of YHWH's awesome power (v. 7a-b):

> Then you shall tell them that the waters of the Jordan were cut off
> > in front of the ark of the covenant of the LORD.
> > When it crossed over the Jordan,
> the waters of the Jordan were cut off.

The second explanation joins past, present and future. In this case, Joshua associates the present event with the crossing of the Red Sea and declares that the event has significance beyond Israel: "so that all the peoples of the earth may know that the hand of the LORD is mighty, and so that you may fear the LORD your God forever" (v. 24). The erection of the stones, then, testifies to the awesome display of YHWH's power and to its significance for all peoples.

The various features of the narrative—the awkward style, the disjointed chronology, the narrator's interruptions, and the multiple viewpoints—work together to produce a sense of disorientation in space, time, and perspective. The text takes the reader back and forth across the Jordan: from the edge of the eastern bank (v. 15b), upstream to Adam and downstream to the Dead Sea (v. 16), back to the middle of the Jordan (v. 17), then to the other side of the Jordan (3:17–4:1), back to the middle of the Jordan (with the twelve men; 4:8a) and across the Jordan once more (4:8b), returning once again to the middle of the Jordan (4:9) before crossing again with the people (4:10c) and then with the priests (4:11), and finally back to the priests in the middle of the Jordan who exit onto the western bank (4:15-18). Instead of a simple, linear crossing from point to point, the narrative goes around and around the river, before settling at a place appropriately named Gilgal ("Circle"). In a similar manner, the text takes the reader back and forth through time. We begin "at the end of three days" (v. 2), at which point Joshua commands the people to sanctify themselves, declaring that *"tomorrow* the LORD will do wonders among you" (v. 5). Yet shortly thereafter YHWH declares that *"this day* I will begin to exalt you," and the action proceeds without reference to any prior sanctification. Impeded by a few interruptions (3:6, 12, 15), the event continues to unfold until we are abruptly taken back in time to an unspecified moment at which Joshua set up stones in the Jordan (4:9). Following this, the temporal sequence rewinds to the beginning of the crossing. The sequence from the crossing to the installation of the memorial stones is then repeated, this time in more detail (4:10-13, 15-24). Perspectives, too, shift back and forth. The themes of communal integrity and priestly prominence configure the story until YHWH offers an alternative perspective (3:7-8, the only words YHWH speaks in this section). The prior themes are taken up after this brief interlude until the competing theme of YHWH's exaltation appears (4:2-8). Priestly performance and Israelite unity then carry the story through 4:19, with another thematic interruption at 4:14. The final perspective, however, shapes the event in terms of YHWH's mighty work (4:19-24).

The disordered character of the narrative has the odd effect of detaching the reader from the action. It is difficult to enter the story when one cannot get one's bearings! By refusing a vantage point in space, time, and perspective, the account suspends the sense that the reader is encountering events as they happen. This textual phenomenon, unique within Joshua, can be explained in part by the highly liturgical cast of the narrative.[5] As we have observed, the crossing of the Jordan is an event of epochal significance for Israel and is thus imbued with deep symbolic import. The various elements of the story reinforce Israel's identity with the land and with YHWH while also legitimating Israel's claim to the land against all other inhabitants. The crossing reinforces

[5] The disjointed character of Joshua 3–5 indicates a complex compositional history. Attempts to describe the sources and process of editing have yielded a variety of explanations. The discussion is summarized succinctly by R. Nelson, *Joshua,* OTL (Louisville: Westminster John Knox, 1997) 55–60, 65–8, who sees issues of national identity and claims to the land at the heart of the narrative. For references to particular positions, see A. G. Auld, *Joshua, Moses and the Land* (Edinburgh: T & T Clark, 1980) 43–4.

Israel's distinctiveness against the other peoples of the land, who simply inhabit the territory. They represent those who have crossed over into the land, as opposed to those who are already there. The event thus constitutes a charter for subsequent generations, bringing together in one event the essential attributes that define the community.[6]

The narrative underscores the significance for all generations of Israelites by giving it a timeless quality and infusing it with the language of myth and metaphor. The journey through the Jordan represents a unique event that requires obedience, for the people do not "know the way" (3:4) The stoppage of the waters is a "wonder" performed by YHWH in response to the obedience of Joshua and the priests (3:5). The stones taken from the Jordan are "signs" (4:6) and "memorials" (4:7) which evoke a retelling of the event. And the connection to the passage through the Red Sea appropriates a powerful symbol which marks this crossing as a formative event which transforms the nation from unformed people to integrated nation.[7]

By crossing the Jordan, Israel not only enters a new land but takes on a new identity, as a settled people joined to the land given by YHWH. This transformation is traced by the movement of the ark and the ritual performances associated with it. The ark, representing YHWH's powerful presence, appears throughout the account and serves as a focal point for the four major themes. The first act of obedience required of Israel is to follow the ark to the Jordan (3:3-4), and the ark remains in the Jordan until the entire nation crosses (4:10, 11). The ark also confirms the sacral status of the priests. While the rest of the nation must keep their distance from it (3:4), the priests bear it into the Jordan and out onto the western bank.[8] Furthermore, the ark elevates Joshua's position as leader of Israel by demonstrating his authority over "the priests who carry the ark" (3:8). Finally, the ark itself stands at the center of the explanation given for

---

[6] R. Polzin offers a detailed analysis of the various shifts in time, space, perspective, and phrasing and sees in these shifts, and in the overall cultic character of the narrative, a reflection on the possibility of interpreting the Mosaic torah; *Moses and the Deuteronomist* (New York: Seabury, 1980) 91–110.

[7] The depiction of YHWH splitting the waters draws on archetypal imagery present in other ancient Near Eastern cultures. In the Babylonian creation story, the *Enuma Elish,* splitting Tiamat (the flood) is an act of creation which results in the establishment of the cosmic order. The imagery is linked explicitly to the passage through the Red Sea in Isaiah 51:9-11, which looks forward to Israel's return from exile in Babylon (cf. Ps 89:5-14, where Rahab [spelled differently in MT than the "Rahab" in Joshua 2] signifies chaos).

[8] The priests are, in fact, characterized repeatedly in this narrative as "those who carry the ark" (3:2, 6, 8, 13, 14, 15, 17; 4:9, 10, 15, 18).

the memorial stones: "then you shall tell them that the waters of the Jordan were cut off in front of the ark of the covenant of the LORD" (4:7).

Ritual by its nature takes the participant out of ordinary time and space into a sphere within which identity can be broken down and reconfigured. The transit through ritual space and time is facilitated by strict adherence to ritual acts which, when performed correctly, bring about a change in status. As we have noted above, the narrative's temporal disorientation evokes the sense of timelessness that signals an entrance into extraordinary time and space. In the midst of chronological confusion, however, the text also focuses on strict adherence to divinely-given commands by which the crossing (and thus communal transformation) will take place. Countering the confusion of space, time, and perspective, the narrative renders a sense of order through a pattern of command and response, prediction and fulfillment. Generally, the narrator reports the execution of commands soon after they are given, and predictions are often noted at later points. The pattern can be discerned by placing the commands and predictions against their execution and fulfillment.

CHART 4: COMMAND AND EXECUTION AT THE JORDAN CROSSING

Command	Execution
To the priests Joshua said, "Take up the ark of the covenant, and pass on in front of the people." (3:6a)	So they took up the ark of the covenant and went in front of the people. (3:6b, cf. v.14)
And (the officers) commanded the people, "When you see the ark of the covenant of the LORD your God being carried by the levitical priests, then you shall set out from your place. Follow it." (3:3)	When the people set out from their tents to cross over the Jordan, the priests bearing the ark of the covenant were in front of the people. (3:14)
Joshua said to them, "Pass on before the ark of the LORD your God into the middle of the Jordan, and each of your take up a stone on his shoulder, one for each of the tribes of the Israelites." (4:5)	The Israelites did as Joshua commanded. They took up twelve stones out of the middle of the Jordan, according to the number of the tribes of the Israelites, as the LORD told Joshua. (4:8a-b)

"When you come to the edge of the waters of the Jordan, you shall stand still in the Jordan." (4:8b)	While all Israel were crossing over on dry ground, the priests who bore the ark of the covenant of the LORD stood on dry ground in the middle of the Jordan (4:17a-b)
Prediction	*Fulfillment*
"When the priests bearing the ark of the covenant of the LORD came up from the middle of the Jordan . . ." (4:18a)	Joshua therefore commanded the priests, "Come up out of the Jordan." (4:17)
The LORD said to Joshua, "This day I will begin to exalt you in the sight of all Israel, so that they may know that I will be with you as I was with Moses." (3:7)	On that day the LORD exalted Joshua in the sight of all Israel. (4:14)
"When the soles of the feet of the priests who bear the ark of the LORD, the Lord of all the earth, rest in the waters of the Jordan, the waters of the Jordan flowing from above shall be cut off; they shall stand in a single heap." (3:13)	So when those who bore the ark had come to the Jordan, and the feet of the priests bearing the ark were dipped in the edge of the water, the waters flowing from above stood still, rising up in a single heap far off at Adam . . . while those flowing toward the sea of the Arabah, the Dead Sea, were wholly cut off. (3:16)

The account of the Jordan crossing is rendered both as an historical event and as a timeless experience that transcends the historical moment. It is both something that "happened" and an event that remains present through the stone memorial and the retelling of the story. The crossing also strongly asserts the unity and transformation of the people. The entire nation, including the eastern tribes, participates in the event and leaves behind the nomadic existence of the wilderness. The narrative thus affirms the strong bonds forged between the tribes, and between YHWH and the nation. Yet the narrative also injects considerable ambiguity into the transforming moment. The sequence of events is difficult to determine. And the particular attention given to the eastern tribes (3:12-13) reminds us that the nation and the promised land are not completely one, and that some tribes will cross the boundary in the other direction and return to a more pastoral existence. "All Israel" takes part in crossing it, but some will cross again, in the other direction, and as the events recounted in Joshua 22 will prove, this will raise new questions about the identity of the nation.

Preparation for the Crossing: 3:1-6

The preparations for the Jordan crossing evoke much the same atmosphere of anticipation as the speeches in Joshua 1. The section begins, as at the book's beginning, with a series of speeches: the "officers" to the people (vv. 3b-4), Joshua to the people (v. 5), Joshua to the priests (v. 6), YHWH to Joshua (vv. 7-8) and Joshua to the people (v. 9, 10-13). The references to the "officers" and the three-day period connect the two texts. This narrative "return" to Joshua 1 restores the sense of Israelite obedience and integrity in contrast to the disobedience of the spies and the promised deliverance of Rahab and her family, setting the story back on course after the digression at Jericho.

Many elements work to reassert Israelite obedience. The account opens with the report that Israel broke camp and journeyed to the Jordan, just as Joshua had commanded (3:1; cf. 1:11). The ensuing speeches issue a series of commands addressed to the leaders, priests, and the nation as a whole which set out the program for the crossing. Subtle allusions to the Sinai narrative reinforce expectations that the event will demonstrate Israelite obedience. The commands that the people sanctify themselves and observe a distance between themselves and the ark recall similar commands at Sinai, where both people and priests were sanctified and warned to keep their distance from the mountain (Exod 19:10-15, 22-23). In addition, the first speech (3:2-4) is framed (in the MT) by references to a three-day span of time, a period also significant in the Sinai narrative (Exod 19:11, 15, 16). A note that the officers went through the camp at the end of three days introduces the officers' proclamation (v. 2a), and an idiomatic expression concludes it (*mittĕmôl šilšôm*, v. 4; literally, "from tomorrow, three days ago"; NRSV "before").[9] Moving outward, the entire series of initial speeches is bracketed by references to carrying the ark before the people (v. 3, 6), a more di-

---

[9] The NRSV changes the sequence of the MT. While the phrase "for you have not passed this way before" concludes the speech in the NT, the NRSV places it after the command to set a distance from the ark.

rect allusion to Israel's three-day journey from Sinai, with the ark at the lead (Num 10:33).[10]

The appearance of the ark in this and the rest of the account is somewhat unexpected. It has not figured prominently in the larger narrative, appearing only with reference to the tabernacle (Exod 40:21; Num 3:31; 4:5; 7:89), the aborted attempt to enter Canaan from the south (Num 14:44), and Israel's departure from Sinai (Num 10:33-36). In these and other biblical texts, the ark constitutes the locus of YHWH's power and presence among the people.[11] The ark is thus a meeting place between YHWH and human intermediaries (Lev 16:2; Num 7:89) and a reminder of Israel's covenantal obligations (Exod 25:16, 21; Deut 10:2, 5). It exudes a perilous holiness (1 Sam 6:6-9) and can put Israel's enemies to flight (Num 10:35). Because of this, the ark has a place within Israel's divine war ideology, at times accompanying Israelite troops into battle (Josh 6:1-16; 1 Sam 4:2-9). In the context which most closely parallels the present one (Num 10:33-36), the ark travels well in advance of Israel as it journeys through the wilderness and designates the next site of encampment. Its prominence here at the outset of the Jordan crossing thus signals that Israel's crossing will take place in response to divine initiative and offers a tangible sign of Moses' promise that YHWH will cross over before the nation and defeat its enemies (Deut 9:3).

The events in this section are joined together by the repetition, in the MT, of various forms of the verb *ʿābar*, which the NRSV renders variously as "crossing over" (v. 1), "went through" (v. 2), "passed" (v. 4), and "pass on" (v. 6). The verb signifies passing through or over something or crossing a boundary. On the surface, the repetition keeps the focal event—the crossing of the Jordan—continually in the foreground. But the verb can also signify an inappropriate boundary crossing, particularly the "transgression" of the covenant (Deut 17:2c-3a; cf. Judg 2:20; 2 Kgs 18:12; Hos 6:7) or the commands associated with it (Ps 17:3; Isa 24:5), a not insignificant nuance given what has just transpired at Jericho.

The account begins, then, by resuming the preparatory activities described in Joshua 1. The preparations confirm that Israel will not enter Canaan in its own way and at its own time. Rather YHWH will

[10] The narrative here, as well, signals careful compliance with the law of Moses by introducing those who carry the ark as "levitical priests" (v. 3). The phrase expresses strict obedience to Deut 10:8, which stipulates that the tribe of Levi has been set apart to carry the ark; cf. Deut 31:9, 25.

[11] The wife of Phinehas commemorates the loss of the ark to the Philistines by naming her newborn son "Ichabod" ("Where Is the Glory?"), because "the glory has departed from Israel" (1 Sam 4:21-22).

lead the people into the land. By responding obediently, Israel will not only display loyalty to its covenant deity but also will acknowledge again that the land is YHWH's gift.

Into the Jordan: 3:7-13

Another set of speeches follows the report that the priests carried the ark before the people. YHWH delivers the first speech (vv. 7-8), which like the one to Joshua in 1:2-9 begins with a promise and ends with a command. The speech introduces the meaning of the event from the divine perspective; YHWH will begin to elevate Joshua in the eyes of the people so that they will recognize that YHWH is with him. The promise of divine presence (v. 7) reiterates that given in 1:5 and answers the proviso of the eastern tribes, who had hinted that their participation in the enterprise was contingent on this very point (1:17). YHWH's explanation of the exaltation of Joshua, "so that they may know that I will be with you as I was with Moses," also plays off the declaration in v. 4 that the Israelites do not know the way they should go. The contrast of the two kinds of "knowing" enhances Joshua's leadership. The Israelites do not know the path they should take, but they will recognize the one who will lead them on it. Joshua will command the priestly vanguard (v. 8), and the people will follow.

The elevation of Joshua to Mosaic stature follows immediately. Joshua commands the people to draw near and then assumes the role of divine messenger: "hear the words of the LORD your God" (v. 9). The phrase echoes a common preface to prophetic oracles (Jer 2:4; 31:10; Ezek 6:3; Hos 4:1; Amos 7:16), although Joshua preserves a measure of distinctiveness by speaking of "words" instead of the conventional "the word." Like Moses before him, Joshua now asserts that the words he speaks are YHWH's words. The significance of this declaration receives particular emphasis from the narrator, who sets it apart by inserting a short tag ("Joshua said") between it and the rest of the speech (v. 10a). The speech itself then continues the prophetic ambiance, moving from a confirmation of the divine promise (v. 10; cf. Deut 7:1), to a declaration of the ark's imminent journey (v. 11), then to command (v. 12), and finally to prediction (v. 13). While YHWH focuses on the exaltation of Joshua as a means of confirming the divine presence with him, Joshua now draws attention to YHWH's sovereignty and power as a means of confirming the divine presence with Israel. The verb signifying "knowing" (*yādaꜥ*) occurs now for a third time (v. 10), linking the recognition of YHWH's presence with Israel to YHWH's presence with Joshua. Israel will learn, during the ensuing events, that YHWH is with Joshua and is present among the people. The change from "not knowing" to "knowing" also provides a verbal link to the story of Rahab, whose "not knowing" the whereabouts of the spies was followed by a confession of her "knowing" that YHWH has given the land to Israel (2:4, 8).

The majesty of YHWH is further embellished by the odd reference to the ark as "the ark of the covenant of the Lord of all the earth" (vv. 11, 13). The exact meaning of the phrase is open to debate, for the phrase translated by the NRSV "all the earth" (*hāᵓāreṣ*) can refer either to the earth as a whole or to the entire land of Canaan in particular. The latter is the more likely focus, given the prior promise that YHWH will drive out the nations before Israel and the spies' declaration that YHWH had given Israel the entire land (2:24). In any case the appellation underscores YHWH's ownership of the land and ability to determine its fate. In contrast to the totality of YHWH's presence and power, the peoples of the land are now listed in their seven-fold plurality (v. 10). The ark will thus demonstrate the supremacy of the God of Israel, who will drive out the many inhabitants of the land.

Between references to the ark Joshua inserts an open-ended command, "so now select twelve men from the tribes of Israel, one from each tribe" (v. 12). The command momentarily diverts the focus from the crossing by introducing another plot line, one that will focus on the future rather than the present. The fact that Joshua neither gives a reason for the command nor specifies what the men are to do builds the suspense of the moment and hints that there will be much more than a simple crossing going on at the Jordan. After the command, Joshua concludes with a prediction that the waters of the Jordan will "stand in a single heap" once the priests who bear the ark enter it (v. 13). The verb "stand" (MT *wĕyaʿamĕdû*) harkens back to Joshua's command that the priests "stand" when they come to the edge of the Jordan (v. 8). The verb thus unites the activity of the priests with the marvelous stoppage of the Jordan. Two things will "stand" when the feet of the priests touch the river: the priests and the waters of the Jordan. The wordplay underscores the liminal (in-between) status of the priests in the narrative; they will become one with the boundary which they enter.

The Crossing: 3:14-17

As we move to the actual crossing of the Jordan, the various themes and motifs flow into a sort of narrative channel which accentuates the transformation of Israel. The main stream of the narrative follows repetitions of the root *ʿbr*; NRSV "to cross over" (v. 14), "crossed over" (v. 16), "crossing over" (2x, v. 17) and of "the Jordan" (vv. 14, 15 [2x], 17), thus keeping the event itself in sharp focus. However, the rest of the words heap up into a clutter of word plays and puns (in the MT) that join characters and concepts in surprising ways. Like the people themselves, the waters of the Jordan seem to recognize the holiness of the ark and keep their distance from it ("far off at Adam," v. 16; cf. v.4). As Joshua predicted, they "stand" (v. 16), as do the priests *(hakkōhănîm),* who remain stationary *(hākēn)* within the dry riverbed (v. 17). The waters "descending from above rise up" at Adam (v. 16, AT), while the waters descending to the Dead Sea are "completely" *(tammû)* cut off, linking them with the people who "completely" *(tammû)* cross the Jordan (v. 17).[12]

The structure and tempo of the account emphasize the wondrous character of the event. References to the priests and people (vv. 14, 17) bracket the description of the stoppage of water, which is related in detail. In order to highlight the moment, the narrator slows the tempo with long sentences punctuated by digressions and descriptive terminology. The sentences emphasize connections between YHWH and the event by the repetition of the cumbersome phrase "the priests bearing the ark."[13] At the climactic moment (when the feet of the priests touch the Jordan) the narrator momentarily builds the suspense by digressing to inform the reader of the Jordan's characteristic flooding at harvest time.[14] Upon returning to the narrative moment, the narrator dramatizes the magnitude of the wonder by using a number of verbs to characterize the stoppage of waters ("stood still," "rising up," "wholly cut off," v. 16), extending the episode through a detailed description of waters upstream and downstream. The description takes the reader a considerable distance, from Adam (probably associated with the present Tel ed–Damiyeh, about eighteen miles due north of Jericho at the mouth of the Jabbok), down to the Sea of the Arabah and is further

[12] R. Hess also sees a word play between the "standing" of waters at "Adam" *(wĕyyaʿamĕdû* and *bĕʾādām* respectively); *Joshua,* TOTC (Downers Grove: InterVarsity, 1996) 105. The unusual occurrence of the infinitive absolute constitutes, in the consonantal form of the text *(hkn),* an anagram of the word for "priest" *(khn).* The word-play is accentuated, in the MT, by the insertion of the *athnach* on the former word.

[13] NRSV disturbs the sequence of the difficult grammar of the MT. The repetition can be appreciated by following the syntax more precisely: "and *the priests who carried the ark of the covenant* were in front of the people. And when *the priests who were carrying the ark* to the Jordan and the feet of *the priests who were carrying the ark* were dipped into the edge of the water" (vv. 14b-15a).

[14] This is syntax of the MT. Again, the NRSV does not follow this sequence but inserts the digression before the entrance of the priests' feet into the water.

attenuated by the inclusion of additional geographical information ("Adam, the city that is beside Zarethan," "the sea of the Arabah, the Dead Sea").

The account concludes by returning to the people, who are again characterized by their "crossing" in contrast to the priests who are characterized by their "standing" (v. 17). The contrast again distinguishes the priests as those who stand in the boundary and facilitate the transformation of the people. Both people and priests tread on "dry ground" *(beḥārābâ)*. The Hebrew term employed here is relatively uncommon, although it occurs in connection to the crossing of the Red Sea (Exod 14:21). The wide swath of dry land temporarily opens the boundary represented by the Jordan, joining the western side to the eastern side and symbolically the nomadic life to settled existence. The one point of reference now is the ark of the covenant, borne by the priests, which remains in its place until the entire people has entered the promised land. The transformation is reinforced by the use of *gôy* ("nation"), rather than the more common *ʿam* ("people") which has previously designated Israel. The change in nomenclature suggests a change of identity. While the latter term is general and indiscriminate, the former signifies a discrete nation, discernable through a common origin, independent government, common religious structures, and connection with a particular territory.[15] While *gôy* appears as a designation for Israel in Deuteronomy (4:6, 8; 9:14), it occurs much more frequently as a designation of the peoples of the land (Deut 7:1; 8:20; 9:1; 11:23; 12:2). Having crossed the Jordan, Israel has left the undifferentiated terrain of the desert and has become like the peoples of Canaan—a settled nation bound to the land. But, we may wonder, how *much* like them?

A Memorial of the Crossing: 4:1-9

While the account of the crossing stresses the wondrous character of the event, the following passage focuses on its significance for the present and future generations. The erection of memorial stones will ensure that the crossing continues to be a formative experience for the nation. They witness to a common, unifying event which both confirms the Israelites' claim to the land and enables them to take their place among the nations of the world. The retelling of the story, which the stones elicit, will itself constitute a unifying activity by reminding

---

[15] R. Clements, *gôy*, TDOT, 2:426–33.

the tribes of their common history and calling. The twelve stones thus paradoxically signify a "oneness" which distinguishes Israel from the "plurality" of the peoples of the land.[16]

The new plot line is joined to the preceding narrative by key structural and thematic repetitions. The opening phrase, "when the entire nation had finished crossing over the Jordan" (4:1a) repeats the last phrase of the preceding section (3:17c), signaling both a change in the direction of the plot and a continuity with the previous story. Repetitions of the verb *ʿābar* continue (NRSV "pass on" [v. 4], "crossed over" [v. 7], "carried them over" [v. 8]), as do recurrences of "the Jordan" (vv. 5, 7 [3x], 8, 9), keeping the crossing at the center of attention. The wordplay involving the noun *kōhēn* (priest) and the verb *(hākîn)* is picked up again and taken in a new direction. Here as well the verb is in the infinitive form but now displays a slightly different spelling. The change in spelling looks forward to a third occurrence of the verb (v. 4), which extends the wordplay by appropriating a finite verbal form *(hēkîn)* to refer to the men appointed to carry the stones.[17] Another verbal link is made through the verb *nûaḥ* ("rest"), which refers to priests' entrance into the Jordan (3:13) but here refers to the putting the stones in their place (4:3, 8).

Like the crossing itself, the erection of the stones takes place in response to YHWH's command, and the narrative continues the sequence that has configured much of the account: YHWH commands Joshua, Joshua commands the people, the people carry out the command. In this case, however, YHWH's commands take a different form. Although speaking to Joshua, YHWH uses the plural form of the imperative to issue the commands (vv. 2-3), for the moment confusing leader and people while reinforcing the communal significance of the instructions. In another subtle shift, Joshua does not relay YHWH's instructions precisely (vv. 5-7). Reversing the previous pattern, Joshua directs the appointed men to "pass on before the ark of the LORD your God" (v. 5; cf. 3:6, 11, 14). He then declares that the stones are to be a "sign" among the people, employing the same term *(ʾôt)* that Rahab had used to request assurance of the spies' loyalty (2:12). In this fashion the fu-

---

[16] R. Nelson remarks: "To retell the story of crossing was to reinvigorate identity and esteem, to reinforce and objectify peoplehood, and to build the unity of the nation. Telling and hearing this story would create self-understanding and identity. The audience would come to see itself as twelve tribes forced into a single nation. Understood in this way, the text is less an etiology for a circle of stones than an etiology for the group identity of Israel." *Joshua*, 68.

[17] The middle verb *(hākîn)* conflates the first and third forms; it shares the first vowel *(patach)* with the first occurrence *(hākēn)* and the second vowel *(hireq yod)* with the third occurrence *(hēkîn)*.

ture "remembering" of the crossing is linked to the "remembering" of
Rahab's future deliverance. Finally, it is Joshua rather than YHWH who
explains the meaning of the stones and formulates the response that
future parents are to give to their children's questions. The response
(v. 7) is rendered in a symmetry that combines the two elements of the
wonder, the entrance of the ark and the stoppage of the waters, with
the ark at the center of the formula.

> The waters of the Jordan were cut off
> > Before the ark of the covenant of YHWH
> > When it passed through the Jordan
> The waters of the Jordan were cut off

This explanation of the stones reinforces the central meaning of the
event; YHWH opened the way into Canaan through an awesome demonstration of power. The designation of the stones as a "sign among
you" (v. 6) and "to the Israelites a memorial" (v. 7) affirms that the
meaning of the event is directed toward those who participated in the
crossing.

After reporting that the Israelites did as YHWH had told Joshua (v.
8), the narrator unexpectedly interrupts the sequence again to report
that Joshua set up twelve stones in the middle of the Jordan, at the
place where the priests bearing the ark stood (v. 9). The meaning of the
comment is uncertain. It may refer again to the previously reported
event, thus providing details about the precise location within the Jordan from which the stones were taken. More probably, it refers to the
erection of a second set of stones within the waters of the Jordan itself,
to commemorate the spot where the priests stood. These stones, it
seems, do not function explicitly to elicit a retelling of the event, for no
one will ever see them. And no explanation is attached to them. They
simply remain within the Jordan, "to this day," marking the spot known
only to YHWH and the participants, where the ark was born aloft while
Israel crossed the Jordan. While the first set of stones invites future
generations of Israelites to subsume their stories within the larger
scope of YHWH's saving acts, these stones emphasize the uniqueness of
Joshua and his generation and stand as a subliminal reminder of the
distance between the current experience of future generations and the
wondrous things experienced during the age of Joshua. While awkward, the comment is not therefore unrelated to its context. On the
contrary, it picks up elements of the previous narrative, particularly
the phrase "the place where the feet of the priests bearing the ark of
the covenant had stood" (cf. 4:3). However, it also makes an implicit
connection to the larger story. The twelve stones set up at the border

region "beneath the standing place" *(taḥat maṣṣab)* allude to the twelve pillars which Moses set up at the border region "beneath the mountain" *(taḥat hāhār)* after Israel had reaffirmed its obedience to YHWH at Sinai (Exod 24:4).[18] The connection is strengthened by the text's assertion that *Joshua* set up the twelve stones, echoing the Exodus assertion that Moses set up the stones at Sinai. The report thus affirms key elements of the story, forges another connection between Joshua and Moses, and confesses that Israel now inhabits the land because of the its obedience to YHWH.

Another Crossing: 4:10-14

With another reference to "the priests who bore the ark" the narrative signals a return to the main plot of the narrative, the crossing itself. Surprisingly, the narrative now doubles back and repeats the crossing. The repetition disrupts the chronological sequence, but disruption does not seem to be its primary purpose. Rather, the retelling constitutes a significant thematic complement to the previous account. In the first instance (3:1-17), the narrative relates Israel's *coming to* the Jordan from Shittim and focuses on the exaltation of YHWH through the miraculous stoppage of the water. This latter account (4:10-19) relates Israel's *coming out* of the Jordan to Gilgal and highlights the obedience of Israel as it follows the commands of YHWH, Joshua, and Moses. The narrative structure itself thus evokes a sense of crossing. The first scene begins on the eastern side, highlights the initiative and power of YHWH, and ends at the Jordan. Like the waters of the Jordan, the story then stops in order to digress on the topic of memorial stones. Once the purpose of the stones is explained the story now returns to the Jordan, depicts the obedience of Israel and the exaltation of Joshua, and concludes on the western side. The Jordan itself stands between the two accounts, linking the stories of entry and exit, with the repetitions of *ʿbr* in 3:14-17 and 4:11-13 tying them together.[19]

---

[18] The "standing place" *(maṣṣab)* also puns on the word for the twelve "pillars" *(maṣṣēbâ;* the Hebrew is singular) which Moses erected.

[19] Besides the four repetitions of the root noted in 3:14-17 (see above), the root occurs five times in 4:11-13. The NRSV translates the various repetitions of the root as "crossed over" (v. 10), "crossing over" (v. 11), "crossed over" (v. 11), "crossed over" (v. 12), "crossed over" (v. 13). In addition the term referring to "the plains of" Jericho *(ʿarabôt)* puns, through metathesis of the consonants, on the root *ʿbr.*

The structural and thematic connections demonstrate that this re-telling of the crossing is not the result of clumsy editing but rather an expansion which develops the significance of the event. In addition to the repetitions of *ʿbr*, this second account repeats important elements of the first, notably the characterization of the priests as the ones "who bore the ark" (v. 10), the reference to their "standing" as the nation crosses (v. 10), and the use of the verb *tam* to signify the completion of the crossing (vv. 10, 11). The repetition of new terms, however, indicates a different thematic emphasis. Three references to Moses (vv. 10, 12, 14) resurrect the themes of obedience and integrity laid out at the beginning of the book, and make the crossing an occasion to reassert these themes. The connection between YHWH, Joshua, Moses, and the people is also reiterated three times. In the first instance, the narrative once again stresses Moses' superiority to Joshua by reporting that the priests remained standing in the Jordan "until everything was finished that the LORD commanded Joshua to tell the people, according to all that Moses had commanded Joshua" (v. 10). The second instance reports that the eastern tribes made up the vanguard of those who crossed and confirms their obedience to Moses' charge (Deut 3:18-20; cf. Josh 1:16). The third instance (v. 14) specifically fulfills YHWH's promise to exalt Joshua (v. 7). Expressed through a commentary on the crossing, the remark asserts that Joshua achieved Mosaic stature in the eyes of the people, "they stood in awe of him as they had stood in awe of Moses, all the days of his life." The location of the comment is notable. Inserted at this juncture, it deflects any sense that Joshua was exalted because of the miracle at the Jordan, which in the text is attributed to the entrance of the ark. Rather, the placement of the comment at this point confirms that Joshua is exalted because he faithfully carries out the commands of YHWH and Moses. His obedience to their commands leads to his exaltation and is the basis of the esteem he receives from the nation.[20]

Out of the Jordan: 4:15-18

The theme of obedience continues to configure the narrative as we return to the priests, who leave the Jordan only at the divine command issued by Joshua. In contrast to the first instance in which YHWH issues

[20] This account also underscores the theme of integrity and wholeness through references to "all that Moses commanded" (v. 10), "all the people" (v. 11), "all Israel" (v. 14) and "all the days of his (Joshua's) life" (v. 14).

a command to the priests through Joshua (3:8), the narrative here explicitly notes Joshua's exact communication of the divine words (4:15-17). The priests respond immediately, resulting in the return of the Jordan's waters. Although the priests are again characterized as those who bear the ark, specific mention is made of their feet. This marks the third reference to the priests' feet, and each one has marked a key point in the crossing. The soles of the priests' feet touch the point at which the waters reach the eastern riverbank, resulting in the stoppage of the waters (3:13, 15). They next mark the middle of the dry riverbed, a place commemorated by the placement of stones (4:9). Now they touch the dry ground on the west bank (4:18), resulting in the return of the waters. [The particular emphasis given to their feet, and particularly to the soles of the feet (3:13; 4:18), hints that this event is a paradigm for the kind of obedience required of Israel if it is to take the entire land, for YHWH's promise, uttered again at the beginning of the book, grants to Israel "every place on which your feet shall tread" (1:3, AT).] By treading on the eastern bank, the western bank, and even the Jordan itself, Israel appropriates the divine promise and claims all the terrain as its own.

The unusual phrase *mittĕmôl šilšôm* (NRSV, "as before") concludes the event, bringing a sense of closure to the convoluted tale. At the beginning of the account, the phrase referred to the novelty of what Israel would experience—an event of transformative power, infused with wonder ("you have not passed this way *before*"). Now, with reference to the return of the waters, it signals the end of the wonder, the completion of the transformation, and a return to "normal" existence.

Crossing Over and Passing Through: 4:19-24

An epilogue fixes the wondrous event in space and time and associates it specifically with the Exodus and Passover. Whereas the first explanation of the memorial stones focused on the stoppage of the waters, this one revolves around the crossing itself, instilling in it a significance that transcends the moment and places it within the context of Israel's larger story. The children's question corresponds to that in 4:6, but the prescribed response now concentrates on the "dry ground" upon which the people crossed and stresses the purpose for the retelling. Besides the explicit connection between this event and the crossing of the Red Sea (v. 23), the passage contains a number of allusions to the flight from Egypt. The narrative only now reveals the date of the crossing, the tenth day of the first month, a date noteworthy for its correspondence to that fixed for obtaining a lamb in preparation for the Passover (Exod 12:3-5). The more familiar term *yabbāšâ*, which signifies the dry ground traveled by Israel through the Red Sea (Exod 14:22) now replaces *ḥārābâ* to denote the dry ground within the Jordan (v. 22). And the purpose ascribed to the retelling, that the nations may recognize YHWH's power, echoes a refrain within the story of the Exodus, that the Egyptians may recognize YHWH (Exod 7:5; 14:4, 18).

While the first explanation for the stones elaborates their significance to Israel, the second expands the scope and articulates their meaning for "all the peoples of the earth." Here again we find an ambiguity in the word translated "earth." As it does in connection with the ark and YHWH (3:11), the term could refer either specifically to the peoples of Canaan or to the peoples of the entire world. Whatever the sense, the declaration reveals that YHWH has a wider audience in mind for the performance of his mighty acts—even for those that are of pivotal significance for Israel's own experience. We now realize that the dry ground, the momentary erasure of the "boundary" signified by the Jordan, connects the peoples of the land to Israel just as it brings Israel into contact with the peoples of the land. Bearing the ark into the midst of the Jordan—lifting up the divine presence—removes the boundary which divides east from west, Israel from Canaan, and Israelites from Canaanites, but the boundary returns when the presence leaves it.

Joshua declares that the stones have two complementary purposes—to reveal YHWH's power and to provoke reverent response—and these are not mutually exclusive purposes, as Joshua himself has intimated (3:10).[21] The peoples of the land, as well as Israel, are called to witness the demonstration of YHWH's might. Will they respond differently than Israel? The question is put subtly but pointedly through the text's echoes of the only "inhabitant" we have thus encountered: "we have heard how YHWH dried up *(hôbîš)* the Red Sea before you" (cf. 4:23). The words, of course, are Rahab's, the only character in the story thus far to offer praise to Israel's God.

[21] The proclamation takes up again the theme of "knowing" which figured prominently at the beginning of this section (3:4, 7, 10) as well as in the story of the spies at Jericho.

Chapter Five
FIRST THINGS FIRST
Joshua 5:1-15

With the nation completely across the Jordan, the narrator lingers at the new encampment. In contrast to the predominance of speech thus far in the book, narration rather than dialogue now carries the action, allowing both narrator and reader to gain a more comprehensive perspective. The chapter comprises four discrete units: a report that the kings of the land were terror-stricken by the wonder at the Jordan (v. 1), an account of mass circumcision at Gilgal (vv. 2-9), the celebration of Passover (vv. 10-12), and an eerie encounter between Joshua and the commander of the divine armies (vv. 13-15). The middle events depict the beginning of a new era by reporting the performance of rites that constitute primary markers of community identity. The first and fourth events frame these observances with reports that foreshadow the victories Israel will soon achieve. The structure of the chapter thus associates community integrity and devotion to YHWH with the imminent campaigns against the peoples of Canaan. Israel transformed is now prepared to wrest the land from its inhabitants.

The Kings Beyond the Jordan: 5:1

The narrator employs a brief report about the kings of the land to clarify points of connection and contrast. Having explained the crossing's significance for Israel, the narrator now reveals its significance for the peoples of Canaan. The report emphasizes the kings' geographical distance (they are "beyond the Jordan to the west") but more importantly confirms their distance from the event itself. The kings do not witness YHWH's miracle or the crossing of the people. Their experience of the event comes from the news they receive from some unknown witness. As with the report of the spies' entrance into Jericho (2:2), we are not told how the kings hear of the crossing into Canaan, but the narrator uses the distinctive language of 4:19-24 (YHWH "dried up" the waters of the Jordan) to confirm that they have heard correctly. As it does with Israel the miracle evidently unites the kings of Canaan ("all the kings of the Amorites" and "all the kings of the Canaanites"), but produces the opposite effect, melting hearts and loss of resolve.[1] Terror- stricken and despairing, they stand in stark contrast to the Israelites, who have been characterized in the previous narrative by their wholehearted compliance to the commands of YHWH, Moses, and Joshua. Israel possesses the promises of divine presence and victory, and, we are led to assume, a determination and courage that the kings do not have.

The report also suggests connections with key points in the story thus far. The narrator's words closely follow Rahab's description of the crossing of the Red Sea (2:11): the kings of the Amorites are located "beyond the Jordan," YHWH's act involves a "drying up" of water, the "hearts" of the inhabitants of the land "melt" and there is "no longer any spirit" in them.[2] The particular language of the narrator's report, in effect a repetition of Rahab's words, has the curious effect of aligning our perspective with that of Rahab, yet linking her on the semantic plane with the kings of Canaan who hear of the crossing; both the narrator and the kings view the crossing in language borrowed from Rahab. Her influence, it appears, extends beyond the spies, who also use her words to articulate their perspective (2:24).[3] Rahab, the spies, the kings, and the narrator now share a common perspective, revealing a four-fold alignment of perspective that breaks down the boundaries which differentiate Israelite and Canaanite, character and narrator, story and narrative. Rahab, the Israelite spies, and the narrator have blended together. They speak the same words. All reiterate the words of Moses (Exod 15:15-16), and all share the same speech and perspec-

---

[1] The term "Amorites" probably designates the inhabitants of the highland areas, while "Canaanites" refers to the coastal inhabitants of the land. For more on these peoples, and the others listed in Joshua, see E.C. Hostetter, *Nations Mightier and More Numerous*, BDS 4 (N. Richland Hills: Bibal, 1995).

[2] The phrases in 2:11 and 5:1 are nearly identical in the MT, although the NRSV translates them differently: *wayimmas lĕbābēk wĕlōʾ-qāmâ ʿôd rûaḥ bĕʾîš mipnēykem* (2:11) and *wayimmas lĕbābēm wĕlōʾhāyâ bām ʿôd rûaḥ mipnēy bĕnēy yiśrāʾēl* (5:1).

[3] The spies' report quotes Rahab's initial declaration (2:9), while the narrator's derives from the rest of her speech (2:10-11).

tive. Rahab thus remains present in the narrative through her words, which now form an *inclusio* around the crossing narrative (2:24; 5:1). Reports of melting Canaanites encompass the story of a stopped-up river, accentuating the effect of the wonder and confirming YHWH's promise to terrorize the inhabitants of the land. Yet, because the language is Rahab's, it also melds images of an obedient Israel with the confessions of a Canaanite prostitute. The *inclusio* therefore provokes a question. Whose side are we on?

The blending of narrative boundaries parallels a confusion of geographical boundaries. The narrator not only links Rahab and Israelites through speech and perspective but also links the sides of the Jordan through a sudden shift of geographical perspective. After multiple "crossings," the narrative has concluded with Israel now encamped on the west side of the Jordan. However, the narrator now spirits the reader back across the Jordan a final time and reports the perspective of the kings *west* of the Jordan while still ostensibly situated on the *east* side. The text creates this confusion through another repetition of the root *ʿbr*, which now specifically designates the kings as "beyond" *(bĕʿēber)* the Jordan. The confusion arises because the term has previously designated the eastern side of the Jordan (1:14, 15; 2:10). The "other side" is *east*. But now, we are explicitly told that the "other side" is *west*. The language of the text thus employs a word which expresses the perspective of those in Canaan and turns it back on the same region, resulting in the transformation of the reader's perspective and location from the *west* back to the *east*. "The other side" denotes the place *opposite* of one's own location. But what *is* this opposite place? The "other side" is now Canaan, not the Transjordan, and we learn of the melting hearts of the Canaanites as if we were standing once again outside the land.

The narrator's comment therefore does much more than report or clarify the action of the story. It evokes a raft of ambiguities that invite further reflection on the "crossing" and its meaning. On the surface, the report affirms that the demonstration of YHWH's power has sufficiently cowed the kings of Canaan, who seem to have given up the fight. But we have seen enough of Canaan to wonder about the melting hearts and loss of spirit. Rahab had spoken of her compatriots in the same terms, but the appearance of the king's men at her door indicated little sense of defeatism. And Rahab, who declared that *"our* hearts melted and there was no strength left in *any of us"* nonetheless proved more than a match for the spies and succeeded in winning concessions which insured her survival. How then are we to understand these melting hearts and fainting spirits? Have the kings of Canaan lost all sense of hope? Are they paralyzed by terror? Is our narrator

simply fond of hyperbole?[4] Does this commentary simply confirm that
YHWH has been at work to prepare the land for conquest? Why has
Rahab not been terrorized? From whose perspective is this story being
told? For whom are YHWH's mighty acts being performed?[5] Is crossing
over the Jordan the defining characteristic of God's people or is there a
place for others who acclaim YHWH's glory?

The Reproach of Egypt: 5:2-9

As we have noted, the crossing of the Jordan signifies the transformation of Israel into a landed and coherent nation. The crossing is an
act of creation, and the Israel now encamped at Gilgal constitutes a new
people. The newly reconstituted nation is marked by the performance
of rites which mark beginnings but also stress continuity with the past.
The rite of circumcision reaches back to the Patriarchal narratives,
which tell of the nation's origins in YHWH's calling and promise, while
the Passover remembers Israel's deliverance from slavery in Egypt, the
event that begins Israel's journey to the promised land. In addition,
both rituals ground the coherence of Israel within the basic units that
comprise the nation. Neither calls the nation to assemble for corporate
confession and performance but rather situates these within the family.

Through the rite of circumcision, the people now mark the fulfillment of the patriarchal promises and affirm their identity as a unique
people bound by covenant to YHWH. The origin of the ritual, recorded
in Gen 17:1-27, establishes circumcision as a transforming act which affirms the people's decision to choose the God who has chosen them. In
this text, YHWH (here called God; MT *ʾelohîm*) begins by establishing a
covenant with Abram and declaring that Abram will become the ancestor of many nations (vv. 2-4). YHWH then changes Abram's name to
"Abraham," an act which implies a transformation of identity. Associated with this new identity is a reiteration of the promises of nationhood, covenant, and land (vv. 6-8):

---

[4] Hyperbole is a common element in the war literature of the Ancient Near East,
as is the appropriation of stock imagery for the terrorized state of the enemy. For
more on this, see L. Younger, *Ancient Conquest Accounts: A Study of Ancient Near
Eastern and Biblical History Writing*, JSOTSup 98 (Sheffield: Sheffield Academic
Press, 1990).

[5] The narrator's report follows immediately after Joshua's assertion that the
stones at Gilgal have been set up as a memorial both to Israel and to the inhabitants
of the land.

I will make you exceedingly fruitful; and I will make nations of you. I will establish my covenant between me and you, and your offspring after you throughout their generations, for an everlasting covenant, to be God to you and to give to you, and to your offspring after you, the land where you are now an alien, the land of Canaan, for a perpetual holding; and I will be their God.

God then institutes circumcision as "sign of the covenant between me and you" (v. 11) which will be carried out "throughout your generations" (v. 12). Circumcision thus marks the reciprocal choosing of God and people, an essential and visible sign of the covenant between Israel and YHWH.

In Joshua, the circumcision of all males follows immediately after the nation has crossed the Jordan and symbolically verifies the transformation of the people. The performance of circumcision in this context signals the fulfillment of the ancestral promises, now realized by the crossing into the land. YHWH has been faithful in bringing Israel into the land. Now, through circumcision the nation responds to YHWH's faithfulness with an act that expresses the devotion that characterized their ancestors.

A lengthy digression reinforces the sense that the performance of circumcision signifies a new beginning (vv. 4-7). The text emphasizes the uncircumcised state of the people prior to the crossing (vv. 5, 7) and asserts the present generation's *discontinuity* with the previous generation. The digression establishes a dichotomy between the people who have "crossed into" the land and those who "came out of" Egypt, intimating a radical break with the wilderness period. The root *yṣ'* (to come out) occurs five times to designate the previous generation, which is linked repeatedly to Egypt and the wilderness (vv. 4, 5, 6); they "came out of the wilderness" and "journeyed through the wilderness" in contrast to those who have "crossed into" (*'br*) the land. The phrases associated with them accentuate their ambiguous, in-between status; they embody both settled existence (Egypt) and nomadism (wilderness), slavery (Egypt) and freedom (wilderness). On another note, the wilderness generation's failure to circumcise those "born during the journey" demonstrates their disobedient nature, for YHWH explicitly commanded the circumcision of all males in the household, including children. Failure to do so amounts to a breach of covenant (Gen 17:11-14). The narrator explicitly draws attention to their disobedient character by commenting that the entire generation came to its end in the wilderness because they "did not listen to the voice of the Lord" (v. 6). In contrast, the generation now in the land gives prompt attention to circumcision. The narrator undergirds their obedient

character by employing the command-execution form which characterized the crossing narrative; YHWH issues a command (this time to
Joshua) and the text promptly reports the execution of the command.[6]
The obedience of the present generation, expressed through their
"crossing into" the land and now by circumcision, constitutes the appropriate response to the promises of nationhood and land, both now
and in the future.[7]

The contrast between the two generations is accentuated by the language of totality. The same holistic terminology that characterized those
who crossed into the land is now applied to the wilderness generation
but emphasizes the totality of their disobedience and failure. Whereas
the repetition of "all" *(kôl)* signified the unity and obedience of the
people as they crossed the Jordan, here its repetition signifies the disobedience and fate of the wilderness generation, "all the males . . . all the
warriors died" (v. 4). "All the people who came out" had been circumcised in Egypt, but they did not observe the covenant by circumcising
"all the people born on the journey" (v. 5). They therefore wandered for
forty years until "all the nation . . . perished" (v. 6). The "perishing" of
the previous generation reflects a translation of the Hebrew verb *tam*,
which appears frequently during the crossing to emphasize the completion of the event (3:16, 17; 4:1, 10, 11) and will occur again to denote the
completion of the circumcisions (5:8). With reference to the wilderness
generation, it now denotes the end of wandering—the death of all who
did so. Ironically it conveys a sense of *in*completeness, for the comments
which follow remind the reader that YHWH had sworn that they would
not see the land. The wordplay occasioned by the various uses of the
verb enhances the contrast between the two generations; the "completeness" of the crossing generation surrounds the "end" of the wilderness
generation. The contrast between the generations suggests that the
negative traits which characterized the latter were left behind as the nation crossed the Jordan. The Israel now encamped in the land will be
everything that the previous generation was *not*. Wilderness Israel came
out of Egypt and perished in the wilderness because of their disobedi-

---

[6] The narrator underscores the significance of circumcision as an act of obedience and communal inauguration by placing it at "Gibeath-haaraloth" ("the hill of
foreskins," v. 3). The site has not been identified; see, for example, R. Boling, *Joshua*,
AB (Garden City: Doubleday, 1982) 189. While the phrase probably refers to a particular site, it also suggests another sight, namely that of a mound of severed foreskins. This gruesome image links the foreskins (signs of their "disobedient" status
before crossing) with the other piles and heaps in Canaan (7:26; 8:28, 29; 10:27).

[7] The transcendent significance of the event is marked by the subtle reference to
"the land that he had sworn to their ancestors to give *us*" (v. 6).

ence. Israel-in-Canaan has come into a land of milk and honey and looks forward to a life epitomized by devotion to YHWH. This Israel is a new nation, whereas the disobedient Israel of the wilderness is completely a thing of the past.

It is in this sense that we should understand the obscure explanation given for the shrine at Gilgal: "Today I have rolled away from you the disgrace of Egypt" (v. 9).[8] The meaning of the declaration cannot be determined with precision. What "disgrace" does the text refer to? A number of possibilities have been suggested. The "disgrace" may refer to the degrading condition of slavery which Israel suffered in Egypt. Or it may have some connection with the previously uncircumcised state or disobedience of the current generation.[9] Whatever the precise sense, the comment clearly asserts that Egypt and everything associated with it have been exorcized from Israel. It is therefore by no accident that this aside occurs immediately after the report that "all the nation" was circumcised (v. 8). The etiological reference explaining Gilgal's name thus commemorates, within this context, the institution of a new nation which will obediently live out the life YHWH offers in the land.

New Food: 5:10-12

Like circumcision, Passover is a rite of beginning. The celebration of the festival, now within the land itself, provides additional confirmation of the nation's reconstitution. "The reproach of Egypt" has been rolled away, and the nation further disassociates itself from Egypt by the festival which commemorates its departure under Moses. During the first Passover, YHWH had made "a distinction between Egypt and Israel" (Exod 11:7) by slaying the firstborn of the Egyptians while sparing the firstborn of the Israelites. The present celebration commemorates that "distinguishing" event now in a new land while gathered on the plains of Jericho. The narrator consolidates the connection by making special note of the date and time at which the festival was celebrated (v. 10; cf. Exod 12:6, 18). But most of the attention is devoted to the people's change in diet, from manna to the produce of the land. The consumption of the food of Canaan at the precise moment when the manna ceases presents a final, dramatic metaphor for the end of the wilderness period and the beginning of life in the land. The significance

---

[8] The name Gilgal puns on the Hebrew root *gll* (to roll).

[9] R. Nelson, *Joshua*, OTL (Louisville: Westminster John Knox, 1997) 76.

of this change in diet (and the change in Israel it signifies) is emphasized through repetition, "on the day after the Passover, on that very day, they ate the produce of the land . . . the manna ceased on the day they ate the produce of the land, and the Israelite no longer had manna."[10] Symbolic connections to Israel's experience through the Jordan are also effected through the MT's elegant wordplay on the root *ʿbr* ("crossing"): "in the evening *(bāʾereḇ)* at the plains *(bᵉʿarbôt)* of Jericho. And they ate from the produce *(mēᶜᵃḇûr)* of the land" (vv. 10-11, AT).

The nation now encamped at Jericho finds nourishment in the fare of a settled people rather than the ephemeral food of the wilderness. The unleavened cakes and parched grain enjoyed near Jericho are foods prepared in haste, hearkening back to the eve of the wilderness experience, when the same diet was consumed by another generation in Egypt. But they are also foods produced from crops that have been cultivated and harvested, the foods of a sedentary people now tied to the land. As such they symbolize the arrival of Israel in the promised land.[11]

The Commander of YHWH's Army: 5:13-15

In the Deuteronomic scheme, YHWH's presence with Israel is predicated on Israel's careful obedience to the laws of Moses. The rites of circumcision and the celebration of Passover have presented unambiguous demonstrations of the nation's fidelity immediately after the Jordan crossing, and we might therefore expect some affirmation of divine presence as Israel prepares for its campaigns in Canaan. The appearance of the "commander of the army of the Lord" ostensibly offers this confirmation and connects the crossing experience with the imminent battle at Jericho. The commander stands with an unsheathed sword, intimating the army's readiness for battle. And like the priests who stand *(ʿōmēd)* on ground sanctified by YHWH's presence through the ark (4:10), both the commander and Joshua stand *(ʿōmēd)* on holy ground (vv. 13, 15).[12]

[10] R. Hess discerns a chiastic structure. See *Joshua*, 124.

[11] There is no mention in the text of the consumption of the lamb for Passover. The omission reinforces the wilderness-land dichotomy. Lamb is a food associated with pastoral rather than agricultural existence. It does not therefore carry the same symbolic resonance as the grain foods associated with permanent inhabitants of the land. Mentioning grain thus enhances the symbolic ambience of the text in a way that the lamb does not.

[12] The participial form of the verb in each of these instances defines the individuals by the action they perform.

The appearance of a divine being before the outset of a battle is an element of the war literature of many Ancient Near Eastern cultures, and commentators almost uniformly understand the apparition as an encouraging sign on the eve of the wars for Canaan.[13] In this view, the encounter reveals that the heavenly armies have been mobilized to fight alongside Israel and endorses Joshua's leadership as the commander of Israel's armies. Joshua's prostration before the commander demonstrates his submission to YHWH and thus reinforces the chain of command for the campaigns. The armies of YHWH will fight the battles for Israel who, under the direction of Joshua, will participate in the victories by fulfilling the commands to slaughter all the peoples of the cities. The encounter thus provides an assurance of Israelite triumph and implicitly commissions Joshua as YHWH's lieutenant. However, many features of the encounter create a sense of ambivalence and uncertainty. The episode begins abruptly "by Jericho" *(bîyrîḥô)*. The NRSV here makes the best of a difficult construction in the MT, for the phrase in other contexts would normally be translated "in Jericho." Only the literary context prompts us to understand the phrase with reference to some unspecified site in the region of Jericho, and while this must certainly be the case, the more "conventional" translation draws a subliminal connection between Joshua and the spies by placing the former at the site of the latter's escapades. Additional territorial ambiguity occurs when the commander declares that the place where Joshua stands is holy. What does this declaration mean? Is holiness confined to the "place" where Joshua stands, now sacred space because of the presence of the divine commander? Or does it mean that the entire land is holy since the presence of YHWH has now crossed over into it?

The demeanor of the divine commander adds to the air of uncertainty. In biblical literature divine beings with drawn swords usually represent adversaries rather than allies, and they usually threaten death and judgment. Such is the case with the angel of the Lord, who stands with drawn sword and blocks Balaam and his donkey (Num 22:21-35). In that instance, the apparition threatens a death which the prophet only narrowly escapes. David, too, sees the angel of YHWH in the midst of a plague, with sword unsheathed over Jerusalem (1 Chr 21:14-16). In both cases, the encounter takes place because the subject has provoked YHWH's anger. We are therefore prompted to ask questions here at Jericho. Is YHWH angry? Does the commander's appearance portend victory or disaster?

[13] See the discussions in Nelson, *Joshua*, 80–83 and P. D. Miller, *The Divine Warrior in Ancient Israel*, HSM 5 (Cambridge, Mass.: Harvard University, 1973) 128–31.

This is precisely the issue Joshua seeks to resolve. He takes the role of a sentry, standing at some distance from the rest of the camp, and he asks the sentry's question, "friend or foe?" The apparition, however, is evasive. Curiously, he refuses to declare his allegiance and simply identifies himself as the commander of the army of the YHWH (v. 14a). His terse and noncommittal response is particularly strange in light of YHWH's unambiguous promise to be with Israel (1:5-9) and YHWH's participation in the Jordan crossing (4:21-24). If the commander has appeared to give Israel assurance of divine presence and victory, why does he not do so, especially on the eve of the first conflict in Canaan?

The story's abrupt and open ending caps the enigmatic atmosphere of the story by leaving the question of loyalty in suspension. The encounter concludes with the kind of command-execution sequence we have seen throughout the last three chapters. The commander tells Joshua to remove his sandals and the narrator reports that Joshua did so. Yet, one has the feeling that something else should follow. Is the purpose of the story simply to inform the reader that divine warriors have entered Canaan (while not confirming their allegiance)? Or to inform Joshua that he stands on holy ground (whatever that means)? Is there nothing more?

Our expectations of a better end are perhaps influenced by the form of the story itself, which appropriates many elements of the call of Moses (Exod 3:1-12). Both stories are theophanies which begin as surprising encounters with divine beings (the commander here, the angel of YHWH in Exodus). In each case the divine being issues the identical command, "Remove the sandals from your feet, for the place on which you are standing is holy ground" (v. 14; cf. Exod 3:4-5). In the Exodus text, the command sets up an encounter during which YHWH will commission Moses to deliver Israel. The commission includes a declaration of YHWH's intent to bring Israel into the land (Exod 3:8)

> I have come down to deliver them from the Egyptians, and to bring them up out of that land to a good and broad land, a land, flowing with milk and honey, to the country of the Canaanites, the Hittites, the Amorites, the Perizzites, the Hivites, and the Jebusites.

With this text in mind, Joshua's encounter with the divine commander raises certain expectations. The command that he take off his sandals strongly indicates that Joshua will be the recipient of a divine charge to lead his people to victory over the inhabitants of the land. YHWH has already exalted Joshua in the presence of the people, so that they esteem him as they did Moses (4:14). As Israel faces the power of Canaan for the first time, we anticipate another demonstration that YHWH is with Joshua as he was with Moses (1:5, 17). Moses had his theophany; now Joshua has his. But the divine instruction is cut short at the crucial moment, immediately before the promise of the land would be affirmed. In other words, what is left unsaid—what is omitted—is precisely that part of YHWH's charge to Moses that pertains to the present situation. YHWH gave strong assurances to Moses and inspired him by pointing to the imminent fulfillment of the ancestral promise of the land. Since Joshua's encounter follows the same pattern, the reader might expect similar affirmations. Yet the story stops before the confirming words can be uttered, leaving the promise unaffirmed and the reader without a sense of closure. The absence of the land promise at this crucial juncture in the story, along with the commander's refusal to commit for Israel, abruptly stops the forward momentum of the story. From forthright expressions of Israel's allegiance to YHWH (through the rites of circumcision and Passover) the story now shifts to an ambivalent expression of YHWH's allegiance to Israel. Why the equivocation here, of all places? Why should the narrator inject any sense of doubt as Israel prepares to take possession of the land?

The chapter thus ends with a profound ambivalence. Israel has explicitly expressed its fidelity to YHWH through circumcision and Passover, but YHWH has not responded in kind. In effect, YHWH has refused an opportunity to declare "for" Israel. Whose side is YHWH on? Why then has the divine commander appeared? If anything, the enigmatic words of the commander challenge any attempt to tie national aspirations too closely to YHWH's purposes. The battles fought on the soil of Canaan will be YHWH's battles, waged to fulfill longstanding promises. The commander is not answerable to any human being, even Joshua. Although obscure, the commander's terse response makes one thing clear. The wars in Canaan will be initiated and conducted by YHWH for YHWH's own purposes. Israel will occupy the land only because it is the beneficiary of divine choosing and faithfulness (cf. Deut 9:4-7).

Chapter Six
GOING IN CIRCLES
Joshua 6:1-27

After its long digression at the Jordan the narrative now resumes with the assault against Jericho. The account gives surprisingly little attention to the actual conflict (vv. 20-21, 24) and concentrates instead on the continuation of two prior themes: Israel's obedient performance of ritual commands and the deliverance of Rahab and her family. The first section relates a series of ritual processions around Jericho which are carried out under the direction of Joshua (vv. 2-15). The middle section, which tells of the destruction of the city (vv. 16-21), concludes this theme while introducing the second. The processions come to an end on the seventh day, when Joshua issues additional instructions concerning the city and the walls fall flat as the people shout and blow the trumpets (vv. 16-20). Joshua also decrees the deliverance of Rahab and her house (v. 17), introducing a second plot line which becomes the focus of the third section (vv. 22-25). The chapter ends with the pronouncement of a curse and a confirmation that YHWH was with Joshua, whose renown spread throughout the land (vv. 26-27).

The events that comprise the chapter thus bring together and complete the two opposing plot lines we have encountered thus far, Israel's expression of fidelity through ritual and Rahab's exemption from the Mosaic ban. Repetitions of the root ʿbr render a continuity with the Jordan crossing and thus with the associated issue of identity, connecting the transit of the ark around Jericho with the ark's transit through the Jordan (NRSV "go forward" [v. 7], "pass on" [v. 7], "went forward" [v. 8]). Here, as at the Jordan, the ark figures prominently in the ritual procession as it is born aloft by the priests.[1] On a deeper level, the ark intimates a symbolic association with the Jordan crossing. Jericho's walls, like the Jordan, represent a boundary which will be dismantled in a spectacular manner. Jericho is the first of the cities of Canaan to be assaulted by Israel and thus represents a prototype for future conquests. The wondrous collapse of the walls confirms that YHWH will indeed fight for Israel and enhances the status of Joshua as YHWH's lieutenant by providing dramatic confirmation that YHWH is with him (v. 27; cf. 4:14).

The command-execution pattern which recurs throughout Joshua 3–5 configures virtually the entire narrative in Joshua 6. By appropriating this pattern to shape the whole of the account, the narrator powerfully demonstrates the nation's complete obedience to YHWH and Joshua. As in the previous events, a description of the execution of commands often follows the particular language of the commands themselves. The technique further underscores the meticulous manner in which the exact words of the command are carried out and reinforces the chain of command. Joshua relays YHWH's commands to the people and the narrator reports that Israel responded "as Joshua had commanded" (v. 8).

CHART 5: COMMAND AND EXECUTION AT JERICHO	
Command	*Execution*
You shall march around the city, all the warriors circling the city once (v. 3).	The ark of the LORD went around the city, circling it once (v. 11a, cf. v. 14a).
Thus you shall do for six days, with seven priests bearing seven trumpets of rams' horns before the ark (vv. 3-4).	The seven priests carrying the seven trumpets of rams' horns before the ark of the LORD passed on, blowing the trumpets continually. . . . They did this for six days (vv. 13a, 14b).
On the seventh day you shall march around the city seven times, the priests blowing the trumpets (v. 4b).	On the seventh day they rose early, at dawn, and marched around the city in the same manner seven times. It was only on that day that they marched

---

[1] The narrative even recreates some of the confusion characteristic of the crossing account; it is difficult to determine whether the trumpets are blown only by the priests or by the priests and the rear guard (vv. 8-9, 13).

	around the city seven times. And at the seventh time, when the priests had blown the trumpets (vv. 15-16a).
As soon as you hear the sound of the trumpet, then all the people shall shout with a great shout; and the wall of the city will fall down flat, and all the people shall charge straight ahead (v. 5).	As soon as the people heard the sound of the trumpets, they raised a great shout, and the wall fell down flat; so the people charged straight ahead into the city and captured it (v. 20b-c).
Take up the ark of the covenant, and have seven priests carry seven trumpets of rams' horns in front of the ark of the LORD (v. 6b).	The seven priests carrying the seven trumpets of rams' horns before the LORD went forward, blowing the trumpets, with the ark of the covenant of the Lord following them (v. 8b-c, cf. v. 13).
Go forward and march around the city; have the armed men pass on before the ark of the LORD (v. 7).	And the armed men went before the priests who blew the trumpets (v. 9a; cf. v. 13).
To the people Joshua gave this command: "You shall not shout or let your voice be heard, nor shall you utter a word, until the day I tell you to shout. Then you shall shout" (v. 10)	Joshua said to the people, "Shout! For the LORD has given you the city" . . . So the people shouted and the trumpets were blown (vv. 16b, 20a).
The city and all that is in it shall be devoted to the LORD for destruction (v. 17a).	Then they devoted to destruction by the edge of the sword all in the city, both men and women, young and old, oxen, sheep and donkeys (v. 21).
So Joshua said to the two men who had spied out the land, "Go into the prostitute's house, and bring the woman out of it and all who belong to her, as you swore to her" (v. 22).	So the young men who had been spies went in and brought Rahab out, along with her father, her mother, her brothers, all who belonged to her—they brought all her kindred out (v. 23).

By utilizing this pattern throughout the episode the narrator conclusively reasserts the wholehearted obedience called for at the beginning of the book.

Opposing this unmistakable demonstration of Israelite fidelity is the delicate matter of the agreement with Rahab and the story of her household's deliverance from death. As with the ritual processions, loyalty and obligation propel Israel's actions, but in this case they are oriented toward a Canaanite prostitute. Here as well the narrator makes a point of noting that Israel honors its commitments, since she and her family are spared the fate suffered by the rest of the population. The attention given to the fate of her family, against repeated demonstrations of Israel's obedience to the commandments, brings to the surface an undercurrent of tension that was initiated by the spies' trip to Jericho (and hinted at by the immediately preceding encounter between Joshua and the commander of YHWH's army). The nation as a whole has been scrupulously obedient to follow the commands of YHWH as they are relayed through Joshua, but the oath that the spies have made with Rahab constitutes a flagrant violation of Moses' commands regarding the inhabitants of the land (Exod 23:22-23; Deut 7:1-6). The conjunction of these opposing situations at this point in the story raises a dilemma which will test Israel's fidelity to YHWH. How will the issue be resolved? Will Joshua disavow a covenant and oath made in the name of YHWH in order to keep the command of Moses? Or will Joshua honor the oath made to Rahab and therefore violate the command of Moses? The matter is of crucial importance. The reader knows that possession of the land depends on adherence to the commands of Moses (Deut 7:12-16; 8:1; 11:22-25), and Moses himself has promised dire consequences for failure to heed his commands (Deut 7:4; 11:26-28). What will be the effect of the spies' oath and on the ruling made with respect to it? And how will YHWH respond?

The conflicting images presented by Israel's ritual observances and Rahab's deliverance render a sense of ambivalence regarding Israel's fidelity to YHWH and thus to the entire enterprise of possessing the land. On the corporate level the reader has encountered a uniformly obedient nation which has entered the land through the power of YHWH and seems poised to realize YHWH's promises. Individual Israelites, however, have not displayed a corresponding attentiveness to the commands of Moses, and the deliverance of Rahab and her family intimates the incursion of the diverse into the ostensibly uniform community.

The destruction of Jericho and the deliverance of Rahab bring the first major section of Joshua (Joshua 2–6) to a conclusion and constitute the last components of a larger structural symmetry which heightens the tension between these two plot lines.

A Israelite spies promise to deliver Rahab at Jericho (2:1-25)

  B Israel crosses the Jordan in ritual procession opposite Jericho (3:1–5:1)

    C Israel's commitment to YHWH is confirmed through rituals on the plains of Jericho (5:2-12)

    C' YHWH's commitment to Israel is unspoken in a theophany near Jericho (5:13-15)

  B' Israel destroys Jericho after ritual processions (6:1-21)

A' Israelite spies deliver Rahab from the destruction of Jericho (6:22-25)

References to Jericho bracket the section and unite the diverse materials which comprise it (2:1, 3; 3:16; 5:10, 13; 6:26-27). Rahab's story (2:2-21; 6:22-25) encloses the accounts of crossing and conquest, countering the repeated demonstrations of Israelite ritual obedience at the boundary regions (the Jordan, the walls of Jericho) with a portrait of wayward Israelites and a pious prostitute. The central episodes articulate the ambiguity rendered by the opposing images of Israel with a bit of irony; Israel confirms its commitment to YHWH through covenantal rites, but YHWH, through the commander of the divine army, refuses to declare for Israel. The ending of the chapter thus offers a sense of closure (for Israel will now leave Jericho for new conquests) but does not resolve the problematic issues of the nation's character and identity.

Preparations for the Procession: 6:1-7

The chapter opens with a series of preparations for the upcoming assault, beginning with the report that Jericho has been tightly shut up (v. 1). Then there follows a sequence of speeches after the pattern in Joshua 1. The longest speech is delivered by YHWH, who speaks first and addresses Joshua. Echoing the initial promise of the land, YHWH declares that Jericho and its king have been delivered to Israel (vv. 2-5; cf. 1:2-9).[2] Also reminiscent of the opening speech, YHWH shifts between second person singular and plural verbs when addressing Joshua. The next two speeches belong to Joshua, who gives commands first to a select group (v. 6; cf. 1:10-11) and then to the people (v. 7; cf. 1:12-15).

---

[2] The verb *nātan* ("give") denotes the "handing over" of Jericho.

By following the pattern of the book's opening scene, the narrative signals a new beginning and reconfirms the unity of YHWH, Joshua, and
the people. The speeches also reiterate the chain of command (YHWH-
Joshua-select group-people) and reinforce the connection between
promise, obedience, success.

The narrator introduces these speeches with a brief introduction that
directs the reader's attention to Jericho and its response to the Israelites.[3]
The city looms before Israel, silent and impenetrable, a formidable obstacle in the path of the nation's aspirations. The population within has
sealed itself off completely from the invaders. It is "shut up inside and
out" and "no one came out and no one went in."[4] A walled city evokes a
number of associations. First, it recalls the trepidation with which the
wilderness generation responded to the opportunity to enter the land.
That generation had forfeited the promise because they feared both the
populace and the cities, "Yet the people who live in the land are strong,
and the towns are fortified and very large" (Num 13:28). Conversely, the
sight recalls the victories in Transjordan won by the present generation.
The cities of Og were fortresses with high walls but the Israelites utterly
destroyed them (Deut 3:5). The wall also emphasizes the difference between Israel and the peoples of the land. The peoples' inactivity stands
in contrast to the Israelites, who will soon undertake a great deal of activity around them. We may also note that this episode marks the only
time in the entire book, save in the story of Rahab (2:15), that walls are
even mentioned. Beginning the story with the description of a seemingly impregnable Jericho accomplishes two things. First, it sets the
scene for YHWH's participation in the ensuing assault by making it clear
that Israel would not be able to take the city by conventional means. Second, it reminds the reader of Rahab (whose dwelling in the wall was
specifically noted) and of the spies' promise to spare her household.

The ensuing speeches draw attention to YHWH's crucial role in the
campaign by blending ritual and military practices. YHWH's speech be-

---

[3] Jericho can be confidently identified with Tel es-Sultan, a large tel located at a
strategic crossing site near fords of the Jordan. A significant body of scholarship
addresses the archaeological record as it relates (or does not relate) to the events
recounted in Joshua. Recent commentaries generally offer an overview of the discussion. For a more extensive overview and bibliography of the archaeological
record of Palestine during the pre-exilic period, see D. Bloch-Smith and B.A.
Nakhai, "A Landscape Comes to Life: The Iron Age I," *NEA* 62 (1999) 62–92,
101–127.

[4] In the MT, the first phrase exhibits an unusual participial construction, *sōgeret
ûmĕsuggeret*. This combination of *Qal* and *Pual* participles emphasizes that routes of
egress and exit have been completely sealed off.

gins with an explicit declaration of victory, utilizing a conventional form, literally, "I have given into your hand Jericho and its king" (AT; cf. Deut 2:25, 30; 3:2, 3; Josh 2:24). The declaration implicitly fulfills YHWH's promise through Moses (Deut 7:24) and reveals that the outcome has already been decided. Here as in other instances throughout the book, proclamation and prediction confirm the power of YHWH's word. YHWH simply declares what will be and subsequent events unfold accordingly. YHWH calls for an unusual sequence of processions around Jericho which will comprise both priests and warriors. Corresponding to the participants, the processions incorporate practices that derive both from ritual and military contexts (v. 3). The initial verb in the MT (*sabbōtem*, NRSV "march around") can refer either to surrounding a city in preparation for a siege or a march around the city. The ambiguity, however, is quickly resolved by a second verb (*haqqēyp*, NRSV "circling") which employs an infinitival form to specify that a procession rather than a siege is meant. The verbal pair conveys a sense of motion in contrast to the static state of Jericho suggested by participial pairs in 6:1. In a reversal of the sequence at the crossing, the warriors lead the procession, followed by seven priests and then by the ark of the covenant, expressing the military character of the activity.

The crossing of the Jordan represents an act of national transformation and cohesion, and this is signaled by the leadership of the priests who stand in the Jordan while the nation passes through. The narrator's description of the event focuses on its visual character. The ark passes repeatedly before the people and is held aloft by the priests as the nation crosses. The spectacular stoppage of water begins with a visual cue. When the feet of the priests touch the edge of the Jordan the water stops. YHWH's instructions for the processions around Jericho also emphasize spectacle but intensify the sensual complexity of the event by joining sound to sight. For six days seven priests blowing seven trumpets will precede the ark as it is carried around Jericho. On the seventh day, however, the people will make seven trips around the city and, at a specific signal from the trumpeters, the people will shout. At this noise, the walls of the city will fall flat. As at the Jordan, the nation thus participates in YHWH's mighty work through the performance of a specific ritual act.[5]

Both the trumpets *(šôpĕrôt)* and the shout *(tĕrûâ)* appear in ritual as well as military contexts. In military situations, the shout is a battle cry

---

[5] In the MT Joshua's command that the people "go forward" (v. 7) is expressed by the verb *ʿābar*, the verb that signified the people's crossing of the Jordan. The use of the verb here reinforces the connection between the two episodes.

which terrifies the enemy and celebrates victory (1 Sam 4:5-6; 17:20; Amos 1:14; 2:2; Ezek 21:22 [MT 27]); Zeph 1:16), while in ritual contexts it is an exclamation of joy or a celebration of YHWH's supremacy (2 Chr 15:14; Pss 47:5 [MT 6]; 89:15 [MT 16]; Ezra 3:11-13). Shouting accompanies the ark in both battle and rituals (1 Sam 4:5-6; 2 Sam 6:15). The Hebrew *tĕrû'â* can also signify a trumpet blast (Num 10:5; 29:1; 2 Chr 13:12), a nuance that fits nicely into the present context. The sounding of trumpets mobilizes troops for battle, warns of impending danger, and signals the beginning of battles and the movement of troops on the battlefield (Judg 3:27; 6:34; 1 Sam 13:3; 2 Sam 2:28; 18:16; Neh 4:18; etc.).[6] The trumpet *(šôpār)* also features prominently in Israel's worship. Blowing trumpets accompany the ark as David brings it to Jerusalem (2 Sam 6:15) and communicate YHWH's majestic presence (Exod 19:13, 16; 20:18). Israel sings the praises of YHWH amidst the sound of trumpets (Pss 47:5-6 [MT 6-7]; 98:5-6; 150:3).

The trumpets here are qualified by the adjective *yôbēl,* a term that occurs almost exclusively in connection with the Year of Jubilee (Lev 25:8-55).[7] In the literal sense, the term probably denotes a ram's horn, but its presence in this text is but one of a number of allusions to the Jubilee Year. According to Leviticus, the sounding of the trumpet inaugurates the observance after "seven sabbaths of years, seven years, seven times" (v. 8, AT). A similar repetition of sevens, in particular the instructions to go around Jericho seven times on the seventh day, occurs in the present story, and the completion of the cycle here as well is marked by a trumpet blast (literally a "shout" [*tĕrû'â*], v. 4). More significant, however, is the common concern of both texts, possession of the land and transference of property. The Jubilee Year calls for the return of all land to its original owners and provides guidelines for the redemption and release of property (Lev 25:10, 25-34). The stipulations stress the permanent tie that exists between a family and its land. The land may be sold but may remain the possession of the new owner only until the Jubilee releases it. However, the practice also denies any

[6] Certain elements of the present account occur again in Judges 7:15-23. In this case, Gideon and a small contingent of select soldiers blow trumpets, shout, and shatter pottery in order to discomfit Midianite marauders.

[7] The name given the year is derived from the Hebrew term. Besides the present text, Exod 19:13 is the only other text in which the term occurs outside its connection with the festival. In this instance, the sounding of the ram's horn at Sinai signals a change of state. Prior to the trumpet blast, no one may touch the mountain. But after the ram's horn sounds, the people may go up the mountain. Here as well the infinitival phrase *bimšōk* (literally "when blowing") signifies a particular sound, distinguished from the other soundings *(yitqĕ'û).*

essential connection between the people and their land, for YHWH declares that "the land is mine; with me you are but aliens and tenants" (v. 23). In addition, the practice enforces a distinction between *claim* and *occupancy*. Claim to the land is legitimized by YHWH and held in perpetuity, even though those who claim the land may not always occupy it. These notions of claim and occupancy unite the Jubilee legislation to the campaign against Jericho. Allusions to the legislation, during this first battle in Canaan, confirm Israel's rightful possession of the land, even though the land has been taken from its original owners by violent means. YHWH hands over the land and its people, confirming Israel's claim and establishing a foundation for the land to be apportioned and occupied. By evoking the Jubilee, the narrator also deflects any notion that possession constitutes ownership. The land is YHWH's to give, and Israel will possess the land only because YHWH has promised that it will be so (Gen 12:7; 15:18-21; 17:8; Exod 3:8; etc.). Like the one who redeems property, YHWH has redeemed Israel from its Egyptian masters, "to become a people of his very own possession, as you are now" (Deut 4:20; cf. 7:8).[8]

Six Days Around Jericho: 6:8-14

The processions begin with an ambiguous comment that nonetheless demonstrates the people's compliance with Joshua's commands. The opening phrase in the MT, *wayyĕhî keʾemōr yĕhôšuaʿ ʾel-hʿām*, may be read as a brief commentary (thus NRSV "As Joshua had commanded the people"), but may also signify a prompt response to Joshua's words (thus "when Joshua had spoken to the people, seven priests carrying seven ram's horn trumpets passed before YHWH"). In any case, the phrase functions as a grammatical link between the instructions of Joshua and the obedience of the people, signaling the command-execution format which will configure much of the story. The ensuing narrative gives a detailed description of the first-day procession around Jericho (vv. 8-11) and an abbreviated account of the second-day procession. The latter account confirms that subsequent processions were conducted in precisely the same fashion as the first. The narrator adds additional confirmation with a concluding report to the same effect.

[8] A significant portion of the Jubilee laws concerns the redemption of slaves (Lev 25:39-55); the practice is tied explicitly to YHWH's work in bringing Israel out of Egypt and into Canaan (v. 38).

Besides the initial phrase, the opening sentence in the MT exhibits an unusual structure consisting of a noun with a long chain of modifiers, followed by the verb.[9] The unconventional syntax puts strong emphasis on the priests and on their role in the narrative. As in the crossing narrative, they are not simply "the priests." They are "seven priests who carry seven ram's horn trumpets before YHWH." The lengthy title corresponds to the one given to the priests at the Jordan—"the priests who carry the ark of YHWH, the lord of all the earth" (3:13; cf. 3:8)—and contrasts their role in this episode with their role during the crossing. At the Jordan the priests carry the ark and thus draw attention to the glory of YHWH by keeping the ark in view of all the people. In the opening sentence of the present episode the priests carry trumpets and blow them, thus drawing attention to the glory of YHWH by creating a thunderous sound.[10] The text accentuates the contrast by pointedly separating the priests from the ark. Although Joshua has commanded that the priests take up the ark (v. 6), the text (while meticulously recording compliance to every other command) does not report that the priests did so. Instead the means by which the ark is transported remains unspecified, "with the ark of the LORD following" (v. 8), "the ark of the LORD went around the city" (v. 11).

The textual focus on the noisy priests infuses the narrative with a dynamic quality that is intensified by the repeated references to circling and marching. The participle *hōlēk* ("going, walking") occurs five times within this section, twice with reference to the vanguard (NRSV "the armed men went," vv. 9, 13), twice with reference to the rearguard (NRSV, "the rearguard came," vv. 9, 13), and once with reference to the seven priests (untranslated by NRSV, v. 13). The third occurrence, in the middle of the sequence, refers to the priests. The pattern of the repetition therefore mimics the order of the procession. The narrative structure, as with the order of the procession, places marching Israelites before and after the marching priests. The use of the participial form produces a number of effects. First, because it describes the action of each of the participants, it conveys the unity and totality of the procession. Second, repetitions of the participle occur in the reports of both the first and second day processions and thus imply the continuity of all the marches throughout the six day sequence. Finally, the particip-

---

[9] Normal Hebrew syntax places the verb first, followed by a simple subject.

[10] The trumpet blast is associated with thunder, an aural manifestation of YHWH's awesome presence. The connection is made explicit in the Sinai narrative when, on the morning of the third day, YHWH descends on the mountain, accompanied by "thunder and lightning, as well as a thick cloud on the mountain, and a blast of a trumpet so loud that all the people who were in the camp trembled" (Exod 19:16).

ial form itself defines the participants by their activity. The characters in the story are described by what they do.[11] The narrator magnifies the sense of energy by employing the infinitive absolute form of the same verb *(hālôk)* and pairing it with the verb which signifies the sounding of the trumpet *(tāqôăᶜ)*. The paired infinitives occur three times, the second time directly following the priestly participle ("those who were marching were marching and blowing," v. 13 AT). The first and third phrases seem to refer to the rearguard, thus doubling the effect of the intensification ("the rear guard was marching [*hōlēk*] after the ark, marching and blowing [*hālôk wětāqôăᶜ*]," vv. 9, 13 AT).[12]

The narrative thus presents the processions around Jericho as a commotion of sound and sight. Countering the noise and activity, the narrator reports (when the procession is well underway) that Joshua directed the people to remain silent until commanded to shout (v. 10). Against the surrounding clamor, Joshua calls for silence with the same repetitive detail that the narrator uses to describe the cacophony of the procession, "you shall not shout or let your voice be heard, nor shall you utter a word"(6:10). The sudden and strident command to silence, in stark contrast to the repeated references to marching and blowing, further heightens the sense of energy and motion until the people return to the quiet of the camp (v. 11).

The confluence of ritual and military themes, along with the many grammatical and structural links to the Jordan crossing, prompts the reader to view the activity at Jericho as a continuation of Israel's national transformation. Both the crossing through the Jordan and the circuits around Jericho are initiated by YHWH and carried out in strict obedience to divine commands. The crossing precipitated a change in status but this remained incomplete. Israel has entered the land and partaken of its produce, but does not *possess* any of the land. The processions around Jericho unite the episode with the crossing by looking toward a completion. Throughout the book, the narrative has marked time: three days until the Jordan crossing (1:11), three days in hiding before a return to the camp (2:22), preparation for the crossing at the end of three days (3:2) and the procession to the Jordan on the next day (3:5), the Passover four days later (5:10; cf. 4:19), with the

---

[11] In the case of the priests *hōlēk* is but one of a number of participial modifiers. In addition to marching, the priests are characterized by "carrying" *(nośᵉʾēy*, vv. 8, 13) and "blowing" *(tōqēᶜ*, v. 9; the participle reflects a *ketibh* which is at variance with much of the manuscript tradition). The clustering of active participles creates a sharp contrast between mobility of the priests here and the immobility of the priests in the middle of the Jordan (4:10).

[12] The latter phrase adds "on the trumpets."

consumption of Canaan's food following the next day (5:11). In a sense, Israel has been in mid-course throughout the story. However, now at the walls of Jericho, Israel will mark a full seven-day cycle, a complete period of time. The seventh day, with its echoes of sabbath and Jubilee, marks a conclusion, the end of a full span of time. On the seventh day, Israel will witness another of YHWH's wonders, one which will complement that performed at the Jordan. There YHWH stopped the waters so Israel could cross into the land and begin its life as a landed people. Now YHWH will bring down another barrier, signaling the possession of the land. Both events carry the important message that YHWH leads, gives, and fulfills. But YHWH's work requires Israel's response. Only through its obedience, will Israel participate in the marvelous works of YHWH and experience the fulfillment of YHWH's promises.

The seventh day and seven circuits will provide the grand demonstration of this theme. But they also, in an ironic sense, allude to matters that remain incomplete. The Hebrew number "seven" *(šeba͑)* derives from the same root as that for the verb which denotes the swearing of an oath *(nišba͑)*, and the words for week *(šābûa͑)* and oath *(šĕbûʿâ)* are virtually homonyms. The repetition of sevens thus brings to mind the matter of oaths, a matter of particular importance not only to the nation of Israel but also to a family sequestered within the walls of the city. Rahab and her family also await a new beginning and the fulfillment of a promise.

Shouts Up, Walls Down: 6:15-21

The pivotal scene at Jericho opens with the report that Israel made seven circuits around the city on the seventh day. At the climactic moment, just after the priests have blown the trumpets, Joshua commands the people to shout and relays YHWH's promise of victory. But the people do not yet follow this command. Instead, Joshua goes on to give detailed instructions for the slaughter of the populace, the deliverance of Rahab and her family and the disposition of the spoil. The digression heightens the suspense of the moment and increases its dramatic impact by introducing Rahab's oath at the very point that Israel's obedience will actualize YHWH's promise to deliver the city. The command (v. 16b) and execution (v. 20a) are thus bisected by additional instructions which articulate the paradoxical nature of Israel's obedience. All living things are to be put to death, except for Rahab, who hid the messengers. While the city and all that is within it is rendered "devoted to destruction," Rahab shall live.

Following the commands of Moses, Joshua declares that the city is to be "devoted to destruction" (cf. Deut 7:2; 20:17) and admonishes the people to "keep away from the things devoted to destruction" (cf. Deut 7:26). The practice of devoting something to destruction is associated with warfare throughout biblical literature and is signified in Hebrew by the root *ḥrm*. The root occurs five times within vv. 17-18, both as a noun *(ḥērem)* and as a verb *(heḥĕrîm)*[13] and has no precise equivalent in English (although NRSV's "devote to destruction" comes close). The verb occurs frequently in connection with the conquest of cities and peoples, often with a qualifying phrase or note that reports the annihilation of a population: "they devoted to destruction by the edge of the sword all in the city" (6:21; cf. 7:24-26; 11:12), "he left no one remaining" (10:28; cf. 10:37, 38; 11:21-22; Deut 2:34; 3:3), "there was no one left who breathed" (11:11). These campaigns of extermination are usually presented as a response to a divine decree and place the conduct of war within the context of the nation's relationship with YHWH. The massacres of populations are cast as acts of careful obedience to the divine decrees and enhance the sense of Israel's covenantal loyalty.[14] Alternatively, failure to execute the full measure of destruction, as stipulated by divine decree, signifies disobedience and threatens dire consequences.[15]

---

[13] Four of the repetitions are nouns, while the only verbal form, *taḥărîmû* ("you will devote"), presents grammatical difficulties. For this reason NRSV follows the Greek text of Joshua and reads "lest *you covet*" (Greek *enthumēthentes;* cf. 7:21).

[14] The sense in which the cities and their inhabitants are "devoted" to YHWH during warfare is the subject of much debate and has been tied to understandings of Israel's theology of war. For a fuller discussion, see S. Niditch *War in the Hebrew Bible: A Study in the Ethics of Violence* (Oxford/New York: Oxford University Press, 1993) and N. Lohfink (*"ḥāram,"* TDOT V. 5:180–99). The literature on the biblical *ḥērem* ("ban") is vast, particularly as the concept fits within Israel's theology of warfare. Particularly informative for our purposes are those discussions that deal with the *ḥērem* in light of the utopian vision of Deuteronomy. R. D. Nelson, for example, proposes viewing *ḥērem* within the context of Israel's culture map and in-group ethic, where it can be understood as a category similar to such terms as "clean," "unclean," "holy," and "profane." Defined in this manner, the *ḥērem* denotes "the state of inalienable Yahweh ownership" and "an entity in the state of inalienable Yahweh ownership"; "*Ḥērem* and the Deuteronomic Social Conscience," *Deuteronomy and Deuteronomistic Literature,* BETL 133, ed. M. Vervenne and J. Lust (Leuven: Leuven University, 1997) 39–54. See also Y. Hoffman, "The Deuteronomistic Concept of the Herem," *ZAW* 111 (1999) 196–210; M. Weinfeld, *Deuteronomy 1–11,* AB (Garden City: Doubleday, 1991) 364–65, 377–84; J. Tigay, *Deuteronomy,* JPSTC (Philadelphia: The Jewish Publication Society, 1996) 470–2.

[15] The rejection of Saul illustrates the dire consequences of failing to execute the full measure of divinely-ordained annihilation. Samuel accuses Saul of failing to

While the root most frequently occurs in military texts, where it refers to destruction or extermination, its usage outside the arena of war suggests that the act of destruction is not central to its meaning. In other texts *ḥrm* designates land, property, livestock, or people that have been placed permanently off-limits. Of particular note are laws which emphasize the radical and irrevocable status of that which has been marked as *ḥērem*. One of these deals with a field that has been consecrated to YHWH. The law states that the field will become "holy to YHWH" as a *ḥērem* at the Jubilee Year if the original owner has not redeemed it (Lev 27:20-21). Because the field has not been redeemed its status changes permanently. It can no longer be redeemed and is transferred into the possession of the priests (cf. Num 18:14; Ezek 44:29). Another law in the same context reinforces the irrevocable nature of the *ḥērem* (Lev 27:28-29):

> Nothing that a person owns that has been devoted to destruction for the LORD, be it human or animal, or inherited landholding, may be sold or redeemed; every devoted thing is most holy to the LORD. No human beings who have been devoted to destruction can be ransomed; they shall be put to death.

This law expresses the sense of the term in a different manner. Whereas the law in vv. 20-21 declares that land not redeemed becomes *ḥērem*, this law decrees that property which has been rendered *ḥērem* cannot be redeemed or sold. Both laws stress that the property in question has been removed from common use and has become YHWH's property. (It is "holy" in v. 21 and "most holy" in v. 28.) In the case of a human being, the result of this transference is death. The law pointedly separates the concept of *ḥērem* from the death itself and implies that death is the consequence of being rendered as *ḥērem* (v. 29).[16]

Deuteronomy stresses the radical, contagious otherness of that which is *ḥērem,* and this explains in part its application to Israel's dealings with the peoples of the land. The most strident of the Deuteronomic texts (7:1-

---

carry out a campaign of extermination against the Amalekites and makes it the basis of his rejection as king (1 Sam 15:1-23). In another instance, a prophet declares that Ahab will forfeit his life for failing to devote Ben-hadad to destruction (1 Kgs 20:42).

[16] In this case, NRSV's rendering of "devoted to destruction" does not quite fit the context. In what sense would a field be "devoted to destruction" and what would be the purpose of stipulating that such a destroyed field cannot be sold or redeemed? The law here refers back to that in vv. 16-25, where the issue is not the destruction of the field but its consecration. For a discussion of the irrevocable character of the *ḥērem* see J. P. U. Lilley, "Understanding the *Ḥērem*," *TynB* 44 (1993) 169–77.

6) contains an emphatic command to "utterly destroy" *(haḥărēm taḥărîm)* the seven nations of Canaan (v. 2).[17] Although clearly intended in a military sense, the verb here lacks any of the qualifiers which in Deuteronomistic literature commonly confirm that those under the *ḥērem* were annihilated. Instead, a sequence of contingent commands follows, proscribing, in detail, any form of social intercourse between Israel and the peoples of the land. These prohibitions against covenants and intermarriage, superfluous if Israel indeed "utterly destroys" the inhabitants of the land, accentuate the *ḥērem* status of the nations and warn of dangerous difference. They serve to underscore and explain the threat to Israelite identity which the nations represent. Israel is to consider these nations out-of-bounds and thus have no contact with them whatsoever, for Israel is a unique nation, one that YHWH has chosen "out of all the peoples on earth to be his people, his treasured possession" (v. 6). Contact with the nations will infect Israel with a toxic difference that threatens this uniqueness (v. 4), a difference so virulent that Israel itself will become like the peoples of the land; embracing that which is *ḥērem*, i.e. Canaanite, will render Israel itself *ḥērem* (v. 26). The command is repeated, with the same intensity *(haḥărēm taḥărîm)* and rationale, when Deuteronomy addresses the rules for war against the cities of Canaan (20:16-18). Unlike cities outside Canaan, with whom the Israelites may negotiate, the law decrees that the peoples of the cities of Canaan must be exterminated and rendered *ḥērem* so that their inhabitants may not teach Israel the ways of Canaan. Deuteronomy also declares that Israelite cities may be rendered *ḥērem* if they go astray to follow "other gods" (13:12-18), thus becoming like the peoples of the land. The situation here is deemed so serious that the city itself is rendered *ḥērem*. In this case, Deuteronomy decrees the slaughter of livestock as well as the people and mandates the burning of the town along with all that is in it.

Rendering something or someone as *ḥērem* marks that thing or person as unalterably off-limits. With respect to YHWH, it signifies permanent transference into YHWH's possession and removal from common use or contact. With respect to the nations of Canaan, it radically separates Israel from the inhabitants of the land. The *ḥērem* establishes a boundary that must not be transgressed if Israel is to retain its unique status as the treasured possession of YHWH. When Joshua declares that Jericho and all that is in it shall be "*ḥērem* to YHWH" (v. 17a) he therefore recapitulates the boundaries that separate Israel from YHWH and Israel from the peoples of the land. Yet immediately after this declaration, Joshua pronounces an exception (again signaled in the MT with the particle *raq*) which

---

[17] The MT utilizes an infinitive construction which intensifies the main verb.

compromises the boundary: Rahab and all those with her are not *ḥērem* and are to be spared (v. 17b). The explanation given for her survival, that "she hid the messengers we sent" hints at the reason. Rahab has decided *for* Israel against her own people, and through her confession, for Israel's God against the gods of the land. Presently, Rahab belongs neither in the city of Jericho nor in the camp of the Israelites. She has collaborated with the invaders against her own people and has praised Israel's God yet remains one of the "peoples of the land." Waiting in the wall-boundary that separates Israelite from Canaanite, her paradoxical identity both reinforces and blurs the distinction between the peoples.

Immediately following his declaration that Rahab shall be spared, Joshua returns to the issue of the city's *ḥērem* state by issuing a command which emphasizes the contagious danger of the city and its contents (v. 18).[18] In the MT, the root *ḥrm* occurs four times, reiterating the Deuteronomic warning that any contact with *ḥērem* (and the difference it represents) will transform Israel itself into the same state: "As for you, be careful of the *ḥērem*, lest you *bring ḥērem* and take from the *ḥērem* and make the camp of Israel a *ḥērem* and bring disaster on it."[19] The construction utilizes the noun form three times, conveying the sense of *ḥērem* as state, and three verbs to signify the transformation and consequences that *ḥērem* threatens: you will cause *ḥērem*, you will make the camp *ḥērem*, and you will bring disaster. The command is important thematically, because it not only asserts the radical otherness of this Canaanite city but also foreshadows Achan's transgression, which will illustrate precisely the consequences of bringing what is *ḥērem* into the community. Joshua then decrees that the plunder is holy and sets it apart for Yhwh's treasury, echoing the language of Lev 27:28-29.

With the end of Joshua's speech the text returns to narration. The narrator reports the action with a brief chiastic construction that conveys the stunning rapidity with which the event takes place. "So the people shouted, and the trumpets were blown. As soon as the people heard the sound of the trumpets, they raised a great shout" (v. 20). The report of the wonder—the collapse of the walls—receives surprisingly little elaboration. In quick succession the wall falls down flat and the people charge into the city and execute the *ḥērem* by slaughtering all the people and the livestock. After the long narrative buildup, the terse lan-

---

[18] The command makes a grammatical link with Rahab by employing again the Hebrew particle *raq*, linking her with the Israelites and setting her fate in vivid contrast to that of the city.

[19] The command declares that contact with *ḥērem* will "bring trouble" on the camp of Israel and thereby foreshadows the sacrilege of Achan (7:1, 25).

guage thus accelerates the action, adding to the sense of surprise. With the instantaneous disintegration of the walls, the Israelites rush into the city and carry out Joshua's orders quickly and efficiently.

Deliverance for Rahab: 6:22-25

The concise report of Jericho's destruction confirms many of the promises that, up to this point, have been potential. The collapse of the walls demonstrates YHWH's power over the formidable cities and nations of Canaan and proves that YHWH is indeed with Joshua. With these matters settled, the narrative shifts to the deliverance of Rahab. Joshua now summons the two spies and directs them to bring Rahab and her family out of the city. The final phrase of his imperative alludes to the oath which the spies have sworn to her, intimating that this is the reason that she and her family have been spared. Joshua has evidently concluded that the violation of an oath sworn in the name of YHWH would be a more serious matter than allowing pious Canaanites to live. Yet there are hints that the act of deliverance is not undertaken without ambivalence. Joshua does not speak her name, but simply calls her "the prostitute, the woman" (in contrast to the narrator, who twice calls her by name). And he mentions the spies' oath but not Rahab's mercy toward the spies. In the presence of the people, Joshua had spoken her name and declared that she would be spared because "she hid the messengers we sent" (v. 17). Now, in private conversation with the spies, Joshua frames the deliverance as an act of obligation, recalling all the disconcerting elements of the rooftop tryst in Jericho.

Reference to the spies as "messengers" again evokes the story of Lot's deliverance from Sodom, for the Hebrew term (*malʾākîm*) is identical to that which signifies the "angels" who visit Lot. The title, used only here to signify the spies, reminds the reader again of the connection between the two stories. Like Sodom and Gomorrah, Jericho has been completely destroyed. And like Lot and his family, Rahab and her household escape annihilation (cf. Gen 19:24-26). The narrator pauses to enumerate those who have taken shelter with Rahab and thus are spared—her father, mother, brothers, and all who belonged to her—and repeats the assertion that her entire family were brought out (v. 23). The listing of family members not only impresses the reader with the number of those who have been spared but also underscores Joshua's faithfulness to the oath, since the listing of people roughly corresponds to the list of family Rahab had set before the spies (2:13). Unlike Lot, who lost his wife, Rahab succeeds in bringing her family through intact.

Joshua then assigns her and her household a place outside the Israelite camp and thus to a marginal status befitting their ambiguous identity.

Joshua's initial command that Rahab be delivered was embedded within instructions for the destruction of the city and contrasted her survival with the city's annihilation (v. 17). In a reversal of this structure, a report of the burning of Jericho is now imbedded within the report of Rahab's deliverance (v. 24), evoking the contrast once more. Israel reduces Jericho to ashes, but the narrator makes a point of noting that Rahab's family "has lived in Israel ever since" (v. 25). The comment strongly suggests that these Canaanites were not assimilated into Israel but retained their identity and lived within the land as a distinct community. It thus has the effect of affirming the identity of Rahab's family, even though it has been marginalized. The exemption of Rahab shatters any idea that the land will be populated only by "Israelites." The narrator reinforces this unsettling situation by reminding the reader of Rahab's occupation. She is "Rahab the prostitute," and with the survival of her family Israel will always deal with the otherness of Canaan within its own borders.

Curse and Acclamation: 6:26-27

The story of Israel's first campaign in the promised land concludes with a short supplement that reports Joshua's curse of Jericho and the narrator's comment that Joshua's renown spread throughout the land. Within the story-world, the city itself has been rendered *ḥērem* and therefore has become permanently off-limits. Joshua reinforces this with a curse on any who would seek to rebuild it (cf. Deut 13:12-18). On the narrative level, the curse represents an instance of foreshadowing that points beyond its context to the larger biblical narrative. Jericho will be rebuilt at a later time, during the reign of Ahab (1 Kgs 16:34), and the report of its construction explicitly mentions the builder of the city and confirms that Joshua's curse took effect, "In his days Hiel of Bethel built Jericho; he laid its foundation at the cost of Abiram his firstborn, and set up its gates at the cost of his youngest son Segub, according to the work of the LORD, which he spoke by Joshua son of Nun." Viewed from this perspective, Joshua's curse takes on the character of a prophetic utterance, the fulfillment of which will be duly noted by the biblical narrator.[20]

[20] The Deuteronomistic History reports the fulfillment of prophetic utterances as a means of creating a sense of coherence and thematic unity. Compare, for example 1 Kgs 13:1-2 with 2 Kgs 23:15-18.

The chapter, as well as the larger unit that began in 2:1, ends with the narrator's confirmation that YHWH was with Joshua and that his fame (or perhaps, "news about him") filled the land (v. 27). The comment works in conjunction with that in 4:14 to confirm both YHWH's faithfulness and Joshua's authority. Earlier YHWH promised to be with Joshua and declared that Joshua would put Israel in possession of the land (1:5-6). Later, the eastern tribes, speaking for the whole nation, raised the issue of YHWH's presence with Joshua (1:17) and thus implicitly called for some corroborative demonstration. The wonders at the Jordan and at Jericho have now provided such a demonstration, and in each case the narrative elevates the character of Joshua by presenting him as a prophetic leader who conveys the directions and commandments of YHWH. The waters of the Jordan stood in a heap just as Joshua said they would (3:13-16) and now YHWH has given Jericho to the Israelites in spectacular fashion, again as Joshua predicted. By conveying his words to the people through Joshua, YHWH has confirmed that Joshua is indeed the successor to Moses, and by confirming his words with mighty acts, YHWH has demonstrated that he is with him and will bring Israel into possession of the land under his leadership. The narrator concludes, then, with a direct confirmation that the concerns suggested in Joshua 1 have now been resolved. YHWH is indeed with Joshua. The question of whether YHWH is with *Israel,* however, remains open (cf. 5:13-14).

Chapter Seven
AI SPY
Joshua 7:1–8:35

The stories associated with Ai feature a series of reversals.[1] The battle at Jericho takes place in an instant and results in a decisive victory achieved by an awesome demonstration of YHWH's power. However, there are two battles at Ai, and YHWH does not actively participate in either one. The first battle brings an ignominious defeat, while the second results in victory through a carefully executed strategy. In addition, the story of Rahab the prostitute encloses the account of the battle at Jericho (2:1-21; 6:22-25), contrasting the slaughter of Canaanites as a whole with the incorporation and survival of a Canaanite family. A different kind of story appears in connection with Ai. In this case battles enclose a story, one that relates the exclusion and extermination of an Israelite family because of an act of treachery. Achan's story itself reverses elements of Rahab's. Rahab gives glory to YHWH and saves her family by an act of faithfulness. Achan, however, condemns himself and his family to death by an act of sacrilege and disobedience. While Rahab's act contributes to a stunning Israelite victory, Achan's act precipitates a shocking defeat (Israel's first at the hands of the land's inhabitants). Rahab, in short, acts like an Israelite should and receives life in the land. Achan, on the other hand, suffers the fate of the inhabitants of the land.

Achan's theft of plunder from Jericho represents something far more serious than the looting of a conquered city. Bringing devoted material into the Israelite camp kindles the wrath of YHWH and introduces a

---

[1] The parallels and reversals are described in more detail in Chapter Two.

foreign contaminant which threatens communal identity. References to YHWH's "burning anger" begin and end his story (7:1, 26), constructing a framework for comprehending the impact of Achan's deed. YHWH is angry that Achan has kept plunder that has been declared *ḥērem* ("devoted") and set aside for the treasury of YHWH's house. As a consequence, the divine presence does not accompany Israel onto the battlefield, leading to a disastrous defeat. On the surface, then, the attempt to assuage anger drives the plot, and once this is accomplished, through the execution of the offending party, YHWH once again ensures an Israelite victory. Beneath the surface, however, the complex of stories associated with Ai attempts to work out the threat of Canaanite presence within Israel (symbolized by the stolen plunder). If it is sometimes difficult to recognize a Canaanite outside the boundaries, how much more so if the "Canaanite" is within, and hidden. Canaanized Israelites are not easily identified, but if they are not unmasked and eliminated, the entire community may disintegrate. The need to deal with an undetected Canaanite presence thus orients the story along a different, though not unrelated, trajectory. This more profound plot finds expression primarily through allusions to the Deuteronomic laws concerning apostasy (Deut 13:6-18). These laws address the same problem, Israelites who threaten communal identity by seducing the nation away from its essential integrity (vv. 6, 13).

The Deuteronomic laws address the problem of Canaanized Israelite at both the individual and communal levels. In the case of an individual, the law declares that the offender be shown no mercy and stipulates stoning as the means of execution (vv. 7-10). The punishment is designed to be a deterrent, "then all Israel shall hear and be afraid, and never again do any such wickedness" (v. 11). The laws concerning communities are more involved. When a report of the town's apostasy is received, the charge must be substantiated by a thorough investigation. If the charge is established, all the inhabitants of the community are declared *ḥērem* and put to the sword, along with their livestock. The legislation stipulates that everything in the city is to be brought to the public square where, along with the city itself, all of it is to be burned (presumably because, since it has separated from the nation, the whole city is *ḥērem*, vv. 12-16). Like *ḥēremized* Jericho, no use may ever be made of the site; it has been rendered irrevocably "other" and must remain a "ruin forever" (v. 17). The severe measures taken against it reinforce the contagious influence of the town's sedition. Deuteronomy asserts that one community's apostasy subjects the entire nation subject to the "burning wrath" of YHWH (13:17; cf. Josh 7:1, 26). By obliterating the town, divine wrath is turned aside and the nation may once again enjoy YHWH's compassionate attention.

Achan's story illustrates the truth of Deuteronomy's warning not to let anything *ḥērem* "stick to your hand" (Deut 13:17a). YHWH depicts the theft of devoted plunder as an act of covenant transgression and orders the casting of lots as a means of identifying the offender and substantiating the offense (Josh 7:14-15). The lot falls to Achan, who, when interrogated by Joshua, discloses the location of the booty. Joshua sends men to retrieve it, and they return and display it in the sight of the assembled community and YHWH (vv. 22-23). The charge now substantiated, Achan and his family receive the particular form of execution prescribed for apostates (stoning), and like apostate towns, are burned, along with their livestock, their possessions, and the devoted items (vv. 24-25). As with the apostate cities, the procedure effectively turns away the burning anger of YHWH (7:26), and the stone heap raised over them serves as a visual deterrent against additional transgressions of this kind. The stone heap also links Achan and his family to the city of Ai, which itself becomes a "ruin forever" *(tēl ʿôlām).*[2]

Such is the threat represented by difference. Like a tiny drop of color in a gallon of white paint, the contagion emanating from the devoted plunder threatens to spread throughout the whole community, thus destroying its purity and transforming it, in subtle shades, into something other. The perceived magnitude of this threat explains the rapid and extreme measures taken against it. Achan and his house have already been contaminated, and the contaminant must be excised before it spreads.

Allusions to another Deuteronomic text (Deut 1:19–3:11) underlie the larger unit and associate Achan's sin and its consequences with rebellion against YHWH. The Deuteronomic text is a narrative which focuses on Israel's rebellion at Kadesh-barnea, when the people refused to enter the land in response to YHWH's command. As at Ai, spies are sent out in advance of military action (Deut 1:22-25), but the campaign is abruptly interrupted by an act of rebellion (Deut 1:26). Israel refuses to trust in YHWH (1:32), who becomes angry at the nation's faithlessness (1:34-40). The Israelites nonetheless attempt to attack the land's inhabitants, even though YHWH is not with them (1:42), but they are routed (1:43-46) and return in shock to their camp. The story is punctuated by references to the Israelites' "melting hearts" (1:28) and their confession of sin (1:41). Victory in battle returns only after the deaths of all those who had rebelled against YHWH (1:46–2:16). With the deaths of the previous generation of Israelites the nation again wins victories (2:31–3:10).[3]

---

[2] In the Hebrew Bible the phrase occurs only in Deut 13:16 and Josh 8:28.

[3] For a more thorough study of these parallels, see C. Begg, "The Function of Josh 7:1–8:29 in the Deuteronomistic History," *Bib* 67 (1986) 320–34.

Through allusions to the Deuteronomic narrative, Joshua's narrator transforms the campaign at Ai into a program for identifying and resolving the problem of Canaanite difference *within*. The allusions to Deut 1:19–3:11 underscore the grave danger posed by Canaanite presence within Israel, expressing this danger in terms of national rebellion and divine anger. The allusions to Deut 13:1-18 point to a program for eliminating Canaanite presence within Israel and restoring national identity and cohesion. The first battle at Ai illustrates the disastrous consequences of the undetected Canaanite within the community. The identification and destruction of Achan (and everything connected to him) prescribes the remedy for the problem. And the victory at Ai portrays the fruit of a restored community realigned with YHWH.

Breaking Faith: 7:1

The campaign at Ai opens with the narrator's report that "the Israelites broke faith in regard to the devoted things." The report separates the reader from Joshua and the Israelites by presenting information unavailable to characters in the story. The reader knows two things before the story even begins: YHWH's anger burns against Israel and Achan son of Carmi is the offender. Achan's story is henceforth propelled by the impulse to uncover these facts, as Israel seeks first to discover why it has suffered a humiliating defeat and then engages in the task of identifying the offender. The tension between the reader's knowledge and that of the characters generates suspense, and the narrator exploits the tension by devoting much of the text to the prolonged process of finding out. By building suspense, the narrative draws the reader deeply into the story and creates a sense of urgency. The reader knows both the problem and the offender and wants the situation resolved. The narrator, however, increases the suspense by attenuating the process of discovery.

The first words of the report implicate the entire nation in an act of "breaking faith in regard to the devoted things" (*wayyim'ălû bĕnê-yiśrā'ēl ma'al baḥērem*). The Hebrew phrase *m'l bĕ* generally signifies an act of unfaithfulness against someone and, since it refers primarily to YHWH as the object, denotes an offense against God, either through the misuse of holy objects (Lev 5:14-16; 2 Chr 26:16-18) or violation of the covenant oath (Lev 26:15; Ezek 17:18, 20). In the former case, the violation entails an encroachment on the domain of the holy, a trespass of the boundary that separates the sacred from the profane. The use of the formula to open the Ai/Achan narrative therefore evokes a sense of foreboding. Achan's theft has taken him across a forbidden boundary. A sacrilege has been committed, and the entire nation now finds itself in peril as the wrath of YHWH burns against it.[4]

The narrator focuses on Achan's ethnicity by introducing him with a series of patronymics: "Achan son of Carmi so of Zabdi son of Zerah, of the tribe of Judah." The concatenation of names locates Achan within the complex network of kinship relations that connects father's houses, clans, and tribes. Achan is a true Israelite insider, one whose ethnic purity is established by patrilineal descent. The narrative's preoccupation with Achan's patrimony, expressed also in the laborious tracing of kinship through the casting of lots (vv. 16-18), reveals that issues of ethnicity and identity are central to the concerns of the narrator. Unlike the Canaanite Rahab, a woman who lived first in the boundary-wall of Jericho and now on the fringes of Israel, the man Achan is the pedigreed scion of a revered tribal patriarch. The structure of the text links the pedigree of Achan to the Israelite community as a whole:

> But the Israelites broke faith in regard to the devoted things:
>> Achan son of Carmi son of Zabdi son of Zerah of the tribe of Judah took some of the devoted things.
> And the anger of the LORD burned against the Israelites.

The text describes Achan's deed as an act of "taking" *(lqḥ)* but charges *Israel* with "breaking faith" *(mʿl)* and identifies the nation as the target of YHWH's burning anger. Both the individual and the community are thus implicated by contact with the "devoted things" *(ḥērem)*. In a sense, the opening statement turns the Deuteronomic concern for unity on its head. Deuteronomy asserts that the unity of the nation is essential for the success and fulfillment of all. In this case, however, the act of one individual leads to defeat and disaster for the entire nation. Achan has crossed a boundary and through the bonds of kinship has brought the entire nation with him. Put another way, Achan has transformed the entire community, shattering its homogeneity by introducing what belongs outside.[5]

---

[4] Throughout the Deuteronomistic History, *mʿl* occurs only here and in Joshua 22. Its use is therefore striking and punctuates the gravity of Achan's act. Furthermore, this instance (again along with Josh 22) constitutes the only time that the object of the formula *mʿl bĕ* is other than YHWH. "Transgressing against the *ḥērem*" (as opposed to YHWH) thus accentuates the act as a violation of a boundary. For more on the concept of *maʿal* see J. Milgrom, *Leviticus 1–16*, AB (Garden City: Doubleday, 1991) 345–56.

[5] J. S. Kaminsky explains the incident, and the influence of the *ḥērem* on the nation, by placing the idea within the larger theological category of holiness; *Corporate Responsibility in the Hebrew Bible*, JSOTSup 196 (Sheffield: Sheffield University, 1995) 67–95.

Rout 36: 7:2-5

The campaign against Ai begins just as the campaign against Jericho does, with Joshua sending men on a reconnaissance mission (cf. 2:1). Joshua gives the spies slightly different instructions than he did on the previous mission; these men are to "spy out" *(wĕraggĕlû)* the land, whereas the men sent to Jericho were told to "view" *(rĕ ʾû)* the land and city. The change in wording is significant, for it evokes Israel's failed attempt to enter the land from the south (Deut 1:24), injecting a note of ambiguity into the enterprise.

Ai presents a starkly different profile than Jericho. While Jericho was enclosed by formidable walls and tightly sealed against the invaders, this site is simply called "The Ruin" *(hāʿay)*. Corresponding to Achan's genealogy, which locates him among his people, references to other towns situate Ai among the cities of Canaan; it lies near Beth-aven (the House of Sin) and Bethel (the House of God).[6] Ai is not at all the prototypical Canaanite city, whose "towns are fortified and very large" (Num 13:28). Perhaps for this reason, the spies return with words that exude confidence, "Not all the people need to go up; about two or three thousand men should go up and attack Ai. Since they are so few, do not make the whole people toil up there" (v. 3).

The spies' plan portends disaster, and the campaign begins badly. Their suggestion that "not all the people need to go up" divides the community, breaking the "all Israel" integrity necessary for success. "All Israel" wins battles against the fragmented Canaanite peoples, but the "not all" character of this attack presages a reversal. This is emphasized through repetition at the end of the report: "since they are so few, do not make the whole people toil up there."[7] These bold declarations carry the force of commands, setting this report in contrast to the report of the spies at Jericho, whose report comprises an enthusiastic affirmation that YHWH has delivered the whole land into Israel's power and

---

[6] While the name "Beth-Aven" may originally have meant something like "House of Riches," the vocalization of the name in the MT prompts the reader to understand the name as "House of Sin" (cf. Hos 4:5; 5:8; 10:5). The names of the two towns, mentioned in connection with Ai, suggest a strange paradox that alludes to Israel's status at Ai; they are both God's people and the locus of sin.

[7] In both instances, the Hebrew phrase *kol-hāʿām* signifies the people. The words contrast the "not all" character of Israel with the "few" character of the inhabitants of Ai, giving the report an ironic twist. Imbedded in one of the key passages enforcing the distinction between Israel and the peoples of Canaan, Moses declares that Israel was chosen by YHWH because it was the "fewest" of all the peoples (Deut 7:7).

that the hearts of the inhabitants are melting with fear (Josh 2:25).[8] The imperatives dictate a strategy for the attack, again a departure from the program necessary for success. Divine initiative plays no role in this campaign. There are no declarations that YHWH has given Israel the land (cf. Josh 2:25; 6:16; 8:1; 10:8; 11:6), nor does anyone consult YHWH through the ark of the covenant (cf. Num 14:44). Joshua remains silent in response and absent during the attack. The narrative thus insinuates that this campaign is undertaken entirely through human initiative and tactics. Israel conducts this battle in a manner resembling the peoples of the land, relying on its own might and ingenuity. When viewed in the context of the introductory comment that "Israel broke faith with YHWH" through Achan's theft, the situation raises certain questions. Are these changes a consequence of contamination with the *ḥērem?* Has the incorporation of Canaanite plunder somehow produced a transformation in the people? Is the burning anger of YHWH behind this?

The battle does not go as the spies had predicted.[9] In a terse summary of the engagement, the narrator reports that "about three thousand of the people went there; and they fled before the men of Ai" (v. 4). The clipped account expresses the utter failure of the attack against the city. The narrator omits any reference to a military engagement. They simply "went up" and "fled," even though there were about three thousand of them! The language of the report enhances the tone of failure by alluding to the disastrous attempt to enter the land a generation earlier:

> But they had the audacity to go up to the heights of the hill country, even though neither the ark of the covenant of YHWH nor Moses left the camp. Then the Amalekites and the Canaanites who lived in that hill country came down, struck them down, and beat them to pieces as far as Hormah (Num 14:44-45, AT).

> So about three thousand of the people went up there; and they fled before the men of Ai. The men of Ai struck down about thirty-six of them, chasing them from outside the gate as far as Shebarim and striking them down on the slope (Josh 7:4-5a).

---

[8] The two declarations exhibit a parallel structure in the MT and take the form of negative commands. The NRSV reverses the syntax of the last command, which (in MT) places the reference to the peoples of the land after the command concerning Israel: "Don't let the whole nation weary itself there, for they are few" (AT).

[9] The spies' prediction of success corresponds to YHWH's declarations hat he has given the enemies into the hands of the Israelites before other battles. The spies' prescience, however, fails just as their strategy does, underscoring Israel's inability to enjoy victory apart from YHWH.

As at Ai, the debacle near Hormah illustrates the connection between sin and defeat, as well as the futility of attempting to possess the land apart from the presence and guidance of YHWH. And in both cases the Israelites flee toward a site which symbolizes the calamity; the enemy pursues them as far as Hormah ("Destruction") in the Numbers account, and as far as Shebarim ("Breaking Apart") in the present instance.[10]

The narrator makes a subtle connection between Israel's temerity and the subsequent catastrophe. Employing a device utilized at a number of points throughout Joshua, the Israelites' "obedience" to the spies is confirmed by a report that echoes the language of the "command." Thus we read that "about three thousand men" (kišlōšet ălāpîm) went up from the camp against Ai (v. 4), an approximation that would be expected given the large size of the force. However, the same language of approximation is then used to refer to the thirty-six Israelites killed during the rout ("about thirty-six," kišlōšîm wěšišâ). The phrase seems awkward in connection to the more exact number but succeeds in drawing the connection between the plan, its execution, and its consequences. More explicitly, the episode concludes with the note that "the hearts of the people melted and turned to water." The phrase has been used previously to describe the inhabitants of the land (Josh 2:25; 5:1). Now it characterizes the Israelites and suggests a disturbing conclusion. Apart from the presence and guidance of YHWH, Israel bears an uncanny resemblance to the peoples of the land.

Uncovering Divine Anger: 7:6-15

The humiliating feat leads to a lamentation that evokes even more allusions to Israel's rebellion at Kadesh-Barnea (Num 14:1-25). Joshua and the elders give public expression to the nation's sin and grief by falling before the ark, tearing their garments, and putting dirt on their heads. Their actions symbolize the state of the nation itself: splintered, disintegrated, and brought low (cf. Num 14:5-6). Like Moses, Joshua intercedes for the nation (vv. 7-9) and attempts to deflect divine anger by arguing that YHWH's reputation is at stake (v. 9; cf. Num 14:13-19). However, in a striking departure from Moses' prayer, Joshua echoes the complaining of the rebellious Israelites.

---

[10] The spies' command not to let all the people go up to Ai alludes ironically to Moses' command to Israel not to go up to the land (Num 14:42). In another irony, the name Hormah derives from the same root as the term ḥērem.

Joshua said, "Ah, LORD God! Why have you brought this people across the Jordan at all, to hand us over to the Amorites so as to destroy us? Would that we had been content to settle beyond the Jordan! O LORD, what can I say, now that Israel has turned their backs to their enemies!" (Josh 7:7-8)

The whole congregation said to them, "Would that we had died in the land of Egypt! Or would that we had died in this wilderness! Why is the LORD bringing us into this land to fall by the sword? Our wives and our little ones will become booty; would it not be better for us to go back to Egypt?" (Num 14:2b-3; cf. Exod 15:11-12)

The narrator pointedly does not report any expression of communal lamentation. Instead, Joshua and the elders articulate the nation's grief and confusion. Absent when the campaign was planned and executed (apart from any consultation of YHWH), they now appear as representatives of the people before YHWH. The ark of the covenant, prominent during the campaign against Jericho but absent during the attack against Ai, becomes now the focus of discouragement rather than inspiration. Joshua himself articulates the people's uncomprehending despondency, and the language of his lament intimates that even he has been affected by the community's sin and rebellion. The complaint of the wilderness generation now issues from his lips, implicitly blaming YHWH for the tragedy. At Kadesh-Barnea, Joshua stood where the elders now stand and attempted to counter the nation's despair with a spirited exhortation to faith (Num 14:5-9). Now he stands (or rather, lies prostrate) where Moses did, but he speaks like one who has lost hope. Filled with resolve at the Jordan and Jericho, he now seems uncertain and diffident. The language of the complaint reverses, for the moment, the geographical progress of the story and redirects the reader back across the Jordan, putting as a question what had originally been given as a command. In the opening scene of the book, Joshua had sent officials throughout the Israelite camp to stir the nation with the following words, "In three days you are to cross over the Jordan, to go in to take possession of the land that the LORD your God gives you to possess" (1:11b). These commands were echoed repeatedly as Israel crossed the Jordan "before the ark of the covenant" (3:11, 14-17). Now, with the same repetition of the root ʿbr *(hēʿăbartā haʿăbîr . . . bĕ ʿēber hayyardēn)*, Joshua questions the crossing, speaks of being given into the hands of the Amorites, and pines for the wilderness.

The appeal which follows continues the connection with Kadesh-Barnea and corresponds to Moses' response to YHWH's threat to destroy the nation (v. 9):

> The Canaanites and all the inhabitants of the land will hear of it, and sur-
> round us, and cut off our name from the earth. Then what will you do
> for your great name?

> But Moses said to the LORD: "Then the Egyptians will hear of it, for in your
> might you brought up this people from among them, and they will tell the
> inhabitants of this land . . . Now if you kill this people all at one time,
> then the nations who have heard about you will say, 'It is because the
> LORD was not able to bring this people into the land he swore to give them
> that he has slaughtered them in the wilderness.'" (Num 14:13-14a, 15-16)

The correspondence is all the more noteworthy because Moses' appeal
looks forward precisely to the context in which Joshua and the people
find themselves. Both appeals express a concern that the nations of the
land will hear of Israel's demise. In the former instance, however, the
appeal comes in response to YHWH's threat to make an end of Israel.
There Moses attempts to mollify YHWH by arguing that the destruction
of the nation will influence the way other nations perceive YHWH and
argues that bringing Israel to an end will lead other nations to the conclusion that YHWH is weak. Joshua's appeal, on the other hand, focuses
on the peril that Israel now faces at the hands of the *Canaanites* and argues that news of Israel's defeat will prompt them to surround and destroy the nation. Only afterward does Joshua bring up the matter of
YHWH's reputation. The differences in the two pleas are significant.
Moses' appeal implies that the scope of YHWH's concern extends past
Israel to other nations (Egypt, the inhabitants of Canaan) and argues,
on this basis, that destroying Israel will work against this concern.[11]
Joshua's appeal, however, seems patently manipulative. Joshua focuses narrowly on the peril faced by the nation and uses YHWH's reputation as leverage in his attempt to incite the deity to protect the nation.

YHWH's response to this attempt at intercession dismisses both the
complaint and the appeal, beginning with an abrupt command, "Get
up! What is this falling-on-your-face business?" (v. 10b-c; AT).[12] YHWH
then hurls a barrage of accusations at Joshua in rapid sequence, with a
clipped phrasing that conveys the intensity of divine anger. The ferocity of YHWH's wrath builds as Israel's God explodes in a series of invec-
tives against the nation, "Israel has sinned; they have transgressed my
covenant that I imposed on them. They have taken some of the devoted things; they have stolen, they have acted deceitfully, and they

---

[11] In a similar appeal at Sinai, Moses reminds YHWH of the promise made to
Abraham, Isaac, and Jacob (Exod 32:11-14).

[12] The opening interrogative in YHWH's response (*lāmmâ*) parallels that of Joshua's
complaint (*lāmâ*; v. 7).

have put them among their own belongings" (v. 11). The first two accusations present sweeping indictments which implicate the entire nation, presenting the act as a crime against God (v. 11a). The charge that "they have transgressed the covenant" clarifies the more general "Israel has sinned" and connects the offense with apostasy. "Transgressing the covenant" (ʿbr bĕrît) is the phrase used in Deut 17:2 to signify the act of serving and worshiping other gods (cf. Josh 23:16; Judg 2:20). The passage in which it is located (Deut 17:2-7) has much in common with Deut 13:6-18 (punishment of apostate individuals and towns) and, like that text, calls for death by stoning after a careful inquiry into the allegations, "to purge the evil from your midst" (ûbiʿart hārāʿmiqqir-bekā; v. 7c).[13] YHWH's charge thus insinuates that, somehow, Israel has been drawn away from its covenant and toward the peoples of the land. The second set of accusations expands the nature of the offense itself. Although the narrator had stated simply that Achan "took some of the devoted things," YHWH views the act as a multi-faceted offense. Echoing the narrator's rendering of the event ("they have taken some of the devoted things") YHWH goes on to accuse the nation of theft, deceit, and unlawful possession.

After specifying the charges against Israel, YHWH presents them as the explanation for Israel's defeat in battle (v. 12). The "explanation" concentrates on Israel's transformed character; Israel not only *acts* like the peoples of the land are supposed to act in battle ("turning their backs on their enemies;" cf. Exod 23:27), but they now resemble Jericho itself, "they have become a thing devoted to destruction" (hāyû lĕḥērem). YHWH thus declares that the status of the entire nation has changed. Under the influence of the Canaanite ḥērem, Israel has acquired a "not-Israel" character. The transformation explains why YHWH did not go with Israel into battle, and it is only now that YHWH declares that he will not be with Israel again "unless you obliterate the ḥērem from your midst" (kî-lōʾtašmîdû ḥērem miqqirbĕkem; v. 12, AT).

Through accusation and explanation YHWH reveals both his anger and the ḥērem state of the nation to a people who had been unaware of either. YHWH now resumes the initiative and prescribes a way for Israel to be restored to its God and to itself (vv. 13-15). In words reminiscent of those spoken before the Jordan crossing, YHWH directs Joshua to command the people to sanctify themselves (v. 13; cf. 3:5). The command

---

[13] The Hebrew verb translated "they have transgressed" (ʿābĕrû) is the same used by Joshua, in his complaint, to ask why YHWH "brought Israel across" the Jordan (v. 7). Through a wordplay on the root ʿbr YHWH therefore turns Joshua's words against himself.

signals a new beginning by orienting the people again to YHWH and
performing a ritual which will begin the movement from their current outsider *(ḥērem)* state back to their original status as the recipients
of YHWH's blessing and gift of the land. YHWH then establishes a procedure whereby the *ḥērem* may be identified and excised (vv. 13-15). The
procedure traces the kinship bonds which unite the nation, reversing
the course by which the *ḥērem* contagion has spread throughout the
entire nation. Beginning with Achan, the incorporated "difference"
symbolized by the Canaanite *ḥērem* has spread from house to clan to
the entire nation (symbolized through the genealogical reference in
v.1). The remedy moves in the opposite direction. Beginning with a call
to sanctification and the announcement that Israel has incorporated
ḥērem within it, the procedure moves inexorably from nation to clan to
father's house to the offender himself. Once exposed, he will be destroyed, enabling Israel to recover its distinctive identity against the
other peoples of the land.

The speech ends, as does the procedure outlined by YHWH, by redi-
recting corporate guilt to that of the individual offender. The offense
is now described in two ways; the offender has "transgressed the
covenant" and committed "an outrageous thing in Israel" *(ʿāśâ nĕbālâ
bĕyiśrāʾēl)*. The first phrase repeats the one YHWH used previously to indict the entire nation at the beginning of the speech (v. 11), forming a
frame which renders the instructions as a procedure for restoring a
wayward Israel back to YHWH. By tracking the kinship network in reverse, from the nation to the individual, the community will be able
identify and distance itself from the source of the contagion. Thus, at
the end of the process, the individual rather than the nation will carry
the guilt for "transgressing the covenant." The second phrase identifies
the offense as an act that has shattered the fundamental bonds which
hold the kinship network together (cf. Gen 34:7; Deut 22:21; Judg 19:23;
20:6, 10; 2 Sam 13:12; Jer 29:23). By eliminating the offending party (and
all directly connected to him) the bond between nation and God may
therefore be restored, and the fractured nation can be reintegrated.

Uncovering Difference: 7:16-23

The narrative now moves on to recount the process of discovery
and elimination, implicitly offering a paradigm for confronting the
problem of difference within the nation. The rest of the story lays out a
procedure: identification (vv. 16-18), confrontation (19), confession (vv.
20-21), confirmation (vv. 22-23), extermination (vv. 24-25). The proce-

dure enables the community to separate itself from the Canaanized party and to affirm publicly that this "not-Israelite" presence has no place within it. The text focuses particular attention on the process of uncovering this difference and swiftly eliminating it. The point of the story is clear; undetected difference constitutes a clear and present danger to communal integration and identity.

The procedure links identification and disclosure with the restoration of communal integrity. The narration of the lot-casting (vv. 16-18) follows precisely the instructions YHWH has given, restoring the command-execution format used previously in the book to confirm the nation's obedience to YHWH. With similar precision, it traces the patriarchal structure which configures Israelite society. By repeating the social hierarchy, from nation to tribe to clan to father's house to individual, the narrative reasserts the importance of the structure for Israelite identity and serves a dual purpose, both affirming the structure of relationships by which the nation is defined and at the same time demonstrating the means by which Israel may distance itself from those now rendered off-limits *(ḥērem)*. By means of the procedure, the nation is gradually united and reintegrated against an offender who is in turn gradually alienated. With surgical precision, the nation separates itself from those within who are "not one of them."

The expanding distance between the nation and the offender is also tracked by the repetition of the verb *lākad* (NRSV "taken") in vv. 17-18. Outside of this context the verb occurs in Joshua only to refer to the capture of Canaanite cities. It receives emphasis here through repetition, thus echoing the many instances in which Canaanite territory is transformed, by conquest, into Israelite territory.[14] In all but one instance, the verb is rendered in the *Niphal* stem, casting the action in the passive mood (in a sense, reversing the direction of the other occurrences, which are active). Israel is once again uniting to make war against "Canaan," but the conflict here is directed toward a Canaanized insider (a subject) who has infected the nation, rather than Canaanite outsiders (an object) whose territory will be possessed by Israel.

The narrative quickly picks up momentum after Achan is identified by the lot, shifting from narration to direct speech and moving rapidly from Joshua's admonition to Achan (v. 19), to Achan's inventory of items plundered from Jericho (vv. 20-21), to the public exposure of the hidden items (vv. 22-23). The focal point of this sequence, and the largest block of text, is Achan's speech, which relates in detailed what has been hidden from the rest of the nation. The speech's concentration

---

[14] Note in particular the formulaic repetitions in Josh 10:28, 32, 35, 37, 39, 42 (cf. 6:20; 8:19, 21; 10:1; 11:10, 12, 17; 15:16, 17; 19:47).

on revealing what is hidden, expressed through opposing references to concealment and exposure, discloses the narrative's fundamental anxiety about difference within. The emphasis deepens the reader's sense of the danger posed by Achan's deed. This is not only a matter of theft, nor even offense against God. Not only has Achan brought what is off-limits *(ḥērem)* into Israel, but *he has concealed its presence within the community*. By keeping the matter secret he has therefore endangered the whole community even more severely. The encounter between Joshua and Achan reveals that the most perilous difference is the one that is not apparent, that lies hidden within the midst of the community. Achan took the Canaanite items into the camp, but on the surface everything seemed the same. The *ḥērem* lay within Israel, but no one was aware of it until disaster struck. The text therefore exposes a crucial issue for a community preoccupied with keeping its communal boundaries intact. How can the nation guard against the contamination of difference if difference is not always apparent? Put another way, how can Israel recognize the presence of Canaan within itself if what is Canaanite is not always open to view?

The narrative underscores this point in a striking and ingenious manner, through the name of the offender himself. The name "Achan" makes no sense in Hebrew. It derives from no known root and is attested nowhere else in the Hebrew Bible.[15] However, the name, along with its root *ʿkn*, constitutes an anagram of *kʿn*, the root from which the name "Canaan" is constructed; *ʿākān* represents the presence of *kĕnaʿan* within Israel, a cryptic presence which must be identified, uncovered, and excised. The hidden presence of Canaan within Israel is personified by this now-Canaanized Israelite. By ridding itself of Achan, Israel rids itself of Canaan.

The narrative therefore manifests a fundamental anxiety; the need to identify and excise what is different. The anxiety is given expression in Joshua's charge to Achan. The charge, configured by a series of four

---

[15] The Chronicler appears to recognize the peculiar character of the name "Achan" and renders it "Achar." The variant spelling changes the nonsensical "Achan" into a name that links it to the offense and its consequences: "Achar, the troubler *(ʿôkēr)* of Israel, who transgressed in the matter of the devoted thing" (1 Chr 2:7). It is sometimes argued that the name reflects a scribal error which mistakes final *nun* (n) for *resh* (r). This would assume that the scribe made this mistake consistently, since the name occurs often in the chapter. For a synopsis of other explanations of the name, see R. S. Hess, "Achan and Achor: Names and Wordplay in Joshua 7," *HAR* 14 (1994) 89–98. It is also interesting to note that the narrator makes a wordplay that evokes this one, although more explicitly in Joshua 3–4, between the noun *kōhēn* (priest) and the verb *(hākîn)*.

commands, opens with an invitation which reflects Achan's ambiguous status as both Israelite and outsider, "My son, give glory to the LORD God of Israel and make confession to him." The paternal "my son" expresses a bond between Joshua and the offender, while the charge itself invites Achan to affirm his allegiance to the God of Israel. Yet the words are directed to one who has already been separated from the community, and the command to confess is a call to self-condemnation, given what the reader knows about the outcome of the procedure (v. 15). The call to confess is also heavily tinged with irony. It recalls the confession of Canaanite Rahab, who gave unsolicited glory to the God of Israel (2:9-11). The second of the two phrases ("make confession to him") is, in Hebrew, a double entendre *(wĕten-lô tôdâ)*. The noun *tôdâ* more commonly refers to an act of praise or thanksgiving (Pss 26:7; 50:14, 23; 95:2; Isa 51:3; Jer 30:19), although it can also refer to the confession of sin (Ezra 10:11).[16] The use of the noun thus blends praise with the confession of sin. Which is Joshua calling for? Here for the first time in the whole affair, we find reference to glory and praise for the God of Israel on the lips of an Israelite, but only as the means to prompt a suspected thief to condemn himself.

Joshua conspicuously levels no accusation at Achan. Instead, he articulates the oppositions which express the issue of undetected difference: "Tell me now what you have done; do not hide *(ʿal-tĕkahēd)* it from me." The two commands parallel the previous commands to "give glory" and "make confession." The former commands prompted Achan to speak to YHWH, but the latter two prompt him to speak to Joshua, again reinforcing both the theological and social elements of the crime.

Achan's reply, however, does not quite correspond to Joshua's commands (vv. 20-21). He does not give glory or make confession to God. Rather, he begins by admitting to a charge that Joshua has not leveled ("It is true;" Hebrew *ʾomnâ*). Achan is surprisingly cooperative and readily confesses that he has sinned against YHWH. The exposed thief then provides Joshua with an inventory of the items he has taken and divulges their location. The plunder is luxuriant and exotic—"a beautiful mantle from Shinar and two hundred shekels of silver" (about seven pounds) "and a bar of gold weighing fifty shekels"—and betokens considerable temptation. The location of the plunder, "hidden in the ground inside my tent" alludes symbolically to the danger of Canaanite influence; it was "hidden in the ground/land" *(ṭĕmûnîm bāʾāreṣ)*.

---

[16] The dual meaning of the English word "confession" approximates the dual sense of the Hebrew term.

Achan's willing cooperation with Joshua may seem puzzling, but his speech plays a significant role within the narrative. His words illustrate the process by which an Israelite may be drawn away by the captivating influence of Canaan, thus introducing perilous difference into the nation. The process is traced by the sequence of verbs which configure the speech: "I saw . . . I coveted . . . I took . . . they are hidden." Achan has not heeded the Mosaic warning about the seductive allure of Canaan (Deut 7:25b-26):

> Do not covet the silver or the gold that is on them and take it for yourself, because you could be ensnared by it; for it is abhorrent to the LORD. Do not bring an abhorrent thing into your house, or you will be set apart for destruction like it. You must utterly detest and abhor it, for it is set apart for destruction.

Moses cautioned that the silver and gold of Canaan are *ḥērem*, possessing the capacity for making the one ensnared by it *ḥērem* as well. Achan's confession therefore warns both the assembly and the reader alike, confirming the uncompromising commands of Moses that brook no contact whatsoever with Canaan.

The location of the plunder now exposed, Joshua dispatches messengers, who run to Achan's tent, excavate the plunder, and display it in plain view of the community (vv. 22-23).[17] The narrative is brief and succinct, conveying a sense of urgency. Joshua's address has articulated the danger of undetected difference, and Achan's words reveal how such a situation could develop. The concise and energetic report of the narrator now serves as a model for quick and effective response to uncovered difference. No time is wasted. Once identified and separated, the contagion must be removed and eradicated.

Achan Ruined: 7:24-26

Achan and his family are physically removed from the Israelite camp, widening the distance between Achan and the Israelite community. Only now does Joshua condemn the offender and his family, "Why did you bring trouble on us? The LORD is bringing trouble on you today." The verdict confirms that the separation is now complete. Achan is one

---

[17] The messengers (*mal'ākîm*) seal Achan's doom when they uncover the plunder. They correspond, in an ironic sense, to the messengers sent by Joshua to save Rahab and her family as they hide within their house at Jericho (6:25).

of "them;" he has troubled "us." And he, instead of the nation, is now YHWH's enemy. The Israelites as a community stone Achan and his family and burn them, along with all their livestock and possessions (cf. Deut 13–16). The violence previously directed toward the inhabitants of Canaan is now directed in equal measure to the erstwhile Israelites who stand alone in the land. By destroying both the family and its possessions, Israel fulfills the Mosaic warning about bringing *any* Canaanite thing into the community. A pile of stones is raised over them, completing the process of "Canaanization." Achan and everything connected to him now resembles Jericho—burned and reduced to rubble. With this final act, the restoration of the nation is completed. The listing of the plundered items, along with Achan's family, livestock, and "all that he had" demonstrates the nation's determination to remove every vestige of threatening difference from its midst. As in the battle reports, "all Israel" acts as one against the Canaanite menace.[18] In so doing Israel reclaims its role as the executor of YHWH's purpose. Joshua tells Achan that "the LORD is bringing trouble on you today," but it is assembled Israel that carries out the threat.

The episode concludes with two etiological notes which enclose a report that YHWH turned from his burning anger (v. 26). The narrative structure thus contrasts the temporary outbreak of YHWH's anger with its permanent effects. YHWH's anger has turned from Israel, but the grave cairn and the place of execution (The Valley of Achor ["Trouble"]) bear mute testimony to its residual consequences. More broadly, reports of YHWH's burning anger now frame the account of Achan's transgression. The phrases "the anger of the LORD burned" (*wayyiḥar-ʾap* [v. 1]) and "from his burning anger" (*mēḥărôn ʾappô* [v. 26]) link the present episode with previous incidents in which divine anger has broken out against Israel (Exod 32:11-12; Num 11:1, 10, 33; 12:9; 25:3-4; 32:14-15) and with the frequent Deuteronomic warnings against apostasy (Deut 6:5; 7:4; 11:16-17; 13:17 [MT 18]; 29:26-27 [MT 25-26]; 31:16-17). Correspondences with the latter reinforce the sense that the episode is primarily concerned with illustrating the seductive peril of Canaan and the means of countering it. Moreover, the manifestation of YHWH's burning anger is unique in this case. In all other instances, the burning anger of YHWH is a destructive presence which threatens to consume the entire community. At Ai, however, YHWH's burning anger is expressed by

---

[18] The unifying nature of the execution by stoning is more striking when compared to the Deuteronomic text which calls for stoning the apostate. In that case, the responsibility of the accuser is emphasized, over and above that of the community: "But you shall surely kill them; your own hand shall be first against them to execute them, and afterwards the hand of all the people" (Deut 13:9).

YHWH's *absence* from the nation. The distinctive expression of YHWH's wrath makes an important point: YHWH's presence with Israel is what distinguishes the nation from the peoples of the land.

Other Secrets: 8:1-9

The assault against Ai demonstrates that the execution of Achan has restored Israel to its former state. As at the beginning of the book and at Jericho, the account begins with the words of YHWH, signaling that Israel once again acts at YHWH's initiative. Reminiscent of the book's opening scene, YHWH encourages Joshua through exhortations ("do not fear or be dismayed," cf. 1:9) and assures him that the inhabitants of Ai have been delivered into the power of the Israelites (cf. 1:3-5; 6:2). As he did at Jericho, YHWH again dictates instructions for the assault (cf. 6:3-5), which Joshua then relays to the people. Likewise, YHWH's assurance that he has delivered the city into the power of Joshua and the Israelites (v. 1b) is reiterated at the conclusion of Joshua's speech to the Israelites (v. 7b), as is the command to set an ambush against the city (vv. 2c, 7a). The peculiar form of YHWH's opening words to Joshua, "see (*rĕʾēh*), I have handed over to you" (v. 8:1b) corresponds to Joshua's concluding words to the people ("see [*rĕʾû*] I have commanded you," v. 8b). The parallel structure (interjection *rāʾâ*—1st person perfect verb—2nd person pronoun) thus encloses the two speeches of YHWH and Joshua by establishing a conceptual link between promise and obedience.[19]

The directions for the assault clarify the lessons learned from the previous debacle. YHWH pointedly declares that the Israelites may keep booty and livestock plundered from Ai (v. 2), in direct contrast to the instructions issued at Jericho (6:16-19). The declaration reconfirms the true nature of Achan's offense. The simple theft of the plunder was not the issue but rather that the plunder had been declared off-limits (*ḥērem*) in accordance with the words of Moses (Deut 7:2), pronounced holy (*qōdeš*) and reserved for YHWH's treasury. The command therefore surrounded the plunder with a boundary which Achan crossed. By

---

[19] The first phrase ("see, I have handed over to you") also parallels the opening of YHWH's instructions to Joshua as Israel prepares to take the city of Jericho (6:2).

YHWH's speech establishes a set of frames for the narrative. The command for the disposition of Ai, its king, and its spoil and livestock (v. 2a-b) anticipates a conclusion that is carefully marked at the end of the episode when the disposition of Ai is related in similar terms (vv. 27-29).

disobeying the direct command of Joshua (and thus YHWH), Achan transgressed a definitive communal boundary. Now, by divine fiat, what was declared *ḥērem* at Jericho is rendered into something that may safely be incorporated into the nation, again demonstrating that Israel's boundaries are defined by YHWH.

The tactical plan for the conquest of Ai yields another lesson. As in the first assault, the plan involves dividing the nation. In the previous instance, the division was made because of the overconfidence of the Israelites, who undertook the attack on their own initiative (7:3-4); the people followed the spies' suggestion that only two or three thousand should go up against the city. Now Joshua, acting at the behest of YHWH, divides the nation again, separating thirty thousand and sending them to lie in ambush against the city. Israel will again flee from the men of Ai, but this time the flight will be a ruse to draw out the warriors so the city can be taken by those waiting west of the city. The stratagem itself is tinged with irony. Achan had hidden what was Canaanite from the rest of the Israelites. Now Israelites will hide themselves from the Canaanites within Ai. And unlike the attack against Jericho, the victory will be accomplished apart from any miraculous intervention. Israel will fight the battle, with YHWH orchestrating the attack. The plans also affirm Joshua's position as victorious conqueror, reestablishing the unity of God, leader, and people. The narration of the battle follows the instructions given by YHWH and expanded upon by Joshua, repeating the command-execution pattern that signified Israel's obedience at the Jordan and at Jericho. YHWH gives the instructions, Joshua relays them to the people, and "all the people" (vv. 3, 4) carry them out just as Joshua has stipulated.

The unit which relates Joshua's preparations for the campaign (vv. 3-9) displays a symmetrical structure which links the concepts of subterfuge, leadership, obedience, and conquest. A series of key terms enclose the specific instructions for the battle: "sending" (vv. 3, 9), "night" (vv. 3, 9), "command" (vv. 4, 8), and "ambush" (vv. 4, 9). The references to night and to the ambush reflect the secretive nature of the operation, while the repetitions of the verbs "send" and "command" assert Joshua's authority and the people's obedience. The instructions themselves focus on the city through a sequence of verbs which detail the steps by which victory will be achieved, "I and all the people with me will approach the city" (v. 5), "until we have drawn them from the city" (v. 6), "you shall rise up from ambush and seize the city" (v. 7), "when you have taken the city" (v. 8), "you shall set the city on fire" (v. 8).

By divulging the plan of attack at the beginning of the episode, the narrator now aligns the reader's perspective with those of YHWH and Israel, against that of the people of Ai. The Israelites now join YHWH

and the reader as those in the know, but the Canaanites remain igno-
rant. The effect is significant because, at the beginning of the campaign, the narrator had introduced information that aligned the reader
with YHWH *against* Israel (7:1); the reader was informed of YHWH's
burning anger but Joshua and the Israelites were unaware. With the re-
alignment of perspectives, the narrator affirms the restored unity of
YHWH, people, and reader against the peoples of the land.

Enticing the Canaanites: 8:10-23

The narrative devotes most of its attention to the preparation for
and execution of the ambush. The amount of textual space devoted to
this stratagem of deception and trickery suggests that the narrative is
continuing to work out the concerns symbolized by Achan's story. The
Israelites hope to envelop and conceal themselves from the unsuspect-
ing Canaanites and then to draw them out from the safety of the city
walls. The success of the plan depends in part on the people of Ai's
willingness to follow the Israelites into an open area and on Israel's
ability to cut off lines of escape. The plan of attack, then, corresponds
symbolically to the very fears which Israel seeks to master. According
to Deuteronomy, the peoples of Canaan are not nothing if not seductive! They are a powerful presence characterized by a capacity to lure
unwary Israelites away from YHWH and thus to their own destruction
(Deut 7:1-5; 12:29-32; 29:17-29). The peoples of Canaan threaten Israel,
who may be tempted to follow their ways instead of YHWH's. And if Israel is drawn outside the protective boundaries which YHWH has established, into unbounded spaces, it may find itself entrapped and
obliterated. The Canaanite threat is all the more perilous because it may
remain undetected until disaster strikes. This is the lesson of Achan's
story. The presence of Canaan cannot always be detected. Like the Israelites concealed in the hills around Ai, "Canaan" surrounds Israel, hidden and calculating, waiting for an opportunity to lure the nation to its
destruction. The story of Achan illustrates the crucial importance of ex-
posing and annihilating the Canaanite presence within the nation. The
stratagem against Ai now turns the focus outward. In a sense, the plan
involves beating the Canaanites at their own game. *Israelites* are now
the hidden ones, hoping to lure the people of the land into following
them, so that they can be ensnared and destroyed. Conquering the
people of the land through beguilement promises mastery over Canaanite seductiveness. By successfully tempting the tempters (and destroying them), Israel frees itself from their power.

The narrator simulates the clandestine operations of the Israelite troops by indulging in a bit of textual legerdemain. We have been informed previously that Joshua selected a contingent of thirty thousand warriors and sent them, by night, to a place of ambush west of the city, between Bethel and Ai (vv. 3-9). However, the procedure seems to be reported again in vv. 12-13, with significant differences. This time the entire Israelite force bivouacs north of the city before a contingent of troops is selected for the ambush, and those selected number only five thousand! Rather than "sending" them to the place of ambush, Joshua now seems to take a more direct hand in setting the trap; he "takes" and "sets" the troops in ambush (v. 12). And all this seems to take place during the day! The operation begins in the morning (v. 10) and is completed with the report that Joshua "spent that night in the valley" (v. 13). Together, the two reports produce a number of effects. The first report (vv. 3-9) allows the reader to view the campaign from the perspective of the hidden group and provides an occasion for revealing the means by which YHWH's command will be implemented. The second (vv. 10-13) relates the campaign from the perspective of the entire nation and moves the narrative forward by relating the execution of YHWH's directions. More importantly, the differences which arise from the repetitions create a sense of confusion in the reader. How many ambushes are laid, one or two? How many troops have been separated out of the main force? And when does the operation take place, during the night or the day? The confusion has the odd effect of placing the reader alongside the king of Ai. Both know that something is up, but neither can see with clarity.[20]

The fluctuation of perspectives becomes more explicit once the trap is set. Following the remark that Joshua spent the night among the people, the narrative abruptly shifts the perspective from Israel to the king of Ai (v. 14).[21] Coming immediately after the reference to the night (v. 13), the report that "the king of Ai saw" underscores the king's inability to perceive the Israelite stratagem. His ignorance is further emphasized by the note that "he did not know that there was an ambush against him behind the city." Like the king of Jericho, he is left in the

---

[20] The repetitions, and the confusion they create, also evoke the narration of the Jordan crossing (3:1–4:24). That narrative as well contains multiple accounts of the events, conflicting information, and bewildering shifts in perspective. The narrative obscurity thus reinforces the sense, rendered by theme and vocabulary, that the campaign constitutes a new beginning for Israel.

[21] The transition is signaled in the MT by use of the verb *wayĕhî* ("and it was," often not translated). The verb conventionally marks the beginning of a new narrative segment.

dark. Israelites have entered by night, but he does not know where they are, and he is ready to send his men out of the city to chase them (cf. 2:2-3, 7). His "not knowing" also recalls the words of Rahab, who was engaged in her own campaign of subterfuge and whose declaration of "not knowing" helped the Israelites to escape their pursuers (cf. 2:4-5).[22]

Having established the king's point of view, the narrative returns to that of Joshua and Israel with the remark that "Joshua and all Israel made a pretense of being beaten before them" (v. 15). The shift here is marked by the verb *wayyinnāgĕ'û*, which alerts the reader to the fact that this rout, unlike the previous one, is a deliberate diversionary tactic. In a reversal of the battle at Jericho, "all the people" of Ai leave the city to pursue a detachment of divided Israel (v. 16). The totality of the pursuit, and the complete abandonment of the city, are emphasized both by repeated vocabulary and by the structure of the narrative itself, which draws the reader's focus to the city's vulnerability (vv. 16-17).[23]

> A They pursued Joshua
>> B They were drawn away from the city
>>> C No one remained in Ai or Bethel who did not go out after Israel
>> B' They left the city wide open
> A' They pursued Israel.

The abandonment of the city leads in turn to a signal to those waiting in ambush. In a command reminiscent of that given to Moses at the Red Sea (Exod 14:16), YHWH commands Joshua to point the sword in his hand toward the city (v. 18).[24] Joshua does precisely as YHWH commands (and here again the narration corresponds to the command), and the focus shifts to those waiting in ambush. With an urgency matching that of the departed king, the hidden Israelites suddenly rush from their hiding places, take the city, and immediately set it aflame (v. 19). Again, the language closely follows Joshua's commands (cf. vv. 7-8), providing additional confirmation of Israel's complete obedience. All of this happens very rapidly, a sense conveyed by the repetition of the root *mhr* (quickly)

---

[22] The verb signifying the king's pursuit of the Israelites *(radāp)* is the same used to signify the pursuit by the king of Jericho's men (cf. 2:5, 7, 22).

[23] Given that the ambush lay in wait between Bethel and Ai, it is curious that no one encounters the hidden Israelites when the call goes out to Bethel to pursue those who have fled!

[24] As at the Red Sea, Israel's enemies pursue the people and are destroyed.

and by the sentence structure, which begins with short verbal phrases and accelerates the action by moving to a simple sequence of verbs ("they captured it, they did it quickly, they set the city ablaze" [AT]).

Again the focus shifts, this time back to the pursuers from Ai (v. 20). The move is accomplished in dramatic fashion and aligns the perspective of the reader with what the men of Ai see, "the men of Ai turned around and they saw and look! the smoke of the city went up to the sky" (AT). Now that those hidden have been revealed, the men of Ai "see" what the king of Ai had trouble seeing, and they see it very clearly (cf. v. 14).[25] The result is discouragement and chaos. With a rhetorical flourish, the narrator conveys the helpless and demoralized state of the pursuers through the use of an idiom, "they no longer had hands among them to flee anywhere" (AT). The phrase (translated "they had no power to flee this way or that" by NRSV) draws a striking contrast between the doomed Canaanites and the victorious Israelites. (The hand often symbolizes power in the Bible). The men of Ai, who have been delivered "into the hands" of the Israelites, no longer have "hands," while Joshua's hand is extended against them. Caught between those who have now taken the city and those who had feigned flight, the situation of the pursuers is now hopeless.

As the battle has progressed, the narrative has shifted focus with increasingly frequency. The shifts now take place with startling rapidity, simulating the confusion of the battlefield. Joshua and "all Israel" now "see" what the men of Ai see (v. 21), but for them the sight of the burning city signals the certainty of victory. Turning on their pursuers, they launch a counterattack. Those from the city attack from the other direction (v. 22a), and the men of Ai find themselves "in the midst of Israelites" *(wayyĕhî lĕyiśrāʾēl bammāwek)*, surrounded on all sides with no place to flee (v. 22b). The Israelites annihilate the force in their midst with a ferocity that is conveyed by the intense language of the report: "they attacked them until not one survivor or escapee was left" (AT). The lone exception is the king, who is captured and brought to the Israelite leader.

Ai Ruined: 8:24-29

Reunited on the battlefield, "all Israel" returns to Ai to finish the destruction of the city and its populace (v. 24). The final scene of the

---

[25] The interjection *hinnēh* ("look!") functions to align the reader's perspective exactly with that of those in the story; the reader sees what the character(s) see.

campaign concentrates, in gruesome detail, on the totality of Ai's destruction. The narrator first recounts the obliteration of the Canaanite force in the field, "when Israel had finished slaughtering all the inhabitants of Ai . . . and when all of them to the very last had fallen by the edge of the sword." Then, with the annihilation of the military force accomplished, the troops turn back to the city and attack it "with the edge of the sword." The devastation of the city is then related from many angles. There is a body count (twelve thousand, both men and women, "the entire population of Ai" [AT], v. 25) and a report that Israel's leader did not stop the slaughter until "the entire population of Ai" had been marked as *ḥērem* (and therefore killed, v. 26). The city is burned to the ground and reduced to rubble (v. 28). And the king is singled out for an ignominious death. He is hanged on a tree, a form of execution that marks him as an accursed criminal (v. 29; cf. Deut 21:22-23).

The narrator makes specific mention that the livestock and plunder of the city were taken as spoils of war (v. 27). The report is calculated to confirm the lines of authority and the people's obedience to them. The theme of obedience is marked implicitly through the language of the report (which points back to YHWH's command at the beginning of the battle [8:2]), and explicitly through the comment that this was done "according to the word of the LORD that he had issued to Joshua." In a similar vein, the references to the destruction of the city and the death of the king fulfill YHWH's command to "do to Ai and its king what you did to Jericho and its king" (8:1). The narrator's conclusion therefore links the totality of Ai's destruction with the nation's complete obedience to YHWH. Israel leaves nothing undone of the commands of YHWH, nor does it deviate from those commands. The nation, Joshua, and YHWH act as one.

The story of Ai's destruction ends with a refrain that connects the destruction of Ai to the death of Achan and his family. Both stories conclude with dual references to sites which remain "to this day." One pair of references explains the names of geographical locations. The Valley of Achor is so called because it marks the site where the "trouble" precipitated by Achan's sin and YHWH's wrath was resolved (7:26c).[26] In a more indirect sense, the name of "Ai" (literally, "the ruin") can be explained by the devastation it experienced (8:28). The other pair of references refers to the cairns raised to mark the ignoble deaths of Achan (7:26a) and the king of Ai (8:29c). This refrain draws the events together

---

[26] The connection is made emphatically in the MT by the repetition of the root *ʾkr* (7:25): *meh ʾăkartānû yaʾkŏrkā* YHWH *bayyôm hazzeh* ("Why did you bring trouble on us? The LORD is bringing trouble on you today.")

and presents them as lessons for the present day. The parallel refrains remind the reader that the stories of Achan and Ai are meant to be read as a single piece. Together they depict the perilous danger of Canaanite presence and the necessity of taking decisive action against it. Achan represents the Canaanite presence within the community, while the king and people of Ai represent the Canaanite presence outside. No matter what the case, whether individual or communal, the narrative urges the same action (illustrated by the parallel fates of Achan and the king of Ai). That which is Canaanite must be drawn from its hidden, secure place, and when exposed it must be completely eliminated. Both stories concentrate on the process of discovery and emphasize the thorough extermination of the Canaanite presence. And both end by affirming that the eradication of Canaanite difference unites the nation. "All Israel" joins in stoning Achan and by doing so restores its relationship with YHWH (7:25-26). And the divided nation is reunited on the battlefield near Ai, from whence "all Israel" proceeds to destroy the city (8:24). These actions are carried out in response to YHWH's commands given through Joshua, and Israel's zeal in executing them demonstrates the nation's uniform and zealous commitment to carry out the full measure of divine direction. At the end of the campaign Israel is reintegrated and obedient, ready to fulfill the mandate to take possession of the land.

Israel at the Altar: 8:30-35

The demonstrations of Israelite unity, homogeneity, and obedience expressed in the destruction of Achan and the city of Ai lead to a capstone event that explicitly confirms the restoration of these qualities. The ceremony at Mts. Ebal and Gerizim affords an occasion for reasserting the distinctive identity of Israel. In terms of the larger narrative context, the ceremony signals both an end and a beginning. The language and substance of the account reassure the reader that the one, great threat to Israelite identity (contact with Canaan) has been successfully mastered. Israel, now chastened by experience, stands united in complete obedience to the Mosaic commandments. On the other hand, the language of the account also resonates deeply with the opening speeches of the book, confirming the "return to the beginning" insinuated throughout the previous episode. For the first time since Israel's entry into the land Moses, not Joshua, dominates the scene. While Joshua's name occurs at the beginning and the end of the episode (vv. 30, 35), the intervening material looks to Moses (vv. 31

[2x], 32, 33, 35).[27] The five occurrences of his name remind the reader of his superior authority. Once again the narrator identifies Moses with the title "the servant of YHWH" (vv. 31, 33; cf. 1:1). References to Moses' commands enclose the episode (vv. 31, 35), and his words provide the impetus and direction for the ceremony. Joshua, for his part, continues his role as the executor of Moses' will. His name occurs in connection with the three main acts of the episode: he constructs an altar, copies the law on stones, and reads the words of the law. With Israel now in the land, the narrator invokes the hierarchy through which Israelite obedience is to be expressed, finishing with an emphatic flourish, "there was not a word of all that Moses commanded that Joshua did not read before all the assembly of Israel" (v. 35).

The episode also reinstates the Deuteronomic paradigm, overshadowing the equivocal Israel of the story with the ideal Israel conceived by Deuteronomy. For the moment, a flawed and irresolute Israel gives way to an Israel that binds itself wholeheartedly to YHWH and to the words of Moses. Gone is the Israel influenced by prostitutes and infatuated with Canaan. The nation now before the reader, its disparate elements united by covenant to YHWH, embodies the vision of Deuteronomy. "All Israel, alien as well as citizen, elders and officers and their judges" stand around the ark, pronouncing blessings (v. 33), and "all the assembly of Israel, and the women, and the little ones, and the aliens who resided among them" hear all the words of Moses (v. 35).

The account itself is rendered as an act of communal obedience in fulfillment of a specific directive of Moses, who had commanded Israel to undertake such a ceremony once it entered the land (Deut 27:1ff). As it has so often within the story, the narrative demonstrates the obedience of Israel by reporting the execution of commands in terms that correspond closely to the commands themselves. The Deuteronomic text, itself configured by references to the commands of Moses (27:1, 4, 10, 11; 28:1), calls Israel to set up stones and erect an altar on Mt. Ebal. Moses decrees that the stones should be covered with plaster and that "all the words of this law" should be written on them (vv. 2-4). He next commands that an altar be constructed of stones that have not been worked by iron, specifying that the stones be "unhewn" (*šĕlēmôt*, vv. 5-6). After constructing the altar, the people are to offer burnt offerings and sacrifices of well-being on it in celebration (v. 7). The command to write "all the words of this law" on the stones is then repeated (v. 8), enclosing altar and sacrifice within the commands of Moses. The sacrifices in turn

---

[27] Joshua is mentioned three times, at the beginning, midpoint, and end (vv. 30, 32, 35).

are to be followed by a ceremony of ritual blessing and curses. Israel is to divide into two groups on Mts. Ebal and Gerizim, with some tribes standing for the blessing and the others for the curse (vv. 9-13).

The implementation of these commands in Joshua follows the program closely, as does the narrator's report, which quotes part of the Deuteronomic text (v. 31b). The narrator summarizes the erection of the altar, the offering of sacrifices, and the recording of the law (vv. 30-32), and then recounts the utterance of blessings on Mts. Gerizim and Ebal (the pronouncement of curses being conspicuously absent, v. 33). However, the episode diverges in small but significant ways from the Deuteronomic text. Joshua assumes a prominent role in the ceremony, while the role of the Levites is diminished; they become the voice of Moses, reciting his predecessor's words to the assembled nation (vv. 34-35; cf. Deut 27:14). The Levitical priests, for their part, are again designated as "those who carried the ark of the covenant of the LORD" (v. 33), effecting a link to the Jordan crossing (3:3, 4, 8, 13, 14, 15, 17; 4:9, 10). As they did during the crossing, the Levitical priests stand in an in-between place, lifting the ark as the focal point of the nation. Finally, the report of the event makes repeated reference to the "book of the law of Moses" (vv. 31, 34), a phrase which, though not found in the Deuteronomic text, alludes, indirectly, to the opening of the book (Josh 1:8). The narration of the ceremony thus focuses the reader's attention on the presence of YHWH and the commands of Moses, just as the opening speeches and the Jordan crossing did.

Another subtle modification signifies a more pronounced divergence. The Deuteronomic command emphasizes the writing of the commands on the plastered stones (Deut 27:2-4, 8). Joshua's narrator, however, directs the reader's focus toward the altar by presenting the episode as an act of altar-building (v. 30). The construction of the altar, not the plastering of stones, receives first mention and assumes priority in the subsequent account. The narrator emphasizes that the altar was constructed to fulfill the command of Moses but summarizes the recording of the law on stones in a phrase (vv. 31-32). The shift in focus evokes a powerful symbol. Throughout the Hebrew Bible altars constitute a metaphor for social coherence and transformation. Transitions in social status or configuration are often marked by the construction of altars (Gen 8:20; 12:7-8; 1 Sam 14:31-35; 2 Sam 24:25; 1 Kgs 18:30-32; 2 Kgs 16:10; Ezra 3:2-3).[28] Building an altar lays implicit claim to the land

---

[28] See also M. Weinfeld, "The Pattern of the Israelite Settlement in Canaan," *Congress Volume Jerusalem 1986*, VTSup 40 (1988) 270–83, who draws parallels with Greek traditions of the foundation of settlements.

on which it is located.[29] Joshua's focus on the construction of the altar on Mt. Ebal therefore symbolically underscores the end of the old, nomadic social order and inaugurates a new social configuration for Israel as the nation prepares to take possession of the whole of Canaan.

Within the account, recording the law of Moses facilitates a transition of focus from the altar, constructed precisely according to the commandments of Moses, to the recitation of blessings and curses and the oral proclamation of the law. With this narrative hinge, the text connects the construction of the altar, representing a new beginning and claim to the land, to a ceremony which unites the community through an expression of devotion to YHWH. The allusions to Deuteronomy 27 and reading of the law suggests a connection to covenant renewal, but this is nowhere explicit in the text.[30] Rather, the account constructs a powerful visual image which portrays what lies at the center of Israel's corporate identity. Israelites oppose each other on Mts. Ebal and Gerizim and invoke blessing. At the center of focus, between the opposing groups, are symbols which represent YHWH's devotion to the nation and the nation's devotion to YHWH: the ark of the covenant, representing the presence and guidance of YHWH (as illustrated at the Jordan crossing and Jericho); the altar, the place of sacrifice; and the stones containing the law of Moses. Hearing and responding to the words of YHWH unites the nation, a point which the narrator emphasizes by defining the corporate "whole" in terms of its parts. "All Israel," on opposing sides of the ark, comprises "alien as well as citizen, with their elders and officers and their judges" (v. 33). And "all the assembly of Israel" includes "the women, and the little ones, and the aliens who resided among them" (v. 35). The dual reference to aliens is particularly significant, for the reader now knows who some of these aliens are and how they have come to be "among them." The concluding phrase, "among them" *(bĕqirbam)*, forges a subtle but unmistakable link to the story of Rahab and her family, who now live "within Israel" *(bĕqereb yiśrāʾēl* [6:25]). By repeatedly alluding to them, the narrator distends Israelite identity from ethnic otherness. "All Israel" encompasses men, women, children, and even Canaanites, indeed all who express obedient devotion to YHWH.

---

[29] Throughout Genesis for example, the patriarchs build altars at various locations in Canaan. The issues of social transformation and land claims will arise later in Joshua as the eastern tribes clash with the rest of the nation over the construction of an altar (22:10).

[30] T. Butler calls this passage "a literary accumulation of citations from Deuteronomy" and discusses the connections to Deuteronomy 27–31 in detail; *Joshua*, WBC (Waco: Word, 1983) 90–5. See also R. Nelson, *Joshua*, 117–9.

Chapter Eight

FOILED AGAIN

Joshua 9:1–10:27

Israel's triumph over Canaanite guile turns out to be short-lived. Having presented the reader with a profile of Israelite integrity and obedience through the covenant ceremony at Mts. Ebal and Gerizim, the narrator now relates a tale that demonstrates Israel's continued susceptibility to chicanery. The themes of deception and discovery that configure the story draw connections to the story of Rahab's deliverance. In both cases, Israel encounters inhabitants of the land and winds up making an agreement to spare them (a situation forbidden by the commands of Moses). The pacts raise issues of obedience and identity which the narrator first expresses through subtlety and suggestion in the story of Rahab. The impropriety of sparing her and her family is hinted at but never articulated, and the narrator softens the impact of the agreement by emphasizing the precarious circumstances in which it is made. In the story of the Gibeonites, however, the forbidden covenant occupies the narrative foreground. The beginning of the story depicts deceitful Canaanites attempting to trick Israel into doing what is specifically proscribed by the commandments of Moses (9:3-5). The covenant's forbidden character is emphasized throughout the episode: in the elaborate preparations undertaken by the Gibeonites (9:3-5), the questions which Joshua and the Israelite elders raise (9:6-8), the grumbling of the congregation (9:18), and Joshua's furious invective (9:22-23). Here as well the Israelites find themselves in a predicament, but one that is the consequence of, rather than the context of, an unlawful agreement. The themes of disobedience and the integration of outsiders therefore acquire greater visibility, all the more so because those who make the covenant are Joshua and the Israelite leadership, as opposed to a couple of bit players. The consequences of the covenant are also more serious, with territorial as well as ethnic implications. The pact with Rahab results in the survival of a small group of Canaanites (Rahab's family [2:12-13]), but the covenant with Gibeon exempts an entire city, along with the villages connected to it, from the campaign of destruction (9:17). And while Joshua assigns Rahab's family to the periphery of the Israelite community (6:23), he locates the Gibeonites at the very center of the community, at the altar (9:27).

As in the corresponding stories, Deuteronomic pronouncements form a backdrop for the action. The Gibeonites borrow language from Deut 20:10-18, which establishes rules for waging war against enemy cities. The passage makes a distinction between warfare against cities outside the boundaries of the land and those possessed by the peoples of the land. In the former case, Moses authorizes a measure of flexibility. Before launching an attack, the Israelites are to offer terms of surrender. If accepted, the Israelites may subject the citizens of the city to forced labor. If rejected, they are to put all male citizens to death but may take women and children, along with everything else in the city, as spoils of war. But cities in Canaan are an exception. The peoples of the land (enumerated in terms of the six-fold list) are to be given no opportunity to surrender. Rather, the Israelites must not "spare anything that breathes" (v. 16). The legislation concludes with a rationale for this exception, "so that they may not teach you to do all the abhorrent things that they do for their gods, and you thus sin against the LORD your God" (v. 18). The Gibeonites seem to be familiar with this distinction, and their scheme for securing survival depends on fooling the Israelites into believing that it applies to them. They therefore present themselves as emissaries "from a far country" (Josh 9:5), knowing that, if their ruse succeeds, Joshua will apply the more flexible scheme in dealing with them. When, too late, Israel discovers their plot, they reveal their knowledge of the Mosaic ordinances and cite them as a rationale for the extraordinary measures they have taken (cf. Deut 7:1-5).

Allusions to the "words of the covenant" in Moab (Deut 29:1-15) prompt the reader to view the Gibeonite pact as an act of incorporation into the Israelite community. The Gibeonites dress in the kind of worn-out clothing that would have characterized Israel in the wilderness, had it not been for YHWH's provision (9:4-5, 13; cf. Deut 29:5), and like Moses they refer to Israel's victories over Sihon and Og (9:10; cf. Deut 29:7). Most significantly, when Joshua discovers their gambit, he declares that they shall be "hewers of wood and drawers of water." The phrase, which is repeated three times in the course of the episode (9:21, 23, 27), explicitly links the Gibeonites with the covenant which unifies the nation in Moab (Deut 29:10-12):

> You stand assembled today, all of you, before the LORD your God—the leaders of your tribes, your elders, and your officials, all the men of Israel, your children, your women, and the aliens who are in your camp, both those who cut your wood and those who draw your water—to enter into the covenant of the LORD your God, sworn by an oath, which the LORD your God is making with you today.

The worn-out clothing, acclamation of victories over Sihon and Og, and consignment as wood-hewers and water-bearers strongly suggest that we may view the Gibeonites as those Moses referred to on the plains of Moab, namely "those who are not with us today," who nonetheless are participants in the covenant community (Deut 29:15).

Canaanites United: 9:1-2

The narrative has created the sense of a new beginning through the victory at Ai and the covenant ceremony at Mts. Ebal and Gerizim. The transitional remarks regarding the kings of the land bolster this sense by evoking a previous point in the story, namely Israel's entrance into the land.[1] After Israel had first crossed the Jordan, the narrator reported the response of the kings of the land (5:1). Now, after Israel has reconstituted itself, the narrator makes a similar report, signaling the resumption of the nation's mission after the disruptive events at Jericho.

> When all the kings of the Amorite who were across the Jordan, westward, and all the kings of the Canaanite who were by the sea heard that YHWH had dried up the water of the Jordan before the Israelites until they had crossed, their hearts melted and there was no longer any spirit in them before the Israelites (5:1, AT).

> When all the kings who were across the Jordan, in the hill country, the Shephelah, and all along the coast of the Great Sea toward Lebanon—the Hittite and the Amorite, the Canaanite, the Perizzite, the Hivite, and the Jebusite—heard, they assembled together for battle with Joshua and Israel, as one voice (9:1-2, AT).

As with the previous report, this one also transports the reader again to the other side of the Jordan. The kings are "across" the Jordan (*bĕʿēber hayyardēn*), a point of view that reflects one standing on the eastern side of the Jordan, viewing the Promised Land from the outside.

---

[1] The reader will later learn that the events take place back at Gilgal, the site of Israel's first encampment in the land.

Against the demonstration of Israelite reintegration (8:30-35), the narrative now again reiterates the characteristic Canaanite plurality. Opposing Israel's one leader (Joshua) are the many kings of the land, who command diverse peoples in contrast to the one unified nation (Israel). Even the geographical description accentuates their plurality, listing the different localities they inhabit. The kings are making their own attempt at unification, but the shape of the report injects a sense of ambiguity into the enterprise. The syntax of the MT connects the phrase "with one voice" (NRSV "with one accord"; *pĕh ʾeḥād*) with Joshua and Israel—"they gathered together to wage war with Joshua and Israel, one voice" (v. 2)—but it seems to refer to the activity of the kings. Who possesses "one voice," the kings (of uncertain number) and peoples or Joshua and Israel? The language of the report thus reminds the reader of the essential difference between Israel and the peoples of the land. Israel has gathered under Joshua's leadership at one place to affirm its covenant with the one God. The peoples of the land gather under the leadership of many kings from many places within the land. An aggressive plurality again threatens Israel.

Let's Make a Deal: 9:3-15

Our introduction to the Gibeonites reveals at once that the Canaanite unification project has not been entirely successful. The Gibeonites, later identified with the Hivites (v. 7), seek to engage the Israelites in a different way. The opening words of the episode imply their divergence from the rest of the peoples by reiterating, in slightly altered form, the words which began the report of the kings' activity: "the inhabitants of Gibeon heard" (*wĕyôšĕbēy gibĕʿôn šāmĕʿû*, v. 3).[2] When the kings hear, they unite to make war against Israel. But when the Gibeonites hear they conspire to make a covenant. More striking, however, is the constitution of the Gibeonite community. While kings dictate the course of action for the peoples of the land, no king does so among the Gibeonites. Instead, "the inhabitants of Gibeon" decide to confront the Israelites with a conspiracy to defraud. Furthermore, the text makes no distinction between these inhabitants and the undetermined number of their community who travel to the Israelite camp. The narrative simply follows the reference to the inhabitants with a string of verbs in the third person plural: "the inhabitants of Gibeon heard . . . they acted . . .

[2] Compare with "when all the kings heard" (*wayĕhî kišmōaʿ kol-hammĕlākîm*, v. 1).

they went and prepared provisions . . . they took worn-out sacks . . . and they went to Joshua and said to him" (vv. 3-6). The ambiguity is accentuated with an emphatic aside: "when the inhabitants of Gibeon heard . . . they, yes those very same ones, acted" (AT, NRSV "they on their part acted," *wayyaʿăśû gam-hēmmāh*, v. 4). A surface reading of the text gives the impression that the entire community speaks to Joshua, but this clearly cannot be the case. Instead, the narrator employs an indefinite form of expression to suggest that those who speak to Joshua, whoever they are, speak for the entire community.

The creation of this impression is crucial for the development of the narrator's rhetorical objective. The delegation which speaks to Joshua cannot immediately be distinguished from the rest of the Gibeonite community. The Gibeonites therefore demonstrate a community integrity and unity that has heretofore marked the Israelite nation. The Gibeonites, from the beginning of the episode, bear an essential resemblance to Israel. As rendered by the narrative, the Gibeonites look more like the Israelites than they do the other peoples of the land. Israel is distinctive in having no king, as opposed to the peoples of the land (cf. 2:3; 5:1; 8:1, 23; 9:1). Apparently the Gibeonites now share this distinctive.

The sense of Gibeonite unanimity becomes more striking when contrasted to Israelite decision-making in the story. Whereas an undifferentiated "they" speaks for Gibeon, the narrative pointedly presents Israelite responses through multiple sources and diverse titles. Initially, the Gibeonites speak to "Joshua and the Israelites," (vv. 6-8) but later "the men" (*hāʾănāšîm*, NRSV "leaders") sample their provisions (v. 14) and the "leaders of the congregation" (*nĕśîʾî hāʿēdâ*) take an oath which seals the covenant (v. 18). In the first instance, the phrase translated "Israelites" is literally "the man of Israel" (*ʾîš yiśrāʾēl* vv. 6, 7). The unusual phrase expresses the integrity of the Israelite community, corresponding to the unanimity of the Gibeonites. In other words, Israel speaks as a single individual to its Gibeonite counterpart: "The man of Israel said to the Hivite, 'Perhaps you live within me. How can I make a covenant with you?'" (v. 7, AT).[3] The question itself, as rendered in the MT, is highly suggestive. Is Gibeon a part of Israel? If so, how can Gibeon be an object? Does Israel see itself in Gibeon?

The allusions to Deuteronomy 29:2-9 (MT 1-8) amplify the Gibeonites' resemblance to Israel. The text emphasizes their appearance, both through a description of their preparations (vv. 4-5), and through the

---

[3] The first person singular forms are indicated by the vowel points in the MT, although certain words in the consonantal text suggest different forms (a phenomenon called *qere-ketibh*).

Gibeonites' riposte to the Israelites' questions about their identity (vv. 12-13). They arrive at the Israelite camp with "worn-out" sacks *(śaqqîm bālîm)*, wineskins *(nōʾdôt yayin bālîm)*, sandals *(nĕʿālôt bālôt)*, and clothing *(śĕlāmôt bālôt)*, as if they have just come from a very long journey, evoking Moses' remarks about YHWH's provision for Israel during the nation's wilderness wanderings (Deut 29:4-6 [MT 3-5]):

> But to this day the LORD has not given you a mind to understand, or eyes to see, or ears to hear. I have led you forty years in the wilderness. The clothes on your back have not worn out *(lō-bālû śalmōtēykem mēʿălēykā)* and the sandals on your feet have not worn out *(wĕnaʿalkā lōʾ-bālĕtâ mēʿal raglekā)*; you have not eaten bread, and you have not drunk wine or strong drink—so that you may know that I am the LORD your God.

The Gibeonites allude even more directly to the passage as they invite the Israelites to sample the provisions (v. 13b): "these garments and these sandals of ours are worn out from the very long journey" *(wĕʾēlleh śalmōtēynû mēʿălēykā ûnĕʿālēynû bālû mērōb hadderek mĕʾōd)*. These explicit semantic connections draw an important connection between the two peoples; the Gibeonites look like the Israelites *would* have looked upon entering the land, had it not been for the presence and provision of YHWH.[4]

The Gibeonites' response to Israelite probing reinforces the connection to the Deuteronomic passage. Echoing Moses, the emissaries declare that they "have heard a report of him (YHWH), of all that he did in Egypt and of all that he did to the two kings of the Amorites who were beyond the Jordan, King Sihon of Heshbon, and King Og of Bashan who lived in Ashtaroth" (vv. 9b-10; cf. Deut 29:2, 7). This brief recitation of YHWH's mighty acts suggests that the Gibeonites may be appropriate candidates for the covenant community, for recognition of what YHWH has done leads to the recognition of YHWH's divine character and commitment, "that you may know that I am the LORD your God" (Deut 29:6).[5] The Gibeonites imply that they have been drawn to Israel

[4] For more on the connection between Deuteronomy 29 and Joshua 9, see R. Polzin, *Moses and the Deuteronomist* (Garden City: Doubleday, 1980) 117–23 and P. Kearney, "The Role of the Gibeonites in the Deuteronomic History," *CBQ* 35 (1973) 1–8.

[5] The recitation of YHWH's mighty acts conventionally precedes an expression of the nation's commitment to the covenant with YHWH (cf. Josh 24:1-15). Deuteronomy itself takes the form of a covenant document. It begins, in a larger way, with the recitation of YHWH's deeds on behalf of Israel (1:6–3:29), followed by an exhortation to commitment to YHWH and to his decrees (4:1-40).

The Gibeonites pointedly do *not* report that they "heard what Joshua had done to Jericho and Ai" (v. 3).

precisely because of the acclaim YHWH has attained, "your servants have come from a very far country, because of the name of the LORD your God" (Josh 9:9a). They have "heard" what Israel has "seen," and wish to join themselves to the community.

The narrator has opened with a description of the Gibeonites that separates them from the plurality of the other peoples of the land and invests them with an Israel-like unity. Then, through allusions to Deut 29:1-7, the text associates them with the Israelite community assembled for the covenant on the plains of Moab. After the covenant between Gibeon and Israel has been forged, the incorporation of Gibeon will be confirmed by the Israelite leaders' decree that they will be "hewers of wood and drawers of water." The semantic link with Deut 29:11 completes the intertextual connection by returning the reader to the earlier covenant ceremony, just at the point that Moses moves from the reminder of YHWH's deeds to a call for the community to unite by entering the covenant of YHWH (vv. 10-15 [MT vv. 9-14]). The Israelites, on the other hand, ironically reflect Moses' assertion that "YHWH has not given you a mind to understand, or eyes to see, or ears to hear" (Deut 29:4 [MT v. 3]) and prove unable to see through the Gibeonites' disguise. Like the spies at Jericho, they seem curiously susceptible to Canaanite wiles and appear passive and reactive during the early stages of the negotiations. For the first time in the book, the Israelite community and leaders join Joshua in the decision-making process.[6] While Joshua and "the man of Israel" seem to act in accord when treating with the Gibeonites, the very fact that both are mentioned together suggests a lesser degree of unity within Israel than within the Gibeonite community.[7]

The Gibeonites exploit the potential separation between leadership and people and, like Rahab before them, forcefully dictate both the conversation and events. Their objective is to secure a place to live within the land, but they do so with the energy and craftiness that ought to characterize Israel. The narrator introduces the Gibeonites by remarking on their ability to act "with subtlety" (*bĕʿormâ*, v. 4) and signifies their quick and decisive response to the Israelites by using a string of verbs to convey an atmosphere of intense activity ("they went and outfitted and took," v. 4 [AT]). Dispensing with trivial pleasantries, the emissaries offer a brief introduction before revealing the purpose of their mission, "We have come from a distant land. Now make a covenant with us" (v. 6b, AT). Though brief, the message is carefully

[6] This dispersal of authority enhances the similarities between Israel and Gibeon.

[7] The fact that the Gibeonites who speak to Joshua constitute a delegation is not explicitly revealed until the sense of their communal unanimity has been well-established.

crafted to deflect Israel's attention away from their identities and to elicit an immediate response. The first sentence, a simple declaration, is rendered in the indicative mood, while the second takes the form of an imperative which, preceded by the particle *ʿattâ* ("now") for emphasis, demands the attention of the Israelites.

At first, the Israelites do not take the bait and respond with comparable craftiness. Beginning with their own declaration, they defuse the force of the imperative by transforming it into a question (thus giving more force to the issue of identity), "Perhaps you dwell very close to us. How can we make a covenant with you (v.7)?"[8] At this, the Gibeonites make a calculated move. Instead of responding to the "man of Israel's" question, they turn instead to Joshua and, in a markedly obsequious gesture, drop the imperative and say simply, "we are your servants" (v. 8a). With this succinct announcement, the Gibeonites acknowledge Joshua's authority and redefine themselves as his subjects, appropriating language conventionally employed to address monarchs and others in high authority (2 Kgs 10:5; Exod 5:15-16; Num 32:5). They direct their words to Joshua and not the nation (as is indicated by the singular form of the pronoun).[9] Thwarted by the Israelites' question, the Gibeonites now turn their appeal toward Israel's leader.

Joshua, however, will not let the issue of identity lie, though his questions are less threatening than those of the Israelites (v. 8b), "Who are you? And where do you come from?" The Gibeonites respond to the softened tone of these questions by repeating their claim that they have traveled from a far country (although they now emphasize the distance by asserting they have come from a *"very* far distance" [v. 9a]). Immediately after this, however, they deftly change the subject again, this time in a direction that strikes at the heart of Israel's self-concept. After acclaiming the renown of Israel's God and the victories over Pharaoh and the Amorite kings, the Gibeonites finally divulge that they have been sent by "our elders and all the inhabitants of our land" (v. 11).[10] The impact of the pronouncement is two-fold. First, it reinforces the "official" nature of the Gibeonites' mission and thus the legitimate character of any agreements they make. Second, the reference

---

[8] As noted above, the "man of Israel's" response is actually rendered in the first person. The introduction to the response—"the man of Israel said to the Hivite"— signals that the two peoples are, for the moment, on equal footing in the negotiation.

[9] The Hebrew language has four forms of the second person pronoun, whereas English has only one.

[10] The Gibeonites' words, however, contrast with the sense rendered by the narrative at first. The reader has therefore been given a picture of Gibeonite community against which to evaluate the emissaries' own description to Joshua.

to "elders and inhabitants" stresses their affinity with Israel and disassociates them from kings who rule the peoples of the land. They then take the edge off their initial imperative by recasting it in a much less aggressive form and prefacing it with their offer of servitude, "We are your servants; come now make a covenant with us" (11b). Here words of submission replace words of identification, and these are now directed toward the entire community ("your servants" now occurs in the plural [*ʿabdēykem*]). Pressing the initiative, the emissaries then ensure that the exploration of their identities will take place on their terms rather than on the Israelites'. They direct attention to the condition of the bread, wineskins, garments, and sandals as evidence that they have indeed traveled on "a very long journey" (vv. 12-13). And they invite the Israelites to have a look for themselves.

The Israelites seem to be caught off-guard by the fast-talking Gibeonites, who had initially seemed so tight-lipped. In response, the Israelites divide. "The men" (*hāʾănāšîm*) sample the provisions, Joshua makes peace with the Gibeonites, and the leaders of the congregation (*nĕśîʾî hāʿēdâ*) swear an oath to them (vv. 14-15). Furthermore, in a brief comment imbedded within Israel's response, the narrator notes that the leaders "did not ask direction from the LORD." Rarely within Joshua does the narrator intrude with such commentary, but this intrusion accentuates an element of the story that the narrator does not want the reader to miss. The Gibeonites have acknowledged YHWH and claim that YHWH's deeds have drawn them to Israel. But the Israelites seem, for the moment, to have forgotten YHWH. Is this just an oversight? Have Joshua and the rest of Israel been so bamboozled that they can do only what the Gibeonites tell them to do? Or have they "neglected" YHWH on purpose? The making of treaties is no small matter and, one would think, ought to be carried out thoughtfully and with the input of divine counsel. How are the Israelites so easily duped regarding the provisions, especially since they had been so perspicuous about the emissaries' identities at first? The narrator's succinct rendering of Israel's response indicates a quick decision, reached with little deliberation. Did the temptation of subjecting another people prove too powerful for Joshua and the Israelite leaders? What would YHWH have said if consulted? Strangely, Joshua and Israel make peace with these emissaries without ever finding out precisely who they are or from whence they have come.[11]

When set against these questions, Joshua's actions in particular hint that there is more to the whole affair than meets the eye. The NRSV gives

[11] J. Liver views the Israelites' quick decision as an indication that they are willingly taken in. See his article, "The Literary History of Joshua IX," *JSS* 8 (1963) 227–43.

the impression of one action, with two aspects, "Joshua made peace with them, guaranteeing their lives by a treaty" (v. 15a). But the syntax of the MT describes two equivalent actions: "Joshua made peace with them and he made a covenant with them to spare them" (*wayya'aś lāhem yĕhōšûa šālôm wayyikrōt lāhem bĕrît lĕhayyôt*). The phrase alludes again to the Deuteronomic laws of warfare, which allow the Israelites to offer peace to distant cities (Deut 20:10-11), but prohibit them from doing so for the peoples of the land (v. 16). The reader, who knows the real identity of the emissaries, understands the import of these words. The last phrase in particular ("to spare them") foreshadows grave consequences. Sparing Canaanites will ensure a plurality in the land that may lead the nation away from YHWH (Deut 20:18).[12]

Now What? 9:16-27

The next episode in the story (signaled by the opening *wayĕhî*) takes place "at the end of three days." By now the reader is familiar with this time frame. Joshua sent messengers throughout the camp three days before the Jordan crossing (1:11), and the spies hid themselves for three days in the hills beyond Jericho (2:16, 22). The entire phrase, *wayĕhî miqṣēh šĕlōšet yāmîm*, reiterates the phrase used to introduce the Jordan crossing (3:1), thereby drawing a semantic link between the two events. The first entailed a boundary crossing, during which Israel entered Canaan and began the transition from nomadic people to landed nation. The present event involves a different kind of boundary crossing, not of geography but of ethnicity, during which members of Canaan will enter Israel (expressed by the three-fold reference to the Gibeonites living "in the midst of" Israel [vv. 7, 16, 22]). The three-day time frame thus establishes a thematic connection between the Jordan crossing, the story of Rahab, and the present episode.

Another "beginning" is evoked by the report that the Israelites "heard" that those with whom they had made peace actually lived near them (v. 16). The reference to hearing corresponds to the words that began the present sequence of events: "when all the kings who

---

[12] The language employed by the Gibeonites, as well as other elements in the encounter, suggests that the covenant between the two parties constitutes a vassal treaty. See the discussions in J. M. Grintz, "The Treaty of Joshua with the Gibeonites," *JAOS* 86 (1966) 113–26 and C. Fensham, "The Treaty between Israel and the Gibeonites," *BA* 27 (1964) 96–100.

were beyond the Jordan . . . heard" (9:1). The kings of Canaan have united "in one accord" to wage war against Joshua and Israel (9:2), and the narrative hints that the Israelites are now ready to do the same. They immediately set out for the Gibeonite cities, which (now discovered) are named with characteristically Canaanite plurality, "their cities were Gibeon, Chiphirah, Beeroth, and Kiriath-jearim" (v. 17b). However, the narrator pointedly states that Israel did *not* attack the city because the leaders had sworn an oath. The abrupt shift away from the expected outcome highlights the dilemma that Israel now faces. Do the Israelites carry out YHWH's commands against the Canaanites and thus profane the oath they have sworn? Or do they honor the oath and thus break YHWH's commands?[13]

The dilemma reveals a fracture within the Israelite community which had been hinted at in Israel's response to the emissaries (the men sampled provisions, Joshua made peace, and the leaders swore an oath, vv. 14-15). The leaders decide to honor the oath at the expense of obedience to the Mosaic commandments, a decision which acquires an ironic sense by the narrator's remark that they have sworn "by the LORD, the God of Israel" (v. 18).[14] But this in turn leads to dissension. The text points to a division within "all Israel" (reintegrated at Mts. Ebal and Gerizim) by setting "all the congregation" against "the leaders" and reporting that the congregation "murmured" (v. 18b). The narrative's choice of language extends the irony of the situation. The congregation's "murmuring" (MT *wayyilōnû*) links them with the wilderness generation, who murmured repeatedly against Moses (Exod 15:24; 16:2, 7; 17:3; Num 14:2, 36; 16:11). Again Israelites complain against their leaders, but this time they do so not because they are rebellious to the commands of Moses but because they want to fulfill them!

The narrator emphasizes the polarized state of the community by using "all" to signify division rather than unity, "all the leaders said to all the congregation" (v. 19). Divided Israel now stands in sharp relief to unified Gibeon; the Gibeonites acted in complete accord with their leaders (v. 11), but the congregation of Israel opposes theirs. Significantly, the leaders still do not turn to YHWH for advice or help in healing the division. Instead, they attempt to reunify the nation through

---

[13] The tensions raised by the narrator are explored in detail by L. Eslinger, *Into the Hands of the Living God*, JSOTSup 84 (Sheffield: Sheffield University, 1989) 24–54.

[14] This marks the first time, within the present series of events, that there is mention of the name of YHWH on Israelite lips. The Israelites did not consult YHWH for counsel on the emissaries' proposal, but they happily invoke YHWH's name to make the covenant.

their own ingenuity. They begin by defining the current state of affairs; they have taken an oath in the name of YHWH which prohibits Israel from attacking Gibeon. Given this situation, they argue, Israel has no choice but to allow the Gibeonites to survive. Using a communal "we" that denies the separation between themselves and the congregation, they present the decision as one that must be made for the best interests of the nation; the oath must be honored so that "wrath may not come upon us" (v. 21b).[15] Having made their point sufficiently, the leaders then recast the proposal as a decree, "let them live" (v. 21a).

At this point the narrator intrudes to inform the reader that the Gibeonites became "hewers of wood and drawers of water for all the congregation, as the leaders had decided concerning them" (v. 21b). The comment softens the straightforward edict of the leaders and prompts the reader to view the final decision as a compromise. The leaders ameliorate the congregation's objections by diminishing the status of the Gibeonites and subjecting them to slavery in the service of Israel. The last phrase is ambiguous in the MT, and could easily mean something like "as the leaders had said to them." Taken this way, the comment fills in more details of the proposal, but in an indirect manner that allows the focus to remain squarely on the issue of the Gibeonites' survival. By repeating the decision to spare the Gibeonites, and downplaying the role assigned to them, the narrative thus keeps the reader's attention on the main issue, that is, the social and theological implications of Israel's decision not to attack. All the while, Joshua remains conspicuously absent, thus remaining at a distance from the implications of the decision. The focus of the deliberations enhances his separation, centering on the oath which the leaders swore rather than the covenant which Joshua made. Although the narrator explicitly implicates both Joshua and the leaders in the agreement (v. 15), the narrator now intimates that responsibility for dealing with the pact and its consequences lies with the Israelite leaders. In this manner, the text safeguards Joshua's character as a leader zealous for carrying out the Mosaic commands to annihilate the Canaanites. (The leaders, not Joshua, make the decision to spare them.)

Insinuating that the leaders are to blame for the survival of the Gibeonites allows the narrator to present Joshua once again in authoritative terms. With communal discontent thus resolved through the mediation of the Israelite leaders, and with the ruling that they are exempt in place, Joshua again assumes center stage. With no mention of the

---

[15] The argument conveniently omits the connection Deuteronomy makes between divine anger and failure to exterminate the peoples of the land (Deut 7:4).

covenant or oath, he summons the Gibeonites and chides them for their perfidy. Then he takes up the compromise suggested by the leaders and transforms it into a curse, "now therefore you are cursed, and some of you shall always be slaves, hewers of wood and drawers of water for the house of my God" (v. 23). The curse turns the emissaries' fawning language ("we are your servants") against them and sets the Gibeonites forever apart from the rest of the nation. However, Joshua modifies the original decree in one more crucial detail. Instead of confirming the leaders' decision to place the Gibeonites in the service of the congregation, Joshua places them in the service of "the house of YHWH." The effect of the decree is to place that which is accursed at the very center of the Israelite community![16]

The Gibeonites, for their part, also demonstrate a penchant for irony. In response to Joshua's questions, they acknowledge their servile status but, with an adroit turn of phrase, forge a semantic association between themselves and Moses, "it was told to *your servants* for a certainty that the LORD your God had commanded Moses *his servant* to give you all the land and to destroy all the inhabitants of the land before you" (v. 24).[17] They then cast their deception as a response to the Mosaic commandments; they heard what YHWH has done and responded by reflecting on and responding to the law of Moses. How different from the first explanations of why they had approached Israel! Originally, the Gibeonites declared that they had come to join themselves to Israel "because of the name of the LORD your God," expressed as a report of YHWH's mighty acts against the kings of the Amorites. Now, however, they attribute their actions to Moses. The shift in focus is highly significant. The Gibeonites "did this thing" because they believed the words of Moses.

In another ironic twist, Israel's new slaves then declare that "we are in your hand." The phrase has been used often with respect to the peoples of the land, where the announcement that YHWH has given the people into Israel's hand foretells the annihilation of Israel's foes (Deut 2:24; 3:3; Josh 2:24; 6:2; 8:1, 7). Standing now before Joshua, these inhabitants of the land, exempted from destruction by covenant and oath, refer to themselves in the same terms, but this time under the protection of oath and covenant. They conclude strongly, with an imperative that communicates submission to Joshua but again raises the dilemma that their deception has created for Israel, "what is good and

[16] Perhaps Joshua intends in this way to maintain their separation from the rest of the community. By assigning them to "the house of YHWH" he ensures that their difference will pose less of a temptation than if they were dispersed throughout the entire congregation.

[17] The NRSV translates the same Hebrew word (ʿebed) as "slave" in v. 23.

proper in your eyes to do to us, do" (v. 25b, AT). At the mercy of Joshua, and having displayed a unity greater than that demonstrated by fractured Israel, the Gibeonites' declaration raises an implicit question. What *is* the good and proper thing to do?

The text picks up the tone of the Gibonites' speech as it concludes the story, reporting succinctly that "this is what he did for them" and then characterizing Joshua's actions in this manner, "he saved them from the Israelites; and they did not kill them" (v. 26). The NRSV here translates an idiom ("deliver from the hand of X," *nṣl miyyad*) which occurs throughout the Hebrew Bible to denote YHWH's deliverance of Israel from its enemies (Judg 6:9; 9:17; 1 Sam 4:8; 7:3; 10:18; 12:11; 14:48; 17:37; Ezra 8:31). In a final irony, Joshua therefore assumes the role of Gibeon's savior, delivering them from the hands of their enemies (the Israelites) so that they are not killed.

The story of Gibeon's deliverance concludes, as do the stories of Rahab and Achan, with an etiological note which records their existence within the land to the present day (v. 27; cf. 6:25; 7:26). In this case the note underscores the status and location of an exempted population within Israel. For the third time, we read that the Gibeonites were made hewers of wood and drawers of water. Only now does the narrative reveal that Joshua endorsed the decision of the leaders (to assign them to the whole congregation) along with his own decree (to assign them to the altar of YHWH). The comment ends with a phrase that would seem to refer to Joshua—"in the place that he should choose"— but which picks up the Deuteronomic stipulation that sacrifices may be offered only at the place "that the LORD your God will choose" (Deut 12:5, 14).[18] The narrator's comment therefore also alludes to the altar, reinforcing the ambiguous status of the Gibeonites, who will serve forever at the unifying center of the nation's life.

The Gibeonites' ambiguous role expresses the paradox they represent throughout the story. They are a cursed people, assigned to the most menial of tasks. Yet they are also a privileged people, set apart for service to the altar, at the very center of the community. Their status epitomizes the ambivalence that Israel itself expresses towards outsiders. From a distance, the peoples of the land are obstacles that must be eliminated in order to claim possession of YHWH's gift of the land. Up close, however, they do not appear all that *different*. The narrator shapes the stories of encounters with Rahab and Gibeon to make just this point. *Corporately,* the peoples of the land are enemies to be de-

---

[18] Although the NRSV translates the phrase differently in the two contexts, the verbal forms are identical.

stroyed, as they are at Jericho, Ai, and, in the following episode, Gibeon. *Individually*, however, the narrator has suggested that, when matched against their Israelite counterparts, the peoples of the land display the same qualities that Israel holds as distinctive of its own identity. Words of praise flow from the lips of a Canaanite prostitute, while Israelite spies seems strangely neglectful of their covenant obligations. Gibeonites display a striking unity and a responsiveness to the commands of Moses, while Israelites squabble over the right thing to do. The stories suggest that the boundaries which establish the people of God may be elastic enough to include some of the peoples of the land. The narrator makes this point with particular emphasis through repeated references to the existence of the Gibeonites "within" *(qereb)* Israel (9:7, 16, 22; 10:1). They like Rahab enter Israel's corporate life. If these stories are representative of Israel's interactions with the peoples of the land, how many others were thus brought into the community?[19]

Five Against Gibeon: 10:1-5

The phrase *wayĕhî kišmōa* ("now when [they] heard"), occurring here for the third time in the book, signals a shift back to the kings of the land (10:1; cf. 5:1; 9:1). In each of the three cases, the reader learns of the kings' response to a report concerning the Israelites. The first instance reveals that the kings were disheartened by word of YHWH's miraculous stoppage of the Jordan (5:1), while the second concentrates on the kings' conspiracy to wage war against Israel in response to an unspecified report. The present case leads to a more elaborate account which combines elements of the kings' response in the first instance ("he became greatly frightened") with elements of the second ("they went up with all their armies and camped against Gibeon, and made war against it"). For the first time, however, the narrator renders the impending conflict as a contest between the kings and Joshua (rather than YHWH or Israel). This subtle change not only gives the reader

---

[19] The allusions to Deuteronomy 29 symbolically connect the Gibeonites with the community that renews the covenant at Moab. In a similar way, allusions in Rahab's story associate her and her house with Passover (a red mark in a portal, which ensures the survival of the family inside [2:18-19]). Through these symbolic associations peoples of the land participate in constitutive events of the Israelite community (Exodus and covenant). In the reverse sense, Achan is symbolically associated with a third constitutive event: the gift of the land. He is cut off from life in the land by the same means that the tribal inheritances will be allotted (7:14-15; cf. 18:10).

another view of the story from the Canaanite perspective but also enhances Joshua's status as a warrior and hero. The great victories at Jericho and Ai are now attributed to him, foreshadowing the role he will play in the miraculous victory to come.[20]

By framing the imminent battle in terms of a conflict between kings, the narrative diverts attention away from the ethnic issues that have been the focus of the previous episodes. Henceforth, the conflict of peoples will be portrayed as a conflict between the leaders of the peoples; Joshua against the kings of the land.[21] The story begins with the activity of one king, Adoni-zedek of Jerusalem. Like the Gibeonites before him, news of Israelite victories has greatly frightened him (v. 2a; cf. 9:24b). But the king responds differently than do the collective Gibeonites. While their fear led them to join themselves to Israel by covenant, Adoni-zedek's fear leads him to instigate a coalition of forces to crush Gibeon. He has good reason to fear, for his strategic position has now become precarious. Israelite victories have secured much of (what would become) the Benjaminite hill country, effectively cutting off hope of support from the powerful kings to the north. And the defection of Gibeon, only a few miles to the north, has transformed a buffer into a threat. The text conveys his apprehension by emphasizing its size (both through syntax and repetition) and the formidable reputation of its citizens, "And he was terrified, because a large city was Gibeon, like one of the imperial cities, and because it was a larger city than Ai and all its men were warriors" (v. 2, AT).

Adoni-zedek is therefore forced to look south for help in opposing the invaders, and he enlists the support of kings who rule four power-

---

[20] The previous episode with the Gibeonites has the rhetorical effect of enhancing Joshua's prestige as well. Parallels with other Ancient Near Eastern documents reveals that such stories (of foreign peoples hearing of the king's deeds and offering themselves as vassals) were utilized to glorify the king's power and beneficence. For more, see L. Younger, *Ancient Conquest Accounts: A Study in Ancient Near Eastern and Biblical History Writing*, JSOTSup 98 (Sheffield: Sheffield Academic Press, 1990) 200–4.

The report that Joshua did "to Ai and its king as he had done to Jericho and its king" also underscores Joshua's obedience to YHWH by confirming the fulfillment of YHWH's commandment concerning the city (v. 8:2).

[21] The kings have been acquiring increasing visibility as the narrative develops. The king of Jericho plays a bit part in Rahab's story (2:2-3) and the ensuing battle (6:2), while the king of Ai plays a more prominent, though still marginal role, in the next campaign (8:14, 23, 29). The summaries of the kings' conduct (5:1; 9:1; 10:1) discloses a gradual strengthening of Canaanite resolve against the invaders, from outright discouragement (5:1) to a decision to wage war (9:1) and now to the formation of a coalition, followed by an attack on Israel's new vassal (10:1).

ful and strategically important cities. The narrator conveys the urgency of his situation through a succinct message which begins in the imperative mode before shifting to the indicative, "Come up and help me, and let us attack Gibeon; for it has made peace with Joshua and with the Israelites" (v. 4). A response returns from the kings, whose Canaanite plurality is highlighted by the listing of their names as well as their cities. The names of the kings themselves manifest the heterogeneity of Canaan; the names Hoham and Piram are particularly exotic.[22] Significantly, they do not direct their hostility against Israel but against a city inhabited by other peoples of the land. Assembled together, they represent an imposing enemy indeed. The kings' massive display of force injects a new level of suspense into the narrative. It is one thing to battle one king. But how will Joshua fare against five?

Hail, Sun and Moon: 10:6-15

Despite the armies encamped around them, the Gibeonites are able to get a message out to Joshua. Again they refer to themselves as "your servants," but this time the epithet implies the obligation that Joshua owes them as their overlord. The heart of their plea echoes Adonizedek's message to the kings, indicating that although they have joined themselves to Israel, they still speak the language of Canaan, "come up to us quickly, save us, and help us; for all the kings of the Amorites who live in the hill country are gathered against us" (v. 6; cf. v. 4). The Gibeonites' message, however, differs in a small but important way from Adoni-zedek's. Adoni-zedek sought kings to join him in an attack against Gibeon. But the Gibeonites pointedly look to Joshua to save them once again from their enemies. They use the language of hyperbole to convey the dire situation they face. From their perspective, it must indeed look as if all the kings of the land are arrayed against them!

Joshua responds immediately, leaving the Israelite base camp at Gilgal with his "mighty warriors," who now march to rescue the "warriors" of Gibeon. The narrator relates the ensuing battle with remarkable brevity when compared to the accounts of the victories at Jericho and Ai. The report begins with YHWH's assurance that he has given Israel's enemies into their hands, although the opponents now are the Amorite kings rather than Canaanite cities (cf. 6:2; 8:1). For good

---

[22] For additional information on the names, see R. Hess, "Non-Israelite Personal Names in the Narratives of the Book of Joshua," *CBQ* 58 (1998) 205–14.

measure, YHWH punctuates this assurance by repeating the declaration, made at the beginning of the book, that no one will be able to stand against Joshua (v. 8; cf. 1:5a). During the battle itself, however, YHWH and Joshua virtually reverse roles. YHWH fights and pursues the enemies, while Joshua stops the sun and moon in their courses in order to allow both YHWH and the Israelites to complete the annihilation of the opposing forces. In this manner, the narrator creates the strong impression that the two work closely together to accomplish the victory. Tactically, Joshua initiates a surprise attack after a forced march during the night (v. 9), but it is YHWH who throws panic into the camps of the enemies (v. 10). The specific nature of YHWH's involvement evokes parallels with the miraculous deliverance of Israel from the Egyptians at the Red Sea (Exod 14:24-25). The same verb *(yĕhummēm)* denotes YHWH's actions in both cases, with similar results. The Egyptians flee because they recognize that YHWH is fighting for Israel against Egypt.[23]

YHWH so thoroughly shocks the Canaanite troops that no military engagement actually takes place. The narrator elaborates only the pursuit and mopping up operations. Although NRSV implies that *Israel* pursued the routed troops, the sense of the MT is less certain. The grammatical structure of v. 10 gives the impression that YHWH, rather than Israel, is the active party, "YHWH threw them into panic before Israel, and he struck them with a mighty blow at Gibeon and pursued them on the way of the ascent of Beth-horon, and he struck them down as far as Azekah and Makkedah" (AT). The narrative then goes on to specify the manner of YHWH's attack. As the terrified troops descend the slope of Beth-horon YHWH rains huge stones upon them, killing more with the stones than the Israelites do with their swords (v. 11).[24] Understood in this fashion, the narrative's rendering of the pursuit of the fleeing Canaanites minimizes Israel's part in the battle by describing YHWH as attacker and pursuer and magnifying the casualties YHWH inflicts over those inflicted by Israel.

Joshua, too, is exalted during the battle. Here again the NRSV alters the syntax of the MT, which begins with a declaration that Joshua "spoke" *(yĕdabbēr)* to YHWH: "then Joshua spoke to YHWH on the day YHWH gave the Amorites over to the Israelites" (v. 12a, AT). The choice of

---

[23] The term signifies the confusion which YHWH unleashes on enemies of Israel (Judg 4:15; 1 Sam 7:10) and here represents the graphic fulfillment of YHWH's promise (Exod 23:27; Deut 7:23). It also occurs in Assyrian and Hittite conquest accounts, where the agent is conventionally a king rather than a deity. See Younger, *Ancient Conquest Accounts,* 73–4, 133–4.

[24] The "great" stones *(ʾăbānîm gĕdōlōt)* forge a semantic link with the "great slaughter" *(makkâ-gĕdōlâ),* strengthening the impression that the subject of v. 10 is YHWH.

terms for Joshua's address is striking. While very common, the verb used here *(yĕdabbēr)* is generally employed in Deuteronomy and Joshua to designate an authoritative pronouncement (Deut 1:1; 5:4; 20:2; Josh 1:3; 4:8; 9:21; 11:23), in the majority of instances with either YHWH or Moses as the speaker. Nowhere in these books, except for this one instance, is it employed to signify an individual's address to YHWH. Adding to the arresting use of the verb is the fact that the text does not disclose what Joshua said to YHWH. Instead, the narrative shifts abruptly to what Joshua said to the sun and moon "in the sight of Israel," before lapsing immediately from prose to poetry (vv. 12b-13a):

> "Sun, stand still at Gibeon
> and Moon, in the valley of Aijalon."
> And the sun stood still, and the moon stopped,
> until the nation took vengeance on their enemies.

The sense of Joshua's command is difficult to determine. Many proposals have been advanced to explain the reference to the sun standing still: the day was actually prolonged, Joshua was seeking a good omen for battle, a solar eclipse occurred which confounded the Canaanites, the sun and moon were perhaps patron deities whose powers were checked, the astral bodies are called upon to stand in shocked amazement at YHWH's great power.[25] None, however, can sufficiently define the event, and perhaps that is what the narrator intends. There is surprisingly little narrative buildup for such a cataclysmic event, apart from a few clipped phrases with jarring shifts of focus. The event happens suddenly, and the befuddlement created by the terse telling of the event reproduces something of the incomprehensibility of the event. Nowhere else in the book does the narrator describe an event through poetry, and this, along with the absence of any further elaboration, preserves its marvel and mystery, leaving the details to the reader's imagination.

The narrator is not so much concerned with exactly what happened as it is with what it means. And that is astounding enough. Joshua commands the sun and moon to assist Israel as it slaughters its enemies, and that is just what happens. (The second half of the poem comprises the voice of "Jashar" and thus weds event to testimony.) The narrator emphasizes the obedience of the sun and moon with the extraordinary method of supplying an in-text citation of a source for additional information (v. 13b), before endorsing the veracity of the poem through a

---

[25] A thorough discussion of these proposals can be found in D. M. Howard, Jr., *Joshua*, NAB (Nashville: Broadman & Holman, 1998) 238–49. See also Nelson, *Joshua*, 141–5 and Hess, *Joshua*, 196–9.

narrative confirmation of the event (which does not do that much to clarify the details, v. 13c). What is crucially important, from the narrator's perspective, is that the event constitutes a singularity in human history; at this one moment in time, YHWH heeded a human voice. (The Hebrew verb *šāmāʿ* ["heeded"] can also signify obedience.) The narrator's summation of the event thus magnifies Joshua's heroism and prestige, imbuing him with a unique eminence previously reserved only for Moses. In the words of the narrator we read echoes of Deuteronomy's closing assessment of Moses, "never since has there arisen a prophet in Israel like Moses, whom the LORD knew face to face" (Deut 34:10).

The final phrase, "for the LORD fought for Israel," caps the account of the battle by again pointing to the strange reversal of roles; YHWH has been the fighter, Joshua commands the heavenly bodies. The reversal anticipates a fusion of roles that will be developed further in the next section and throughout the remaining accounts of Israel's battles against the kings of Canaan. As of this point, Joshua will gain increasing prominence in the narrative. (Joshua's name appears thirty-six times in 10:28–11:23, compared to fifteen references to the name of YHWH.) YHWH's victories will be presented as Joshua's victories. With the report that Joshua returns to Gilgal, with "all Israel," the narrative signals the effective end of the threat posed by the Canaanite forces as well as the nation's complete obedience to Joshua (v. 15).

Joshua and the Kings: 10:16-27

The narrator introduces the battle at Gibeon as a contest between Joshua and the five kings (10:1-5). The ensuing battle, however, pits YHWH against an anonymous "them" (presumably the Canaanite forces arrayed against the city). After reporting that the Israelites returned to Gilgal (v. 15), the narrator digresses in order to relate the conflict on its original terms, giving considerably more attention to the capture and execution of the kings (vv. 16-18, 22-27) than to the annihilation of their forces (vv. 19-21).

By bringing the contest of peoples down to the level of a contest between leaders, the narrator magnifies the heroic stature of Joshua and demonstrates his authority, zeal, and power. During the episode Joshua's role as Israel's leader merges with YHWH's (who virtually disappears from the narrative).[26] The narrator accomplishes this through a number

---

[26] The only references to YHWH are made by Joshua (v. 19, 25).

of lexical connections with 10:6-15. Joshua now relays the assurance *(ex post facto)* that YHWH has given the enemy forces into Israel's hands (v. 19, cf. 10:8) and exhorts his troops in the same terms that YHWH had once used to encourage him (10:25; cf. 1:6, 9). And Joshua commands that large stones *(ʾăbānîm gĕdōlôt)* be rolled against the mouth of the cave where the kings are hiding, recalling the large stones with which YHWH had pelted their armies (vv. 11, 18). Along with the Israelites he strikes the Canaanites down with "a very great slaughter" *(lĕhakkôtām makkâ gĕdôlâ-mĕʾōd,* v. 20), corresponding to the great slaughter inflicted by YHWH (v. 11). Connections to the stoppage of sun and moon are made less explicitly. Joshua orders his army "not to stand" *(ʾal-taʿămōdû,* NRSV "do not stay," v. 19), in contrast to his command to the sun and moon (v. 12), and not to let the survivors "enter" *(lābôʾ)* their towns, echoing the narrator's statement that the sun did not hurry "to set" *(lābôʾ,* v. 13).[27] In addition, the narrator's remark that the slaughter continued until the Canaanites were "wiped out" *(tummām,* v. 20) alludes to the comment that the sun did not set for a "whole" *(tāmîm)* day (v. 13) and puns on the panic YHWH inflicts on the assembled armies *(yĕhummēm,* v. 10).

On a more abstract level, the episode again illustrates the supremacy of the one (Joshua) against the many ("the five kings," vv. 16, 22, 23) and reinforces the thrust of the stories of Achan and Ai: Canaanite difference must be exposed and destroyed. Like Achan's plunder, the five kings are hidden in the earth and, when discovered, are "excavated" and brought into public view. As they come out of the cave, the narrator stresses their Canaanite plurality: "the five kings . . . the king of Jerusalem, the king of Hebron, the king of Jarmuth, the kings of Lachish, and the king of Eglon" (v. 23). In an act that exemplifies utter supremacy, Joshua summons "all Israel" (v. 24) and instructs his military commanders to place their feet on the necks of the kings. While in this posture, Joshua exhorts them, "Do not be afraid or dismayed; be strong and courageous; for thus the LORD will do to all the enemies against whom you fight" (v. 25). Though directed toward the chieftains of Israel, the militant rhetoric carries a deeper symbolic resonance. The imperatives echo those at the beginning of the book (1:6, 7, 9), where YHWH admonishes Joshua to diligence in the strict execution of the commandments of Moses. The real enemy of Israel is the plurality and heterogeneity that the five kings represent, and neither leaders nor people should be slack in eliminating it.

To illustrate the point, Joshua kills the kings and, in another act of symbolic import, hangs them on five trees. The exposure of the kings'

[27] Hess, *Joshua*, 200.

bodies creates a visual image which links "cursed" (hanging, cf. Deut 21:22-23) with "plural" (the five trees), and associates the defeated kings with the king of Ai (8:29). After sunset, they are cut down and thrown back into their hiding place, which is sealed (and thus rendered inaccessible) by the same "large stones" that entrapped them (v. 27). In this way the kings (symbolically their hidden plurality) are removed from the sphere of Israel's life in the land. The concluding remark, that the stones "remain to this very day," testifies to the lasting success of the operation.

Exposing Kings and Difference

The stories connected with Gibeon combine themes associated with those at Jericho and Ai. The story of the Gibeonites recapitulates the themes of Rahab's story but does so more boldly. Both stories focus on mercy and inclusion and suggest that peoples of the land may indeed join themselves to the people of God, despite the strict demands of Moses. Others may have the same concerns and commitments as Israel, and they may acclaim the same God. If so, the stories intimate, there is room for them in Israel. The battle against the five kings, on the other hand, illustrates how Israel should deal with the threat of Canaanite difference. In this case, the themes involve extermination and exclusion, and the narrative parallels extend to the stories of Achan and Ai. The kings are characterized by plurality, belligerence, and a tendency to "go underground." Like the people of Ai, the kings are brought into the open and slaughtered, illustrating the decisive and uncompromising action required to neutralize the peril they represent to the community. The five kings, like the king at Ai, are "cursed" by hanging and buried under a pile of stones that announces their presence and impotence to one and all, even "to this very day" (8:29; 10:27). Canaanites who "look like" Israelites may thus take their place among the people of God, but those who do not "look like" Israel, whether inside or outside the community, must be eliminated. The stories therefore illustrate both the elasticity of Israel's national boundaries and the critical importance of preserving them intact.

Chapter Nine
CONQUERING CANAANITES
Joshua 10:28–12:24

The stories of Rahab, Achan, and the Gibeonites take place on the individual level and contest notions of identity based on ethnic separation, obedience to the commands of Moses, and possession of territory; peoples of the land survive to live among Israel while Israelites who have entered the land are put to death. The associated battle reports take place on the corporate plane and illustrate the twin themes of YHWH's initiative, power, and faithfulness and Israel's obedient response; YHWH gives kings, cities, and peoples into the hands of the Israelites and brings victory, while the Israelites in turn follow YHWH's commands. By setting these plot lines against each other the narrator creates a series of destabilizing tensions. Israel enjoys life in the land to the extent that it executes divine directives. Yet YHWH continues to fight for Israel, even when the commandments of Moses are broken. The Israelites annihilate the peoples of the land but also permit some to live among them. Israel takes the entire land but allows territory to remain in the possession of indigenous peoples.

Having raised these tensions through this narravite triptych, the narrator now summarizes the remaining campaigns of conquest, with one small but significant modification: Joshua, rather than Israel, gradually becomes the exemplar for the themes of initiative and response. Although Israel fights the battles, the focus is on Joshua. "Joshua and all Israel" win victories at Libnah, Lachish, Gezer, Eglon, Hebron, and Debir (10:29-39), but Israel virtually fades from the picture when the entire campaign is summarized (10:40-42), appearing only at the end as "Joshua and all Israel with him" return to Gilgal (10:43). Here it is Joshua who does all "the LORD God of Israel commanded" (v. 40). The reorientation of the command-obedience-victory pattern to Joshua becomes even more pronounced in the summary of the northern campaign (11:1-15) and the narrator's concluding summary (11:16-23). The command-execution pattern that previously confirmed Israel's obedience now is applied to Joshua (11:6, 9), and the narrator emphatically relocates the theme of obedience to Joshua through repeated comments that he did all that he was commanded to do (11:9, 12, 15, 23; cf. 1:1-9).

The campaigns and summaries are linked by a series of catchwords and repetitions. The first summary, recounting victories in southern Canaan (10:28-43), begins with the report that Joshua took Makkedah, the city near the cave where Joshua executed the five kings (10:28; cf. 10:16-17). It concludes, after the listing of cities taken, with additional connections to the battle at Gibeon, through reports that "the LORD God of Israel fought for Israel" (10:42; cf. 10:14) and "Joshua returned, all Israel with him, to the camp at Gilgal" (10:43; cf. 10:15). Three additional summaries then expand the scope of Israel's victories: the cities of northern Canaan (11:1-15), the whole land of Canaan (11:16-23), and all the lands acquired by Israel, both east and west of the Jordan (12:1-24). The narrator unites the segments thematically by portraying the conquests as Joshua's victories over the kings of the land. Joshua and the kings thus personify the continuing conflict between Israelite integrity and Canaanite plurality. Joshua, the epitome of the Deuteronomic ideal, conquers the entire land and defeats all its kings (10:40; 11:16, 23; 12:7). He is able to do so because YHWH fights for Israel (10:42) and he in turn acts with full obedience to the commandments YHWH gave through Moses (11:15, 21). The succinct listing of one conquest after another accelerates the narrative tempo, creating the sense that Joshua achieves his victories rapidly and without difficulty.

The language of totality configures all the material in this section. The Hebrew particle *kôl* ("all, every, whole") appears forty-five times in the MT, asserting Israelite integrity, comprehensive conquest, and obedience to YHWH and the commands of Moses.[1] It occurs with particular density in connection with Israel's sweeping victories and the nation's extermination of the inhabitants of the land; the Israelites defeat all the kings arrayed against them (10:40, 42; 11:15, 12, 13, 17, 18; 12:24) and

---

[1] The particle signifies the unanimity with which the nation goes into battle (10:29, 31, 34, 38, 43; 11:7), the cities and land taken by Israel (10:37, 39, 40, 41; 11:12, 16, 16, 23; 12:1), and the meticulous and thorough manner with which the cities were destroyed (10:32, 37) and the commandments of Moses implemented (11:15, 23).

slaughter every living thing in the captured cities (10:28, 32, 36, 37, 38, 39; 11:11), leaving nothing alive to draw breath (10:40; 11:11, 14). This tendency to depict the conquest in hyperbolic terms follows ancient Near Eastern conventions for reporting conquests[2] but also affirms that the nation now embodies the holistic vision of Deuteronomy. The narratives and summaries bring closure to Israel's campaign of conquest by confirming the final collapse of Canaanite resistance and the complete obedience of Israel to the God who has given the land.

Excursus: The Framework of Conquest

The battle reports in Joshua are modeled after the Deuteronomic account of the Transjordanian conquests (Deut 2:24–3:11). The structure and vocabulary of the pattern established in Deuteronomy is followed precisely in relating the battles at Ai (8:1-29) and against the coalition of northern kings at the waters of Merom (11:1-15), as well as the summaries of the southern and northern campaigns (10:40-42; 11:16-23). The battle at Jericho (6:1-25) and the list of southern conquests (10:28-39) also make heavy use of elements of the program, although to a lesser extent. By appropriating the structure and language of Deuteronomy's version of the victories over Sihon and Og, the book of Joshua forges a unique connection between Israel's conquests on the east and west sides of the Jordan, rendering a continuity that enables the reader to view the separate operations (under Moses and Joshua, respectively) as components of a single endeavor.

The Deuteronomic version of the campaigns against Sihon and Og recapitulates events presented in Num 21:21-31 but represents a more expansive and stereotyped account. The two versions share many common elements: Sihon and Og initiate the conflict (Num 21:23; Deut 2:23; 3:1), Israel strikes *(nākâ)* the kings so that no survivor remains (Num 21:24, 35; Deut 2:34; 3:3), and YHWH gives an assurance of victory against Og, directing Moses to do to him what he had done to Sihon (Num 21:34; Deut 3:2). Deuteronomy, however, exhibits a number of distinctive features. While Numbers relates the defeats of Sihon and Og in different terms, Deuteronomy harmonizes the two campaigns by the use of a common structure and stereotypical vocabulary. Deuteronomy,

---

[2] This feature is amply demonstrated by L. Younger, *Ancient Conquest Accounts: A Study of Ancient Near Eastern and Biblical History Writing*, (Sheffield: JSOT, 1990) 190–2, 241–9.

for example, utilizes the verb *lākad* ("capture") to denote both conquests, while Numbers uses it along with *lāqaḥ* ("take") to signify the
victory over Sihon but uses neither with reference to Og. Deuteronomy
relates the campaigns in more detail, provides a fuller description of the
number and location of captured cities, and presents the campaigns in
overtly theological terms. YHWH directs Israel to take possession of their
lands (Deut 2:24-25) and hardens Sihon's heart in order to deliver his
kingdom to Israel (Deut 2:30). Israel in turn devotes the populations of
the captured cities to destruction (*wannaḥărēm*, 2:34; 3:6).[3] Finally, while
Numbers reports the immediate possession and settlement of the kingdoms of Sihon and Og (Num 21:31, 35), Deuteronomy intimates that
the possession of the eastern territories was not actually completed
until Israel had settled in Canaan.[4]

Deuteronomy introduces the campaigns with a three-fold command ("arise, break camp, and cross the Arnon"), followed immediately by a divine assurance of victory (2:24b-25):

> See, I have handed over to you King Sihon the Amorite of Heshbon, and
> his land. Begin to take possession by engaging him in battle. This day I
> will begin to put the dread and fear of you upon the peoples everywhere
> under heaven; when they hear report of you, they will tremble and be in
> anguish because of you.[5]

After this pronouncement, Moses sends messengers to Sihon, who refuses to allow Israel passage through his territory. Deuteronomy attributes this response to YHWH, who "had hardened his spirit and made
his heart defiant" in order to hand him over to Moses (Deut 2:30). The
ensuing battles against Sihon and Og then assume a common configuration: a) YHWH declares that he has delivered the king and his land to
Moses; b) the king sallies forth against Israel; c) YHWH delivers the king
to Israel; d) Israel defeats him; e) Israel captures the king's cities; f) the
cities are devoted to destruction and g) are plundered; h) Israel takes
the entire territory of the defeated king.

---

[3] The Numbers account makes no mention of YHWH's involvement in the campaign nor the devotion of the populace to destruction.

[4] The Deuteronomic account concludes with a summary which reviews the extent
of Israel's acquisitions but does not affirm the possession of the lands (Deut 3:8-10).

[5] The designation of Sihon as an "Amorite" distinguishes him from the other nations which inhabit the Transjordan (the Moabites, Ammonites, and Edomites) and
links him with the inhabitants of the promised land (cf. Josh 2:10; 3:10; 5:1; 7:7; 10:5,
etc.).

CHART 6: THE CAMPAIGNS AGAINST SIHON AND OG

Sihon (2:31-36)	*Og (3:1b-7)*
a The LORD said to me, "See, I have begun to give Sihon and his land over to you. Begin now to take possession of his land (2:31)"	b King Og of Bashan came out against us, he and all his people, for battle at Edrei (3:1b).
b So when Sihon came out against us, he and all his people for battle at Jahaz (2:32),	a The LORD said to me, "Do not fear him, for I have handed him over to you, along with his people and his land. Do to him as you did to King Sihon of the Amorites, who reigned in Heshbon" (3:2)
c the LORD our God gave him over to us (2:33a)	c So the LORD our God also handed over to us King Og of Bashan and all his people (3:a).
d and we struck him down *(wannak)*, along with his offspring and all his people (2:33b).	d We struck him down until not a single survivor was left.
e At that time we captured *(wannilkōd)* all his towns (2:34a),	e At that time we captured all his towns (3:4a);
f and in each town we utterly destroyed *(wannaḥărēm)* men, women, and children. We left not a single survivor (2:34b).	h there was no citadel that we did not take from them—sixty towns, the whole region of Argob, the kingdom of Og in Bashan. All these were fortress towns with high walls, double gates, and bars, besides a great many villages (3:4b-5).
g Only the livestock we kept as spoil for ourselves, as well as the plunder of the towns that we had captured (2:35).	f And we utterly destroyed them, as we had done to King Sihon or Heshbon, in each city utterly destroying men, women, and children (3:6).
h From Aroer on the edge of the Wadi Arnon (including the town that is in the wadi itself) as far as Gilead, there was no citadel too high for us. The LORD our God gave everything to us (2:36).	g But all the livestock and the plunder of the towns we kept as spoil for ourselves (3:7).

A summary then integrates the separate reports into one sweeping account of Israel's victory and includes a curious reference to the Rephaim, the gigantic former inhabitants of the area (3:8-11a). As in Joshua, the king serves as a virtual eponym for his people:

> So at that time we took *(wanniqqaḥ)* from the two kings of the Amorites the land beyond the Jordan, from the Wadi Arnon to Mount Hermon (the Sidonians call Hermon Sirion, while the Amorites call it Senir), all the towns of the tableland, the whole of Gilead, and all of Bashan, as far as Salecah and Edrei, towns of Og's kingdom in Bashan. (Now only King Og of Bashan was left of the remnant of the Rephaim.)

The campaigns related in Joshua appropriate the same pattern and language to varying degrees. The action begins in Joshua, as it does in Deuteronomy, with the command to cross a watercourse and a declaration that YHWH has given the land ahead, "Now proceed to cross the Jordan, you and all this people, into the land that I am giving to them, to the Israelites" (Josh 1:2; cf. Deut 2:24). When the text shifts to narration, Joshua sends spies into the land (2:1), recalling the messengers that Moses sent to Sihon (Deut 2:26-29).[6] The ensuing battles against the kings and cities of the land then follow the program of the Transjordanian victories and utilize the same vocabulary. In the case of the battles at Ai and the waters of Merom the program is followed precisely.

CHART 7: THE BATTLE AT AI (JOSH 8:1-29)
Deuteronomic components are marked by italicized script.

A *The* LORD *said to Joshua, "Do not fear* or be dismayed; take all the fighting men with you, and go up now to Ai. *See, I have handed over to you the king of Ai with his people, his city, and his land. You shall do to Ai and its king as you did to Jericho and its king* (8:1-2a, cf. Deut 2:31; 3:2a)."

B When *the king of Ai* saw this, *he and all his people,* the inhabitants of the city, hurried out early in the morning *to the meeting place facing the Arabah to meet Israel in battle* (8:14; cf. Deut 2:32; 3:1b).

C Then the LORD said to Joshua, "Stretch out the sword that is in your hand toward Ai; *for I will give it into your hand*" (8:18; cf. Deut 2:33a; 3:3a).

E They entered the city, *captured it,* and at once set the city on fire (8:19b; cf. Deut 2:34a, 3:4a).

D *Israel struck them down until no one was left who survived* or escaped (8:22b; Deut 2:33b-34; 3:3b).

---

[6] The narrative later refers to the spies as messengers (6:25).

F For Joshua did not draw back his hand, with which he stretched out the sword, *until he had utterly destroyed all the inhabitants of Ai* (8:26; cf. Deut 2:34b; 3:6).

G *Only the livestock and the spoil of that city Israel took as their booty,* according to the word of the LORD that he had issued to Joshua (8:27; cf. Deut 2:35; 3:7).

CHART 8: THE BATTLE AT THE WATERS OF MEROM (11:1-15)
Deuteronomic components are marked by italicized script.

B *They came out, with all their troops,* a great army, in number like the sand on the seashore, with very many horses and chariots (11:4).

A *And the LORD said to Joshua, "Do not be afraid of them, for tomorrow at this time I will hand over all of them, slain, to Israel (11:6a)."*

C *And the LORD handed them over to Israel (11:8a).*

D *They struck them down, until they had left no one remaining (11:8c).*

E *Joshua* turned back *at that time, and took (wayyilkōd)* Hazor and *struck its king down* with the sword (11:10a).

F *And they put (wayyakkû)* to the sword *all who were in it, utterly destroying them;* there was no one left who breathed, and he burned Hazor with fire (11:11b).[7]

E *And all the towns of those kings,* and all their kings, *Joshua took (lākad,* 11:12a),

D *and struck them* with the edge of the sword (11:12b),

F *utterly destroying them, as Moses the servant of the LORD had commanded (11:12c).*

G *All the spoil of these towns, and the livestock, the Israelites took for booty* (11:14);

D *but all the people they struck down* with the edge of the sword, until they had destroyed them, and they did not leave any who breathed (11:14b).

Although the battles differ significantly (and the battle at Ai is elaborated with striking detail), an overview of each reveals that the

---

[7] The reference to "everything that breathed" *(kôl něšāmâ)* substitutes for the programmatic "no one was left who survived." The substitution picks up the language of Deut 20:16, which stipulates the extermination of those in captured Canaanite cities and reinforces the account's assertion that Joshua carried out the campaign in complete obedience to the commands of Moses (v. 15).

Deuteronomic pattern provides the overall framework for the presentation of the battle.[8]

The battle at Jericho and the list of battles against the cities of the south also adhere closely to the Deuteronomic paradigm, although they do not manifest the same degree of dependence. In the case of Jericho (6:1-25), certain features of the battle cannot be appropriated into the paradigm. The people of Jericho do not leave their city to attack Israel (b), and the verb *nakkâ* ("strike") is not used to signify Israel's assault against the city (d). The rest of the program, however, follows the common pattern: YHWH promises victory by delivering the city, along with its king and people Joshua's hands (a, v. 2), Joshua declares that the city has been delivered to Israel (c, v. 16), Israel captures the city (e, v. 20c) and devotes the populace to destruction (f, v. 21), and the people burn the livestock and plunder rather than taking it (in response to Joshua's command, g, v. 21; cf. vv. 17-19).

The account of battles against cities in the south comprises little more than a listing of victories, followed by a summary which expands the scope of Joshua's conquests to encompass the entire southern region. The list maintains a fixed form that resists an attempt to harmonize it too closely to the Deuteronomic scheme. Yet, although the structure shows a good deal of variation from city to city, the configuring influence of Deuteronomy is still discernible.

CHART 9: THE SOUTHERN CAMPAIGN (10:28-39)
Deuteronomic components are marked by italicized script.

MAKKEDAH (10:28)

E *Joshua took (lākad) Makkedah* on that day,

D *and struck it and its king* with the edge of the sword;

F *he utterly destroyed every person in it; he left no one remaining.*

A *And he did to the king of Makkedah as he had done to the king of Jericho.*[9]

LIBNAH (10:29-30)

B Then Joshua passed on from Makkedah, and all Israel with him, to Libnah, and fought against Libnah.[10]

---

[8] See also N. Lohfink, "Geschichtstypologisch Orientierte Textstrukturen in den Büchern Deuteronomium und Josua," *Deuteronomy and Deuteronomic Literature: Festschrift C. W. Brekelmans*, eds. M. Vervenne and J. Lust (Leuven: Leuven University, 1997) 133–60.

[9] In Deuteronomy, this occurs as a command from YHWH to Moses, with reference to Og (Deut 3:2b).

[10] While Sihon and Og are depicted as the aggressors in Deuteronomy, Joshua and Israel initiate the attacks against the southern cities.

C *The* LORD *gave it also and its kings into the hand of Israel;*

D *and he struck it* with the edge of the sword, and everyone in it; *he left no one remaining in it;*

A *and he did to its king as he had done to the king of Jericho.*

LACHISH (10:31-32)

B Then Joshua passed on from Libnah, and all Israel with him, to Lachish, and laid siege to it and *attacked it (wayyillāḥēm bāh).*

C *The* LORD *gave Israel into the hand of Israel*

E *and he took it (wayyilkĕdāh)* on the second day,

D *and he struck it* with the edge of the sword, and every person in it

A *as he had done to Libnah.*

GEZER (10:33)

B Then King Horam of Gezer came up to help Lachish;

D *and Joshua struck him and his people, leaving him no survivors.*

EGLON (10:34-35)

B From Lachish Joshua passed on with all Israel to Eglon; and they laid siege to it, *and they assaulted it (wayyillāḥămû ʿāleyhā);*

E *and they took it (wayyilkĕdāh)* that day,

D *and struck it* with the edge of the sword,

F *and every person in it he utterly destroyed that day,*

A *as he had done to Lachish.*

HEBRON (10:36-37)

B Then Joshua went up with all Israel from Eglon to Hebron; *they assaulted it*

E *and took it,*

D *and struck it* with the edge of the sword, *and its king and its towns, and every person in it; he left no one remaining,*

A *just as he had done to Eglon,*

F *and utterly destroyed it with every person in it.*

DEBIR (10:38-39)

B Then Joshua, with all Israel, turned back to Debir *and assaulted it*

E *and he took it with its king and all its towns;*

D *they struck them* with the edge of the sword,

F *and utterly destroyed every person in it; he left no one remaining;*

A *just as he had done to Hebron, and, as he had done to Libnah and its king, so he did to Debir and its king*

In Deuteronomy, reports of specific campaigns over enemy kings include summaries which expand the scope of territorial conquests (h) in

hyperbolic and comprehensive terms. Similar summaries follow the catalogue of victories in the south (10:40-42) and the victory over the coalition of northern kings (11:12-15). The former concentrates on the extent
of territory taken, while the latter places emphasis on the towns of the
kings which Israel defeated (cf. Deut 2:36; 3:4-5). Both make heavy use of
Deuteronomic vocabulary and phrases, rendering a continuity between
the battles waged in Canaan and those waged in the Transjordan:

> *So Joshua defeated (wayyakkeh) the whole land,* the hill country and the
> Negeb and the lowland and the slopes, *and all their kings; he left no one re-*
> *maining, but utterly destroyed all* that breathed, as the LORD God of Israel
> commanded. *And Joshua defeated them* from Kadesh-barnea to Gaza, and
> all the country of Goshen, as far as Gibeon. *Joshua took all these kings and*
> *their land* at one time, because the LORD God of Israel fought for Israel
> (10:40-42).

> *And all the towns of those kings, and all their kings, Joshua struck* with the
> edge of the sword, *utterly destroying them,* as Moses the servant of the
> LORD commanded. But Israel burned none of the towns that stood on
> mounds except Hazor, which Joshua did burn. *All the spoil of these towns,*
> *and the livestock, the Israelites took for their booty; but all the people they struck*
> *down* with the edge of the sword, until they had destroyed them, *and they*
> *did not leave* any who breathed (11:12-14).

The stories of conquest in Joshua conclude with an additional summary that elaborates the full measure of Joshua's victories throughout
the land (11:16-23). Like the corresponding summary in Deuteronomy
(3:8-11), this one comprises two parts. The first (vv. 16-20) gives a detailed geographical survey of the land which Joshua "took" (*lāqaḥ,* v.
16; cf. Deut 3:8) and parallels the survey of Og's land. But the narrator
goes beyond the Deuteronomic prototype to emphasize Joshua's thorough execution of Moses' command to deny mercy to the land's inhabitants and to report that YHWH hardened the hearts of the kings in
order to devote them to destruction. The latter comment, coming at the
end of Israel's conquests in Canaan, reiterates the claim made by Deuteronomy at the beginning of the battles against Sihon and Og. Taken
with the Deuteronomic text, the declaration that YHWH hardened the
kings against Israel thus forms an *inclusio* around the entire program
of conquest, reinforcing the sense that YHWH is at work throughout to
accomplish the fulfillment of the promise to bring Israel into the land.

The second part of the summary reports that Joshua drove out the
Anakim from the hill country of Judah, so that none remained except
in Gaza, Gath, and Ashdod (11:21-22). The Anakim represent the western counterparts of the Rephaim, of whom King Og is said to be the
last (Deut 3:11). By concluding the campaigns with footnotes regarding

the gigantic former inhabitants of the conquered territories, the narrators of the respective books are able to communicate the impressive grandeur of Israel's accomplishments and to affirm that the victories left the nation without rival in the land.

Deuteronomy thus provides the narrator of Joshua with a paradigm by which to render Israel's conquest of Canaan. Following this program, the conquest begins when Israel crosses a prominent geographical boundary. The battles for Canaan portray the kings as the enemies of Israel and utilize stereotypical language to report their defeat and the annihilation of their subjects. Summaries then elaborate the scope of campaigns in the various regions (south and north), as well as the entire program of conquest. The language and structure of Deuteronomy unites the conquests east and west of the Jordan, creating a sense of continuity between the victories won under Moses and Joshua.

Going South: 10:28-43

The campaign against the cities of southern Canaan is rendered in an annalistic style reminiscent of other ancient Near Eastern literatures.[11] By use of this form, as opposed to the narrative style of the previous accounts, the narrator elevates Israel's status by linking it with the great powers of the ancient world; Israel too is a mighty nation with an impressive catalogue of victories. The terse account also intimates that victories against all the cities of the Canaanites were achieved with the same rapidity and ease that characterize the battles at Jericho, Ai, and Gibeon.

Although individual entries display variation, structural features unite vv. 28-39 into a tight unit. The list comprises seven entries, the first of which (v. 28) is a transitional piece which connects the victories in the previous section (through the reference to Makkedah, cf. 10:16) to those in the following list (through the reference to Jericho, cf. 10:30c). Notes about kings occur at the beginning (v. 30), middle (v. 33), and end (vv. 38-39) of the remaining list, with the last report explicitly creating a sense of closure by correlating Debir (the sixth) with Libnah (the second).[12] The list creates a sense of movement by connecting the

---

[11] R. Hess, *Joshua*, TOTC (Downers Grove: InterVarsity, 1996) 202–205.

[12] The remark that "he did to its king as he had done to the king of Jericho" (v. 30, cf. v. 28) is obscure. While the narrative gives detailed information of what Joshua "did" to the king of Ai, it provides no direct confirmation of what Joshua "did" to the king of Jericho.

individual entries by reports that "Joshua" and "all Israel" went from city to city. In each case, the entries employ the verb *nākâ* ("strike") to denote Israel's victory, supplementing it with the phrase "with the edge of the sword" in all cases except that of Gezer (where the object of "striking" is not a city but a king). In geographical terms, the campaign involves cities within the general vicinity of Makkedah, traveling from northwest to southwest, then around to the east.[13]

Beyond these features, the list displays a variation in vocabulary and content that stresses the distinctiveness of each victory. Different phrases denote the slaughter of the peoples. Joshua "left no one remaining" (vv. 28, 29, 37, 39) of the cities of Makkedah, Libnah, Hebron, and Debir and of King Horam's forces (v. 33, echoing the victory at Ai, 8:22), but the same is not affirmed with regard to Lachish and Eglon; the inhabitants of Lachish, in fact, are not said to be devoted to destruction *(heḥĕrîm)* as is the case with all other cities.[14] Different operations as well are suggested by the report that Israel "laid siege to" Lachish and Eglon, and Horam's city (Gezer) is not listed as captured even though the decimation of his army is reported (v. 33).

The summary (vv. 40-43) depicts the campaign in holistic terms and attributes the swiftness of the victories to the fact that "the LORD the God of Israel fought for Israel." In addition, the narrator presents the massacre of indigenous populations as an act of obedience to the commandments of Moses, with particular reference (through the phrase "all that breathed") to Deut 20:16. A geographical description of the land reinforces the impressive catalogue of victories by delineating the scope of Israelite hegemony. Yet at the same time, the references to Gibeon and Gaza undercut the sense of totality which the survey ostensibly makes; Gibeon of course now enjoys a protected status, while Israelite power stops at Gaza, which lies within the area later allotted to Israel (15:47).

Heading North: 11:1-15

With the central and southern regions firmly in the hands of the Israelites, the action turns to the north. As he did at Gibeon, Joshua encounters the combined might of several Canaanite kings. The account of the

---

[13] R. Nelson, *Joshua*, OTL (Louisville: Westminster John Knox, 1997) 146-8. See also K. L. Younger, "The 'Conquest' of the South (Jos 10, 28-30)," *BZ* 39 (1995) 255-64.

[14] The Hebrew verb here is the same translated "devoted to destruction" in 6:21 and "utterly destroyed" in 8:26.

campaign falls into three sections: a description of the kings and their forces (vv. 1-5), a report of Israel's victory at the waters of Merom (vv. 6-9), and the capture of Hazor and other cities in the region (vv. 10-15).

The opening formula *wayĕhî kišmōa* ("now when [he] heard") introduces the action of the Canaanite kings for a fourth and final time (cf. 5:1; 9:1; 10:1) and precedes a report that combines elements of the other instances. As in 10:1 one of the kings of the land responds to "hearing" by "sending" to other kings in the region and is identified along with his city (Jabin king of Hazor), as are other kings and their cities (although only one other king is named [Jobab]). This time, however, the list trails off after naming four of the participating cities and concludes by referring to an undetermined and unidentified group of confederates, who (in the manner of 9:1) are associated with various areas of the land. The description of the regions creates a bit of geographical confusion, for some of the terms employed in the MT ("the Arabah," "Negeb" [NRSV "south"], "the Shephelah" [NRSV "the lowland"]) conventionally refer to areas in the south of Canaan.[15] Thus, while the action appears to be localized in the north, it suggests a conflict of much greater magnitude, against innumerable kings from all over the land. The plurality of kings, cities, and geographical areas is further amplified by another listing of the diverse peoples of the land, this time with notes that connect them to the various regions of Canaan, "to the Canaanites in the east and the west, the Amorites, the Hittites, the Perizzites, and the Jebusites in the hill country, and the Hivites under Hermon in the land of Mizpah" (v. 3). The structure of the report thus suggests a growing and massive concentration of force: from two kings to four cities to many regions to all the peoples of the land. The subtle hyperbole of the report is then capped by more overt exaggeration, "They came out, with all their troops, a great army, in number like the sand on the seashore, with very many horses and chariots" (v. 4). The awesome power of the kings receives emphasis in the MT through a three-fold repetition of the root *rb* ("many"), while the reference to the armies "like the sand on the seashore" completes the picture of an overwhelming force arrayed against Joshua and Israel. The use of hyperbole not only heightens the suspense but also presents the coming conflict in climactic terms, as though all the kings and peoples of the land are gathering for a final attack against Israel.

The report of the battle at the waters of Merom follows a roughly chiastic structure which connects YHWH's initiative and Joshua's obedience to YHWH:[16]

---

[15] Nelson, *Joshua*, 152. The terms, however, effect a stylistic link between this summary and those that follow (11:16; 12:8).

[16] The site of the battle cannot presently be identified with confidence.

A And the LORD said to Joshua, "Do not be afraid of them, for tomorrow at this time I will hand over all of them, slain, to Israel; you shall hamstring their horses, and burn their chariots with fire (v. 6).

B So Joshua came suddenly upon them with all his fighting force, by the waters of Merom, and fell upon them (v. 7).

C And the LORD handed them over to Israel (v. 8a),

B' who attacked them and chased them as far as greater Sidon and Misrephoth-maim, and eastward as far as the valley of Mizpeh. They struck them down, until they had left no one remaining (v. 8b-c).

A' And Joshua did to them as the LORD commanded him; he hamstrung their horses, and burned their chariots with fire (v. 9).

The beginning and ending segments follow the command-execution format that signifies Israel's and Joshua's obedience throughout the book. YHWH commands Joshua to hamstring the horses and burn the chariots (v. 6) and the narrator reports that he did so (v. 9). The narrator's comment that "Joshua did to them as the LORD commanded him" (v. 9) answers YHWH's exhortation at the beginning (v. 6), linking divine initiative with human response in a more implicit fashion. The second and fourth segments report Joshua's surprise attack (following the tactics of 10:9) and the subsequent rout of the kings (vv. 7, 8b-c). At the center stands the declaration that "the LORD handed them over to Israel" (v. 8a), attributing the victory, via its centrality, to YHWH's (unspecified) participation.

The reader may be surprised that so little information is provided about such a decisive victory, the greatest yet given the sheer numbers arrayed against Israel. A detailed account of the battle, however, would not fit the rhetorical purposes of the narrator, who has elaborated previous campaigns in light of Israel's need to establish its own internal boundaries. The narrator has crafted the accounts of previous campaigns (at Jericho, Ai, and Gibeon) into a symmetrical reflection on the contours of Israelite identity. With this purpose in mind, the narrator has been more concerned to convey the *meaning* of the battles than to relate the details of *what happened*. Within the narrator's program, the battles become object lessons for the reader and illustrate a powerful message: YHWH's initiative joined with faithful obedience brings victory over Canaanite power. The episodes at Jericho, Ai, and Gibeon are carefully constructed to establish this point, and once established the details of additional battles are superfluous. It is enough now to sketch the battle and reiterate the basic theme: YHWH promised victory and brought about what he had promised, and Israel realized this victory through obedience to YHWH's commands.[17]

The final section (vv. 10-15) summarizes the capture and destruction of Hazor as well as the "towns of those kings." The summary relates the capture of Hazor first and then establishes a sense of continuity by using the same terms to describe the conquest of other cities in the north. Joshua "took" Hazor and the other cities (vv. 10a, 12a), whose kings and inhabitants were "struck with the edge of the sword" (vv. 10a, 11a, 12a, 14a). The inhabitants of Hazor and the other cities were "utterly destroyed" (*haḥărēm*, v. 11b; *heḥĕrîm* 12b), so that "no one who breathed" survived (vv. 11b, 14c). The subject of the action shifts fluidly between Joshua and Israel, reinforcing the unanimity of leader and people: Joshua (v. 10a), Israel (v. 11a), Joshua (v. 11c), Israel (v. 13a), Joshua (v. 13b), Israel (v. 14), Joshua (v. 15).

Hazor is singled out for special emphasis. Since "Hazor was the head of all those kingdoms" (v. 10), its destruction signifies the demolition of the massive threat exemplified by the chariotry and vast numbers of the enemy force and, ultimately, of Canaanite power within the land. Their defeat is intimated in the previous section by the route taken by the fleeing troops of the kings (v. 8), who are chased up to the border points that will mark the farthest extensions of Israelite settlement.[18] The burning of Hazor (v. 11), the most prominent of the cities of northern Canaan, now confirms the dominance of Israel in the land, and the narrator keeps the image of the incinerated city before the reader by drawing explicit attention to it while reporting the capture of other cities (v. 13).

The special attention given to Hazor contrasts with the indeterminate nature of the rest of the summary. Israel's conquest of southern cities is recounted in meticulous and formulaic detail, thus providing specific confirmation of the narrator's claim that "Joshua took all these kings and their land at one time" (10:42). However, in the corresponding campaign for the north, the narrator reports the conquest of no cities other than Hazor, leaving the reader to wonder just what towns and kings are being referred to (11:12). The indefinite report of northern conquests, in contrast to the specificity of those in the south, anticipates another contrast which will arise during the description of tribal territories. There as well the southern region (represented by

---

[17] The narrator emphasizes Israel's obedience by noting that "they left no one remaining" and Joshua's obedience by reporting his precise execution of divine commands.

[18] Great Sidon constitutes the outer limit of the territory later apportioned to Asher (19:29). Misrephoth-maim also marks the boundary of Sidon (13:6). And the valley of Mizpeh probably denotes a northern point close to Mt. Hermon. Nelson, *Joshua* 153–54.

Judah and Benjamin) is described in expansive detail (15:1-12, 20-61), while the corresponding territories of the northern tribes are characterized by vague descriptions of cities and boundaries, as well as notes of large areas not possessed (19:10-39).

The summary (vv. 12-15) also echoes the tensions raised by the first three campaigns in Canaan. Reports of exceptions undercut the unambiguous reports of total victory that surround them. We are told that Joshua struck all the towns and their kings with the edge of the sword, subjecting them to the *ḥērem* (v. 12). However, we are then informed that the Israelites took all the spoil and livestock from those cities for themselves. This creates confusion, for Joshua previously declared the city of Jericho (and everything in it) to be *ḥērem* (6:17), and Achan's trouble occurred precisely because he took some of the spoil for himself. The Israelites were subsequently allowed to take spoil and livestock from Ai, but in that case only the population, and not the city and its contents, were declared *ḥērem* (8:26-27). In other words, the Israelites did not violate the *ḥērem* by keeping livestock and plunder from Ai, because it was extended only to the populace. In the case of the cities of the north, just *what* was the *ḥērem* applied to? If only to the people (against the plain sense of the text), then the Israelites acted obediently. If to the cities themselves, then the Israelites did not.

As if to accentuate by contrast the problematic nature of the excepting comments the narrator concludes the overview of Israel's northern conquests with a concise but emphatic declaration that returns to the beginning themes of the book, "As the LORD had commanded his servant Moses, so Moses commanded Joshua, and so Joshua did; he left nothing undone of all the LORD had commanded Moses (v. 15)." Once again the hierarchy of command is articulated, and once again Moses, rather than Joshua, is the dominant figure. YHWH communicates his will through "his servant" Moses, Moses conveys the divine will to Joshua, and Joshua carries out YHWH's commands to Moses. This commentary, following immediately on the narrator's confirmation that Israel has carried out the commandments to exterminate the peoples of Canaan, represents the most emphatic statement thus far of the vital link between divine initiative and human obedience. Joshua has achieved victory after victory because he has been careful to do all that YHWH had commanded Moses.

Joshua's Conquests: 11:16-23

The narrator utilizes summaries to reinforce themes that configure the stories of Israel's conquests. In general, these accentuate YHWH's role in Israel's victories and magnify Joshua's military exploits. An overview of the southern campaign asserts that Joshua achieved his victories because YHWH fought for Israel (10:42), while the corresponding review of northern conquests emphasizes Joshua's attention to the commands of Moses (11:15). The present summary combines these two emphases and associates them with a comprehensive geographical survey of the land now controlled by Israel. All three summaries present Joshua's victories in dual terms, as a defeat of kings and an acquisition of their territories (10:42; 11:12; 11:17). This more generalized summary picks up the geographical language of the southern summary (v. 16, cf. 10:40) and supplements it with a description of territory acquired in the north (v. 17).[19]

The summary is divided into two sections (vv. 16-20, 21-23) and enclosed by the declaration that "Joshua took the whole land" (vv. 16a, 23a).[20] Each section begins and ends with a description of conquered territory and reiterates in forceful terms the extermination of the land's inhabitants. At the heart of each, however, the narrator points to exceptions which reveal the incompleteness of the conquests. In the first case, a series of statements qualifies the sense of rapid and total victory. While prior summaries have given the impression that Joshua achieved victories swiftly and easily (e.g. "Joshua took all these kings and their land at one time," 10:42), the narrator now remarks that Joshua in fact waged war against the kings for a long time (11:18). Between this comment and a confirmation that "all were taken in battle," the narrator inserts a qualifying remark which counters a comprehensive claim ("there was not a town that made peace (*hišlîmâ*) with the Israelites") with a conspicuous exception ("except the Hivites, the inhabitants of Gibeon," v. 19a). Together, the statements sensitize the reader to the rhetorical character of the language of totality and raise again the larger issues of inclusion and exclusion from the Israelite community and the land. They are followed by a third comment which declares that YHWH hardened (the kings') hearts so that they would engage Israel in battle. Gibeonites exempted by Israel are thus contrasted with kings destroyed by YHWH, reminding the reader of the Gibeonites' dissimilarity with the other peoples of the land; they do not have

[19] References to the hill country, the Negeb, and the Shephelah occur in the comprehensive and southern summaries, as well as the description of territory possessed by the kings of the north (11:2). In addition, the comprehensive summary includes the seemingly out-of-place references to the Arabah (in the north, 11:2) and Goshen (in the south, 10:41).

[20] Although the NRSV shows a slight variation between the declarations, the language of the MT is identical.

a king for YHWH to harden and thus do not represent the aggressive
threat of Canaanite difference that the kings symbolize.[21] They remain
in the land, among the Israelites, and YHWH seems to have approved
the arrangement by not injecting them with the same belligerence. The
structure thus suggests that YHWH does not oppose the peoples of the
land *per se* but rather the aggressive power of Canaanite difference
which the kings represent.

The second section reports the eradication of the Anakim from the
highlands of Canaan but their survival in the coastal areas of Gaza,
Gath, and Ashdod. As in the previous section, a conspicuous exception
follows a strong affirmation of the total victory. We are informed that
Joshua wiped out the Anakim who lived in "all the hill country of Judah"
and "all the hill country of Israel," with the result that none remained
in the territory now controlled by Israel. Yet the narrator goes on to report that Anakim remain outside the realm of Israelite hegemony. The
first statement conveys a sense of closure by affirming that all of the
Anakim were removed from Israel's land.[22] But the second intimates
that the overall program has not yet been achieved. The coastal plain
of Canaan is part of the land promised to Israel (Num 34:1-12; Josh 1:4)
and is marked as such by the listing of Ashdod and Gaza among the
cities allotted to the tribe of Judah. The comments thus confirm that Israel has succeeded in obliterating indigenous peoples from the land
but also caution against viewing this operation as the end of the program. Israel may have taken "the whole land," but what *is* the whole
land? Does it include Gaza, Gath, and Ashdod?

By confirming the defeat of kings and the extermination of the
Anakim, the symbols of Canaanite power, the narrator attests to Israel's superiority in the land. The indigenous peoples no longer enjoy

[21] L. G. Stone comes near the point when he argues that the kings are destroyed
because their attacks on Israel represent rebellion against YHWH's will; "Ethical and
Apologetic Tendencies in the Redaction of the Book of Joshua," *CBQ* 53 (1991) 25–36.

One wonders why YHWH must precipitate battles by stirring up the kings of the
land. Has Israel lost some of its resolve?

[22] In Deuteronomy, the Anakim symbolize the formidable might of the peoples
of the land. They are noted for their great stature (Deut 2:10; 9:2) and are associated
with the Rephaim of the Transjordan (Deut 2:11). Deuteronomy 9:1-3 renders them
as an amalgamation of the Canaanite cities ("great cities, fortified to the heavens"),
peoples ("nations greater and mightier than you," "a strong and tall people"), and
military invincibility. ("Who can stand up to the Anakim?") Their obliteration constitutes an indirect confirmation of YHWH's participation in the conquest and a fulfillment of Moses' declaration that YHWH "will defeat them and subdue them
before you" (Deut 9:3b).

dominion over Canaan. This is perhaps the import of the concluding comment, that "the land had rest from war." The remark suggests the end of the period of conquest but, in view of the incomplete status of the program to take the land, also introduces a note of uncertainty. Why does the land have rest from war when the peoples of the land still occupy much of the territory promised to Israel?

Conquered Kings: 12:1-24

A final set of summaries effects a transition from the program of conquest to the allotment of tribal territories. Joshua's conquests are here set within the entire compass of Israel's territorial acquisitions by joining them to a summary of Moses' conquests in the Transjordan. Connections extend back through references to the defeat of kings and the close correspondence between the summary in vv. 7-8 and that of 11:16-17. Others, however, extend forward through detailed descriptions of the eastern acquisitions (which anticipate the descriptions of tribal allotments) and the report that Joshua gave the land to the tribes as a "possession" (*yĕruššâ*, v. 7). "Possession" of the land, signified more commonly by the verb *yāraš*, signifies the end toward which the story moves (Josh 3:11) and the completion of Deuteronomy's program for Israel (Deut 11:31; 12:29; 16:20; 17:14; 19:1; 26:1). It represents a second stage in the process, which is made possible only when the dominion of the Canaanites is broken. The transition between the operations of victory and possession is anticipated by the opening remark about the acquisition of the eastern territory (12:1), where the focus of the first stage ("striking," *nākâ*) gives way to that of the second ("possessing," *yāraš*), "Now these are the kings of the land, whom the Israelites defeated *(hikkû)*, whose land they occupied *(wayyiršû)* beyond the Jordan toward the east."

The chapter comprises three distinct units. The first (vv. 1-6) recounts the victories over Sihon and Og and gives a brief survey of the land acquired during the campaigns. The second (vv. 7-8) presents itself as an introduction to the list of defeated kings and provides a concise description of the extent of the land, including a proleptic statement that Joshua gave the land as a possession to the tribes. The third section (vv. 9-24) consists of a list of defeated kings.

The summaries forge a close affinity between Moses and Joshua but carefully preserve the distinction between the two great leaders. Both Moses and Joshua defeat kings and give the tribes of Israel land as a possession. But Moses does so in the Transjordan, while Joshua does the same in the Promised Land, thus preserving Moses' association with the eastern territories. Furthermore, Moses is twice called "the servant of the LORD," a title which he bears as military leader and giver of the land to the eastern tribes (v. 6). Joshua, as yet, bears no such epithet.

The list of defeated kings represents a final recapitulation of Israelite victory over Canaanite plurality. It is introduced by a formulaic description of the plural peoples of the land (the Hittites, Amorites, Canaanites, Perizzites, Hivites, and Jebusites) which corresponds to a six-fold description of their territory (v. 8). The cities associated with the kings mark Israel's first conquests (Jericho and Ai) and then move geographically from the southern to the northern regions of the land. The kings defeated during the southern campaign are listed next, but within these are four others who were not counted in 10:28-39 (Geder, Hormah, Arad, Adullam). Likewise, another group of kings located in the central region (vv. 16-18) are named for the first time (Bethel, Tappuah, Hepher Aphek, Lasharon). The trend continues with the expansion of the list of northern kings (of Madon, Hazor, Shimron-meron, and Achshaph) by an additional seven. The addition of these kings to the list of those "whom Joshua and the Israelites defeated on the west side of the Jordan" (v. 7) continues the escalating scope of conquest begun in 11:1-15 and gives the impression that Joshua's victories took place on a vast scale.[23] Like the extensive description of the Canaanite forces arrayed against Joshua in 11:1-5, the repetitive listing of defeated kings creates a cumulative effect much greater than the sum of its parts. The kings of the land, here revealed in all their multiple majesty ("thirty-one kings in all," v. 24), have been overcome by unified Israel under the command of Joshua. All that remains is for the people of Israel to occupy the rest of the land.[24]

---

[23] The name of the second king in v. 23 of the NRSV ("the king of Goiim in Galilee") diverges from MT (which reads *gôyîm lĕgilgāl*) and follows the reading preserved in the Septuagint. The confused witness of the manuscript tradition does not allow for the name to be reconstructed with any certainty. However, given the narrative's focus on the incorporation of ethnic groups into Israel, the version of the name in MT acquires an ironic sense. "Goiim" is the plural form of the Hebrew word for a large (usually landed) people group, while Gilgal marks the site where Israel crossed the Jordan and became a "goy." The name of this king may this be translated as "the nations at Gilgal."

[24] The structure of the list opposes the kings' diverse plurality to the "oneness" that symbolically refers to Israel. Each entry in the list is answered by the word "one," a scheme that is represented by MT as well as NRSV. On one side, the reader encounters thirty-one different names. On the other, an unchanging integer. The list thus sets the multiplicity of Canaan against the constancy of oneness.

Chapter Ten
ORGANIZING ISRAEL
Joshua 13:1–21:45

YHWH's declaration that "much land still remains to be possessed" inaugurates the second major task before Israel, that of occupying and dividing the land. The battles against the kings and cities have illustrated that transformation of "the land of Canaan" into "the land of Israel" must be a mutual enterprise, characterized by divine initiative and dynamic response. In Deuteronomic terms, the Promised Land is the land which YHWH "gives you to possess" (Deut 5:31 [MT 28]; 12:1; 19:2, 14; 21:1; cf. 4:5; 9:4).[1] YHWH has brought the nation into the land and overpowered the kings who dominate it, while Israel for its part has carefully executed the commands of YHWH (at least on the battlefield [11:15, 20]). In this manner Canaanite power has been shattered, making it possible for Israel to complete the acquisition of the Promised Land. Possession of the land also entails an interaction between YHWH and the nation, but the narrator concentrates more explicitly on Israel's role. YHWH initiates the process with an exhortation to "divide this land for an inheritance" (13:7) and concludes it through commands to establish cities of refuge and Levitical cities (20:1-6; 21:1-2). But YHWH does not appear in the intervening material and communicates indirectly through the casting of lots. The task of settling the land which YHWH gives is Israel's responsibility, under the leadership of Joshua. The narrator develops this scheme through elaborate descriptions of tribal territories interspersed with stories of individuals who demonstrate exemplary initiative and thus receive places to live: Caleb (14:6-15), Achsah (15:13-19), the daughters of Zelophehad

---

[1] The phrase occurs with particular frequency throughout Deuteronomy and in a few other contexts (e.g. Gen 15:7; Lev 20:24; Num 33:53).

(17:3-6), and Joshua (19:49-50). Other stories put an ironic spin on the theme by telling of tribes which display initiative by taking land not originally assigned to them, but only because they have not succeeded in securing their apportionments (the Joseph tribes, 17:14-18, and Dan, 19:40-48). And intermittent commentary makes the point in the negative, by reporting the failures of tribes to eliminate the peoples of the land from their territories (15:63; 16:10; 17:12).[2]

The Hebrew verb *yāraš*, which signifies the idea of possession, expresses the dual nature of the process by which Israel will replace the indigenous peoples as the inhabitants of the land. In the *Hiphil* form, it denotes the elimination of the peoples, generally with a destructive force not conveyed by NRSV's "drive out."[3] Within Joshua it usually occurs in the positive sense with reference to YHWH (to report YHWH's elimination of the peoples of Canaan; 3:10; 13:6; 23:5, 9) but in the negative with reference to Israel (to mark Israel's failure to do the same; 13:13; 15:63; 16:10; 17:12-13).[4] The *Qal* form, on the other hand, generally denotes occupation of territory through the displacement of the indigenous populations, a sense which Deuteronomy conveys by pairing it with the verb for inhabiting or dwelling (*yāšab*; Deut 12:29; 16:20; 17:14; 19:1; 26:1; cf. Josh 21:43). Together "displacing" and "dwelling" signify the program by which Israel will acquire the land that YHWH has promised and fulfill the divine commandments and ordinances. This sense is communicated explicitly in the programmatic statement which concludes Moses' opening exhortation (Deut 11:31-32):

> When you cross the Jordan to go in to occupy the land that the LORD your God is giving you, and *when you occupy it and live in it,* you must diligently observe all the statutes and ordinances that I am setting before you today.

In Joshua, the *Qal* form acquires a more active sense ("take possession"). In the opening scene it introduces the central focus of the narrative, through Joshua's command that Israel prepare itself to "cross over the Jordan, to go in to take possession of the land that the LORD your God gives you to possess" (1:11). But it also anticipates the end which Israel hopes to achieve. By declaring that the eastern tribes may only possess their land when they have succeeded in helping their kindred secure

---

[2] The note regarding Judah (15:63) is a special case, since it reports the tribe's failure to take Jerusalem, which in fact lies outside its tribal allotment.

[3] N. Lohfink, "*yāraš*," *TDOT*, VI: 374–6.

[4] Notable exceptions draw a contrast between Caleb's initiative and courage (14:12) and the trepidation of the Josephites (17:18).

possession of Canaan (1:15), Joshua points to a specific event that will signal (both to Israel and the reader) the successful completion of the program. "Taking possession" thereafter reiterates the anticipated conclusion at strategic junctures throughout the book and functions as a thematic bridge which introduces the summary of conquests, east and west (12:1) and connects the conquests to the occupation of tribal territories, east and west (13:1). The verb appears again in Joshua's exhortation to the remaining seven tribes, in the form of a question which raises the issue of Israel's resolve (18:3). Two final occurrences articulate the paradoxical nature of the book's claims regarding the fulfillment of its task. The narrator confirms that Israel took possession of and settled the land YHWH had given (21:43), but Joshua subsequently reveals that the task remains incomplete; YHWH will *displace (Hiphil)* the land's inhabitants so that Israel may *possess (Qal)* the Promised Land (23:5).[5]

Tied to the notion of land as possession is the concept of land as inheritance *(naḥălâ)*. In Deuteronomy "possession" and "inheritance" are used interchangeably with reference to the gift of the land. The phrase "which YHWH your God has given/is giving you" can be completed either by "to possess it" *(lĕrištāh;* 3:18; 5:31 [MT 28]; 12:1; 19:2, 14; 21:1) or "as an inheritance" *(naḥălâ;* 4:21; 19:10; 20:16; 21:23; 24:4; 26:1), and the two terms are combined in 15:4 and 25:19 ("the land that the LORD your God is giving you as a possession to occupy/as an inheritance to possess," *bāʾāreṣ ʾăšer* YHWH *ʾĕlōheykā nōtēn lĕkā naḥălâ lĕrištāh).*[6] In Joshua, however, the terms serve distinctively different purposes. As the previous survey has shown, the concept of land as possession serves as a structural marker which unites the beginning to the anticipated end. The description of land as *inheritance,* however, appears almost exclusively in the second main section (13–21), where it expresses the central concern of the unit. The narrator utilizes it to connect the apportionment of land to the conquest of cities by inserting it within the summary of Joshua's victories (11:23). "Inheritance" thereafter becomes the dominant descriptor for the land allotted to the tribes.[7]

---

[5] The *Hiphil* and *Qal* forms occur together in Josh 23:5 to express the two-fold nature of possession: "The LORD your God will push them back before you, and drive them out *(wĕhôrîš)* of your sight; and you shall possess *(wîrištem)* their land, as the LORD your God promised you." The introduction of the formula at this point in the book is striking, because the event which forecasts completion of the story (the eastern tribes' return to their lands) has already occurred (22:1-6).

[6] NRSV translates the phrase differently in the two contexts.

[7] The term does not occur before this reference ("Joshua give it for an inheritance to Israel according to its tribal allotments") but appears forty-two times in 13:1–21:45.

The English word "inheritance" does not quite capture the full sense of the Hebrew term and can be misleading. The latter *(naḥălâ)* does not center so much on the concept of *transference* of property from generation to generation as it does the notion of rightful and legitimate *claim* to property. Its frequent pairing with the noun *ḥēleq* ("part, share, portion") indicates that it has to do with the division and ordering of property and thus, on a deeper level, with one's place or role within the community and world.[8] The act of dividing property and assigning inheritances thus serves the purpose of ordering the community, establishing the place of social units within it, and permanently fixing the resultant configuration. YHWH's involvement in the process invests the ordering of land and nation with a legitimacy that ensures its enduring character. The Israelites are the rightful inhabitants of the land because YHWH has given it to them, an assertion driven home through the frequent references to "YHWH your God who gives you the land" and by YHWH's declaration, at the beginning of the book, that he has given the land to Israel (1:3-5). Reports of YHWH's victories over the kings of the land establish YHWH's authority and power to give the land of Canaan to Israel (cf. Exod 23:27-31; Deut 9:3). This claim established, the narrative now proceeds to the business of dividing the land among the new inhabitants. Here again claims to territory are legitimized by divine decree. Through the casting of lots YHWH divides the land among the various tribes and decrees the place that each will occupy within the nation. Through the lot, YHWH assigns each tribe a territory, and each territory becomes an inheritance. In essence, the divine will, communicated through the lots, authenticates the tribes' claims to their lands. The thematic priority of *organizing the nation* as opposed to *describing territorial possession* is emphasized throughout the section by intermittent reminders that the tribe of Levi received no land as their inheritance (13:14, 33; 14:3-4; 18:7) and by the institution of Levitical cities within the territories (21:1-40). While the conquest of the kings establishes Israel's claim to the land as a whole, the allotment of territories endorses each tribe's permanent claim to a particular piece of the land and thus to perpetual participation in the life of the entire community. The *claim* exists apart from, but not independent of, each tribe's *occupation* of its specific tribal allotment. The narrator carefully makes this distinction by describing the boundaries of each tribe, but relating the settlement of only a few areas and noting that some tribes did not succeed in occupying the whole of their apportionment. This tension, between the program of allotment and the process of possession, points to the deeper tension that exists between divine

---

[8] N. C. Habel, *The Land Is Mine: Six Biblical Land Ideologies*, OBT (Minneapolis: Augsburg Fortress, 1995) 33–5.

promise and human obedience. YHWH gives Israel a place to live and establishes an order for life in that place. It falls to Israel to occupy it.

The overall structure of the section stresses this tension by placing heavy emphasis on what Israel does once the kings of the land have been crushed. It consists of an elaborate system of narrative frames which divide and subdivide the contents into pairs of units and subunits.

CHART 10: THE STRUCTURE OF 13:1–21:45

A YHWH's words: Promise and command to possess the remaining land (13:1-7).

  B The allotment of tribal territories (13:8–19:51).

    C The lands of the eastern tribes (13:8-33)

    C' The lands of the tribes in Canaan (14:1–19:51)

      D Lands and stories connected to Judah and Joseph (14:1–17:18)

      E Judah's possessions (14:1–15:63)

      E' Joseph's possessions (16:1–17:18)

      D' Lands of the seven remaining tribes (18:1–19:51)

  B' The designation of special cities (20:1–21:42)

A' YHWH's acts: YHWH's words fulfilled, Israel in possession (21:43-45)

References to YHWH enclose the descriptions of lands and cities, reasserting divine initiative and participation, first through YHWH's promise to displace the indigenous inhabitants from the remaining lands (13:1-7) and finally through a report that YHWH did all that he promised (21:43-45). The intervening material comprises two main units which elaborate the division and occupation of tribal lands (13:8–19:51) and the designation of cities of special status (20:1–21:42). The first of these units makes up the bulk of the section and is itself subdivided into three units which are joined thematically by references to dividing the land for inheritances to the tribes (13:7; 19:51).[9] Within this frame, the description of the territories which Moses assigned to the eastern tribes constitutes a self-contained unit (13:8-33) marked by a summary introduction and

---

[9] YHWH's command that Joshua divide the land into inheritances for the tribes (13:7) is a narrative hinge that concludes YHWH's speech and inaugurates the program of allotment and possession.

conclusion. A corresponding description of territories allotted to the tribes west of the Jordan (14:1–19:51) is also enclosed by a chiastic set of narrative frames; the outer frame consists of a discrete introduction (14:1-5) and conclusion (19:51) which is matched by an inner frame that relates the stories of Caleb (14:6-15) and Joshua (19:49-50), the only two figures to span the wilderness and the entry into the land (Deut 1:34-40). The material within these frames comprises another two subsections, the lands apportioned to Judah and the Joseph tribes (14:1–17:18), and the territories allotted to the remaining tribes (18:1–19:51). The second of these is marked off by references to the continuation of the program at Shiloh (18:1-10; 19:51), while the former consists of two units (Judah, 14:6–15:63 and the Joseph tribes 16:1–17:18) which are themselves framed by stories which present contrasting portraits of courage (14:6-15) and trepidation (17:14-18) as groups take the initiative to possess their territories.[10] This elaborate network of frames not only unifies the diverse materials in the section but also reasserts themes prominent in the stories of conquest (e.g. Israel's obedience/disobedience to the commands of Moses, the completion/incompleteness of possessing the land).

The defeat of the Canaanite kings and the conquest of their cities constitutes the first phase of the campaign to take Canaan. Yet even though the kings (and the power they represent) have been defeated, the peoples of the land yet remain. YHWH has given the land and defeated the kings and now promises to drive out the native populations (13:6). Now YHWH requires Israel to fulfill its part and complete the program. As the concluding summary (21:43-45) intimates, YHWH brings his promises to completion, but fulfillment of the promises will depend on the nation's determination to actualize them.[11]

The Land That Remains: 13:1-7

The narrator opens by drawing attention to the long passage of time between the story's beginning and the present narrative moment.

---

[10] As is apparent, certain texts serve multiple functions; they may correspond structurally to one framing component but thematically to another.

[11] R. Polzin has observed that the process of possessing the land is connected to the themes of obedience to the law and the separation from outsiders. He remarks that the spatial contrast between the land God has given and the land still to be to be possessed matches the contrast between the law which Moses gave and the law which Israel must still live out, representing Israel's ambivalence toward the notions of insiders and outsiders. See *Moses and the Deuteronomist* (New York: Seabury, 1980) 133–4.

Joshua's advanced age ("old and advanced in years") is noted first by the narrator and then emphasized by repetition when YHWH addresses Joshua (13:1). The dual references link the text with a similar construction that introduces Joshua's farewell address (23:1ff) and for this reason many interpreters have viewed them as superfluous and out of place.[12] In literary terms, however, this reference to Joshua's advanced age serves an important purpose, signaling the transition from the first phase (subjugation of Canaan) to the second (apportionment and settlement). Settlement can begin in earnest only when the kings' potent threat has been removed and the land enjoys rest. The concluding summary of the conquest phase states emphatically that this did in fact happen but also adds that it took place after "a long time" (*yāmîm rabbîm*, 11:18). The declaration that Joshua is old and "advanced in years" (*bāʾ bayyāmîm*) picks up the sense of this remark and redirects it to the beginning of the occupation. A long time has passed, the land has rest, and settlement may begin in earnest.

The unusual structure of the opening, wherein YHWH repeats the words of the narrator, also effects a stylistic connection to the book's beginning. The construction initiates the second main section of Joshua just as it does the first (13:1-7; cf. 1:1-9).

After the death of Moses, the servant of the LORD, the LORD spoke to Joshua son of Nun, Moses' assistant, saying, "My servant Moses is dead" (1:1-2a).	Now Joshua was old and advanced in years; and the LORD said to him, "You are old and advanced in years" (13:1a).

The content of the ensuing speech then follows that of YHWH's first speech to Joshua. As in the beginning of the book, YHWH refers to the task ahead (13:1b; 1:2), defines the extent of land to be taken (13:2-5; 1:3-4),[13] assures Joshua that he will ensure success against the inhabitants of the land (13:6; 1:6-8), and concludes with a command (13:7; 1:9). Through these parallel speeches, the narrative reinforces the continuity between the campaigns of conquest (2:1–12:24) and the apportionment of territories (13:6–21:45). On the other hand, the speech

---

[12] The perceived awkwardness of the construction in the present context has led many scholars to the conclusion that it is a secondary insertion. R. Nelson, for example, remarks that the two references to Joshua's advanced age are implausible in a plot which expresses a single authorial perspective; *Joshua*, OTL (Louisville: Westminster John Knox, 1997) 164.

[13] The description of territory in this context appropriates the same "from-to" structure that characterizes the first description.

tempers the optimism that characterizes its counterpart. At the beginning of the book, YHWH speaks in expansive terms about the territory Israel is about to possess; YHWH has given Israel every place it walks (1:3), "all the land of the Hittites" (1:4). Now, however, YHWH employs the same expansive language is employed to characterize the land that yet remains, "all the regions of the Philistines, and all those of the Geshurites" (13:2), "all the land of the Canaanites" (13:4), "all the Lebanon" (13:5), "all the inhabitants of the hill country" and "all the Sidonians" (13:6). This comprehensive description of what has yet to be possessed collides with the claims of conquest made at the end of the previous section (11:16–12:24), reorienting the narrative from triumphal euphoria to the pragmatic realization that the greater part of the task still lies ahead.

The description of the land's boundaries also intimates a scaling down of expectations. At the beginning of the book YHWH declares that the boundaries of the land extend as far as the Euphrates River (1:4), but the claim of land here is more modest, with Lebo-Hamath marking its northernmost extent.[14] The survey seems to encompass three successive zones, a southern area (Philistines, Geshurites, and Avvites, vv. 2-3), a second area of unknown location associated with the Canaanites (v. 4), and a third located somewhere to the north of Misrephoth-maim, the site of Joshua's victory over the Hazor coalition (vv. 5-6a).[15] Unlike other territorial descriptions, though, this one describes the regions of the land primarily in terms of the peoples who inhabit them ("all the regions of the Philistines," "all the land of the Canaanites," etc.) rather than in geographical terms.[16] The survey thus focuses as much on the peoples that inhabit the land as on the land itself. Territory must be taken and peoples must be dispossessed in order for Israel to enjoy fullness of life in the land. The peoples of the land in particular stand between Israel and the fulfillment of the ancestral promises, and YHWH encourages Joshua with the promise that he will destroy them (v. 6b).

YHWH concludes by assigning roles for the task ahead. YHWH describes his role through a promise (v. 6b) which is set off grammatically through the use of an independent pronoun ("as for me, I will destroy them before Israel" [AT], *ʾānōkî ʾôrîšēm mippĕnēy bĕnēy yiśrāʾēl*). Joshua's

---

[14] The description of territory approximates that in Num 34:1-12 and corresponds roughly to the erstwhile Egyptian province of Canaan.

[15] Nelson, *Joshua* 165–7.

[16] The reference to the Philistines is a literary anachronism. The Philistines were one of a number of peoples who invaded the coast of Syria and Palestine some time after the era of Joshua. The mention of them here reveals that the narrator stands at some distance from the events themselves.

role is defined by commands focusing on the theme of inheritance, the first of which (v. 6c) is introduced by the strong disjunctive particle *raq* ("only"). Joshua is to allot the land "as an inheritance" (i.e. serve as YHWH's authorized representative [v. 6c]) and to divide the land "for an inheritance" (i.e. organize the nation within the land).[17] The promise/command structure of these concluding remarks once again articulates the thematic relationship between divine initiative and human response necessary for the successful completion of the program.

The Territory of the Eastern Tribes: 13:8-33

The conquest and occupation of the Transjordan exemplifies the Deuteronomic program of possession. As we have noted in the previous chapter, Deuteronomy's account of the conquests of Sihon and Og (Deut 2:24–3:7) establishes a comprehensive paradigm for the conquests in Canaan. Israel soundly defeats the kings, takes all their cities, and wipes out the indigenous peoples (including the last of the Rephaim). The thorough execution of the program makes possible the kind of occupation envisioned by Deuteronomy; Israelite tribes hold the land without heterogenous elements within their territories. In a similar fashion, Deuteronomy's description of the Transjordanian possessions (Deut 3:8-17) establishes a paradigm for the distribution of tribal lands related in Joshua. The completeness and homogeneity achieved in these territories is reiterated in Joshua by the frequent repetition of *kôl* ("all, entire"), which occurs twelve times in this section.[18] In addition, the text combines elements of the Deuteronomic account with elements of a previous report of the victories over Sihon and Og (Josh 12:1-6), thus accentuating the comprehensive character of the territory claimed and settled.[19]

The segment opens abruptly in the MT with the phrase "with him" (*ʿimmô*), followed by "the Reubenite and the Gadite." The grammatical antecedent of the pronoun "him" is "the half-tribe of Manasseh," which ends the previous sentence (13:7). However, the *referent* of the pronoun is different, for while "the half-tribe of Manasseh" in 13:7 refers to that segment of the tribe *west* of the Jordan, the pronoun actually

---

[17] Though translated by different prepositions in NRSV, the two phrases are identical in the MT (*běnaḥălâ*).

[18] Vv. 9, 10, 11 (2x), 12, 16, 17, 21 (2x), 25, 30 (2x).

[19] Nelson, *Joshua* 171.

refers to that part of the tribe located *east* of the Jordan (the subject of the ensuing passage).[20] The arresting construction draws attention to the divided geographical situation of Manasseh and, in a larger sense, that of Israel itself. Here again, the Jordan seems to create a stark separation between the tribes. The two parts of one tribe bear the same name yet are separate entities.[21] The import of this paradox (Manasseh as both "one" and "two"), and the problems it presents for notions of national identity, are hinted at (at the beginning of this section) but not yet addressed explicitly. The issue will be raised again at the beginning of the last section (22:1-34), where it will become the occasion for addressing fundamental issues of community definition.

The unit comprises four segments, an introduction which recapitulates the full extent of the eastern lands (vv. 8-14), followed by successive descriptions of the territories of Reuben (vv. 9-23), Gad (vv. 24-28), and half-Manasseh (vv. 29-33). Parallel comments about the Levites conclude the introduction and the unit as a whole (vv. 14, 33), breaking up both literary and tribal homogeneity. Like the tribe of Manasseh, Levi is a liminal ("inhabiting the boundary") tribe, although it inhabits existential rather than geographical boundaries. Levi is *like* the rest of the tribes in that it derives from the eponymous ancestor Israel, yet it is *distinct* from the rest in that it receives no land as an inheritance. In both instances, the narrative expresses this status in paradoxical terms. On the one hand it straightforwardly asserts that Moses gave no inheritance to Levi. Yet immediately thereafter it reports that Levi *does* possess an inheritance; its perpetual share is YHWH (v. 33), and particularly the offerings by fire (v. 14). Among the description of tribal territories, reference to the Levites is made only here, so that the Levites are paired with the eastern tribes as elements within Israel that cannot be easily situated within the polarities of unity/separation and possession/non-possession (cf. 18:7).[22]

Statements which reinforce the connection between these anomalous tribal groups bracket the initial overview (vv. 8-14): "with the other half-tribe of Manasseh the Reubenites and the Gadites received their inheritance, *(naḥălâ)*, which Moses gave them" (v. 8), "to the tribe of Levi alone Moses gave no inheritance" (*naḥălâ*, v. 14). Both of the bracketing

---

[20] Nʀsv resolves the ambiguity with a more expansive translation of *immô:* "with the other half-tribe of Manasseh."

[21] "The half-tribe of Manasseh" refers to the clans that settle east of the Jordan in 1:12; 4:12; 12:5,6; 13:29; 18:7; and 22:1, 7, 9–15, 21, but to those that settle west of the Jordan in 13:7; 21:5-6 (see also 14:2-3).

[22] For an excellent discussion of the liminal nature of priesthood, see R. Nelson, *Raising Up a Faithful Priest: Community and Priesthood in Biblical Theology* (Louisville: Westminster John Knox, 1993) 83–8.

comments divide the subject tribes from the rest of the nation. The first sets the eastern tribes off from the rest of Israel by reminding the reader, through repetition, that their land has been given and allotted by Moses, rather than Joshua ("their inheritance, which Moses gave them, beyond the Jordan eastward, as Moses the servant of the LORD gave them," v. 8).[23] The second reminds the reader of the Levites' unique status. In this manner the survey of eastern lands infuses the concept of "inheritance" (rightful claim, ownership) with a level of uncertainty.

The sense of ambiguity is heightened by references to the Geshurites and Maacathites (vv. 11, 13). According to the Deuteronomic summary upon which this one is based, Israel's conquests extend as far as the borders of these peoples (a territory which probably approximates the present-day Golan Heights [Deut 3:14; cf. Josh 12:5]). In the present instance, however, the description of the "inheritance" given by Moses is stated less clearly (v. 11), although a similar phrase is employed. The problem is the omission of the small preposition *ʿad* ("up to, as far as"), which occurs in the other lists but not in this one (which reads *ûgĕbûl haggešûrî wĕhammaʿăkātî* ["and the border/territory of the Geshurite and the Maacathite"]). The Hebrew word *gĕbûl* can refer either to a boundary or to a territory possessed by a particular people. When used in conjunction with the preposition *ʿad* it signifies the former, and NRSV translates accordingly in Deut 3:14 and Josh 12:5. The phrase *ûgĕbûl* (*gĕbûl* with conjunction, as here) may also denote a border and in these instances may be translated "as a boundary" (cf. Num 34:6; Deut 3:17; Josh 13:23, 27; 15:12, 47).[24] In these cases it follows and modifies another noun. However, in the present text *ûgĕbûl* precedes the nouns it qualifies. To add to the confusion, the larger phrase is linked with Gilead, Bashan, and Mt. Hermon (the last of which also is a boundary point in the other contexts), suggesting that it does not refer to a boundary but to the territories possessed by the Geshurites and Maacathites. The ambiguous sense of the phrase implies that Israel's *claims* in the Transjordan (the "inheritance" given by

---

[23] The statement that "Moses gave" in connection with the apportionment of territory suggests a subtle contrast with the land "YHWH gave/gives," a phrase which is used frequently with the reference to Canaan. The eastern tribes requested the Transjordan lands but were initially rebuffed with a scathing rebuke from Moses (Num 32:1-32). However, when they agreed to participate in the conquest of Canaan, Moses "gave" them the former lands of Sihon and Og (Num 32:33). Deuteronomy does not refer to the situation, except to report that Moses awarded the lands to these tribes (Deut 3:12-22). The Deuteronomic account is concerned instead with legitimating claims to the Transjordan and carefully equates the land "Moses gave" (vv. 12, 15) with the land "YHWH gave" (v. 18).

[24] See Magnus Ottosson, "*gᵉbhûl*," *TDOT*, II: 364–6.

Moses) may even here exceed the areas conquered and settled, encompassing territories outside the present extension of Israel's power.[25] How far do the boundaries extend? What lands are actually claimed?

The second of the two references reinforces the indeterminacy, "the Israelites did not drive out the Geshurites or the Maacathites; but Geshur and Maacath live within Israel to this day" (v. 13). The structure of this declaration is identical to that which reports that Judah could not "drive out" the Jebusite inhabitants of Jerusalem (15:63). But this only complicates matters for that comment is also an anomaly; Jerusalem lies *outside* the territory allotted to the tribe of Judah (cf. 18:28). Does the failure to drive out the Geshurites and Maacathites thus endorse a later (unsuccessful) attempt to extend Israel's boundaries in the Transjordan, undergirded by pronouncements of Moses? Or does the comment point us back once again to the issue of inclusion and exclusion of other ethnic groups within Israel? The comment that "Geshur and Maacath live within Israel to this day" forges a direct thematic link with the stories of Rahab (6:25) and the Gibeonites (9:27), which as we have seen are paradigms for the extension of Israel's internal boundaries towards other peoples. The report injects a note of incompleteness into an otherwise exemplary account, and the consequent sense of uncertainty and unfinished business undercuts the whole enterprise of establishing boundaries. How can geographical (and ethnic) boundaries be fixed when they cannot be clearly determined?

The descriptions of the tribal lands (Reuben [vv. 15-23], Gad [vv. 24-28], and half-Manasseh [vv. 29-31]) counter the shifty ambiguity of the introduction with a symmetrical organization which brackets geographical details with parallel phrases:

> "Moses gave an inheritance to" (vv. 15, 24, 29)
> "according to its clans" (vv. 15, 24, 29)
> "their territory was" (vv. 16, 25, 30)[26]
> "this is the inheritance" (vv. 23, 28, 32)[27]
> "according to their clans, with their towns and villages" (vv. 23, 28)[28]

---

[25] Verse 11 is disconnected grammatically from its context and bracketed by parallel references to the territories of the Amorite kings: "all cities of King Sihon" (v. 10) and "all the kingdom of Og" (v. 12).

[26] In the first instances the phrase is *wayĕhî lāhem haggĕbûl;* the third reference (to Manasseh) omits *lāhem.*

[27] The phrase is plural in the last case and summarizes all three distributions rather than Manasseh's territory.

[28] The NRSV translates *lĕmišpĕḥōtām* as "according to their families" in v. 23 but "according to their clans" in v. 28.

The delineation of each tribe's borders tends to follow the same "from
. . . to" pattern that characterizes the definition of geographical regions
throughout the book (1:4; 11:16-17; 12:1-5; cf. Deut 3:7, 16-17), and each of
the descriptions lists cities enclosed within the borders. The sequence of
the three accounts moves from south to north, beginning at the Wadi
Arnon (Reuben's southern boundary) and then northward through
Gilead to an unspecified area associated with King Og of Bashan. Corresponding to this move from south to north is a deterioration from the ordered and complete presentation of Reuben's territory to the vague and
terse presentation of half-Manasseh's. The territory of Reuben (vv. 15-23)
receives a relatively extensive and coherent treatment, marked by a full
description of the area given by Moses and the listing and location of
many of the towns within it. It also includes reports that the Israelites defeated several Midianite chieftains and put Balaam son of Beor to death
(vv. 21b-22). These reports reinforce the integral character of Reuben's
territory by evoking the connection between homogenous possession of
land and safety from the dangerous plurality of the peoples of the land.
The reference to the Midianites reminds the reader of the incident at Baal-
Peor, where Israelite men succumbed to the seductive powers of Midianite women (Num 25:6-18). Like the peoples of Canaan the Midianites
undid Israel's distinctive integrity through trickery and deceit (vv. 17-18),
kindling the anger of YHWH and bringing a plague which threatened to
destroy the nation (vv. 8, 9, 18; cf. Deut 3:3-4; 7:1-6). The narrator of
Joshua reminds the reader of the threat the Midianites represent by symbolically listing them in the plural terms that characterize the peoples of
the land ("the leaders of Midian, Evi and Rekem and Zur and Hur and
Reba, as princes of Sihon, who lived in the land" [v. 21; cf. 3:10; 9:1; 10:1-
5, 22-23; 11:1-4; 12:9-24]). The narrator presents Balaam son of Beor (a
patronymic that sounds very close to "Peor") as a similar threat by defining him as one "who practiced divination" (v. 22).[29] By reporting the
elimination of these menacing plural elements from the land, within the
context of a coherent and well-ordered description of tribal inheritance,
the narrator undergirds the connection between fulfillment, order, and
the elimination of heterogeneous elements in the land. By defeating the
Midianites and putting Balaam to death, Israel eradicates the plural and
diverse. Reuben thus embodies the utopian Deuteronomic vision.

The description of Gad's territory is more succinct and contains
no reports such as those included in the account concerning Reuben.

---

[29] The Midianite chieftains represent diversity through their ethnicity, while Balaam represents the notion through the "otherness" of the diverse practices of divination. (Balaam's story also includes the construction of many altars for sacrifice,
another expression of Canaanite/Amorite plurality; Num 23:1-2, 14-15, 29-30).

Although pared down, it closely follows the pattern of the previous account and also indicates a land configured by coherent boundaries which enclose a number of towns. Half-Manasseh, however, represents a further degeneration of the paradigm. The description of the half-tribe's lands offers few fixed points, and the "from . . . to" pattern which defines the borders of other territories is absent. The territory thus assumes a nebulous character, encompassing Bashan and "half of Gilead." The towns of Ashtaroth and Edrei are noted but others are more vaguely identified as "the settlements of Jair . . . sixty towns." The compromise of tribal integrity and territory which characterizes Manasseh is reiterated by the repetition of *ḥăṣî* ("half"), which denotes further subdivisions in the concluding remarks: "half of Gilead" and "half of the Machirites" (v. 31). In addition, the structure of the account exhibits a corresponding breakdown of textual parameters. While it begins the same way as the other accounts, it omits the concluding reference "with their towns and villages" and the formulaic closing ("this is the inheritance of"). Instead the formula, in the plural, closes the entire segment, "these are the inheritances that Moses distributed" (v. 32).

The particular structure of the section, which moves geographically from south to north and thematically from integrity to disintegration, sets the pattern for the two remaining phases of tribal allotments west of the Jordan. The territories of Judah and Joseph begin with elaborate descriptions of Judahite boundaries and cities but give way to vague reports of borders and cities where Joseph is concerned (16:1–17:18). In a slight twist on the scheme, the third phase begins with a correspondingly detailed description of Benjamin's allotment (18:11–28) before moving south to bracket the remaining allotments with accounts of those for Simeon (19:1-9) and Dan (21:40), two tribes which embody additional territorial paradoxes.

Judah and Joseph: 14:1–17:18

The allotment of land in Canaan begins with the inheritances apportioned to Judah, Ephraim, and Manasseh. In terms of subject matter, the section comprises two main subsections which deal first with Judah (14:6–15:63) and then with Ephraim and Manasseh (16:1–17:18). Structurally, however, it is diverse, placing stories of settlement against the backdrop of territorial description, much as the earlier part of Joshua places anecdotes against the backdrop of conquest accounts. The main body of the segment consists of territorial surveys interspersed with narratives: a description of Judah's territory (15:1-12), the tale of Achsah (15:13-19), a list of Judah's towns (15:20-63), the territory of Ephraim (16:1-10), and the territory of Manasseh (17:1-13), with a digression which relates the story of Zelophehad's daughters (17:3-6). The stories of Caleb (14:6-15) and the Josephites' request (17:14-18) frame this material with contrasting depictions of the possession of the land. A brief introduction (14:1-5) prefaces the corpus.

As in Joshua 2–12 the narrator employs a paratactic structure which alternates between Israel on the corporate and individual planes, prompting reflection on the central focus of the section (here the division and occupation of the land) and ultimately destabilizing notions of kinship, land, and obedience. The four stories follow a common four-part plot centering on a grant of land in response to an act of initiative. Each of the main characters demands a place in the land with a forcefulness that illustrates the vital importance of this quality for the successful possession of the land which YHWH gives.

CHART 11: THE COMMON PLOT OF THE STORIES OF OCCUPATION[30]

Confrontation: Israelite/s approach a superior/s.

Caleb and the Judahite elders approach Joshua (14:6a).
Achsah urges Othniel to ask Caleb for a field (15:18).
Zelophehad's daughters come to Eleazar, Joshua, and the leaders (17:3-4a).
The Josephites speak to Joshua (17:14a).

Case and Request: The protagonist/s demands territory and gives a convincing rationale.

Caleb demands Hebron and invokes the promise of Moses (14:6b-12).
Achsah demands springs for her land in the Negeb (15:19a).
Zelophehad's daughters demand the inheritance promised through Moses (17:4a).
The Josephites demand the hill country because the cities are too powerful (17:14b-16).

Land Grant: The superior accedes to the demand and gives the requested territory.

Joshua gives Hebron to Caleb (14:13).
Caleb gives the upper and lower springs to Achsah (15:19b).
Joshua gives Zelophehad's daughters an inheritance among their kinsmen (17:4b).

---

[30] This scheme follows that of R. Nelson (*Joshua*, 177–8), as do the labels (confrontation, case and request, land grant, summary of results). Nelson gives the title "land grant narrative" to the common form.

Joshua allows the Josephites to clear and settle the hill country
   (17:17-18a).

Summary of Results: The implications of the decision are reported.

Hebron, formerly Kiriath-arba, becomes the inheritance of Caleb
   (14:14-15).
Zelophehad's daughters receive ten portions in Gilead as
   an inheritance (17:5-6).
Joshua exhorts the Josephites to drive out the Canaanites (17:18b).

Like the stories of Rahab, Achan, and the Gibeonites, these stories confuse concepts of territorial possession, kinship ties, and obedience to
YHWH in various ways. Caleb represents the ideal Israelite, undaunted
by Canaanite might and anxious to take the land promised to him. He
is, however, an Israelite of questionable ancestry, a detail hinted at by
his identification as a "Kenizzite" (14:14), the name of a clan which in
other contexts is associated with the Edomites (Gen 36:11, 15, 42; 1 Chr
1:36, 53). The second and third stories assail the connection between
land and kinship by relating land grants awarded to women. By reporting the giving of land to women, the stories of Achsah and Zelophehad's
daughters challenge the patriarchal structures which reinforce both
property rights and kinship relations (structures explicitly articulated
in the story of pedigreed Achan [7:1]). Possession of land by women
undermines the "male-territory" equation and subtly integrates the
"other" gender into an Israelite community that traces the promise of
the land only through those whose are marked by circumcision (Gen
17:1-14).
   The negative side of the program (here the failure to occupy promised
land) is expressed, as it is in the story of Achan, by a story about pedigreed Israelites. In this case, the subjects are members of Joshua's own
tribal group, who command the special attention of the nation's leader
(17:14-18). The story sets "the tribe of Joseph" against Joshua and turns
the exemplary quality of initiative on its head.[31] The Josephites also request lands, but with less than noble motives. Because they are numerous, they want more than their share, declaring that the hill country is
insufficient but rejecting the plains because Canaanites with iron chariots live there. The Josephites thus stand in stark contrast to Caleb, who
requests the kind of territory that the Josephites refuse. Given prior reports that Ephraim and Manasseh failed to take many of the Canaanite

---

[31] Like the story of Achan, this one pits Israelites against Joshua, reverses elements of the other stories, and communicates a sense of failure and disobedience.

cities, Joshua's command that they drive out the Canaanites concludes the episode on a note of failure.

The stories of Caleb and the Josephites exemplify a larger contrast between the associated tribes. The territory of Judah, the tribe of vigorous Caleb, receives the most extensive and detailed treatment of any of the tribal descriptions. The description of its boundaries is accomplished with a precision that signifies an integrated and coherent geographical unit, in full possession of the tribe which inhabits it (15:1-12), and this is supplemented by an equally extensive list of cities, arranged in a carefully-ordered scheme (15:20-63). On the other hand, the lands of the irresolute Josephites are described in correspondingly indefinite terms, with few details and a confusion of boundary lines and cities. While the cities of Judah are enclosed within discrete borders, the cities of the Josephites are a hopeless jumble; unnamed Ephraimite cities lie within the territory of Manasseh (16:9; 17:8-9) while the only cities associated with Manasseh lie within the boundaries of Asher and Issachar (17:11-12)!

The overall account thus presents a study in striking contrasts. Caleb, the energetic Kenizzite-Judahite hero, represents the tribe of Judah, which demonstrates the integrity and coherence to which all Israel aspires. Conversely the Josephites, who are both one tribe and two, exhibit a diminished resolve and an associated openness in the demarcation of land and cities. And two of the four stories in the section concern women who display the determination of Rahab, securing their place within the land and thus the community. Hints of disobedience to the commands of Moses appear in the reports that the Judahites and Josephites did not destroy the inhabitants of the land (15:63; 16:10; 17:12-13). The resulting portrait of Israel compromises the status of all boundaries—ethnic, religious, and territorial—which construct community identity.

Introduction to the Inheritances in Canaan: 14:1-5

The account of the allotments in Canaan begins in a strange way, with a listing of prior exceptions and ambiguities involving inheritance. The topic of Israel's claim to the land, along with the orderly apportionment of shares to the tribes, is advanced by the repetition of the root *nḥl* ("legitimate share"), which occurs five times within the first three verses. The narrative emphasizes the legitimacy of the tribal claims by reporting the involvement of various authority figures: the priest Eleazar, Joshua, and the heads of the ancestral households, the basic Israelite social units (literally "the heads of the fathers of the tribes of the

Israelites"),[32] and indirectly YHWH (through the lots) and Moses. The
three-fold repetition of Moses' name, twice through the phrase "as the
LORD commanded Moses" (vv. 2, 5), casts the allotment of lands as an
act of corporate obedience, reiterates the lines of authority, and demonstrates the integrity of the community and its unity with YHWH (cf.
Num 33:50-56).[33] Lest the reader miss the implications of these narrative cues, the narrator explicitly links the division of territories to the
commands of YHWH through Moses (v. 5).

A number of ambiguous situations serve as focal points of the passage. First, the narrator recalls the divided geographical situation of Israel: the nine and one-half tribes in Canaan and the two and one-half
tribes "beyond the Jordan" (vv. 2b-3a). Although the text asserts Moses'
direction over the whole procedure of casting lots (cf. Num 26:52-56), it
also reminds the reader of Moses' direct role in determining the inheritances of the two and one-half tribes (versus Joshua's role in allotting
the remaining lands).[34] This leads in turn to a reminder that Moses gave
the Levites no inheritance among the other tribes (v. 3b). The comment,
something of a non-sequitur, represents the third time the status of the
Levites is mentioned, and the rationale given is strikingly different
than in the previous instances. The earlier references to the Levites explain their unique situation in theological and functional terms; Moses
gives no land to the Levites because offerings to YHWH constitute their
inheritance (13:14) and, more directly, YHWH is their inheritance (13:33).
In this context, however, the narrator explains Levi's status in more
pragmatic terms; Levi receives no inheritance because of the ambivalent composition of Joseph (14:4a): "for the people of Joseph were two
tribes, Manasseh and Ephraim." One tribe (Joseph) is also two tribes
(Ephraim and Manasseh), a situation that potentially wrecks Israel's
symmetrical twelve-tribe social configuration. The narrator's explanation implies that Israel's symmetrical twelve-tribe configuration would
be dismantled were Levi to be given a "portion" *(ḥēleq)* as an inheritance. One anomaly thus gives way to another; the tribe with no portion yields to the tribe with two. But the matter doesn't end there, for
the text goes on to report that although Levi receives no portion in
Canaan, it does in fact receive cities and pasture lands. The note effec-

---

[32] The phrase articulates the patriarchal structure which configures the Israelite
kinship system.

[33] The emphasis on Israel's obedience to YHWH through Moses connects the dividing of territory to the crossing of the Jordan and the conquest of kings and cities.

[34] The difficulty that the eastern tribes represent for Israelite self-identity can be
gauged by the frequency with which they appear in the larger narrative (Num 32:1-
40; 34:15-16; 36:1-12; Deut 3:18-22; Josh 1:12-18; 4:12).

tively separates the notion of "portion" from ownership of property, breaking the sense of equivalency between "inheritance" and "land." The resulting bifurcation muddles the intricate conceptual network that undergirds the possession of the land. Tribes may occupy lands that they do not have claim to, and conversely tribes may claim lands that they do not occupy. If the concept of possession combines the notions of claim, legitimate ownership, and occupation, it does so apart from the strict lines of demarcation which seem to be the focus of all that follows. With these ambiguities noted, the narrator proceeds to describe the delineation of tribal allotments.

JUDAH'S INHERITANCE: 14:6–15:63

The account of Judah's allotment exhibits a paratactic structure which alternates between stories about Caleb and Achsah (14:6-15; 15:13-19) and descriptions of Judah's territory (15:1-12, 20-63). The structure encourages the reader to connect the qualities of courage, perseverance, and initiative illustrated by the stories with the comprehensive and integrated portrait of tribal territory depicted in the delineation of boundaries and the list of cities.

Caleb's Demand (14:6-15)

The comments which introduce the inheritances in Canaan prepare the reader for a description of tribal lands after the fashion of the eastern apportionments (13:8-33), but this is not immediately the case. Instead, the account begins with a story which illustrates, through the character of Caleb, the relationship between initiative, obedience, and successful possession of the Promised Land. That Caleb is something of a poster boy for the Deuteronomic agenda is indicated through structural cues and careful attention to characterization. His story is divided into parts; the first (14:6-15) revolves around themes of obedience, promise, and the gift of land, while the second relates the fulfillment of his request for a portion in Judah (15:13-15). The two parts of the story enclose the description of Judah's allotment, by far the most complete and detailed description of all the tribal territories (15:1-12), and the second precedes a correspondingly extensive list of Judahite towns. The interplay of these texts discloses the wider significance of Caleb's story. Judah's elaborate and coherent boundaries demonstrate the consequences of the energy and obedience that Caleb symbolizes, while the encyclopedic list of cities shows what can be accomplished by those who eagerly assault the cities of giants. In an even larger sense,

Caleb represents the nation itself. The Mosaic promise that motivates him, that "the land on which your foot has trodden shall be an inheritance for you and your children forever" (v. 9), corresponds to YHWH's promise to Israel at the beginning of the book, "every place that the sole of your foot will tread upon I have given to you, as I promised to Moses" (1:3). Both promises, significantly, measure fulfillment in terms of response; the extent of territory "given" depends on how much the subject will "walk" (cf. Deut 11:24-25).

The narrator presents Caleb as the embodiment of obedience, zeal, and initiative. The episode consists mainly of a speech, during which the Judahite leader confronts Joshua with the promise that YHWH and Moses made to him at Kadesh-barnea (vv. 6-9) and speaks of faithfulness, courage, and trust. He begins with a retrospective which reminds the reader that Caleb and Joshua, alone among the twelve spies sent into Canaan, exhorted the people to enter the land (Num 13:1-33). On that occasion ten of the spies discouraged the nation by reporting the presence of large and fortified cities within Canaan and a diverse population made up of the descendants of Anak and the Amalekites, Hittites, Jebusites, Amorites, and Canaanites (vv. 25-29). Caleb, however, encouraged the people to go up and take possession of the land (*wĕyārašnû ʾōtāh* [v. 30]) but could not overcome the negative report of the other ten, who emphasized the strength, size and ferocity of the peoples of the land (vv. 31-33). His speech to Joshua encloses his own words on that occasion with the words of Moses, implicitly joining obedience and promise. He begins by recalling what "the LORD said to Moses the man of God in Kadesh-barnea concerning you and me" (v. 6) but does not reiterate what was said until he first reminds Joshua of the "honest report" which he gave in opposition to the demoralizing words of the other spies (vv. 7-8).[35] He then returns to the words of Moses and quotes the promise of an inheritance made "on that day" (v. 9). Throughout this recapitulation Caleb emphasizes his own unhesitating devotion to YHWH by declaring that he "wholeheartedly followed the LORD my God" (vv. 8, 9), supporting his claim by recalling Moses' consequent promise to him (v. 9).[36]

---

[35] The "honest report" of NRSV translates the idiomatic phrase *dābār kaʾăšer ʿimlĕbābî* ("a word as it was in my heart"), the wording of which confirms Caleb's personal integrity. Caleb declares that the other spies "made the heart of the people melt" (v. 8), drawing an implicit connection between the effect of their words on the nation and the effect of Achan's sin on the next generation (cf. Josh 7:5).

[36] Caleb demonstrates the consequences of obedience to YHWH; Moses swears his oath in response to his honest report and because of his wholehearted devotion.

Caleb shifts decisively from the past to the present with "and now, as you see" (*wĕ'attâ hinnēh* [v. 10]), and his words now acquire a sense of urgency and force. The particle *'attâ* is repeated three more times within the rest of the speech (vv. 10, 11, 12), which shifts rapidly back and forth from "that day" (vv. 11, 12) to "this day" (vv. 10, 11, 12). Caleb's words now assert his undiminished vigor (v. 11) even as they underscore the vast expanse of time that separates the two "days." YHWH's faithfulness is demonstrated by the fact that Caleb remains alive forty-five years after the promise was first uttered. Caleb too is faithful. Despite the long gap between promise and fulfillment, Caleb remembers the promise and recognizes that the time has come to actualize it. Even though he is now eighty-five, Caleb claims to have lost none of his strength, a point that he makes with particular emphasis (v. 11). With remarkable forcefulness, he now demands the hill country where the Anakim dwell "with the great fortified cities," the very places that had intimidated his companions forty years earlier! He ends by reiterating the program for possession of territory in modest but straightforward terms: YHWH being with him, he will displace the inhabitants, as YHWH has promised (v. 12c).

The episode concludes with a report, repeated for emphasis, that Caleb received Hebron as an inheritance (vv. 13-14). The repetition of *lĕnaḥălâ* ("as an inheritance"), together with a third reference in v. 9, brings together various concepts associated with land as inheritance; inheritance is linked with promise in v. 9, gift and blessing in v. 13, and obedience in v. 14. A third reference to Caleb as one who "wholeheartedly followed the LORD the God of Israel," this time by the narrator, accentuates the crucial import of these associations. In contrast to the trepidation of his companions, Caleb wholeheartedly followed YHWH (v. 8) and for this reason Moses promised him an inheritance (v. 9) which Joshua now grants (v. 14).

Caleb possesses the mettle required of Israel as it prepares to undertake the occupation of Canaan, a wholehearted devotion to YHWH and a determination to snatch the land from its inhabitants, with a zeal and ardor unabated by forty years of wandering in the desert and another five in conflict with the peoples of the land.[37] Like Caleb, Israel ought to be a people who relies on YHWH's promises and understands that even giants and cities will fall before them. In order to receive the full

---

[37] The numerical scheme of Caleb's speech implies that Israel has been in the land for five years. He declares that he was forty when he received the promise at Kadesh-barnea (v. 7) to which we must add forty years (the wilderness period [Josh 5:6]). It is now forty-five years hence (v. 10), indicating another five years in the land.

measure of their inheritances, the tribes must follow Caleb's lead. To punctuate this point the narrator adds a postscript (v. 15) which further enhances Caleb's heroic zeal by reporting that Hebron was formerly called Kiriath-arba ("Arbaville"), after Arba, the greatest of all the Anakim (cf. Deut 9:1-3). The report then concludes with the comment that "the land had rest from war," a duplicate of the comment which ends the account of Israel's victorious campaigns against the kings and cities of Canaan (11:23). By ending the story this way, the narrator suggests that Caleb was in fact successful in breaking the formidable powers of the land granted to him and that he carried the campaign through to completion.

Caleb exemplifies Judah in particular and Israel in general, even though his bloodline cannot be clearly traced to the tribe's eponymous ancestor. The narrator hints at Caleb's extra-Israelite paternity by referring to him, at the beginning and end of the episode, as "Caleb son of Jephunneh the Kenizzite" (vv. 6, 14). The references form a narrative frame against which to comprehend Caleb's request; in the manner of other "outsiders" in the book, he displays courage, initiative, and remembrance of YHWH to secure a place in the land. The narrator confirms his connection with these outsiders, namely Rahab and the Gibeonites, through the same kind of etiological note that marks the end their stories: "so Hebron became the inheritance of Caleb son of Jephunneh the Kenizzite to this day" (v. 14). Caleb's story thus continues the same theme, in the context of the second phase of possession, that the stories of Rahab and the Gibeonites do in the first phase.[38]

Judah's Land (15:1-12)

The opening phrase, "the lot for the tribe of the people of Judah according to their families reached" *(wayĕhî haggôrāl lĕmaṭṭēh bĕnēy yĕhûdâ lĕmišpĕḥōtām)*, connects the allotment of land to Judah with the others in Canaan through a common reference to the lot (cf. 16:1; 17:1; 18:11; 19:1, 10, 17, 24, 32, 40). However, it also effects a discontinuity between this territory and the lands apportioned to the tribes across the Jordan, the descriptions of which begin with the phrase "Moses

---

[38] Caleb's name means "dog." This has generated considerable discussion among scholars, some of whom see it as a totemic reference or, in the positive sense, as an expression of devotion. Given the low view of dogs in the Hebrew Bible (e.g. Deut 23:19 [MT 18]; 1 Sam 17:43; 2 Sam 3:8; 1 Kgs 21:19-24; 2 Kgs 8:13; Ps 22:16 [MT 17]; Pro 26:11; Qoh 9:4; Isa 56:10), however, it is difficult to see how the name could hold any such positive connotations in the canonical text. The disreputable sense of his name enlarges Caleb's heroic stature through contrast.

gave an inheritance" (13:15, 24, 29). The delineation of the territory assumes a narrative tone, with verbs such as going, crossing, ascending,
descending, and turning connecting many of the border points.[39] This
"quasi-narrative" survey creates the sense that the reader is traversing
the circumference of the territory, perhaps with the promise of Josh 1:3
(and the recent allusion in 14:9) in mind. The description focuses on the
southern and northern boundaries, the latter of which is defined with
meticulous precision. Overall, the survey indicates a clearly-defined
geographical unit.

Caleb, Othniel, and Achsah (15:13-19)

The stories of Rahab and the Gibeonites destabilize the kinship network that configures Israel by relating the incorporation of other ethnic groups in the Israelite community. The narrator broaches the
topic surreptitiously through the story of Rahab, advancing it with
suggestion and subtlety while relating the exemption of a basic social
unit (an ancestral household), which is assigned to a relatively
harmless location at the community's periphery (2:12-13; 6:22-25).
Having thus set this contentious issue before the reader, the narrator
then addresses it directly through the story of the Gibeonites' ruse.
Here the topic is given explicit treatment with results that more seriously damage the ethic of ethnic separation. In this case, an entire
complex of cities is allowed to survive and its people are placed at the
very center of the community's life (9:14-27). The story of Caleb continues this strategy within the context of the division of the land, but
the next two stories (Achsah and Zelophehad's daughters) challenge
Israel's social configuration in a different way. By relating stories about
women who possess land, the narrator undercuts the patriarchal network by which property is legitimized and transferred. Together the
stories challenge the notion that "Israel" is to be defined in exclusively
masculine terms; severing the male-land equation also cuts the male-
Israel equation which undergirds it. If women possess land, women are
also Israelites in the most fundamental sense.[40] Like the stories of Rahab,

---

[39] Nelson, *Joshua*, 186.

[40] This simple affirmation is not self-evident within the Hebrew Bible. The
promise of the land is first given to the patriarch Abraham (Gen 12:7) and is transferred from father to son (through Isaac and Jacob) and thence to the eponymous
male ancestors of the tribes. The promise is codified through a divine-human covenant which sets circumcision as the sign of obedience, a further indication that it is
directed toward the male members of the community. The tribal inheritances, given
"according to their clans," reinforce the system by invoking the authority of Joshua

the Gibeonites, and Caleb, the stories of Achsah and Zelophehad's daughters deal with the extension of Israel's internal boundaries, in this case to those of other gender rather than other ethnicity.[41]

The same strategy used to introduce the issue of ethnic otherness is employed again to confront that of gender otherness. The first story introduces the topic in an indirect manner and relates a modest outcome (the gift of springs to Achsah), while the second confronts the issue head-on and concludes much more dramatically (ten "portions" awarded as "inheritances" to the daughters of Zelophehad). The narrator begins unobtrusively by directing the reader's attention again to Caleb. The scene opens with a succinct repetition of the previous episode's concluding remarks (thus picking up the story where it left off [v. 13, cf. 14:14-15])[42] before moving rapidly to finish the story with a terse report that Caleb "drove out" *(wayyōreš)* the three sons of Anak (who are identified with characteristic Canaanite plurality ([v. 14]).[43] The narrator does not devote much attention to the campaign but continues the story past its completion. After reporting the conquest of Hebron, an elaborate transition carefully redirects the reader's focus from Caleb to Achsah (vv. 15-17). An additional campaign against Kiriath-sepher/Debir provides the context for this transition. It begins when Caleb declares that he will give his daughter Achsah as a wife to whoever attacks and captures Debir.[44] The narrator then repeats his words and substitutes the

---

the nation's leader, Eleazar the nation's priest, and the "heads of the fathers of the tribes" (14:1). In this manner, the ownership of property is legitimized and claims to property are traced patrilineally from YHWH to tribe to clan to father's house.

[41] Rahab, of course, embodies "otherness" in the fullest sense (in ethnicity, gender, and social station). It is therefore significant that hers is the first story which treats the issue of Israel's social definition. A reversal of conventional gender roles is evident throughout her encounter with the Israelite spies (2:1-21); she determines the course of action, exhibits a remarkable forcefulness of character, and tells the males in the story what to do and where to go. The end of her story suggests that she, not a male, heads her house ("Rahab the prostitute, her family, and all who belonged to her") and becomes the eponymous ancestor of an established social unit within Israel ("she has lived in Israel ever since" [6:25]).

[42] The text, however, makes a small but strategic modification, replacing "inheritance" with "portion."

[43] Anak surrounds his children in the structure of the report: "the three sons of Anak: Sheshai, Ahiman, and Talmai, the descendants of Anak." The structure reinforces the formidable might of the "sons" whom Caleb destroyed and but also reiterates the father-son connection (here associated with the peoples of the land).

[44] The verbs Caleb uses ("strike " [*nkh*], "capture" [*lkd*], and "give" [*ntn*]) also characterize Joshua's conquests of the Canaanite kings and cities, the first two with

words "Othniel the son of Kenaz, the brother of Caleb" in place of "whoever attacks Kiriath-sepher":

> Whoever attacks Kiriath-sepher and *takes it, to him I will give my daughter Achsah as wife* (v. 16).

> Othniel son of Kenaz the brother of Caleb *took it; and he gave him his daughter Achsah as wife* (v. 17).

The identification of Othniel as kin to Caleb assures the reader, ahead of time, that the land given to Achsah will remain safely within Caleb's patrimony, while the land taken (Debir) implicitly differentiates the land she will acquire from Caleb's inheritance (Hebron).

Othniel, however, remains little more than a bit player in the drama, becoming a pronoun as the story completes the transition by shifting abruptly to Achsah (v. 18). Although her story is told with brevity, it nonetheless communicates her force of character through action and speech.[45] The narrative highlights the quality of initiative which she exemplifies, first reporting that she urged her husband to ask her father for a field and then immediately thereafter relating the request she makes of Caleb. Her drive and demand are so vital to the story that the narrator provides none of the details which we might expect (e.g. Othniel's response to her urging, how and when she came to Caleb on her donkey, why she later asks for a spring when she earlier urges her husband for a field); the focus is squarely on her request and determination. Her words possess power as well. Speaking imperatives in response to Caleb's question, she emphatically demands springs of water:

> Give me a present;
>> since you have set me in the land of the Negeb,[46]
> give me springs of water as well.

---

reference to Israel's actions and the second with reference to YHWH's. The verbs implicitly associate Caleb with YHWH, for like YHWH Caleb now issues an exhortation to "attack" and "capture" while declaring what he will "give."

[45] The terse narration, however, may yield a variety of understandings about Achsah's character and action. See particularly D. N. Fewell "Deconstructive Criticism: Achsah and the (E)razed City of Writing," *Judges and Method: New Approaches in Biblical Studies,* ed. Gale A. Yee (Minneapolis: Fortress, 1995) 119–45.

[46] "The land in the Negeb" can also be understood in a metaphorical sense. ("You have given me as Negeb-land"). From this point of view Achsah may be comparing her marriage to Othniel with the grant of land ("you have given me away like a piece of land") or complaining that she has been given in marriage without a dowry. See Fewell, "Deconstructive Criticism," 134 and Nelson, *Joshua,* 184.

Achsah seeks both blessing and life-sustaining property. Her first words, "give me a present" (*běrākâ,* translated elsewhere as "blessing"), unite her with Caleb, who receives both land and blessing from Joshua (14:13). However, she is even more like Rahab; though initially excluded from her own place in the land, she secures it through the force of her imperatives (2:1-24). As with Rahab, the narrator reports that she received exactly what she requested (v. 19b).

The presence of Achsah on the roll of Israelite land-owners disturbs the patriarchal configuration of the community, and the narrator tempers the implications of the story by a variety of means. The pace of the story is brisk and details are sparse. Instead of a "portion" Acshah asks for a "field" and requests a "blessing" rather than an "inheritance." The land she is given lies on the outskirts of Judah's allotment (just as Rahab is given a place on the periphery of the camp). The narrative imbeds her story securely within Caleb's by beginning and ending with similar constructions; a declaration introduced by direct speech and immediately repeated by commentary (vv. 16-17, 19). Nonetheless, the issue of property ownership by women (and the more fundamental issue of women's status) has been broached. It will appear again, more explicitly and on a wider scale, within the account of Joseph's allotment.

Judah's Towns (15:20-63)

A profuse list of Judahite towns follows Acshah's story, implicitly illustrating the consequences of the initiative she exemplifies just as the detailed description of Judah's territory endorses Caleb's. While the delineation of the land begins with a formula that connects Judah with the other tribes in Canaan (14:6), the list of towns begins with one that connects Judah more generally with all the tribes, although the phrase "this is the inheritance of" generally concludes rather than begins the accounts (13:23, 28; 16:8; 19:8, 16, 23, 31, 39, 48).[47] As with the other units in this section, this one is clearly defined by introductory and concluding remarks, and the cities themselves are organized into a symmetrical twelve-part scheme. Each segment of the scheme is clearly demarcated from the others with a summary that records the total number of towns listed along with the phrase "with their villages" (vv. 32, 36, 41, 42, 48, 51, 54, 57, 59, 60, 62).[48] These segments are in turn grouped within four

---

[47] The one exception is 14:1, where the phrase (in the plural) introduces the apportionment of all lands in Canaan.

[48] The exception (Ekron, Ashdod, and Gaza) will be addressed in the next paragraph.

major geographical regions: the extreme South (v. 21), the Lowland (v. 33), the hill country (v. 48), and the wilderness (v. 61).

The organizational program and attention to detail are quite impressive, yet even within this tight and careful schematic the reader encounters some untidiness. The first has to do with a fifth group (vv. 45-57), which breaks the schematic form in a conspicuous fashion. The grouping includes few geographical details, no summation of cities at the end of the segment, and repetition of the phrase "with its towns and villages."[49] The peculiarities of structure and vocabulary draw explicit attention to the cities mentioned: Ekron, Ashdod, and Gaza. Historically speaking, Israel never "possessed" these cities nor the area (Philistia) in which they were located, although Judges affirms that Judah "took" them. The anomalous structure of the segment thus insinuates a measure of failure in Judah's attempt to occupy the lands allotted to it, despite the inspiring examples of Caleb and Achsah and the magnificent survey of territory and cities. This sense of failure is punctuated, at the end of the list, with the report that "the people of Judah could not drive out the Jebusites, the inhabitants of Jerusalem; so the Jebusites live with the people of Judah in Jerusalem to this day" (15:63). The comment is all the more remarkable because it seems unnecessary; Jerusalem will be apportioned to Benjamin, not Judah (18:28). The rhetorical impact, however, is decisive, turning the focus once again to issues of ethnicity rather than geography and thus to the lasting survival of other groups within Israel (6:25; 9:27; 14:14). The note also looks ahead to reports connected with Ephraim and Manasseh (16:10; 17:12-13) and implies Judah's affinity with its northern counterparts.

JOSEPH'S INHERITANCE: 16:1–17:18

In contrast to the coherence and completeness of Judah's section, that concerning the tribes of Joseph is incomplete, confused, and fragmented. It comprises four subunits: a survey of Joseph's allotment (16:1-4), Ephraim's territory (16:5-10), Manasseh's territory (17:1-13), and the request of the Joseph tribes (17:14-18). Certain repetitions suggest a semblance of organization ("the lot went out/was" [16:1; 17:1], "the territory of X was" [16:5; 17:7], X "could not destroy" the Canaanites [16:10; 17:12]), but none are strictly parallel. The first and last units, which concern "Joseph," enclose texts which deal individually with

---

[49] Although NRSV reads "with its dependencies and its villages" in v. 45 the phrase in the MT is identical to those in v. 47 *(ûbĕnōteyhā wĕḥăṣēreyā)*.

Ephraim and Manasseh, but beyond this no organizational pattern unites the various texts, and the transition from one text to another is more often than not an awkward one.

The disjointed and diverse structure of the section mirrors the fragmented make-up of Joseph itself. Joseph is both an integer and a duality, a situation that presents particularly thorny problems for establishing a clearly-defined geographical and social identity. The issue presents itself in the first and last subunits, which refer to Joseph as a unit and establish a framework for the description of territories (16:1-4; 17:14-18). The first describes the allotment in vague terms, outlining Joseph's territorial claim before expressing its paradoxical character (16:4), while the last attempts to resolve the conflicted status of Joseph through a story which relates the possession of its territory. Significantly, "Joseph" is not designated as a "tribe" in either of these sections, the term being reserved for the two constituents which comprise it (16:8; 17:1). In between, the descriptions of Ephraim and Manasseh's lands appropriate terms that have been closely associated with reference to the land but split them among the two groups. The pronouncement that "Joseph" receives a single allotment (*gôrāl*, 16:1; 17:14) receives indirect confirmation with the puzzling mention of an allotment only in connection to Manasseh (17:1). Along similar lines, the language of "inheritance" (*nḥl*) occurs only with reference to Ephraim's territory (16:5, 8, 9) and to the land apportioned to Manassite women (17:3-6).[50] Manasseh is further subdivided along kinship lines (17:1-2) and then according to gender (17:3-6), making it all the more difficult to fix a foundation for constructing tribal identity. The business of sorting out "who gets what and why" becomes all the more difficult in the MT by the incongruous and ambiguous state of the text. In all these respects, the account presents a view of tribal integrity that contrasts markedly from the organized and lucid portrait of Judah's acquisitions.

The Josephites' Allotment (16:1-4)

The reader encounters textual, geographical and ethnic ambiguity right from the start. The opening words, "the allotment of the Josephites went" (*wayyēṣēʾ haggôrāl libnēy yôsēp*), make a subtle distinction between the allotment of this territory and that of Judah ("the lot for the tribe of the people of Judah . . . reached," *wayĕhî haggôrāl lĕmaṭṭēh bĕnēy yĕhûdâ* [15:1]) but also link Joseph with the remaining tribes in Canaan (cf. 18:11; 19:1, 10,

---

[50] The separation of "lot" and "inheritance" further loosens the tight interconnection which legitimizes claims and ownership of property.

17, 24, 32, 40). The phrase itself may have multiple senses, referring to the lot "coming out" of its container, the extension of the boundary which the lot defines, or the territory designated by the lot. The description of the land is surprisingly brief and incomplete (vv. 1-3). The text delineates only the southern border of the allotment, and although it begins with the detail we might expect, it becomes increasingly vague, concluding with "it ends at the sea." More surprising than this is the fact that the description is peppered with references to strange peoples and places. After a precise beginning, underpinned by a three-fold reference to Jericho, the delineation gives way to a series of uncertainties. The first involves the extension of the border from Bethel to Luz, a particularly odd note given the fact that the two names elsewhere explicitly denote the same city (Gen 28:19; 35:6; Judg 1:23).[51] From here "it crosses the territory of the Archites at Ataroth" (AT).[52] The Archites are a people of unknown origin, who nowhere appear in lists of Israelite clans or genealogies.[53] A reference to the Japhletites, a similarly obscure people, follows. This group may be associated with the tribe of Asher (1 Chr 7:33), but if so its presence here, as a point of reference for the southern boundary of Ephraim, is at odds with the eventual location of Asher northwest of Manasseh's territory. The notation therefore presents either an ethnic anomaly (the Japhletites are an indigenous group) or a geographical one (they are located far from the region said to be claimed by their tribe). From here the boundary extends to the region of lower Beth-horon and then to Gezer (which, the reader will soon learn, could not be wrested from its indigenous inhabitants [v. 10]). The description of Joseph's boundary, therefore, has the peculiar effect of drawing attention to the presence of peoples of indigenous or uncertain origin, who are mentioned as though they exist as discrete entities within the land.

A report that "the Josephites—Manasseh and Ephraim—received their inheritance" (v. 4) makes a transition between the general survey of Joseph's territory and the particular lands apportioned to Manasseh. Its terse wording reminds the reader of the dichotomy between the social unit and territorial claim represented by Joseph: one allotment, two tribes.[54]

[51] However, see Judg 1:26, which relates the rebuilding of a second "Luz" after the first was captured by "the house of Joseph" (Judge 1:23).

[52] NRSV reverses the syntax and views "the territory of the Archites" (ʾel-gĕbûl hāʾarkî) as an appositive.

[53] David's trusted advisor, Hushai, is identified as an Archite, indicating eventual assimilation into Israel (2 Sam 15:32; 16:16; 17:14; 1 Chron 27:33).

[54] The plural form of the verb, wayyinḥălû ("they received inheritance") emphasizes the plural and divided sense of the term in this context.

Ephraim's Inheritance (16:5-10)

Although Manasseh is mentioned first (v. 4) and later identified as the "firstborn of Joseph" (17:1), the narrative begins with Ephraim. The opening formula approximates that which introduces Judah's apportionment but replaces "allotment" *(gôrāl)* with "territory" (or boundary, *gĕbûl*). The substitution of terms ensures that only one "allotment" will be described. References to inheritance enclose the survey of the territory, beginning with "the boundary of their inheritance" (v. 5b) and concluding with a formal closing ("such is the inheritance of the tribe of Ephraim by their families" [vv. 8b]). The southern and northern boundaries are coherent if not always precise. The description begins roughly at the midpoint of the southern boundary, at Ataroth,[55] and proceeds westward, generally following the path laid out in v. 3 and ending at the sea (v. 6a).[56] It then shifts abruptly to the northern boundary, beginning at Michmethath and heads in the opposite direction toward the east, ending at the Jordan (vv. 6b-7). Returning to the center at Tappuah the border follows an unspecified path to the Wadi Kanah and then ends at the sea (v. 8a).[57]

The report of Ephraim's cities presents a sharp contrast to Judah's spectacular town list (15:20-63). While it concludes with a similar formula ("all those towns with their villages"), the description does not name any town within Ephraim's territorial boundaries. Instead, it mentions the location of Ephraimite cities within the inheritance of Manasseh (v. 9), again without naming any of them. The succinct note has two important implications. First, it anticipates the failure and loss of resolve illustrated by the Josephites' request that Joshua grant them additional land, an anecdote that will suggest that the two tribes have no cities because they do not *want* them (17:16). Second, the location of Ephraimite cities within Manasseh confuses both the boundaries and the process of allotment by which they are fixed. If the lot defines and divides the tribal lands, how does it designate cities for one tribe within the "allotment" of another? And if the cities of one are located in other allotments, how can apportionments be viewed as distinct, coherent entities? These questions acquire more acuity through an addi-

---

[55] The name Ataroth-adar probably represents a fuller version of the name than in 16:3, in order to distinguish it from another Ataroth that lies on the northern border (v. 7).

[56] "Beth-horon" exhibits the same divided status as Joseph; here the reference is to an Upper Beth-horon as opposed to a Lower Beth-horon (v. 3).

[57] Ephraim's borders are therefore not traced from end to end but from the middle, outward in both directions: westward—eastward—westward.

tional reference that the Ephraimites did not drive out the Canaanites who lived in Gezer (even though the narrator reports the defeat of Gezer's king in 10:33). Of particular import is the comment that "the Canaanites have lived within Ephraim to this day," which corresponds, in form, exactly to the report of Rahab's survival (6:25), in effect adding the inhabitants of Gezer to the ever-expanding list of peoples who survive the Israelite onslaught.[58] The final comment, that the Canaanites were subjected to forced labor only begs the question. Why didn't Ephraim exterminate them as Moses commanded?

Manasseh Divided (17:1-13)

Manasseh is a mess—textually, socially, and geographically. Reflecting the tribe's divided state on both sides of the Jordan, the text shifts back and forth between east-Manasseh and west-Manasseh with such rapidity and confusion that the reader may find it difficult to identify which is which (vv. 1-6). The account opens with the same formula that introduces Judah's allotment (cf. 15:1) but then digresses suddenly and shifts focus repeatedly with a chain of catchwords (vv. 1-2). The note that Manasseh is the firstborn of Ephraim leads to the topic of another firstborn, Machir the father of Gilead. The reference to Machir is then picked up and modified (in the MT) to report that Machir was a warlike man.[59] The mention of Gilead son of Machir introduces the topic of the eastern territories of Gilead and Bashan and provides the basis for the enumeration of the "rest of the tribe" west of the Jordan.[60] The "rest of the tribe" is then identified with the same plurality that characterizes the peoples of the land throughout the book; the ancestral families are listed seriatim. The list of names is followed by an explicit (if seemingly redundant) pronouncement that it comprises "the male descendants of Manasseh son of Joseph." The MT expresses the point in a more direct manner than NRSV; "these are the sons of Manasseh the son of Joseph, the males *(hazzĕkārîm)* according to their clans" (AT). The brief aside explicitly directs the reader's focus to the issue of gender and highlights the patriarchal makeup of the kinship network that constitutes Israel's basic social configuration.

---

[58] NRSV translates as plural what in the MT is singular ("the Canaanite").

[59] The phrase *kî hāyâ ʾîš milḥmâ* ("because he was a man of war") keys off the earlier phrase *kî-hûʾ bĕkôr yôsēp* ("for he was the firstborn of Joseph"). The comments above follow the sequence of the MT, which has been modified in NRSV.

[60] The rapidly shifting focus is given the semblance of continuity through a three-fold repetition of *wayĕhî* ("and it was").

The narrator then takes another unexpected turn and presents the story of Zelophehad's daughters (vv. 3-6). As in the story of Caleb, the case involves a promise which Moses made during the wilderness period (Num 27:1-11). Zelophehad, a Manassite, died but had no sons. His daughters approached Moses, Eleazar, the leaders, and all the congregation with a petition to grant them a possession (*ʾăḥuzzâ*) among their brothers (v. 4). Moses brought the matter before YHWH, who validated the daughters' case and decreed that they were to be allowed to "possess an inheritance among their father's brothers" (vv. 5-7). The present account relates the conclusion of the story. A short preface, which follows the pattern of the original story, introduces the daughters' request. The narrator first traces Zelophehad's genealogy and gives the names of his daughters (Josh 17:3; Num 27:1). As in the first instance, the daughters then boldly approach an assembly that includes Joshua, Eleazar, and the community's leaders (*hannĕśîʾîm* [Josh 17:4; Num 27:2]). By utilizing this literary *deja vu*, the narrator evokes the promise/fulfillment scheme and thus an implicit connection to the story of Caleb; both illustrate the daring and initiative required to possess the promised land.

In its Pentateuchal context, the daughters' request is a free-standing episode which provides the context for the presentation of legislation. A second episode (Num 36:1-12, also free-standing) addresses certain contingencies related to the initial pronouncements and expands the legislation. The story's resolution in Joshua, however, contains no legislation and is firmly imbedded within the division of Manasseh's inheritance. The preceding reference to the "males" of the tribe (v. 2) puts the reader's focus squarely on the story itself and on the issue implicit in the previous episodes: the inclusion of women within Israel's patriarchal social system. Within this context, the naming of Zelophehad's daughters (Mahlah, Noah, Hoglah, Milcah, and Tirzah [v. 3]) establishes a structural equivalency with the enumeration of Manasseh's sons (Abiezer, Helek, Asriel, Shechem, Hepher, and Shemida [v. 2]) and thus suggests a social equivalency as well. The narrator wastes no time getting to the point, but also accentuates it by repetition. The daughters' request succinctly articulates the issue of gender and inclusion: "The LORD commanded Moses to give us an inheritance along with our male kin" (*ʾaḥēnû*, "our brothers," [v. 4b]). The narrator then reports that "according to the commandment of the LORD he gave them an inheritance among the kinsmen of their father" (*ʾaḥēy ʾăbîhen*, "the brothers of their father" [v. 4c]) and concludes by stating again that "the daughters of Manasseh received an inheritance along with his sons" (*bānāyw* [v. 6a]). Within the brief account, then, we are informed three times that the daughters received an "inheritance" alongside "brothers" and "sons." The repetition of this information strongly asserts the daughter's integration into a structure defined in male terms and in so doing challenges the strict social boundaries articulated by the listing of Manasseh's sons, the genealogical pedigree of Zelophe-had, and the assembly of Israelite males. Women who claim and own land demonstrate essential participation in the life promised by YHWH and thus in the community that occupies it. The daughters thus personify what Achsah anticipates, that "Israel" cannot be identified fundamentally in male terms only.[61]

The ownership of land by women destabilizes the essential structures which define and organize the tribes, clans, and ancestral houses, and the narrative structure conveys a corresponding sense of befuddlement. References to Gilead and "the rest of" Manasseh bracket the larger account (vv. 2a, 6b) but mean different things. In the first instance, the title designates the tribes in Canaan whose portions will soon be determined, but in the second it denotes that part of the tribe which settles east of the Jordan. Furthermore, the land given to the daughters remains unspecified, compounding the confusion. Although the references to Gilead link them to the east side of the Jordan (where allotments have already been made), their request is made during the allotment of lands west of the Jordan. The text explains that the ten portions for Manasseh (*ḥablēy-měnaśśeh*), besides Gilead and Bashan, were granted because of the daughters' request, insinuating that their land is located to the west. Yet if so, their land is separated from the land given to the rest of their clan (Machir, located east of the Jordan).

Following this confusing digression, the narrative returns to the topic of Manasseh's allotment (vv. 7-13). The bewildering textual disorientation continues as the text jumbles Manasseh with Ephraim (vv. 7-10) and then Manasseh with Issachar and Asher (v. 11). The section is loosely organized by the repetition of *wayěhî* ("and it was"), which signals the beginning and completion of the territorial survey (vv. 7, 10) and introduces the description of Manasseh's cities (v. 11) and the concluding comment (v. 13). As with Ephraim, the boundaries seem

---

[61] It is true that the patriarchal structure is ultimately confirmed in the story, for the daughters receive land only by appeal to the community's male leadership. But the narrative also explicitly authorizes their inheritance in the same way as all other inheritances, by divine decision. The narrator specifically reports that the inheritance was granted "according to the command of the LORD" (as opposed to "the command of Moses," a phrase that occurs more frequently in Joshua); the decision on the matter is made by YHWH, who also constitutes the authority which legitimizes the claim. The story is not concerned with dismantling the patriarchy, but with demonstrating that it does not constitute an essential element of Israelite national identity.

porous and incomplete, and a northern border is lacking.[62] A southern
boundary is laid out (vv. 7b-10a), but not completed, incorporating
fragments drawn from the description of Ephraim's northern boundary (cf. 16:6b-8). Throughout the survey, "Ephraim" appears almost as
often as "Manasseh," expressing the single/dual status of the tribes.
Towns appear in the description of the boundaries, promising fixed
points of reference, but these create even more perplexities. "The land
of Tappuah" belongs to Manasseh, but Tappuah itself (a border town)
belongs to Ephraim (v. 8). The text also notes Ephraimite towns among
those of Manasseh (v. 9b; cf. 16:9) and concludes by designating land
south of the Wadi Kanah as Ephraimite and that north of it as Manassite (vv. 9c-10).[63] The description of Manasseh's territory thus proceeds
in all directions—north (Asher), south (Ephraim), west (the Sea), east
(Issachar)—but remains indistinct. In essence, Manasseh's territory is
defined by other tribes.

A list of Manassite towns follows the amorphous elaboration of its
territory. But as with Ephraim, the only cities noted are those which lie
outside Manasseh's assigned territory.[64] The narrator lists Manasseh's
towns but then reports that the Manassites could not take possession
of them (v. 12a) and concludes by noting the continued survival of the
inhabitants of the towns (vv. 12b-13). The note corresponds to the
comments of failure which conclude the accounts of Judah (15:63)
and Ephraim (16:10) but offers a more sweeping indictment:

> A Yet the Manassites could not take possession of those towns;
>
>> B but the Canaanites continued to live in the land.
>
>>> C But when the Israelites grew strong
>
>> B' they put the Canaanites to forced labor,
>
> A' but did not utterly drive them out.

The chiastic structure of the note underscores Manasseh's failures through
various associations. The first and last components negate possession of

---

[62] The text notes only that Manasseh's territory extends from Asher (in the north)
to Michmethath (in the south).

[63] The sense of MT in v. 9 is extremely difficult to decipher. For a more complete
discussion see Nelson, *Joshua*, 202–3 and Z. Kallai, *Historical Geography of the Bible:
The Tribal Territories of Israel* (Jerusalem: Magnes, 1986) 148–55.

[64] Kallai (*Historical*, 167–76), however, argues that v. 11 refers to cities abutting
the territories of Asher and Issachar and thus to border cities belonging Manasseh.
Discussion of the issue is complicated by many textual and grammatical difficulties
in the MT.

the land in emphatic terms: "yet the Manassites could not take posses-sion *(wĕlōʾ yākĕlû bĕnēy mĕnaśśeh)* of those towns" and "they by no means destroyed them" ([AT] *wĕhôrîš lōʾ hôrîšô)*. The second and fourth affirm the Canaanites' survival in the land, even though they were subject to forced labor (cf. 16:10; 9:27). The middle component characterizes the entire nation, not at this point in the story but in the future. "When the Israelites grew strong" constitutes an implicit indictment of the conquest generation. When is the time to "be strong" if not during the time given to take possession of the land (cf. 1:6, 7, 9; 10:25; 23:6)?[65]

The descriptions of the territories of Manasseh and Ephraim display a tension between differentiation (through the definition of borders) and conglomeration (through references to cities located elsewhere). The territories the tribes inhabit, like the tribes themselves, comprise identifiable, bounded units which demarcate but do not separate. Joseph's territory, like Joseph itself, is both one and two. The permeable charac-ter of the geographical boundaries thus reflects the equivocal makeup of the tribal unit itself, a situation exemplified by the situation of half-Manasseh and the story of Zelophehad's daughters.

The Josephites' Protest (17:14-18)

The story of the Josephites' request, which concludes this section, represents the thematic opposite of the story of Caleb with which it be-gins (14:6-15). The central concerns of both stories involve initiative and grants of land, but the present story puts an ironic spin on the theme and links it with the theme of failure which has been building throughout the unit. Caleb requests land because he remembers the promise of Moses and YHWH. He embodies the qualities of faithfulness, courage, and energy that are crucial to the possession of the land which YHWH has promised. Although eighty-five, his strength and zeal are not diminished; he seeks the cities of giants and prevails. Because of these qualities, Joshua blesses him and awards him land in Judah. The Josephites, on the other hand, challenge the assignment of lots by which the land is apportioned (and thus, implicitly challenge YHWH whose will is expressed through the lots). They seek land, not in re-sponse to divine promises, but because they are not satisfied with what they have been given. The Josephites want more land because

---

[65] The particular verbal construction which characterizes the Canaanites' pres-ence in the land in v. 12b ("but the Canaanites continued to live in the land") may convey a sense of tenacity. If this is the case, their determination to live in the land accentuates Israel's lack of resolve.

they are "a numerous people," but unlike Caleb they seem intimidated by the cities around them. They in fact prefer the unsettled tracts of land in the hill country to the more populated areas of Beth-shean and the Valley of Jezreel. Unlike Caleb, they do not receive a blessing because of their faithfulness but rather declare themselves blessed because of their great numbers (v. 14).

The issue of Joseph's divided status also configures the episode. The account consists mainly of a dialogue between Joshua and the "house of Joseph" and begins when the Josephites (who speak of themselves in singular terms) confront Joshua with a request for more land. They begin with a question which immediately raises the issue of their perplexing identity, "why have you given me but one lot and one portion as an inheritance?" The answer would seem to be obvious: because that's the way system works—an inheritance consists of one portion designated by one lot. However, the rationale intimates complications. Joseph supports his demand by arguing that he is too numerous for the assigned allotment and then associates his great size with blessing, "since we are a numerous people, whom all along the LORD has blessed." Is numerical strength (and with it power and influence, v. 17) what it takes to acquire land in Canaan? Is this the basis for initiative?

Joshua responds by recasting the rationale in a conditional form which implicitly challenges Joseph's claims, "if you are a numerous people."[66] He then issues a command with its own implications, "go up to the forest, and clear ground there for yourselves in the land of the Perizzites and the Rephaim, since the hill country of Ephraim is too narrow for you." The response suggests how numerical size ought rightly to be perceived. Joshua does not endorse the Josephites' claim of blessedness but directs them to land which can be cleared for habitation. If all the land is to be settled, the larger tribes have the resources to do so.

The Josephites in turn seize on Joshua's assessment that the hill country alone is insufficient, but one cannot be sure what lies behind their words. Is the hill country unsatisfactory because it is too small an area to support the population? Or is it unsatisfactory because the Josephites do not wish to clear it in order to settle it? The latter question takes on added weight in light of the following complaint, that the Canaanites who live in the plain have chariots of iron (v. 16). The statement implies that the hill country is too constrictive for the group because Canaanite might restricts Josephite expansion. The complaint therefore offers an explanation (in the words of the Josephites them-

---

[66] The syntax of the MT reverses that of the Josephites' claim: "if a numerous people are you" in response to "I am a numerous people."

selves) for the failures to take the cities mentioned earlier (17:11-13; and by implication 15:63 and 16:10); the Josephites are discouraged by Canaanite chariotry.

Joshua concludes the encounter by confirming the numerical size of Joseph, this time as an assertion rather than an equivocation. With a markedly hortatory tone, he then issues three pronouncements which synthesize the various facets of the interchange. The first makes a connection between size and power ("you are indeed a numerous people and have great power") as a basis for a ruling that the house of Joseph (here expressed in both singular and plural terms) shall not have just one lot (v. 17). The second (18a), presses the exhortation to clear the hill country, adding for emphasis "to its farthest extent" (AT).[67] The third (v. 18b) reiterates the central task of driving out the Canaanites. Whether this last declaration constitutes a prediction ("you shall drive out") or exhortation ("you are to drive out") cannot be determined from the form of the verb *(kî-tôrîš)*, but in either sense the allusion to v. 13 intimates what Joseph *should* accomplish given their present state of affairs. Joshua here speaks in the positive sense about driving out the Canaanites as opposed to the previous report that Israel did not utterly drive them out. His reference to the strength of the Canaanites only accentuates the not-presently-strong state of Israel.

Additional Allocations at Shiloh: 18:1–19:51

The distribution of land to the remaining seven tribes represents the final stage in the allotment of tribal territories. While the previous two stages comprise loose organizations of diverse forms and texts, this one presents its material in a coherent and orderly format. A short exposition, which reports the gathering of the congregation at Shiloh (18:1), opens the account and is balanced at the conclusion with the report that "they finished dividing the land" (19:51). References to the tent of meeting and Shiloh enclose the allotment of lands within a narrative framework that unifies the action and sets it within a sacral context.[68] A pair of narrative units which feature Joshua (18:2-10; 19:49-50)

---

[67] Although the exhortation, in NRSV, includes a command to "possess" (which would connect it to the comprehensive program of the book), the MT is less emphatic; *yāraš* in the *Qal* ("to possess") is not actually present.

[68] The setting of the scene at Shiloh differentiates this stage of the allotment from the previous one, that presumably took place at Gilgal (14:6).

constitute a second set of brackets and reinforce Joshua's role as national leader and divine agent. The descriptions of individual allotments, which form the main body of the unit, each begin with a reference to the lot and conclude with a reference to inheritance.

The organized structure of the section cannot, however, hide inconsistencies within individual units, nor can it divert a growing sense of failure and incompleteness. Joshua opens the account with a question that strongly suggests that the rest of the nation suffers from the same trepidation associated with the Josephites, "How long will you be slack about going in and taking possession of the land that the LORD the God of your ancestors, has given you" (18:3)? Two of the tribal territories (namely Simeon and Dan) display the lack of territorial integrity that characterizes those of Ephraim and Manasseh. In fact, the entire section follows the pattern of the previous one, beginning with a full description of one tribe's land (Benjamin) and a complete listing of its cities (18:11-28) but devolving quickly into muddled and incomplete descriptions (19:1-48).

THE ASSEMBLY AT SHILOH: 18:1-10

The third stage in the allotment of land opens with a strong affirmation of Israelite unity and integrity (v. 1). The holistic description of the community ("the entire congregation of Israelites") and the specific mention of the tent of meeting combine to present Israel as a coherent community in union with YHWH. The unity between people and God is then reinforced by a report that suggests a correlation between people and land, "the land lay subdued before them." However, this image of completeness is soon shattered by Joshua's "how long?" (v. 3). The question reiterates the theme of Israel's lack of resolve and explicitly connects it to the land that remains by repeating the programmatic verb *yāraš* (here as a *Qal* infinitive construct, *lārešet* ["to possess"]; cf. 13:1). The episode thus begins on the same thematic note that ended the previous one; the lack of Israelite determination and the presence of land yet to be occupied (cf. 17:14-18).

Joshua then proposes a program to get things moving. He lays it out first in a general sense through a series of verbs that infuse the scene with energy and animation (v. 4). After calling the assembly to "provide" three men Joshua declares, "I will dispatch them and they will get up and walk throughout the land and record it" (AT).[69] The

---

[69] The translation follows the syntax of the MT, which places the verbs in close sequence. The second verb "arise" combines with "walk" to form a hendiadys which NRSV renders "they may begin to go."

land is to be trod specifically for the purpose of providing a survey for inheritance and, this accomplished, the travelers are to return to Joshua. The procedure recalls the promise of land articulated at the beginning of the book (1:3) and recently alluded to in the story of Caleb (14:9), reminding both Israel and the reader that the nation will possess just as much of the gift of the land as it cares to traverse. Against the backdrop of this larger program, Joshua then fills in the details (vv. 5-6). During their journeys, the travelers will divide the land into seven parts, taking into account the land already allotted to Judah in the south and Joseph in the north.[70] The "written description" of the land, referred to in the previous verse, will consist of a record of these divisions, which the men will bring to Joshua. In a surprising turn, Joshua then declares that he will cast lots for the tribes "in the presence of the LORD." The pronouncement is unexpected because the casting of lots conventionally lies in the purview of the priesthood (and indeed, the end of the account will record Eleazar's participation in the procedure; 19:51). The declaration, however, reinforces the thematic concerns of the broader narrative, which has carefully constructed the flow of divine authority through Joshua to the nation.

Joshua concludes the careful division of the land with yet another reference to the Levites and the eastern tribes (v. 7). They appear together, as they do in the passage that introduces the earlier allotments (14:2-4), prefacing the promise of ordered division with images of discontinuity and paradox (cf. 13:14, 33). Levi's "no-portion" status receives yet another explanation, "the priesthood of YHWH is their inheritance." The explanation, rather than clarifying matters, actually creates a greater sense of incongruity, for the Levites have been curiously absent amidst mentions of the tent of meeting, Shiloh, and the presence of YHWH. And in the eastern tribes the reader once again encounters the problem of those Israelites who live "beyond the Jordan eastward" and who will forever be defined as those who live "in the land Moses gave."

The rest of the episode repeats the program in a command-execution format that restores a sense of unity between Joshua and the people and suggests a new beginning. The narrator evokes the relationship between success and obedience by repeating the verb *hōlēk* ("go"). Paired with *qûm* ("arise") and then with *ʿābar* ("cross, traverse") it describes the

---

The sending of spies can hardly inspire confidence at this point, given the outcomes of previous missions (Num 13:1ff; Josh 2:1ff).

[70] The verb which NRSV translates "they shall divide" *(wĕhithallĕqû)* puns on the verb translated "go throughout" in the previous verse *(wĕhithallĕkû)*, reinforcing the connection between walking and acquiring the land.

activity of the men selected for the reconnaissance mission (vv. 8a, 9a).
Three more repetitions occur in v. 8 in connection with Joshua's charge
to the men. The repetitions smooth out an otherwise awkward sequence, in which the report of the mission is interrupted by a seemingly
gratuitous reiteration of Joshua's charge, now introduced by the language of command: "Joshua charged those who went" *(wayĕṣaw yĕhôšua
ʾet-hahōlĕkîm)*. The repetition of the command stresses that obedience is
central to the enterprise and provides a succinct synopsis which the narrator then appropriates to demonstrate the men's careful and obedient
response.[71] Thus, as in similar constructions throughout the book, the
narrator reasserts Israel's obedience by reporting the execution of the
command in precisely the terms it is given (vv. 9-10a). A concluding remark, that "there Joshua apportioned the land to the Israelites, to each a
portion," consolidates Joshua's connection with the division of the land,
uniting the phases of conquest and allotment through his character.

The Seven Remaining Tribes: 18:11—19:48

The description of Benjamin's allotment is set off from the rest by a
tight organization and attention to detail that rivals that of Judah's territory. As with Judah, the boundaries of the territory are delineated
first (18:11-20) and then followed by a list of towns (18:21-28). Both
sections comprise clearly-defined units. The territorial survey begins
with an expanded introduction which communicates precision by
neatly differentiating between the two senses of *gôrāl* (v. 11) while
stressing the unity of procedure and outcome; the first phrase ("the lot
went up") refers to the casting of the lot, while the second ("the territory of their allotment") signifies the land designated by the lot.[72] It
concludes with corresponding exactness, "this is the inheritance of the
tribe of Benjamin, according to its families, boundary by boundary all
around" (v. 20b). The borders themselves are drawn meticulously and

---

[71] The verbal pair in v. 9a repeats the sense of v. 8a, establishing a continuity after
the interruption. However, *ʿābar* ("cross, traverse") replaces *qûm* ("arise"). The use
of the two verbs, in a construction that establishes continuity, recalls their pairing in
the command which opens the book, where YHWH commands Joshua to "arise and
cross this Jordan" (1:2a). The repetitions of "going" (five times) and "writing"
(three times) also evoke allusions to YHWH's initial speech, which emphasizes the
importance of adhering to what is written so that Joshua may succeed wherever he
goes (1:7-8).

[72] The allotment of land "according to their families" also links the description of
Benjamin's territory with those of Judah (15:1) and the eastern tribes (13:15, 24, 29).

elaborated in all directions. The text traces each side *(pēᵓâ)*, beginning in the north (vv. 12-13), then to the west (v. 14), onward to the south (vv. 15-19) and finally to the east (v. 20a).

The list of cities displays a comparable coherence. It also is bracketed by introductory and concluding remarks: "now the towns of the tribe of Benjamin according to their families were" (v. 21a) and "this is the inheritance of the tribe of Benjamin according to its families" (v. 28c).[73] The same schematic which organizes Judah's towns also divides the cities of Benjamin into two discrete sections (vv. 21b-24, vv. 25-28b); the listing of towns in a group precedes a summation of the number of the towns, along with the phrase "with their villages." As with Judah, the allotment of Benjamin communicates fullness, order, and coherence.

The reader is therefore not prepared for the disordered and fragmented presentation of the last six allotments. The six, though united by the formulaic comment "this is the inheritance of the tribe of" (vv. 9, 16, 23, 31, 39, 48), display diverse structures and various states of cohesion.[74] Geographical concerns seem to determine the order of presentation, which proceeds from Simeon in the far south (vv. 1-19) and ends with Dan in the extreme north (vv. 40-48). However, the nebulous situations of Simeon and Dan also constitute a thematic frame which encloses the fragmented but still homogenous lands of Zebulun, Issachar, Asher, and Naphtali, suggesting the confusion of boundaries and, symbolically, of tribal identities.

Simeon's allotment raises particular problems for the program of tribal definition and organization. Its inheritance consists only of towns, nine of which are also included in the allotment of Judah.[75] The lack of boundaries and the towns with dual claims pose difficulties for the program of tribal definition. The narrator draws attention to these ambiguities by enclosing the list of towns with comments which clarify their implication for the wider agenda. The narrator twice remarks that Simeon's "inheritance" is located within the "inheritance" of Judah, once at the beginning (v. 1b) and then more emphatically at the conclusion (v. 9). The latter remark exhibits a chiastic construction which explains the intermingling of inheritances by reporting that Judah's portion *(ḥēleq)* was too large for the tribe.

[73] The latter phrase repeats the concluding remark of the boundary section (v. 20b), connecting the two segments into a coherent unit.

[74] The formula also sets the six within the broader framework of all inheritances (14:1; 15:20; 16:8; 18:20, 28).

[75] The nine are Moladah (15:26), Hazar-shual (15:27), Ezem (15:29), Eltolad (15:30), Hormah (15:30), Ziklag (15:31), Ain (15:32), Ether (15:42), and Ashan (15:42).

> The inheritance of the tribe of Simeon formed part of the territory of Judah;
> because the portion of the tribe of Judah was too large for them,
> the tribe of Simeon obtained an inheritance within their inheritance.

The central element of the construction recalls another circumstance of territorial modification, namely the Josephites' claim that their lot and portion is insufficient because they are a "large" *(rab)* people and their assigned place too constrictive (17:14-18). In a reversal of that situation, we are now informed that Judah's portion was too large *(rab)* and that the tribe needed help in occupying their land; thus Simeon's inheritance. Both instances, however, imply a common attitude; a reluctance to settle the land (cf. 17:16). The depiction of a territory with no boundaries and an inheritance within an inheritance renders the whole enterprise of identification-through-inheritance problematic. How can lands (and tribes) retain their distinctiveness without definitive boundaries? How can inheritances define the connection between tribe and land if inheritances are indefinite?

The account of Dan's allotment (vv. 40-48) elicits additional difficulties. Here the issue is not intertribal intermingling but tribal possession and occupation apart from allotment and inheritance. Like Simeon, Dan's inheritance consists mainly of cities, which are enumerated by a simple list (vv. 41b-46). The account, however, goes on to report the loss of the tribe's territory. With an extraordinarily ironic flourish, the narrator relates this failure by employing the same verbal construction that introduces the tribal allotments (v. 47): *wayyēṣēʾ gĕbûl-bĕnēy-dān* ("and the boundary/territory of the Danites came out/was lost" [cf. 16:1; 19:1, 17, 24, 32, 40]).[76] The narrator then relates the conquest of Leshem, using the same verbs, in the same sequence, which signify the larger program of the book: "they went up" *(wayyaʿălû)*, "they fought against it" *(wayyillāḥămû)*, "they captured it" *(wayyilkĕdû ʾōtāh)*, "they put it to the sword" *(wayyakkû ōtāh lĕpî-ḥereb)*, "they took possession of it" *(wayyiršû ʾōtāh)*, "they settled in it" *(wayyēšĕbû ʾōtāh)*, and "they renamed Leshem 'Dan,' after the name of their ancestor Dan." The last verbal phrase confirms that Dan carries the program to completion; the tribe achieves the ideal correspondence between the tribe and the territory possessed. Yet the campaign of possession, the only one yet recorded in its entirety, occurs apart from any divine initiative or authorization. The land that Dan settles is not the land allotted to it. Dan thus

---

[76] The second verb in the sentence, *wayyaʿălû* ("they went up") is the same that used alternatively in place of *yāṣāʾ* to introduce the tribal allotments in the section (18:11; 19:10).

represents both failure and initiative taken to the extreme. In this respect, the concluding remark, that "this is the inheritance of the tribe of Dan, according to its families," acquires a sense of indeterminacy, for the case of Dan completely separates conquest, occupation, and unity with the land from the legitimacy of a divinely-authorized claim through the lot. Dan succeeds in securing a tribal possession but does so apart from the system that legitimates its claim to land. What then defines Israel in the land, occupation or claim?

The descriptions of the remaining allotments develop the sense of tribal and territorial incoherence. Zebulun (vv. 10-16) contains a relatively coherent boundary and a list of towns but displays an accounting anomaly. The narrator states that the number of its towns is twelve, but seventeen are actually listed within the account, twelve of them as border points. Issachar (vv. 17-23) consists of a list of towns, with only the vague fragment of a boundary. Asher (vv. 24-31) offers a detailed boundary and full lists of towns, but both sets intermingle (rather than occurring separately as in other descriptions). Naphtali (vv. 32-39) offers a border description that is difficult to make sense of and communicates a bit of geographical disorientation; the abrupt shift of the boundary as it turns west from the Jordan (v. 34a) is difficult to pinpoint. The description of its land concludes with (correct) references to Zebulun in the south and Asher to the west, but "Judah on the east of the Jordan" (v. 34b)!

The structure of the section thus parallels that of 14:1–17:18, beginning with a model tribe which expresses a coherent territorial unit but immediately countering it with fragmentary and ambiguous descriptions which depict the breakdown of boundaries, territorial indeterminacy, and the intermingling of tribes. A parallel theme, which raises the issue of Israel's courage and resolve, offers an implicit explanation for territorial and tribal incoherence (18:3; 19:9, 47); the tribes either do not carry the program to its completion or modify it to suit their own ends. In the process, the fine distinctions promised by the allotment and division of territories become hopelessly muddled. Boundaries do not enclose or define. Tribes do not succeed in acquiring homogenous territories in which to dwell. Legitimate claims are splintered from the circumstances of settlement. Inheritances, which define and organize Israel's life in the land, fail to do either completely.

EPILOGUE: 19:49-51

The apportionment of land draws to a close with two notes that tell of Joshua's inheritance (vv. 49-50) and offer a formal conclusion (v. 51).

The two segments form a unit, enclosed by programmatic remarks that the task of distributing the land has been finished (*wayĕkallû* [vv. 49a, 51c]). The succinct account of Joshua's inheritance reverses the program whereby Joshua gives lands to the tribes and authorizes their claims. Instead, the Israelites give Joshua an inheritance among them. The grant of land is legitimized by a parenthetical note that this was done "by the command of the LORD."[77] The text leaves until last the report that Joshua asked for the town he is given, as well as its location in the hill country. And it concludes by noting that he "rebuilt" the town and settled in it. The last note conveys an uncertainty not communicated by NRSV; it could just as easily be translated "he built the town and settled in it." The reference to "re/building" a town and settling the hill country associates Joshua closely with his Josephite kinsmen, whom he had charged with clearing the area. And it sets him apart from Caleb the "Judahite," who seeks a formidable territory, inhabited by giants. Joshua asks for a town away from the more densely-populated areas of Canaan and takes it (and not one of the formidable towns assigned to Joseph) as his inheritance. A final comment signals the completion of the allotment phase by evoking all the symbols and structures which have given legitimacy to the division and apportionment of the territories: the priest Eleazar, Joshua, the heads of the ancestral houses of the tribes, the lot, the presence of YHWH, and the tent of meeting.

DESIGNATED CITIES: 20:1–21:42

The establishment of cities of refuge and Levitical cities signals the completion of the program which defines Israel's inheritance but further complicates the organization signified by it. Both apply Mosaic commandments which are to take effect once Israel enters the land (Num 35:1-15; Deut 19:1) and begin by invoking Moses (Josh 20:1-2; 21:2). The designation of the cities displays a systematic presentation that conveys a sense of order, but the inhabitants of the cities point to ambiguity within the now-defined territorial lands.

The list of cities of refuge is enclosed by commentary that emphasizes the marginal character of those who will settle within them (20:1-6, 9). The cities provide a place in the land for members of the community who represent a particular paradox. These individuals are responsible

---

[77] The wording of the note, *ʿal-pî* YHWH ("by the mouth of YHWH") employs virtually the same idiom which, in the beginning section, denotes the travelers' recording of the land "with a view to their inheritances" (*lĕpî nahălātām*; 18:4).

for the shedding of human blood.[78] That they are culpable for the death of another is implicitly confirmed by repeated references to the "avenger of blood" (vv. 3-5, 9) who, we may assume, seeks a measure of justice by killing them. However, in another sense they are also *not* responsible, for they did not kill the other intentionally. The text emphasizes this aspect of their status by combining distinctive terminology from both Numbers and Deuteronomy; the offender did so "without intent" (*bišgāgâ* [vv. 3, 9; cf. Num 35:11, 15]) or "by mistake" (*biblî-dāʿat* [vv. 3, 5; Deut 4:42; 19:4]), with no preexisting enmity *(śōnēʾ hûʾ lî mitmōl šilšôm).* Thus the individual is both responsible for the death of another and not liable for the act (cf. Deut 19:6).[79] The conflicted status of the refugee is reinforced by the procedure which allows the individual to live in the land. Neither YHWH nor Joshua determine whether that person may live within the city. With verbs that echo the thematic equation between gift and settlement, the text declares that the elders shall "give" the offender a "place" in the city in which to "settle" (v. 5), pending approval by the entire citizenry (vv. 6, 9).[80] Paradoxically, the death of another individual (the high priest) resolves the subject's conflicted status, allowing reintegration into the community (v. 6b-c).

The allotment of Levitical cities (21:1-42) reiterates another set of perplexities, namely those involving the status of a tribe whose inheritance is YHWH rather than land. The designation of their towns, while confirming obedience to YHWH and Moses, also intensifies their paradoxical situation. As in the previous section, the list of towns is set within a narrative that refers to the problematic status of the towns' inhabitants (vv. 1-3, 41-42). Reminiscent of other stories of initiative, the Levites approach Joshua, Eleazar, and the heads of the ancestral houses and remind them of Moses' decree that they be given towns to

---

[78] The verb used to characterize them *(rôṣēāḥ)* refers only to the killing of another human being (Deut 22:26; 1 Kings 21:19; Jer 7:9; Hos 4:2).

[79] The Deuteronomic legislation implies a conflict between the Mosaic commandments and the ethics of the family or clan. Deuteronomy is concerned about the blood that may be spilled by the avenger of blood, which would challenge its ruling that the offender has done nothing to deserve a death sentence. However, the family or clan (of whom the avenger is the agent) obviously considers the offender guilty and subject to death. The very fact that Deuteronomy anticipates such avengers intimates another discontinuity between the nation and the Mosaic commandments.

[80] The transmission of authority from YHWH through Moses and Joshua to the elders is conveyed thematically by the repetition of the verb *nātan*, which denotes first what Joshua is to do at the command of YHWH through Moses ("Appoint the cities," *tĕnû lākem ʿārēy* [v. 1]) and then what the elders are to do ("they will give him a place and he will settle with them" (AT, *wĕnātĕnû-lî māqôm wĕyāšab ʿimmām* [v. 5]).

live in, along with pasture lands (vv. 1-2).[81] A report that the Israelites did so then presents the procedure as yet another expression of national obedience to the commands of Moses (v. 3). Though Joshua and Eleazar appear in the scene, the narrator again avoids associating either of them with the business of designating habitations for a group which is so ambiguous, reporting instead that the nation itself gave the towns for the Levites to settle in "by the command of the LORD" (cf. 19:49-50; 21:5). The ambivalence arises from the fact that, like the other tribes, the Levites are given portions of land (as pastures) and towns, even though their inheritance is YHWH, thus breaking the inheritance-land equivalency which undergirds the allotment of tribal territories. The procedure disrupts the system which unites the tribes and their lands, a circumstance the narrator highlights by noting that the towns and pasture lands are taken "out of the inheritance" of the other tribes.

In the manner of other allocations, the lot determines the assignment of towns, this time in two phases. The first, enclosed by references to the lot (vv. 4a, 8), designates the regions in which each of the Levite clans will receive their allotments. The process begins with the same formula as that used to specify tribal territories. The phrase "the lot came out" (cf. 16:10; 19:2, 17, 24, 32, 40) prefaces a schematic description of apportionment. However, the distribution itself is asymmetrical; Kohathites who descend from Aaron (the priests) receive towns within a large, coherent block of land, while the rest of their clan and the other clans receive towns located in widely dispersed lands. In addition, the inclusion of both "halves" of Manasseh yields thirteen divisions, which results in Gershonites receiving towns in four tribal areas rather than three (v. 6). An enumeration of towns (vv. 9-40) also links Levi's apportionment to those of the other tribes. As in other town lists, each listing concludes with a note that reports the total number of towns within it (vv. 19, 26, 33, 40). However, these are further subdivided by additional notes that specify the number of Levitical towns within the respective tribal lands (vv. 16, 18, 22, 24, 25, 27, 29, 31, 32, 35, 37, 39). The anomaly represented by the descendants of Aaron receives additional attention by the inclusion of Kiriath-arba/Hebron as the very first entry (vv. 11-12). The inclusion necessitates an explanation. Thus, we learn, the town of Hebron is not to be considered Calebite (cf. 14:13-14; 15:13) nor Judahite (15:54) but Levite. The narrator offers a way of resolving the conflicted status of the town by declaring that the town and its lands are

---

[81] The structure of the terse account approximates that by which the stories of Caleb, Achsah, Zelophehad's daughters, and the Josephites are told. See Nelson, *Joshua* 177-8.

given to Levi, while the "fields of the town" and its villages are given to Caleb. A chiasm shapes the report, enclosing the ruling with statements that validate it. Following the syntax of the MT it reads:

A They gave *(wayyittĕnû)* them

   B Kiriath-arba (Arba being the father of Anak), that is Hebron, in the hill country of Judah, along with the pasture lands around it.

   B' But the fields of the town along with its villages

A' they gave *(nātĕnû)* to Caleb son of Jephunneh as his property.

The verbs point to the same process by which the apportionment of all Levitical towns is authorized by the community as a whole (v. 3), while the divisions neatly designate areas for Caleb that do not figure in the scheme of towns and pastures.

The note, however, only succeeds in driving an additional wedge between concepts closely associated with the conquest and possession of the land. It reveals that *conquest* of a town does not necessarily lead to *inheritance* (cf. 19:47), nor does the fact that it is *given* by Joshua (14:13-14). *Allotment* does not necessarily stipulate *inheritance*, for the lot sometimes identifies property that is not an inheritance. And *inheritance* is not to be equated with *portion*, for one tribe will possess portions within the inheritances of others. *Inheritance* does not entail *occupation* or even communal endorsement of property. The program for the possession of the land assumes a tight interconnection between concepts of inheritance, gift, conquest, lot, and occupation, but by the end of the section the connections are tenuous.

The many ambiguities that configure the program of allotment have a cumulative effect that not only challenges the distinct organization of Israel in the land but also the network of kinship relationships that lie behind it. Gaps in geographical boundaries reveal a permeability in the social boundaries which configure Israelite society. Women join men in claiming and occupying land, while peoples of the land intermingle with the people of YHWH. Like the land itself, the nation of Israel does not display a thoroughgoing homogeneity, purity, or coherence. And like the possession of the land, the makeup of Israelite society seems to remain in a state of openness. Not all the land *given* has been *allotted as inheritance*, for land promised to the south (to the Shihor, 13:3)[82] and to

---

[82] The identification of the Shihor is the subject of debate. Other biblical references link it to an eastern arm of the Nile (Isa 23:3; Jer 2:18).

the north (Lebo-Hamath, 13:5, and up to the Euphrates, 1:4) still lies outside the boundaries set for the tribes. In a similar sense, the reports of
other peoples within the land (when read with the stories of Rahab and
the Gibeonites) point to a continuing process of social reconstitution.

Everything Came to Pass: 21:43-45

The narrator concludes the second phase of the book with a brief
summation that signals the completion of the entire program. The summary begins with two declarations (vv. 43-44) which create a sense of
closure by affirming the fulfillment of the promises which have driven
the plot up to this point. The first declaration (v. 43), that YHWH gave the
land to the Israelites, who settled and possessed it, precisely answers
the language of promise which initiates the larger narrative. In Deuteronomy, Israel's story begins with Moses' command that the nation
leave Horeb and journey to the land of the Canaanites (Deut 1:6-7). The
command is followed by an exhortation comprising three components:
a proclamation that YHWH has given the land to Israel,[83] a command to
enter and take possession, and a reference to the oath sworn to the ancestors (v. 8). These three elements reappear in YHWH's opening speech
to Joshua (Josh 1:6) as Israel prepares to cross the Jordan into the promised land, articulating the thematic connections between divine faithfulness and human response which will configure the story of conquest.
The second declaration (v. 44), that YHWH gave Israel rest from its enemies, picks up a prominent Deuteronomic cue for the conclusion of the
conquest. The Mosaic declaration that the eastern tribes may return to
their lands when "the LORD gives rest to your kindred, as to you" (Deut
3:20) establishes an implicit signal that the nation has accomplished its
objectives. The declaration serves the same function in the opening
scene of Joshua, where it again looks forward to the successful completion of the story (Josh 1:15). A third declaration (v. 45) shifts the focus
from fulfillment to faithfulness by emphasizing that all of YHWH's
promises to Israel have come to pass.

The sense of completion, however, stands in stark contrast to the
sense of failure and incompleteness which characterizes the preceding
material. How can the possession of Canaan be affirmed when the occupation of the land remains incomplete? And in what sense does Is-

---

[83] Although NRSV reads "behold, I have set the land before you," the verb is *nā-*
tattî, the verb used to signify the giving of the land.

rael enjoy rest, given the presence of "determined" peoples with iron chariots? At no point in the book do narrated reality and the narrator's perspective seem so far apart. What are we to make of commentary that seems to contradict all that we have just read? A number of possibilities suggest themselves. Perhaps the narrator is engaging in hyperbole in order to put the best possible spin on the events. Or the narrator may be affirming the significance of the ideal vision, even though it is never accomplished. On the other hand, we may have to entertain the possibility that the narrator is engaging in an exercise of high irony, perhaps to accentuate Israel's failure or to bring into question all expansive claims of conquest and obedience.

While all of these possibilities contribute to a sense of the summary's meaning, we may find firmer ground by recognizing the *thematic* contrast which it draws with the preceding material. The apportionment of the land consists mainly of *Israel's* actions, YHWH being immediately present only in the beginning and concluding segments.[84] The description of tribal lands puts Israel in the foreground and demonstrates repeatedly the nation's halting and incomplete response to YHWH's promises and commands. The concluding summary, however, emphasizes YHWH's actions, with only a passing reference to the nation's response. It asserts YHWH's initiative, power, and faithfulness and stresses the divine commitment to do everything necessary to bring matters to a successful completion. The Hebrew particle *kôl* ("all, every"), which throughout Deuteronomy and Joshua signals an ideal totality and wholeness, occurs six times to express the comprehensive scope and completion of YHWH's acts on behalf of Israel. The verb *nātan* ("give"), signifying divine initiative and power, frames the description of YHWH's deeds in vv. 43-44. And the repeated reference to what YHWH had sworn to Israel's ancestors asserts a divine determination to accomplish all that was spoken, a commitment to fulfill words uttered long ago. By concentrating on YHWH and emphasizing these attributes, the narrator powerfully attributes Israel's successes to YHWH and accentuates divine resolve in the face of national trepidation. In contrast to Israelite inconstancy, YHWH does not waver from commitments made to the nation. Whereas Israel may fail to follow through on its part, YHWH does everything that he has promised.

The final comment (v. 45) punctuates this contrast by explicitly affirming the fulfillment of every word which YHWH spoke. Divine

---

[84] It is significant in this respect that at Shiloh, at the middle of the section, Joshua speaks and exhorts the people and sends out a reconnaissance mission, all at his own initiative; YHWH does not appear in the scene (18:1-10).

stability and consistency are thus set against Israelite instability and inconsistency. In this way the summary achieves a powerful rhetorical impact which acclaims YHWH's crucial role in the possession of the land against Israel's failures and flaws. Within the larger narrative, this emphasis on divine initiative and faithfulness, contrasted with Israelite inconstancy, brings to the surface a theme which, though implicit in the preceding narrative, will acquire more prominence in the final section of the book.

Chapter Eleven
ALTAR EGOS
Joshua 22:1-34

Although the concluding remarks on the tribal allotments (21:43-45) would seem a good place to end, the story nevertheless continues through a series of farewells. The sense of ending is thus drawn out, as if to work through issues that still await resolution. The story of the eastern tribes' return home offers an ending, for their dismissal signals the completion of the story (cf. 1:12-15). And Joshua's declaration that YHWH has given the nation "rest" (*hēnîăḥ;* v. 4) not only confirms the endpoint which Joshua had set for the conclusion of the conquest (1:15) but also connects the return to the previous commentary (21:44) and to Joshua's farewell address (23:1).

This happily-ever-after ending, however, quickly degenerates as the eastern tribes head off into the sunrise. When they reach the environs of the Jordan, they build an altar. The act inflames the rest of the tribes, who immediately unite to inflict upon their kindred the same measure of violence previously reserved for the peoples of the land. Before hostilities begin, however, the tribes in Canaan send a delegation led by Phinehas the priest. What becomes clear during the ensuing flurry of charges and countercharges is that the two groups have very different ideas about what constitutes obedience to YHWH, possession of the land, and membership in the Israelite nation. The delegation views the construction of the altar as a gross and blatant act of rebellion, an affront to YHWH which will certainly bring divine wrath on the nation once again (vv. 16-20). Linking the construction of the altar with the sin of Baal-Peor and Achan's transgression, they seem to throw the book at their kindred, accusing them (directly or by implication) of treachery, rebellion, apostasy, defilement, and breaking faith. They also insinuate that the Transjordanian territories are not really part of the land of Israel, suggesting that the land is "unclean" and that (only) the land west of the Jordan comprises "the LORD's land."

In response, the eastern tribes deny that any such motives lay behind the construction of the altar. Instead, they bring issues of identity and inclusion to the forefront (vv. 21-29). They argue that the charges, innuendos, and warlike response of the Cisjordanian tribes are symptomatic of precisely the concern that led to them to build the altar, namely the fear that the tribes in Canaan would become overly preoccupied with setting boundaries. Looking to the future, the eastern tribes anticipate that the descendants of the other tribes will view the Jordan as the eastern boundary of the promised land. And if this ever comes to pass, they will inevitably view those on the other side as outsiders. The altar, they claim, will not be used for sacrifice but will be a "witness" to their place within the nation. They then conclude with an emphatic declaration of their fidelity to YHWH.

The intense exchange explicitly raises many of the identity questions that have run just below the surface of the narrative. The eastern tribes appear throughout the book as implicit reminders of the ambiguities that complicate the formation of a distinctive Israelite community. The present episode raises these questions by making them the focus of the action. Is Israel to be equated with the land west of the Jordan? If so, what is the status of the two and one-half tribes in the Transjordan? Are they outsiders or insiders? What are the marks of national unity? How is loyalty to YHWH and to the community to be expressed? What constitutes the obedience that YHWH requires? And how is disobedience to be detected and confronted? What, in essence, constitutes the community's internal boundaries, and how are they to be safeguarded when motives are not apparent in actions? Who and what is "Israel?"

The construction of the altar provides a metaphor for addressing these issues within the context of the narrative. An altar, as a place of sacrifice, constitutes the symbolic center of the community, the place where the polarities of communal life are united and mediated. Sacrifice itself is an exercise in paradox, a place joining such tensions as guilt and innocence, life and death, inclusion and exclusion, and the individual and the community. Thus an altar provides a place where the untidy oppositions of communal life converge.[1] Since sacrifice often marks and facilitates a change in the state of the community, the construction of altars marks social transformations throughout the Hebrew Bible (Gen 8:20-22; 12:6-7; Exod 24:1-8; Josh 8:30-35; 2 Sam 24:15-25; 2 Kings 16:10-15). An altar

---

[1] The connection is more explicit in Hebrew, where the word for altar, *mizbēăḥ*, derives from the verb for sacrifice, *zābaḥ*. For a summary of sacrifice's role in the Israelite community, see R. D. Nelson, *Raising Up a Faithful Priest: Community and Priesthood in Biblical Theology* (Louisville: Westminster John Knox Press, 1993).

therefore constitutes the perfect symbol and setting for this story which attempts to negotiate the difficult issues of community identity.

The polarities within the story also explain why cultic themes and language are so pervasive. The easterners construct the altar, appropriately, in a boundary-region, "the region near the Jordan," while the rest of the nation gathers at Shiloh, a shrine located in the hill country of Ephraim. The delegation which raises the issues is led by a priest (Phinehas), the individual charged with guarding existential boundaries and empowered to traverse them. Within the dialogue, the delegation appropriates cultic language to characterize the easterners' land ("clean and unclean," vv. 17a, 19a) and to assert that the construction of the altar is an act of sacrilege (*maʿal* [vv. 16, 20]). The eastern tribes for their part repeatedly refer to the various sacrifices offered by the community (vv. 23, 26, 28) and associate participation in the nation with participation in those sacrifices (v. 27).[2]

The crux of the story revolves around different perceptions of how the nation is to be defined and held together. The tribes west of the Jordan equate national identity with *the possession of land*, particularly the land west of the Jordan. From their viewpoint, the tribes inhabiting lands east of the Jordan are unclean outsiders. The construction of the altar at the Jordan reinforces this perception and serves as the catalyst for the expression of these sentiments. Since "YHWH's tabernacle" is on the west side of the Jordan (presumably at Shiloh, and since Deuteronomy specifies that sacrifices may only be offered at the (one) place that YHWH chooses, the altar at the Jordan introduces a dangerous *plurality* into the nation. If Israel should offer sacrifice at *many* sites, its distinctive integrity and unity will be lost, rendering it indistinguishable from the other peoples of the land and subjecting it to the devastating visitation of divine anger. The tribes to the west thus see the erection of the altar as a divisive act and ironically divide the nation by setting themselves against their eastern kindred, gathering to "make war" *(laʿălôt ʿălêhem laṣṣābāʾ)* against them just as they earlier gathered to make war against the peoples of the land.

On the other hand, the eastern tribes regard *bonds of kinship* as more definitive for Israelite identity than the possession of a specific territory and are concerned to preserve these bonds. For them, settlement in the Transjordan is not problematic. However, they recognize the difference in perception between themselves and their kindred to the west and seek to preserve these ties into the future. The construction of

---

[2] The priestly tone of the episode (vv. 10-34) is perhaps due to the editing of the story by priestly circles. See J. Kloppenborg, "Joshua 22: The Priestly Editing of an Ancient Tradition," *Bib* 62 (1981) 355–62.

the altar is not a divisive act from their point of view. On the contrary it represents an attempt to hold the nation together throughout its generations. Both tribal groups agree that fidelity to YHWH (here expressed as the proper offering of sacrifices) is also a vital component of national identity, but the whole course of the episode points out the difficulties in pinpointing what obedient actions look like. The easterners' explanation that they have constructed the altar "as a witness" seems a bit too facile. What is an altar if not a place of sacrifice? If the easterners wanted to establish a "witness" of their membership in the nation, why not erect a stone monument, as Joshua will do later after the covenant renewal ceremony at Shechem (Josh 24:25-27; cf. 4:1-7, 19-24). Their claim that the altar is only a "copy" *(tabnît)* could be viewed as a case of special pleading, but it satisfies the delegation and resolves the conflict. Phinehas even remarks that the eastern tribes "have saved the Israelites from the hand of the LORD" (v. 31), an oblique compliment to the tribes for supplying an explanation that eases the tension.

The language of the text influences the reader to view the story as a case of "insiders" vs. "outsiders." The Deuteronomic language of wholeness appears frequently throughout the episode. The tribes of Canaan refer to themselves as the "entire community of YHWH" (vv. 16) and the "entire community of Israel" (vv. 18, 20), indicating that they now view themselves as the full embodiment of the nation, as opposed to those in the Transjordan who are, by implication, *not* part the whole community. (Significantly, the eastern tribes do not refer to themselves in this way.) The narrator reinforces this perspective by using similar terms to denote the tribes in Canaan: "the entire community of Israel" (v. 12) and "each of the tribes of Israel" (v. 14).[3] On the other hand, the narrator employs the language of plurality (hitherto associated with the peoples of the land) to denote the Transjordanian tribes, "the Reubenites, the Gadites, and the half-tribe of Manasseh" (vv. 9, 10, 13, 15, 21). The easterners themselves recognize the divided state of the nation (against the exclusivistic claims of the delegation) and express the western tribes' perception of them in the same plural terminology, "for the LORD has made the Jordan a bound-

---

[3] In all cases, the word translated "entire" or "each" is the programmatic term *kôl.* For a more extensive discussion of the use of vocabulary and perspective, see R. Polzin, *Moses and the Deuteronomist: A Literary Study of the Deuteronomic History* (New York: Seabury, 1980) 134–8. Polzin sees significance in the fact that a similarly programmatic term, *ʿābar* ("cross, pass through") does *not* occur in the episode except in the delegation's "invitation" to the easterners to "cross over into the LORD's land" (v. 19). If Hebrews *(ʿibrîm)* are quintessentially those who have "crossed over," then the delegation's words insinuate that the tribes of the Transjordan are not full members of the nation (because they have not crossed over the Jordan to live in Canaan).

ary between us and you, *you Reubenites and Gadites.*"[4] The nomenclature continues even after the situation is resolved. "The clans of Israel" (v. 30, cf. v. 21) and "Israelites" (vv. 31, 32, 33) still refer only to the western tribes, while the tribes east of the Jordan are listed according to their diverse membership, "the Reubenites, the Gadites and the Manassites" (v. 31, 32, 33, 34).[5] However, the terminology of totality and wholeness is conspicuously absent after the conflict, hinting that a fundamental unity has not been achieved. In a sense, the altar symbolizes this appearance of unity apart from substance. It is a copy, a non-functional altar that stands as a witness between two separated parties.

The story of the confrontation (vv. 10-34) is rendered as an elaborate chiasm which concentrates on the building (at the ends) and function of the altar (in the middle).

CHART 12: THE STRUCTURE OF THE JORDAN CONFLICT[6]

A Eastern tribes build the altar (vv. 10-11)

  B Western tribes gather for war (v. 12)

    C Delegation selected and sent to the eastern tribes (vv. 13-15a)

      D Delegation accuses the eastern tribes (vv. 15b-20)

        E Eastern tribes deny the allegations (vv. 21-23)

          F Eastern tribes explain the altar (vv. 24-28)

        E' Eastern tribes deny the allegations (v. 29)

      D' Delegation is satisfied with the explanation (vv. 30-31)

    C' Delegation returns to the other tribes (vv. 32)

  B' Plans for war are called off (v. 33)

A' Eastern tribes name the altar (v. 34)

---

[4] The plurals are rendered in the MT with the phrase "the sons of" *(bĕnēy).* Although this is a conventional way of denoting tribal plurals, its "plural" character stands out because of the contrast with the singular form which signifies the tribes in vv. 1-8.

[5] The Manassites are listed only in the first instance.

[6] This description of structure modifies the chiasm identified by D. Jobling, "The Jordan a Boundary: Transjordan in Israel's Ideological Geography," *The Sense of Biblical Narrative II: Structural Analyses in the Hebrew Bible,* JSOTSup 39 (Sheffield: JSOT Press, 1986) 88–147. Jobling's trenchant analysis of the episode and related texts elucidates the importance and meaning of perspectives in the story.

The structure promotes the role of the altar as a metaphor for Israel's life as a settled people. An altar is the site of sacrifice which orders and unifies the community through ritual, mediating and holding together various tensions and oppositions. Since notions of inclusion and exclusion lie at the heart of sacrifice, this place of sacrifice serves as a fitting backdrop for working through these issues. Who is to be included in the people of God? Who will be excluded? On what basis? Where and how are the boundaries to be drawn and maintained? The altar at the Jordan, however, only appears to be a place of resolution. It promises communal integrity by glossing the questions. Like the Israelites in the story, it expresses religious sentiments that are little more than a veneer which mask as yet unresolved questions, the chief among which is the question of whether Israel will succeed in holding together at all.[7]

Fond Farewells: 22:1-6

The eastern tribes' departure to their tribal lands makes heavy use of Deuteronomic vocabulary and themes to affirm the group's obedience to Joshua (and thus to Moses and YHWH) and the strong bonds of loyalty between the tribes. It consists mainly of a speech by Joshua, which once again holds up the tribes as the epitome of the Deuteronomic program of obedience and fulfillment. The narrator introduces the tribes in a way that anticipates the Israel/not-Israel questions that swirl around them (v. 1). In the MT, they are "the Reubenite, the Gadite, and the half-tribe Manassite." Each is a corporate "one" yet a part of a list. The narrator thus presents the eastern tribes with a plurality that subtly associates them with the nations of Canaan.

Joshua's speech (vv. 2-6) not only signals the completion of the program of conquest and apportionment (cf. 1:12-15) but also endorses the tribes' determined fidelity to the commands of Moses. Although Joshua appears at the frames of the speech (vv. 1, 6), the speech itself once again reiterates the notion that obedience entails careful attention to the commands of Moses. The three-fold reference to "Moses the servant of the LORD" reiterates the lines of authority established at the beginning of the enterprise (cf. 1:1-18). And the glowing accolades bestowed

---

[7] R. Nelson observes that the altar itself is transformed from a center of conflict to an instrument of reconciliation; *Joshua*, OTL (Louisville: Westminster John Knox, 1997) 249. But this is the case only insofar as the metaphor itself has been compromised and coopted.

on the easterners restore an atmosphere of optimism in contrast to the many notes of incompleteness and reluctance lacing the description of tribal lands.

In the first part of the speech (vv. 2-3) Joshua unambiguously endorses both the eastern tribes' obedience to YHWH and their loyalty to their kindred with a construction marked by the repetition of the root ṣwh ("command"). His words confirm their recognition of the authority structure ("you have observed all that Moses the servant of the LORD commanded you, and have obeyed all that I have commanded you") and the fulfillment of obligations ("you have not forsaken your kindred these many days, down to this day, but have been careful to keep the charge of the LORD your God"). By associating the commands *(miṣwâ)* of YHWH's chosen leaders (Moses and Joshua) with the charge of YHWH *(miṣwât yhwh)*,[8] the declaration asserts the solidarity of God, leaders, and people. It also expresses the comprehensive character of the tribes' obedience both positively ("you obeyed") and negatively ("you have not forsaken"). Joshua's words thus directly testify to the eastern tribes' fidelity to YHWH and to the nation, both of which will be severely challenged in the upcoming conflict.

The second part of the speech consists of a dismissal (v. 4) and an exhortation (v. 5). The shift in tone is marked by the use of *wĕʿattâ* ("and now"), while the connection with the previous declaration is made through the catch phrase "the LORD your God." The phrase *("your* God") reinforces the tribes' obedience and devotion, and thus their membership within the larger national unit. Having affirmed their devotion, Joshua reiterates the marker that establishes the completion of the program and thus the fulfillment of their obligations: YHWH has given rest to their kindred (v. 4). The eastern tribes' return home is thus implicitly linked to YHWH's promise; now that YHWH has fulfilled the promises, they may settle their lands. However, while the opening reference to "the LORD your God" points to the easterners' unity with the nation, an equally pointed reference to "the land where *your* possession lies, which *Moses* the servant of the LORD gave you on the *other* side of the Jordan" reminds the reader of the group's separation from the rest of the nation and thus of their conflicted status.

[8] The commands of Moses and Joshua are subtly distinguished from each other through the use of noun form of the root ṣwh in connection with Moses and the verbal form in connection with Joshua. Associated vocabulary also links Moses' commands more directly with YHWH. The verb *šāmar* (NRSV "observed," "be careful to keep" respectively) denotes observance of both Moses' and YHWH's words, while the verb *šāmāʿ* (NRSV "obeyed") marks the observance of Joshua's.

An exhortation (v. 5) appropriates phrases which Deuteronomy employs to exemplify loyalty to YHWH. It is governed by an imperative form of the same verb used previously to affirm the tribes' loyalty (suggesting a continuity between what they have done in the past and what they will do in the future).[9] A chain of infinitival phrases follows: "to love the LORD your God" (cf. Deut 6:5; 10:12; 11:1, 13, 22, etc.), "to walk in all his ways" (cf. Deut 5:30; 10:12; 11:22), "to keep his commandments" (cf. Deut 5:10; 7:9; 8:11; 13:4 [MT 5], etc.), "to hold fast to him" (cf. Deut 4:4; 10:20; 11:22; 13:5, etc.), "to serve him (cf. Deut 6:13; 10:12, 20; 11;13; etc.) with all your heart and with all your soul (cf. Deut 4:29; 6:5; 10:12; 11:13, etc.)."[10] The piling up of these phrases forcefully underscores the theme of fidelity to YHWH, introducing the subject in the most positive terms. "Eastern tribes" and "fidelity" are therefore tightly joined by the rhetoric of the narrative.

The episode concludes with a terse report that Joshua blessed and dismissed the tribes, who then returned to their tents (v. 6). The blessing of Israel's leader puts the finishing touch on the portrait of the eastern tribes as model Israelites, linking them to Caleb, another model Israelite and the only other recipient of Joshua's blessing (14:13).

Taking Sides: 22:7-9

After presenting the theme of obedience through the dismissal of the eastern tribes, the narrator raises the issue of Israel's compromised tribal configuration with a digression that focuses on the half-tribe of Manasseh. Manasseh represents in miniature the tensions within Israel's social structure. By deliberately drawing attention to Manasseh's divided state the narrator thus evokes troubling issues of national identity (v. 7a-b). We are reminded that half the tribe receives land which "Moses gave," while the other half receives land that "Joshua gave." To complicate matters, the narrative contains a shift in perspective. The "other side" of the Jordan (a designation usually connected with the Transjordan) now refers to Canaan. The narrator accentuates the shift

---

[9] The verb *šimrû* (NRSV "take good care to observe") is an imperative form of *šāmar*. The imperative is set off from the prior words of dismissal by the disjunctive particle *raq* (left untranslated in NRSV) and is followed by the emphatic particle *mĕʾōd*.

[10] A fuller listing of Deuteronomic references can be found in M. Weinfeld, *Deuteronomy and the Deuteronomic School* (Oxford: Oxford, 1972; reprinted Winona Lake: Eisenbrauns, 1992) 332–6. The imperative phrase which precedes the infinitive chain also derives from Deuteronomy.

(in the MT) by pointedly inserting the phrase "westward" *(yāmmâ)* after "the other side of the Jordan." The text thus adopts an "eastern tribe" point of view immediately after the tribes have been dismissed by Joshua. This play with perspective corresponds to the difficulties that occur because of the divided state of Manasseh. The two segments of the tribe evidently hold different points of view regarding ties of land and kin. One contingent settles in the land along with their Josephite kindred, intimating a view of community that defines identity in terms of possession of land west of the Jordan and (as we will see) placing greater priority on ties to the land than on ties to kin. The other contingent, however, is willing to break territorial integrity in order join other, more distantly-related tribal groups across the Jordan. From their perspective, bonds of kinship play a greater role in uniting the nation than possession of particular territory. For them, crossing a geographical boundary (such as the Jordan) does not threaten tribal or national integrity. Manasseh is thus torn in two. One fragment of the tribe will join others in the west in ostracizing "others" of their own kindred and gathering for war to exterminate them. The other fragment will join others across the Jordan to construct a "witness" to national unity. The two halves of the same tribe simply do not see eye to eye.

The narrative returns to Joshua's blessing and dismissal (v. 7c), but in this case the blessing is not associated with obedience itself but with the results of obedience promised by Deuteronomy. With an effusiveness that matches his previous exhortation to fidelity, Joshua catalogues the wealth acquired by the eastern half of the tribe (v. 8). As in the first instance (v. 5), Joshua begins with an imperative ("go back to your tents") before piling up phrase upon phrase to describe all that the half-tribe now possesses (repeating for emphasis that their plunder is "much" [*rabbîm*], "very much" [*rab mĕʾōd*], and "great" [*harbēh mĕʾōd*]). The copious inventory of half-Manasseh's great wealth further confirms their sterling character, the implication being that greatness of their wealth derives from their diligent loyalty to YHWH and to their kindred. This is affirmed even though their decision to possess lands east of the Jordan has splintered the tribe (thus the constant reference to "the half-tribe"). In another irony, Joshua himself initiates a process of division; he instructs the tribe to divide the booty among their kindred (although who is meant by the term "kindred" remains unspecified).[11]

---

[11] The NRSV "divide" translates the verbal equivalent of the noun which signifies the portions of each tribe's inheritance *(ḥilqû)*, thus effecting a thematic connection between the "dividing" that Manasseh undertakes and the broader dividing of the nation through tribal allotment.

The digression concludes by reporting the separation of the entire tribal group from their kindred (v. 9). The structure of the report accentuates the separation. The easterners part from the Israelites at Shiloh (where the nation as a whole assembled to apportion the land) "in the land of Canaan," and travel to Gilead, "the land of their possession."[12] All of this language implies a movement "to the outside." This time, however, the narrator does not describe the possession of their territory in terms of what is given (cf. v. 7a-b) but as an act of obedient response to YHWH "their own land of which they had taken possession by command of the LORD through Moses." The structure of the digression thus articulates the paradoxical status of the eastern tribes. Reminders of the separated location of the Transjordanian tribes enclose the inventory of Manasseh's wealth, intimating that the possession of their territory follows the gift/possession program by which the lands west of the Jordan have been acquired. In terms of receiving gift and blessing, and responding with loyalty and obedience, they are quintessential Israelites. But by settling across the Jordan, they have also separated themselves from "the Israelites." The digression joins issues of obedience with those kinship and territory, preparing the reader for the intersection of these themes in the ensuing intertribal (and in the case of Manasseh, intra-tribal) conflict.

The Altar in Between: 22:10-12

Conflict erupts when the eastern tribes construct an altar in the area of the Jordan. The text offers no rationale for the act, leaving the reader to ponder its purpose and significance. The narrator remarks only that the altar is conspicuously large. It is *meant* to be seen.[13] This bit of information deepens the mystery. Seen by *whom?* Has the altar been erected as a place of assembly or sacrifice for the eastern tribes? Or is it perhaps a challenge to the tribes in Canaan, an implicit assertion of power on the part of the tribes in the Transjordan?[14] Is the altar meant to unify or divide?

---

[12] The Hebrew term which the NRSV translates as "possession" (*ăhuzzātām*) is not the programmatic term for possession (*yĕruššâ*) but is associated with priestly literature.

[13] MT characterizes the altar as "big-looking" (*gādôl lĕmarʾeh*).

[14] R. Boling points to a number of sanctuaries which serve as centers for tribal leagues but which are located in border regions. He suggests that the erection of the

Whatever the motives, the other tribes clearly perceive the altar as a threat and gather at Shiloh to make war against their kindred. As we will soon learn from their own lips, they view the eastern tribes as outsiders and themselves as Israelites. But the narrator, with a skillful turn of phrase, reverses this point of view, "when the people of Israel heard of it, the whole assembly of the Israelites gathered at Shiloh, to make war against them" (v. 12). The language of the report corresponds closely to that which relates the preparations made by the kings of Canaan to wage war against Israel, "when all the kings who were beyond the Jordan . . . heard of this, they gathered together to fight Joshua and Israel" (9:1). The *phrasing* of the report thus associates the tribes of west of the Jordan with the kings of Canaan, and the eastern tribes with the Israelites! "The other side of the Jordan" is again a matter of perspective. Who inhabits the land "beyond the Jordan?" Who are Israelites?[15]

The narrator gives little information to pinpoint what constitutes "beyond the Jordan" or even the location of the altar. The narrator seems intent on specifying the site of the altar, repeatedly making reference to its geographical situation: "the region of the Jordan (*gĕlîlôt hayyardēn*) that lies in the land of Canaan" (v. 10), "by the Jordan" (*ˁal-hayyardēn*, v. 10), at the frontier (*ˀel-mûl*) of the land of Canaan, in the region of the Jordan (*gĕlîlôt hayyardēn*), on the side that belongs to the Israelites (*ˀel-ˁēber bĕnēy yiśrāˀēl*) (v. 11). Yet the terminology is determinedly indefinite. Does *gĕlîlôt* ("districts") signify a proper name (cf. 18:17) or a general area? Does *ˀel-mûl* refer to the "edge" of the Jordan (cf. 9:1; 18:18) or an area beyond or opposite (cf. 8:33; 19:46)? And just what constitutes "the other side" (*ˁēber*), the region west of the Jordan (5:1; 9:1; 12:7) or that to the east (1:14-15; 2:10; 7:7; 9:10; 13:8)? In other words, is the altar on the edge of the land owned by the Israelites (the tribes in Canaan) or in a region opposite the land owned by the tribes? With every clarifying note, the location of the altar becomes increasingly obscure!

Packed tightly with these inscrutable geographical directions are references to the polarized state of the nation: the Reubenites, the

---

altar may have constituted a violation of a boundary and thus a threat to the western tribes; *Joshua*, AB (Garden City: Doubleday, 1982) 511–2. This intriguing hypothesis may illuminate the conflict of perspectives that precipitates the crisis. The western tribes seem to regard the Jordan as a boundary and the altar as a threat. However, if the eastern tribes do not view the Jordan as a boundary, they may not have constructed the altar with an intent to threaten.

[15] The parallel structure of the accounts links them together. The MT utilizes different terms in the respective reports.

Gadites, and the half-tribe of Manasseh (vv. 10, 11) opposing the Israelites (vv. 11 [2x], 12), and the altar (11, 12) opposing Shiloh (v. 13). The
geographical and national indeterminacy creates a bewildering sense
of confusion befitting the issues of identity raised by the story itself. A
kaleidoscope of shifting perspectives swirls around the construction of
the altar. Israel finds itself in a border region where it must face the
paradoxes and oppositions of its own national identity, a space where
perspectives on land, obedience, and tribal loyalties vie with each
other. Ironically the altar, a powerful unifying symbol for the community, has become the opposite: the symbol and site of division.

The Charge: "You Are Rebels!" 22:13-20

Before hostilities begin, the tribes in the west send a delegation
headed by Phinehas the priest, a fitting choice since the issue concerns
polarities and boundaries. As it has throughout, the narrative represents the Cisjordanian tribes as a collective ("the Israelites") and the
Transjordanian tribes as a collection ("the Reubenites and the Gadites
and the half-tribe of Manasseh"). The narrator breaks the western contingent into smaller units with a confusing structure and novel terminology (vv. 13-15). Phinehas is joined by ten "chiefs" *(něśî'îm)* who
are given a set of titles which denote the nation's largest and smallest
subdivisions: "an ancestral household for all the tribes of Israel" *(lěbēyt
'ab lěkōl maṭṭôt yiśrā'ēl* [AT]) and "every one of them the head of a family
among the clans of Israel" *(rō'š bēyt-ăbōtām hēmmâ lě'alpēy yiśrā'ēl).*
Though many, they speak with one voice and deliver a message from
"the whole congregation" (v. 16).

The message begins and ends with rhetorical questions which brand
the construction of the altar as a forbidden transgression of boundaries
(ma'al) and link it with events which previously threatened the destruction of the community (the sin of Peor [v. 17], which occurred east
of the Jordan and Achan's transgression [v. 20], which occurred west of
the Jordan). The speech actually begins with two questions (vv. 16-
18a); the first lists the charges (treachery, apostasy, and rebellion), while
the second warns of a disastrous outcome, with Peor as a precedent.
The basic charge of "treachery" *(ma'al)* recalls Achan's appropriation
of Canaanite plunder which resulted in the visitation of divine wrath
upon the nation. It is clarified by two other charges, that of apostasy
("turning away today from following the LORD") and rebellion. The
delegation points to the probability of national catastrophe at the end
of the speech by linking the altar with Achan's "breaking faith" *(mā'al*

ma'al) and asserting, by analogy, that the whole nation will likely suffer the same fate that he and his family did (v. 20). The two precedents cited by the delegation present the issue in terms of national survival; the eastern tribes have brought the nation to the brink of disaster, just as Achan and the apostates at Peor had done. But there is more behind these stories than fear of divine wrath. Both precedents relate catastrophic encounters with difference, in the case of Peor by going outside communal boundaries after the many gods of Moab (Num 25:1-3) and in the case of Achan by bringing the off-limits plunder of Canaan inside the community (Josh 7:1).

The delegation gets to the heart of the issue in the core of the speech (vv. 18b-19). They accentuate the thrust of the initial allegations by repeating the assertion that the eastern tribes have made the nation subject to divine wrath. The force of the repetition communicates a strong distancing between themselves and those they confront, hinting that the real bone of contention lies not with the altar, nor with fears of divine wrath, but with the perception that the tribes' decision to settle in the Transjordan has fractured the nation. Parallel phrases express an us-them mentality by employing the independent pronoun *ʾattem* ("you" [plural]) for emphasis: "*you* are turning away from YHWH" (*ʾattem tāšubû hayyôm mēʾaḥărēy yhwh* [v. 18a, AT]) and "*you* are rebelling against YHWH today" (*ʾattem timrōdû hayyôm bāyhwh* [v. 18b, AT]). The sense of separation is ungirded by the declaration that the effects of the easterners' actions threaten "the whole congregation of Israel," a designation the speakers have just used with reference to themselves (v. 18c; cf. v. 16a). If the tribes in Canaan now comprise the whole congregation of Israel, who (or what) are the tribes of the Transjordan?

A conditional statement puts the issue more bluntly, "but now, if your land is unclean, cross over into the LORD's land where the LORD's tabernacle now stands, and take for yourselves a possession among us" (v. 19a). By insinuating that the Transjordan is unclean, the delegation implies that only those living west of the Jordan are "pure" Israelites (even though, ironically, they have just implied that they themselves are not yet clean [v. 17b]). The invitation to "cross over" (*'ibrû*) implies the same. Crossing the Jordan (Joshua 3–4) is the constitutive event for the formation of the Israelite nation, an event that transforms Israel from a nomadic people to a landed nation (hence the dense repetition of the root *'br* throughout the episode). When Israel began the conquest, the Jordan was the site of national unification. Now that the nation has received its promised rest, the Jordan divides the nation. The delegation insinuates that the crossing over which shaped national identity on that occasion is to be viewed in light of those who have crossed over *to stay*. For the ten and one-half tribes, the possession of Canaan thus constitutes the essence of Israelite identity. The land west of the Jordan is YHWH's land, the site of YHWH's tabernacle. And, by implication, only those inhabiting YHWH's land are YHWH's people. By refusing to live in Canaan, the two and one-half tribes have (in their view) demonstrated their intent to be other-than-Israel.

Thus, when the easterners construct the altar, they seem to confirm this point of view, for the altar at the Jordan represents an alternative to YHWH's altar. The delegation expresses this perspective with another imperative that combines the theological rationale for the accusation with the core issue, "only do not rebel against the LORD, or rebel against us by building yourselves an altar other than the altar of the LORD our God" (v. 19b). This puts the whole matter succinctly. Since YHWH's people live in YHWH's land, challenging the western tribes challenges YHWH. Theological language thus cloaks anxiety over identity; the eastern tribes have rebelled against YHWH's people and thus against YHWH.

The Rebuttal: "Says Who?": 22:21-29

The eastern tribes (again depicted as a plurality) respond with an explanation (vv. 24-28) encased within denials (vv. 22-23, 29). While the delegation begins their speech with an expression of totality and singularity ("thus says the whole congregation of Israel" [v. 16a]), the eastern tribes open with words that communicate both singularity and plurality, clarity and ambiguity, "The LORD, God of gods! The LORD, God of gods!" The exclamations, in the MT, consist of a simple listing of divine names: a singular form of the name translated "God" (ʾēl), a plural form of the name also conventionally translated "God" (ʾĕlōhîm) and the divine name itself (yhwh). Singular names for deity thus enclose a plural name for deity. One deity is denoted by multiple names (three, corresponding to the three-fold listing of the eastern tribal group). And the appellations are uttered not once but twice! Furthermore, although all terms are clearly associated with one and the same deity, the relationship between the terms cannot be definitively discerned. The NRSV offers one possible understanding ("The LORD, God of Gods"), but the phrase could as easily be translated "El! God! YHWH!" or "YHWH is the God of gods!" The phrases have a distinctively creedal tone, which deepens the ambiguity, for creeds generally clarify and specify. But the meaning of this creedal formulation is not definite. The eastern tribes thus open by expressing themselves in a manner commensurate with their own paradoxical status within the nation.

The confession serves as a means for confronting the delegation's implicit claim of unity with YHWH (v. 22b). YHWH "knows" (presumably that the altar was not constructed with malicious intent), and so should Israel. The MT distinguishes between the two "knowers" by employing a participle form with reference to YHWH *(yōdēăʿ)* but an imperfect form with reference to Israel *(yēdāʿ)*. By appropriating different verbal forms, the eastern tribes surreptitiously undercut "Israel's" claim to unity with YHWH by suggesting a contrast between what YHWH knows (the participle) and what Israel will or should know (the imperfect). They then issue a categorical denial of the allegations leveled against them (vv. 22c-23), all the while chipping away their accusers' "cleaner-than-thou" claims. The first denial (vv. 22c-23a) is directed toward the delegation and forcefully refutes the charges of sacrilege *(maʿal)*, rebellion *(mered)*, and apostasy *(lāšub mēʾaḥărēy yhwh)*. It is set off in the MT by the repetition of the conditional particle *ʾim:* "if for rebellion or if for sacrilege against YHWH" *(ʾim-bĕmered wĕʾim-bĕmaʿal bayhwh* [AT]). Following these refutations they challenge Israel to action (negatively) if the charges are true ("do not spare us"). A second denial, also marked by the repetition of *ʾim,* speaks to the purpose of the altar and calls upon YHWH to take action (positively). As in the first case, the rebuttal takes the form of a conditional declaration in three parts; "if to offer burnt offering and grain offering on it or if to make sacrifices of well-being on it" (AT). These are charges implicit in the delegation's accusation, and they directly concern YHWH, who is now called upon to judge the crime, "let YHWH himself see to it" (AT). Here again the language of the text implies different areas of concern. The tribes west of the Jordan are concerned with the transgression of communal boundaries, while YHWH is concerned with the correct performance of sacrifices. In a sense, the easterners defuse the force of the delegation's argument (that the altar may kindle divine wrath against "the whole congregation") by inviting retaliation against *themselves* if any infraction has been committed.[16]

A forceful negation of the particle *(ʾim-lōʾ;* NRSV "No!") signals a transition from denial to explanation. Responding to the implicit agenda of the delegation's speech (v. 19), the easterners declare that they constructed the altar out of a deep sense of turmoil *(dĕʾāgâ;* v. 24). The explanation which follows (vv. 24-28) is extensive, giving elaborate testimony to their apprehension and, on the narrative level, revealing the thematic center of the story. It begins with a straightforward presentation of the issue (vv. 24-25). In a rhetorical tour de force the easterners cut through

---

[16] Some have seen echoes of oath language in the rebuttal, e.g. T. Butler, *Joshua,* WBC (Waco: Word, 1983) 247–8.

the dissembling and articulate what the delegation is *really* saying by quoting words that the delegation has not spoken, "the LORD has made the Jordan a boundary between us and you, you Reubenites and Gadites; you have no portion in the LORD" (v. 25a). But they do so with uncanny diplomacy, displacing the message into the less-threatening arena of the future, where it becomes a matter between "your children and our children." Framed in this manner, the easterners can safely put words in their accusers' mouths, particularly those which (as they see it) are at the heart of the problem, "What have you to do with the LORD, the God of Israel?" and "You have no portion in the LORD." The two expressions of exclusion articulate a sense of complete alienation. As has been amply demonstrated in the preceding section (Joshua 13–21), a "portion" (*ḥēleq*) is precisely what situates a tribe within the established boundaries of land and community and legitimates its participation in the life of the nation.

Sandwiched between these expressions of exclusion is the declaration that YHWH has made the Jordan the (eastern) boundary of the land given to Israel. The statement, of course, is in considerable tension with the narrator's own declaration, earlier in the story, that the lands of the Transjordan are to be occupied "by command of the LORD through Moses" (v. 9). The tension, however, enables the reader to cut through the rhetoric and comprehend the catalyst for the conflict. The tribal group in the west, *and not YHWH*, has made the Jordan a boundary between the tribes. The words of western children to eastern children thus point not only to a tension in perspectives but to a tendency on the part of the tribes themselves to construct communal boundaries not initiated or endorsed by YHWH. By implication the western tribes, not the tribes in the Transjordan, bear responsibility for the fracturing of the nation.

Putting the matter as a concern for the future, between "your descendants and our descendants," also provides a way to resolve the conflict (vv. 26-28). The easterners go on to claim that they constructed the altar to ensure future *unity*, not division. The altar will be a "witness between us and you, and between the generations after us" (v. 27a). They press the explanation with particular emphasis, so as to affirm, both positively and negatively, that they wish to continue as members in good standing of the Israelite community. Declarations that the altar is a witness (vv. 27a, 28c) enclose a restatement of the attitude which the altar is to prevent ("you have no portion in the LORD"), putting the best possible light on its construction. Countering these explanations are pointed denials that the altar has been constructed for what would seem its obvious purpose, to offer various kinds of sacrifices. Given the highly charged nature of the conversation, the repetition of these denials seems a bit forced. Do the repetitions simply clarify a genuine misunderstanding? Or do the repeated denials and convoluted justifications reveal an explanation on the fly?

The tensions within the response come to a head with the assertion that the altar is actually a "copy of the altar" (v. 28) rather than "an altar" (v. 26). The word translated "copy" *(tabnît)* is sometimes employed in the Hebrew Bible to denote a design or pattern for the construction of some edifice (Exod 25:9; 2 Kg 16:10 [MT 9]; 1 Chr 28:11). But such cannot be the case here, for the "model" is conspicuously large (perhaps larger than the original) and seems to be constructed *after* the altar which presumably is in use at Shiloh. Furthermore, why construct the facsimile of an altar as a witness of cultic fidelity, when such is sure to be regarded as an expression of cultic infidelity?

With the future still in mind, the eastern tribes make a final, impassioned defense (v. 29). Repeating the language of their earlier denial, which took the uncertain form of a conditional statement (v. 23), they now vehemently declare that they would never offer any sacrifices at any altar other than "the altar of the LORD our God that stands before his tabernacle." The declaration concludes their defense on a markedly conciliatory note. First, the declaration that no sacrifices will be offered on the altar reinforces the easterners' claim that it was not built with sacrifice in mind. Second, it acknowledges the altar at the tabernacle (among the ten and one-half tribes) as the only proper place of sacrifice for all the tribes by appropriating the language of unity, "the altar of the LORD *our* God." With this response, the eastern tribes thus ameliorate the concerns of the rest of the tribes, that a dangerous plurality (and consequent divine anger) threatens the community and that the special status of the land west of the Jordan is not recognized by those on the other side.

The reader can assess the original motives for the altar only through the response of the eastern tribes. By waiting until this point to disclose the motives, through the lips of the eastern tribes, the narrator puts the reader in the same position as the tribal delegation. Neither possesses any prior information about the purpose for the altar. Whether the eastern tribes originally constructed it as an actual (and more accessible) place of sacrifice or as facsimile-witness does not receive independent confirmation from the narrator. The device of withholding explanations of motive until now thus creates a space for doubt. The "why" of the altar is overshadowed by the altar's role in raising and resolving a fundamental set of polarities within the nation. What matters is whether the explanation succeeds in resolving a conflict which threatens to tear the nation apart.

Satisfied Minds: 22:30-34

The explanation does in fact defuse the impending conflict between the tribes. The narrator confirms this with a brief note ("they were satisfied") that is the corroborated by the words of Phinehas (v. 31). The narrator, however, employs a particularly vague term to characterize the attitude of the delegation. The phrase in the MT is *wayyîtab běˁêynêyhem* ("and it was good in their eyes"). The idiom generally communicates approval, often in connection with a decision (Gen 41:37; Lev 10:19; 1 Sam 18:15; 2 Sam 3:36; 1 Kgs 3:30; Est 1:21). In this context, however, it only suggests an attitude. Whether they believe the explanation or not, the delegation endorses it as a satisfactory response to the issues raised, allowing them to return across the Jordan with a report of peace. What is most important, as the words of Phinehas reveal, is that the explanation has been efficacious. Phinehas begins by declaring that "today we know that the LORD is with us" (v. 31), in effect declaring that Israel is *not* in a state of enmity with YHWH and thus need not fear destruction. This declaration is followed by a second which exonerates the eastern tribes of the main charge of treachery *(maˁal)*.[17] Phinehas then concludes with a sort of backhanded compliment for the ingenuity of the easterners' defense, "now you have saved the Israelites from the hand of the LORD." The means of this salvation is clearly the explanation that they have given regarding the purpose of the altar. Phinehas implies that Israel was in a state of danger prior to the confrontation between the tribes but that the rationale offered has successfully saved the nation from destruction.[18] He then adds YHWH's endorsement to his; the explanation is "good in YHWH's eyes" as well. Phinehas's words, however, are double-edged. Who is the "us" that YHWH is among? And what "Israel" has been saved?

The narrative concludes with hints that, while the immediate conflict has been resolved, the attitudes which underlie it have not changed. The narrator continues to refer to the eastern tribes in list form and even reinforces their continued "plural" status through repetition (five times within this short section). And "Israelites" still refers to the tribes west of the Jordan (v. 33). The breach between the two tribal groups contin-

---

[17] The eastern tribes exonerate themselves of the contingent charges of rebellion and apostasy by their forceful denial (v. 23). The main charge, however, has awaited a decision from the delegation.

[18] Phinehas' declaration has the curious effect of casting the eastern tribes as saviors and YHWH as an adversary. His reference to being saved from the hand of YHWH recalls the many instances in which the peoples of the land have been given "into the hand of Israel" for the purpose of destruction (2:24; 6:2; 8:1, 7; 10:8, 19, 39, 32; 11:8).

ues through reports which reveal the contrasting perceptions of the tribes. The narrator reports that the "Israelites" endorsed the report of the delegation and decided against "destroying the land where the Reubenites and Gadites were settled" (v. 33c).[19] Living in the right place, it seems, has been and will continue to be an issue for the tribes which have settled in Canaan. The eastern tribes, however, look toward the altar at the border as a witness to continued fidelity and inclusion, a testimony to theological and thus national unity (v. 34).

The altar stands not only as a witness that "the LORD is God" but also as a reminder that Israel is held together by mutually-agreed upon constructs. Like the altar, rationales like that given by the eastern tribes keep the tribes from each others throats by providing a "model" for resolving conflicts. But these constructs are only cosmetic. They fail to address the substantive polarities which continue to tug and pull beneath the facade of national unity. The altar is a symbol of unity but only apparently so; it is also a witness that something stands "between us." As long as some segments in the nation link inclusion to possession of the right land, performing acts in the right way, or maintaining the right social connections, Israel remains in danger of disintegrating.

---

[19] As has been the case throughout the episode, the listing of the eastern group sometimes includes the half-tribe of Manasseh and sometimes omits it (as here), once again underscoring the tribe's conflicted identity as an entity inhabiting both sides of the Jordan.

Chapter Twelve
UNFINISHED BUSINESS
Joshua 23:1-16

Joshua continues the sense of ending through a farewell address that recapitulates the main themes of the book and projects them into the future. From a vantage point near the end of his life (v. 14), Israel's leader looks back and offers a "state of the nation" speech which both affirms Israel's accomplishments and charts a course for the ultimate fulfillment of its objectives. The speech contains strong echoes of the speech that introduces the apportionment of tribal lands (13:1-7). As in the previous instance, the narrator prefaces the speech with a reference to Joshua's advanced age and a repetition of the remark by the speaker (13:1; 23:1-2). Both speeches focus on "what remains" and on YHWH's promise to drive out the indigenous inhabitants. Together the two addresses enclose the apportionment and settlement of tribal lands with words of retrospect and exhortation.[1]

The narrator also creates the sense of an ending by making connections with the summary of the tribal allotments (21:43-45) and the opening speech of the book (1:2-8). The three texts are united by the report that YHWH gives Israel rest *(hēnîaḥ)* and, when taken together, bring the viewpoints of YHWH (1:2-8), the narrator (21:43-45) and Joshua (23:1ff) into dialogue. Joshua's address modifies the hyperbolic claims of possession in 21:43-45 and qualifies its optimistic tone. Whereas the narrator has spoken of the possession of the land as a *fait accompli* (21:43),

---

[1] Joshua's address has a strong testamentary character which links it to the parting words of other significant figures in Israel's history (Gen 48:1–49:28; Deut 33:1-29; 1 Sam 12:1-25).

Israel's leader now speaks of possession as something yet to be achieved
(23:5). And while the narrator mentioned only the "good things" which
YHWH had brought about (21:45), Joshua now mentions the evil with
the good (23:14-16), transforming the glorious certainties of the past
into the troubling openness and incompleteness of the future.[2] Links to
YHWH's opening speech bring the story full circle. Through the words
of Joshua the reader once again encounters a land yet to be possessed
and assurances of victory (23:9; cf. 1:5), as well as admonitions to obey
strictly "this book of the law" (23:6-7; cf. 1:8). But the narrative *déjà vu*
also manifests some striking differences. Though both speeches link
obedience to the Mosaic torah with fulfillment, the goals have changed,
from conquest of the land (1:6-8) to separation from the peoples of the
land (23:6-8). Moreover, the speakers and audience have changed.
YHWH delivers the first speech and directs it primarily to Joshua (although the incidence of plural pronouns in 1:2-4 extends the address to
the nation). In the present context, however, Joshua is the speaker, and
the assembly of Israelite leaders is the audience (23:1). By evoking the
themes of YHWH's speech to Joshua, now presented as Joshua's words
to Israel, the address functions as a hinge between Israel's past under
Joshua and its future without him. The promises and admonitions
made initially to Joshua are now extended to the entire nation. Joshua's
advanced age, along with the rest the land enjoys, marks the completion of his charge. Israel must now rely on Moses just as Joshua has
done, fulfilling its mandate under the guidance of divine promises and
admonitions.

An intricate interweaving of themes and vocabulary give the speech
a distinctly oral character. Words, phrases, and leitmotifs emerge, disappear, and reappear with new meanings, creating a dynamic rhythm
that unites the past with the future and confession with admonition.
Israel has "seen" *(rĕʾîtem)* what YHWH has done to the nations (v. 3) and
is called to "see" *(rĕʾû)* that Joshua has allotted the nations as an inheritance (v. 4).[3] YHWH has fought for Israel (v. 3) and, because YHWH
fights, one sends a thousand fleeing (v. 10). Indeed, YHWH has done so
just as he promised (vv. 5, 10). Joshua made (the lot) fall *(hippaltî)* for Israel (v. 4), while none of YHWH's words have fallen *(lōʾ-nāpal* [v. 14]).
YHWH has driven the nations out before Israel (v. 9) and will continue
to do so (v. 5), but not if Israel joins itself to the surviving nations (v.

---

[2] Joshua pointedly omits the summary's declaration that Israel possessed and
settled the land (21:43b), thereby ascribing all that has happened to the work of
YHWH and projecting the issue of settlement and possession into an open future.

[3] The second instance, an interjection, is left untranslated by the NRSV.

13). Israel should "know" this (v. 13), just as it knows that everything that YHWH has spoken has come to pass (v. 14). The nation must not worship or serve their gods (v. 8), for if it does so YHWH's anger will be kindled (v. 16). Then it will "perish from this good land" (v. 13, 16, cf. v. 15), having seen the fulfillment of "all the good things the LORD your God promised" (vv. 14, 15). Israel must carefully perform all that is written in the book of the law of Moses so as not to *(lĕbiltî)* turn to the right or left (v. 6), so as not to *(lĕbiltî)* be mixed with the nations which are left (v. 7). Rather *(kî-im)* Israel is to hold fast *(tidbāqû)* to YHWH (v. 8) instead of *(kî-im)* joining *(ûdĕbaqtem)* with the rest of the nations (v. 12). Holding fast to YHWH will ensure that no opposing force will prevail, as has been the case "to this day" (vv. 8, 9). The years have passed for Joshua *(bāʾ* [v. 1], *bāʾtî* [v. 2]), who admonishes the nation not to "mix" *(bôʾ)* with the other nations (v. 7) nor allow the nations to do so with them *(ûbāʾtem* [v. 12]). All that YHWH has spoken has come to pass *(bāʾû* [v. 14]), and just as the good things have come to pass *(bāʾû* [v. 15]), so will YHWH bring *(yābîʾ)* the bad ones (v. 15). After Joshua has gone *(hôlēk)* the way of all flesh (v. 14), the nation must not go *(wahălaktem)* after the gods of the land (v. 16).

Because of this interlocking matrix of words and themes, the speech does not display a clearly-defined structure. Generally, it seems to comprise two main sections: vv. 2b-13 and vv. 14-16.[4] The first comprises two subsections (vv. 3-7 and 8-13), both of which recall the victories achieved by YHWH (vv. 3-5 and 8-10) before moving to an exhortation to loyalty and obedience (vv. 7-8 and 11-13).[5] The pattern of recital-exhortation enhances the Deuteronomic ambience of the speech and reemphasizes the importance of human response to divine initiative necessary for the fulfillment of YHWH's promises. The twice-repeated pattern prepares the way for the second section, which also begins with a declaration of the good things YHWH has done (v. 14). In this case, however, the speech takes on a distinctively ominous tone, warning of bad things to come and the dire consequences of divine anger if Israel transgresses the covenant. The change of direction has the effect of putting Israel's *choices* squarely in focus and elaborating the consequences of both alternatives (worshiping and serving YHWH or the "other gods").

---

[4] The definition of structure generally follows R. Nelson, *Joshua*, OTL (Louisville: Westminster John Knox, 1997) 255–7.

[5] The second subsection actually begins with an exhortation, which constitutes the initial component of a chiasm, and ends with two exhortations, the first of which completes the chiasm.

Joshua's central concern in the address is with "those nations that remain" (vv. 4, 7, 12). In its earlier counterpart (13:1-7) YHWH drew Israel's attention to the land that remained. Now YHWH has given rest to the nation. The land is subdued, but the nations remain. They continue to threaten Israel, no longer by their power but by their mere *presence*. With their kings and armies defeated, the peoples of the land cannot mount an effective challenge to Israelite supremacy in the land. However, they still remain a formidable adversary simply because of their difference. As long as they stay within the land, Israel is in danger of becoming like them, thus losing its distinctive identity as the people of YHWH. The power of Canaanite difference thus exceeds the power of Canaanite kings. To emphasize this point, Joshua repeatedly refers to the powerlessness of the peoples of the land (vv. 3, 4, 5, 9, 10) but also portrays them *as an active force* in opposition to Israel (vv. 7, 12, 13). Earlier in Joshua, the kings of the land threaten to destroy Israel by what they *do* (5:1; 11:1-5), but now the peoples may destroy the Israel by what they *are*, "they shall be a snare and a trap for you, a scourge on your sides, and thorns in your eyes, until you perish from this good land that the LORD your God has given you" (v. 13b). The task before Israel now involves overcoming the threat of difference represented by the peoples. Joshua speaks of this task in the same terms employed previously to signify the occupation of the land. In a variation of the preceding program, he now declares that "I have allotted to you as an inheritance *those nations that remain* along with all the nations that I have already cut off, from the Jordan to the Great Sea in the west" (v. 4). Significantly, Israel's "inheritance" is now framed in social rather than geographical terms.

In a sense, Joshua redefines the manner in which Israel will achieve future success or failure in the land. The respective roles of both God and people are clearly delineated. YHWH's role is oriented toward the remaining nations, which he will drive out before Israel (v. 5). Israel's role, however, is directed toward YHWH. Positively rendered, this means that the nation must carefully observe the book of the law of Moses (v. 6), hold fast to YHWH (v. 8) and love God (v. 11). Negatively expressed, Israel must not turn aside to other gods (v. 16). The delineation of responsibilities conveys a powerful message for Israel's life in the land. YHWH will take care of any remaining opposition. Israel's sole charge is to remain loyal to YHWH in the face of remaining Canaanite difference.

The entire speech vigorously asserts the Deuteronomic themes of land, obedience, and ethnic separation that have configured the whole of the book of Joshua, ostensibly countering the sense of failure, trepidation, and incompleteness created by the division of the land (Joshua 13–21). It undergirds these themes by evoking the particular cadences of Deuteronomic speech (e.g. "be very steadfast to observe and do all that is written," "be very careful to love the LORD your God"). Deuteronomy 7:1-5 and 11:16-28 in particular form a conceptual backdrop for the exhortations and warnings Joshua gives. The warnings of Moses in Deut 7:1-5 lie behind Joshua's linkage of intermarriage and apostasy (along with the consequent potential for divine anger) in vv. 12-16, although the command to "show them no mercy" is pointedly not taken up. The admonitions of Deut 11:16-28 are appropriated to a greater degree. The promise that YHWH will drive out the inhabitants of the land, conditioned upon Israel's commitment to love YHWH, walk in all his ways, and hold fast to him (Deut 11:22-23), is now rendered unconditionally (Josh 23:5). The Deuteronomic association of promise with response is also articulated in the past tense (23:8-11) and placed within a chiastic structure that demonstrates the vital relationship between divine initiative, obedient response, and continued success:

A But hold fast to the LORD your God, as you have done to this day (v. 8).

B For the LORD has driven out before you great and strong nations (v. 9a);

C and as for you, no one has been able to withstand you to this day (v. 9b).

C' One of you puts to flight a thousand (v. 10a),

B' since it is the LORD who fights for you, as he promised you (v. 10b).

A' Be very careful, therefore, to love the LORD your God (v. 11)[6]

Joshua's modification of the Deuteronomic text reshapes the relationship between divine initiative and human response, so that the call to "hold fast" and "love" YHWH is presented as a *response to* rather than a *condition of* YHWH's activity on behalf of the nation. This point made, Joshua then places a condition on the divine promise; YHWH will not continue to drive out the nations if Israel insists on joining with them (vv. 12-13). Linking YHWH's continued activity with the issue of separation then leads to an elaboration of consequences (vv. 14-16) that picks up the Deuteronomic passage's "either-or" representation of life with YHWH (Deut 11:26-28). Just as Moses pronounces a blessing for obedience and a curse for turning "to follow other gods that you have not

---

[6] The beginning and end points of the chiasm are signaled by the phrase *kî-im* (vv. 8a, 11a).

known," so Joshua warns that YHWH can bring bad things if Israel turns
to other gods, just as he has brought good things. The appropriation
and reworking of Deut 11:22-28, through the three-fold reiteration of
the divine promise to drive out the nations, therefore clarifies the tension between the unilateral and conditional character of YHWH's promises. YHWH will continue to act on behalf of the nation (v. 5), which must
hold fast *(tidbāqû)* to its God (vv. 8-11). However, should the nation turn
and join itself *(ûdĕbaqtem)* to the surviving nations, YHWH will no longer
drive out the nations, and Israel will perish (vv. 12-13).

The address stridently reinstates the themes of possession of land,
separation from the nations, and obedience to the commandments, but
it does so within the context of the choices Israel must face: to be loyal
to YHWH or to follow other gods. Through the words of Joshua the
themes thus take on a penultimate status. Israel must not leave its prescribed boundaries to join with the other nations, because to do so
would entail serving their gods. The promises of YHWH render it distinctive and require fidelity to the God who gives the promises. If Israel
gives this loyalty to the many gods of Canaan, it will become like them
and will disappear from the good land which has been given to it.
Joshua thus leads the reader to view Israel as a *people defined by choices,*
signified by a covenant which constitutes a metaphor for the reciprocal
choosing of YHWH and the nation. If Israel remains a viable nation, it
will not only be because YHWH defeats its foes but also because it continues to choose YHWH over against the gods of the peoples.

Joshua's address effects a crucial transition between the whole of
the preceding narrative and the final episode of the book, a renewal of
the covenant which formalizes YHWH's choosing of Israel and Israel's
choosing of YHWH (Josh 24:1-28). The themes that have configured
the narrative and the sense of Israelite identity (land, separation, obedience) have steadily been dismantled by both the stories and the
rhetoric of the previous episodes. Now forcefully restated, they are
shown to be derivative rather than essential marks of national identity. Choosing to follow the God who has fought for the nation, and
who promises to continue to fight, establishes the foundation of a distinctive Israelite identity. And if Israel chooses others, it will vanish.
YHWH will not fail Israel. Will Israel hold fast to YHWH?

A Gathering of Leaders: 23:1-2a

The address opens with an introduction that asserts a long passage
of time, although no point of reference is given by which to assess it.

Does "a long time afterward" occur *after* the confrontation over the altar at the Jordan? Or should we take the reference to YHWH's granting of rest as a clue that we are in same general period of time (cf. 22:4). Joshua is "old and well advanced in years," but we have been told the same before tribal lands are allotted (13:1). These ambiguities, and the lack of any real orientation in time, give the ensuing address a timeless quality. Joshua's words are words for all time (a sense reinforced by the speech's rapid shifts between past, present, and future). They have a universal quality that is undergirded by the absence of any reference to the place in which they are delivered (as opposed to the final episode, which takes place explicitly at Shechem). When and where are thus not important aspects of this speech. Its message applies to all.

The audience consists of an assembly of dignitaries who will lead Israel after Joshua's death. The listing of their titles portends a transformation in the entire pattern of national leadership. After Joshua's death the community will no longer be united and led by a single charismatic figure, as it has since leaving Egypt. Once settled in the land, leadership will be dispersed through various channels of authority, with consequences that will become apparent in the subsequent book of Judges.[7] Plurality of leadership within the nation will function well as long as YHWH remains Israel's one true leader. But if (as Joshua warns) the nation turns away from YHWH, a plural leadership structure may not be able to maintain communal integrity. The list itself suggests yet another structure for determining the course of national affairs (cf. 7:16-18; 8:33; 9:14-15; 19:51; 22:14, 30), one that is essentially a hodgepodge of titles employed throughout the book: elders (7:6; 8:10, 33; 9:11; 20:4), heads (of families? tribes? [14:1; 19:51; 21:1; 22:14, 21, 30]), judges (8:33), and officers (1:10; 3:2; 8:33). All now are united as they gather to hear the words of Joshua.

Back to the Future: 23:2b-7

Joshua begins by investing his words with the authority of a perspective achieved by virtue of a long life (v. 2b). He then calls the assembly to acknowledge its present state, punctuating his words with the use of the independent pronoun *'attem* (left untranslated in NRSV). The call consists of two parts, a declaration that the listeners have

---

[7] Compare, for example, Judg 19:1; 21:25.

seen for themselves what YHWH has done to the nations in the past (v. 3) and a summons to recognize the present state of affairs; Joshua has allotted all the remaining nations to Israel (v. 4).[8] For the first time in the book, the peoples of the land are not signified by a list but by the single term "nations" *(gôyyîm)*. Used with reference to the peoples, the term is striking, for it occurs elsewhere only in connection with Israel (3:17; 4:1; 5:6, 8; 10:13). A sense of equivalence between Israel and the nations is thus suggested, and this sense becomes more striking in light of the fact that the term unites the peoples of the land into an integrity that contrasts vividly with the pluralistic designation of the Israelite assembly (23:2a). The reversal of designations interacts with the warnings against mixing with the peoples, a focal point of the address. Previously, the peoples of the land have been designated by lists while the Israelites have been described by single terms. Now we encounter the opposite. The tensions raised by this device are heightened by the repetition of the term *gôyyîm* seven times within the address (corresponding to the seven-fold listing of the peoples of the land [Deut 7:1; Josh 3:10]).[9]

References to "the nations that remain" *(haggôyyîm hanniš²ārîm hā²ēlleh)* enclose a reiteration of YHWH's promise to drive them out and an admonition to obedient response to the book of the law (vv. 4, 7). The first reference appropriates the terminology used previously to signify possession of the land (allotting as an inheritance) and redirects it towards people rather than territory (cf. 13:6). The shift is arresting. What does designating the other nations as Israel's inheritance signify? In the apportionment of tribal lands, inheritance signifies the legitimacy of a tribe's claim to the territory it receives, carrying with it the concept of ownership in perpetuity. It is one of the complex of terms that constructs the symbolic matrix within which the Israelite community is organized and structured. In this context, however, the term extends outside Israel to other nations, suggesting an assertion of Israelite dominance over the peoples of the land. Now that the land has been apportioned into inheritances, the remaining peoples who inhabit the land are allotted. Remarkably, however, nothing is said about *destroying* them. Having been "allotted" to Israel, the remaining nations do just that; they *remain*. Israel may "own" them or determine their place in the land, but there is no longer any command to exterminate them. The statement thus makes a tacit admission that the peoples of the land will always remain part of the land, and that being the case,

---

[8] The two parts are united in the MT by the repetition of the verb *rā²â* (*rĕ²îtem* ["you have seen"] and *rĕ²û* ["see!"]).

[9] The seven occurrences of "nations" are located in vv. 3, 4 (2x), 7, 9, 12, 13.

the nature of Israel's interaction with them changes. Ethnic separation no longer finds expression through overt violence against the peoples of the land but rather through a strict admonition to maintain communal boundaries.

This does not mean, however, that the whole program has changed. YHWH's promise to displace the nations is not abrogated, and the task of realizing the promise to possess the land still lies before Israel (v. 5). But the *reason* for obedient response to the commands of Moses has shifted (v. 6). Before Israel entered the land, YHWH explicitly linked strict performance of the law of Moses with "putting this people in possession" of Canaan.[10] If Joshua was to be successful leading Israel to victory in the land, he would have to do all that Moses commanded, turning neither to the right nor to the left (1:2-6). Victory achieved, Joshua issues a similar injunction to the assembled leaders of the nation, admonishing them in the very same terms (v. 6).[11] However, strict performance of everything written in the book has acquired a very different purpose, "so that you may not go out to these nations that remain among you" (v. 7 [AT]). Now at the end of the program the issue is longer subjugation or occupation, but separation. The book of the law of Moses now sets the boundaries within which Israel must live in the land. They are boundaries that Israel must preserve. To go outside these boundaries means becoming one of "them," and being one of "them" inevitably entails embracing their plurality (expressed theologically) and forsaking the integrity of relationship with YHWH. Leaving the internal boundaries set by Deuteronomy is thus tantamount to forsaking YHWH and worshiping the gods of Canaan. The second, enclosing reference (v. 7) elaborates the new program of separation articulated in v. 4 by making it consequent on observing the book of the law. Strict performance of the law of Moses is necessary for keeping the community intact.[12]

[10] The NRSV "you shall put in possession" translates the Hebrew *tanḥîl*, the verbal counterpart of the noun translated "inheritance" in 23:4.

[11] The exhortation begins with the same verb (*ḥāzaq*) that is repeated three times in 1:6-9, *waḥăzaqtem* ("be strong"). The particle *mĕʾōd* ("very") intensifies the verb, just as it does with reference to observance of the law of Moses in 1:7.

[12] The connection is made more forcefully in the MT by the repetition of *lĕbiltî*: "Be very firm in observing and performing all that is written in the book of the law of Moses *so that* you will *not* turn from it either to the right or to the left, *so that* you may *not* go to these nations that remain among you" (AT). The pronouncement also effects a contrast through a repetition of infinitives, between "turning" *(lĕbiltî sûr)* and "going" *(lĕbiltî-bôʾ)*.

Back to the Future II: 23:8-13

The new focus on staying within the boundaries is reiterated by another symmetrical structure set off from the preceding material by the disjunctive *kî-ʾim* (see p. 251). The first and last components of the symmetry (vv. 8 and 11) comprise terse imperatives which enjoin fidelity to YHWH in distinctively Deuteronomic terms: "holding fast" *(dābaq)* and "love" *(ʾahăbâ)*. The terms are closely associated and are paired in Deut 11:22; 13:3-4 [MT 4-5], and 30:20. Here they are separated in order to provide a rhetoric frame within which to articulate YHWH's deeds and their benefits for Israel. The second and fifth components (vv. 9a and 10b) declare what YHWH has done for the nation, dispossessing great and powerful nations and fighting for Israel. The third and fourth components (vv. 9b and 10a), at the center of the structure, elaborate the favorable consequences of YHWH's involvement and restate Israel's current situation, though not without a bit of irony. Because YHWH has dispossessed mighty nations, no one has been able to withstand the invaders "to this day." In the course of the book "to this day" has acquired some unsettling connotations, most of which are associated with the peoples of the land, who remain among Israel "to this day" (cf. 6:25; 9:27; 15:63). The phrase thus reminds the reader that the issues Joshua presents remain open well into the future. Taken as a whole, the structure reinforces the vital connection between loyalty to YHWH and the enjoyment of YHWH's continued participation in the life of the nation.

An extensive admonition follows the chiasm and redirects the focus of loyalty *(dābaq)* and turning *(sûr* [v. 6b]) from YHWH and the book of the law to the other nations, in effect countering the positive expression of the point with a negative one (vv. 12-13). The issue of internal boundaries acquires an even sharper focus through the presentation of exogamy as the quintessential act of "joining" with the remaining nations. Marriage, the basic bond by which social units are connected, becomes paradigmatic for the issue of communal boundaries faced by the nation as a whole. This is made clear by Joshua's description of intermarriage, "and you go to them and they to you" (AT).[13] The construction employed in MT, the verb *bôʾ* followed by the preposition *bĕ*, occurs earlier in the speech to signify Israel's "going to" the remaining nations (v. 7). Exogamy is "going to" the nations in microcosm. Going out to what is "other" or bringing what is "other" into the community entails a violation of boundaries that jeopardizes the nation's relationship with YHWH. And why should YHWH dispossess the other nations when Israel insists

---

[13] NRSV: "so that you may marry their women and they yours."

on clinging to them?[14] For this reason, Joshua warns, the nations will become a snare, a trap, a scourge on the sides and thorns in the eyes. The stack of metaphors, piled one after the other for emphasis, draws on two biblical texts that warn of danger in the land. The "snare" is taken from Deut 7:16, where it signifies the result of serving the gods of Canaan. The scourge and thorns recall Num 33:55, where they characterize the trouble the peoples will bring Israel if they are not dispossessed.[15] Intermarriage represents a confusion of the basic bonds of the community and will lead to pain, trouble, and eventually the disappearance of the nation itself, which will "perish from this good land that the LORD has given you." Having begun with a relatively positive tone and assurances that YHWH will drive out the nations, Joshua now adopts a more sinister tone, intimating a tragic future if Israel loses its distinctive identity by mingling with them.[16]

Back to the Future III: 23:14-16

The address concludes with a third discourse on fidelity and separation, this time with emphasis on the consequences of the respective choices facing the nation. As in the previous sections, Joshua moves seamlessly between past and future. The image of "the good land" (v. 13) is taken up again and becomes the focal point of the discourse. A sense of continuity is established through the repetition, at the beginning and end of the section, of the same verbs that bracket the previous admonitions in vv. 12-13 ("know" and "perish"). Moreover, Joshua's announcement that he is "about to go the way of all the earth" returns to the more positive atmosphere which began the address, an impression enhanced by a reaffirmation of YHWH's faithfulness, this time in effusive and repetitive terms (v. 14). The open and ominous future threatened in vv. 12-13 is thus countered, for the moment, by an exuberant acclamation of all that YHWH has done for Israel. The declaration that YHWH has fulfilled all the good things he has promised, without fail, parallels

---

[14] The MT emphasizes the point by introducing it with an infinitive absolute and imperative: *yādôaʿ tēdĕʿ* ("know assuredly").

[15] YHWH declares through Moses that "they shall trouble you in the land where you are settling. And I will do to you as I thought to do to them" (Num 33:55c-56).

[16] The verb *ʾābad* ("perish") often signifies nomadic existence or aimless wandering (Lev 26:38; Deut 7:20; 8:19, 20; 11:17; 26:5; 28:20; 30:18). Its use to signify Israel's disappearance from the land thus also intimates the return to a landless and thus disintegrated existence.

the optimistic and decisive assessment of the apportionment of tribal lands:

> Not one of all the good promises that
> the LORD had made to the house of
> Israel had failed; all came to pass (21:45).

> Not one thing has failed of all the good
> things that the LORD your God promised
> concerning you; all have come to pass for
> you, not one of them has failed (23:14c-d).

In the context of the address, however, these assurances no longer stand by themselves. In a stunning reversal, Joshua renders them again in the opposite terms, declaring that YHWH will just as surely bring all the "bad things" he has promised (v. 15). The sense of the pronouncement is hard to pinpoint. It would appear from the context that the words are an implicit *warning* which confirm the consequences of intermarriage and apostasy spelled out in vv. 12-13. Yet they also take the form of a *prediction,* echoing the declarative structure of the affirmations immediately preceding: in the past, YHWH brought the good things to pass, but in the future YHWH will bring the evil things to pass, just as he promised. The positive momentum gained by repeating the affirmations of 21:43-45 is thus stopped cold by an opposing prediction. YHWH's faithfulness to fulfill his promises, an unabashed proclamation of completion in the narrator's summary, now becomes an ominous precedent which anticipates Israel's ultimate failure to inhabit the land. YHWH indeed fulfills all that he speaks. And for this reason, YHWH will just as certainly fulfill his promises to destroy the nation. Particularly shocking is the assertion that YHWH will "destroy" *(hašmîdô)* Israel, for YHWH applies to Israel a term used previously to signify the eradication of the peoples of the land (Deut 4:26; 7:4, 23; Josh 9:24; 11:14, 20).[17] The force of these parallel yet polar pronouncements sets up a new tension between the unconditional and conditional character of YHWH's relationship with Israel. The unconditional and unilateral elements of YHWH's involvement assure Israel that he will certainly fulfill what he has spoken. On the other hand, the gift of the land, rendered in unambiguous terms throughout the book, now acquires a conditional quality. As Joshua looks into the future, he watches Israel vanish from the land.

---

[17] The verb is also used in connection with the deaths of Achan and his family (Josh 7:12).

The tension is not resolved by Joshua's concluding remarks (v. 16), despite the fact that the NRSV renders them in conditional terms. In the MT, the sentence begins with an infinitive construct phrase introduced by the preposition *bĕ (bĕ‛obrĕkem)*, a construction which can express a condition, but can also introduce a causal clause or, more commonly, a temporal clause.[18] It could therefore be understood not only to mean "if you transgress" but also "because you will transgress" or even "when you transgress" the covenant. The emphatic rendering of the clause ("transgress the covenant of the LORD your God, which he enjoined on you") makes its indeterminacy all the more pronounced. Is Joshua speaking in terms of warning or prediction?

The subsequent admonition synthesizes the various themes of the address. Joshua explains transgressing the covenant in terms of going, serving, and bowing down to other gods, forging a terminological link with the violation of the nation's internal boundaries (v. 7) and implicitly restating the fundamental threat the nations pose to Israel. The outcome of such transgression is defined by a restatement of the consequences which Joshua declares will befall Israel for intermarriage, "you shall perish quickly from the good land that he has given you" (cf. v. 13c). Intermarriage, violation of communal boundaries, and transgression of the covenant are thereby joined together as Joshua concludes his address. The two new words which Joshua now introduces, transgression of the covenant and the kindling of YHWH's anger, cement the connection by alluding to the story of Achan, the only other context in the book where the two concepts occur together (cf. 7:1, 11).

Far from bringing closure, Joshua's farewell address therefore leaves the reader with a sense of foreboding. Having begun with rest, it ends with wrath. The charge of apostasy, so recently leveled against the eastern tribes (22:18), now recoils against the entire nation. And the threat of YHWH's anger, so feared by the tribes in Canaan (22:20, 31), still looms large on the horizon. The various tensions within the address—past/future, loyalty/apostasy, good/bad, rest/expulsion—crystallize at the end around the concept of the covenant, preparing the reader for the book's final, climactic episode. At the ceremony at Shechem, the covenant will signify YHWH's choosing of Israel (24:2-13) and Israel's choosing of YHWH (24:16-18). The latter will be expressed particularly in terms of putting away foreign gods (24:23) and will be countered by

[18] A close parallel in both form and content is 1 Kings 18:18: He (Elijah) answered, "I have not troubled Israel; but *(kî-im)* you have, and your father's house, because you have forsaken the commandments of the LORD *(ba‛ăzabkem ’et-miṣwōt yhwh)* and followed the Baals." Here the phrase introduces a causal clause.

Joshua's declaration that Israel is incapable of serving YHWH (24:19). By taking up the themes of land, obedience, and separation, and framing them within the nation's fundamental choice of serving YHWH or the gods of Canaan, the address effects a crucial transition between the thematic emphases of the previous material and the decisions which unite and define the nation. The events of the book have steadily dismantled notions of identity based on kinship, possession of territory, and strict obedience to the Mosaic commandments. Joshua's address now prepares the reader to understand the people of God differently, as a people who chooses the God who has called them into being.

Chapter Thirteen
DECISIONS, DECISIONS
Joshua 24:1-33

The final episode of Joshua relates a covenant ceremony which portrays Israel as a nation constituted by its choice for YHWH as opposed to all other gods. The ceremony takes place at Shechem, a site associated with other occasions of choosing. Israel (in the person of Jacob) put away "foreign gods" there before going on to Bethel (Gen 35:1-4), and Joshua recited the law as Israel invoked blessings in the vicinity of Shechem (Josh 8:30-35). In addition to these associations, Shechem recalls the circumstances surrounding the rape of Dinah, a story that raises tensions similar to those that configure the book of Joshua (intercourse with the people of the land and extermination of the peoples; Gen 34:1-31). The setting of the episode thus creates an atmosphere infused with memories of confrontation (with the peoples and their gods) and commitment (to YHWH), a scenic ambience that magnifies Joshua's challenge that Israel choose whom it will serve (v. 15).

The covenant ceremony completes the thematic program developed in the course of the last two chapters. The story of the eastern tribes (22:1-34) dismantles notions of identity founded on possession of land, obedience to the commandments of Moses, and bonds of kinship by demonstrating how these notions mean different things to different tribal groups (dividing rather than uniting the nation). The confrontation over the Jordan altar reveals that, while views of kinship, land, and obedience may differ, all tribes share the conviction that loyalty to YHWH is crucial for national survival. The delegation from the tribes west of the Jordan raises the issue negatively, charging the eastern tribes (a heretofore exemplary tribal group) with sacrilege, rebellion, and turning away from YHWH. These crimes, they declare, threaten the survival of the nation, which as a consequence is now subject to the visitation of YHWH's anger (22:16-20). The eastern tribes respond first by denying the charges leveled against them (vv. 22-23) and then affirming their unqualified loyalty to YHWH (again in negative terms; v. 29). Their expression of loyalty (or more precisely, their denial of disloyalty) is enough to satisfy the concerns of the delegation and the conflict is thereby resolved (v. 31).[1]

The perception that loyalty constitutes the core element of Israel's national identity assumes greater emphasis in Joshua's address (23:1-16), which redefines the association between ethnic separation and obedience to the law. The speech portrays observance of the Mosaic commandments not as an end in itself but rather as the means by which Israel may remain separate from other nations. Likewise, separation from the other nations is not presented as an end in itself. Instead of calling for the extermination of the nations and the possession of their entire land, Joshua lifts possession of land completely out of the sphere of Israel's responsibility (vv. 3, 5, 9-10) and explains that separation is necessary in order to keep Israel from turning to other gods (vv. 6-7). Retaining its distinctive identity through loyalty to YHWH, rather than occupying territory, now constitutes the basic challenge before Israel, with consequences that will lead to the survival or death of the nation (vv. 14-16). Holding fast to YHWH will bring success in the land (v. 8), while holding fast to the surviving nations will bring bondage and death (vv. 11-13). As the speech concludes, this challenge finds explicit expression through the medium of the covenant. Once again fidelity is defined negatively; transgression of the covenant means serving and worshiping other gods and will ignite YHWH's anger and bring destruction upon Israel (v. 16). In this manner the whole of Joshua's address transforms an understanding of what it means to possess the land, obey the commands, and remain separate from the nation. These are no longer cast as prime directives but as expressions of Israel's choice to follow YHWH exclusively; all flow from the community's decision to devote itself to God. By choosing YHWH Israel will prosper in the land. By turning aside to other gods, Israel will vanish from the land. All is dependent on Israel's response to what YHWH has done. Joshua's address thus prepares the reader for a more explicit constitution of the nation through its decision to serve YHWH at Shechem (24:1-28).

The narrator relates the entire episode in a crisp, straightforward narrative. The account begins with a retrospective of Israel's experi-

---

[1] The structure of Josh 24:1-28, which frames discourse with narrative units, corresponds to the structure of Josh 22:1-34.

ence with YHWH, from the calling of Abraham through the deliverance from Egypt and up to the present moment (vv. 2-13). Although Joshua is the speaker, the words are YHWH's. The comprehensive scope of the review suggests that the current episode represents the crowning event of Israel's story, but the first person point of view makes Israel the story's object rather than its subject. In essence, YHWH tells Israel's story in terms of what YHWH has done for the nation. YHWH declares that he has been at the center of Israel's story from the very beginning. Before YHWH took Abraham from beyond the River, Abraham and his ancestors were no different than all the others, who served other gods beyond the Euphrates (vv. 2-3). But YHWH did something unique in the life of Abraham and his descendants, removing them from their dwelling, granting them victory over their enemies and bringing them into the land of the Amorites. Throughout the summary, the constant repetition of first person verbal forms drives home the point that Israel exists as a nation only because of divine initiative. YHWH brought the nation into existence. YHWH brought it out of Egypt and through the wilderness. YHWH fought for Israel against the Amorites on both sides of the Jordan. In a sense, Israel has been a relatively passive participant in its own story, a point made vividly by YHWH's concluding remarks, "I gave you a land on which you had not labored, and towns that you had not built, and you live in them; you eat the fruit of vineyards and olive yards that you did not plant" (v. 13).

The mood shifts from the indicative (what YHWH has done) to the imperative (what Israel must do) with Joshua's demand that Israel serve YHWH and put away the ancestral gods (vv. 14-15). The sudden shift in tone directs attention to the core of Israel's national identity. The narrative preamble demonstrates that Israel is unique among all other peoples only because YHWH has brought it into being and shaped it through experiences of rescue and gift. Joshua now sets before the people (and the reader as well) the response necessary to preserve the integrity of the community: "revere and serve the LORD in sincerity and faithfulness." To choose the gods of Egypt, the Amorites, or those beyond the River is tantamount to returning to undifferentiated plurality; following other gods means becoming one of the many other nations of the world and losing the basis for community integrity. Israel will be One only if it devotes itself exclusively to the One God. On the other hand, Israel will be no more if it embraces the Many. By setting these two alternatives before the nation and the reader, Joshua therefore powerfully demonstrates that *choosing* YHWH is at the heart of what it means to be "Israel."

The focus on choosing is reinforced thematically by the repetition of the verb ʿābad ("serve") throughout the episode. The verb appears first to characterize Israel's ancestors before YHWH brought the nation into being ("they served other gods" [v. 2]). Joshua then repeats it seven times as he lays out the alternatives between serving YHWH or serving the gods of their ancestors or the surrounding nations (vv. 14-15). This leads to another seven-fold repetition during the ensuing interchange (vv. 16-24). After the people choose to serve YHWH (vv. 16, 18), Joshua pointedly debunks their declaration by denying that they are able to serve YHWH (v. 19) and intimating that they will serve foreign gods (v. 20). The people counter by confirming their intention to serve YHWH (v. 21), and Joshua then endorses their confession by repeating their decision once again (v. 22). The dialogue finally concludes with the people's third declaration that they will serve YHWH (v. 24).

"Serving YHWH" signifies acceptance of the distinctive destiny articulated by YHWH's version of Israel's story. "Serving other gods," on the other hand, signifies a return to a pre-Israel state (v. 2) and the rejection of all that YHWH has done for the nation. The people initially respond by endorsing YHWH's rendition of their story and proclaiming, in both negative and positive terms, their decision to serve YHWH (vv. 16-18). Joshua's shocking rejoinder, however, ostensibly short-circuits the connection just forged between God and nation (vv. 19-20). Although taking the role of a covenant mediator (like Moses), he adopts an adversarial stance, accusing the people of transgressing the covenant (as many of the prophets would later do) even before it is completely ratified. In an abrupt turnabout, Joshua no longer speaks of the graciousness of the giving God but of the harm that will be inflicted by the holy and jealous God. The arrangement will never work, he asserts, because YHWH will not forgive the nation's transgressions (specifically defined as forsaking YHWH and serving other gods). This refutation brings the forward momentum of the episode to an unexpected halt but also produces three significant rhetorical effects. First, it reminds the reader of the consequences of this decision and thus of all future decisions. The choice before Israel is a serious one, and dire consequences will follow if the people of Israel reject the God who has chosen them. Second, it establishes the genuine character of the people's response by prompting them to repeat their decision to serve YHWH (v. 21). Not even their leader's rebuke will dissuade them from their decision to serve YHWH! Finally, Joshua's repudiation of the people's commitment implicitly reinforces the point of YHWH's narrative preamble (vv. 2-13); ultimately Israel's existence as a people depends more on what YHWH does than on what Israel does. In choosing YHWH, the people affirm their identity as a nation formed by YHWH (vv. 17-18a), but this does not mean that *what they do* keeps the community intact. Even Israel's fidelity is derivative and reactive, a response to YHWH's deeds. Israel is a nation constituted by

YHWH and thus a nation which may have a hope of survival even if it joins the other nations, forsakes YHWH, and disappears from the land.

A second rejoinder (v. 22a, 23) leads to a third and final declaration of loyalty (v. 22b, 24). As he did at first, Joshua admonishes the people to put away other gods and then enjoins them to "incline your hearts to the LORD, the God of Israel" (v. 23). This final command stresses that devotion to YHWH comprises both attitude and action. Putting away other gods confirms the inward disposition to revere and serve YHWH; Israel's fidelity will be confirmed by its deeds.[2] Following this exhortation the people reaffirm once more their intention to serve and obey YHWH (v. 24).[3]

Joshua formalizes the people's response by making a covenant and setting up a large stone as a witness to their words (vv. 25-27). Within the context of the episode, both the covenant and the stone acquire metaphorical significance. Joshua makes a covenant with the people in direct response to their decision to choose YHWH. Covenant thus represents Israel's response to God, in contrast to the notion of covenant as that which "the LORD your God, which he enjoined on you" (23:16). Covenant confirms choice. Israel has chosen YHWH over against all other gods and, in response, Joshua codifies the decision in the form of a covenant. Likewise, the stone which Joshua sets up stands as a visible reminder of the decision. It "has heard all the words of the LORD which he spoke to us" and stands as a witness against the nation if it ever reneges on its decision (v. 27). Whereas the covenant formalizes Israel's response, the stone directs attention to the notion that Israel's decision is essentially a response to YHWH's graciousness. "All the words of the LORD which he spoke to us" may refer to the statutes and ordinances connected to the covenant, but they may also refer to the earlier retrospective (vv. 2-13), the only words which YHWH speaks in the present episode. The possibility of the latter leads the reader once again to appreciate the significance of Israel's decision. The stone has heard all that YHWH has done for Israel, and it will bear witness against the nation if Israel does not respond with commensurate loyalty. As in his farewell address, Joshua's last words to the congregation set a somber tone. Instead of looking ahead into a future rich with the fullness of life with YHWH, Joshua again ends on a negative note.

---

[2] Joshua's speech (excluding YHWH's review) encloses Israel's declarations of loyalty with imperatives to action (vv. 14, 23).

[3] The people declare their intention to serve and obey (v. 24), but the narrator does not report that they put away the foreign gods as Joshua has (now twice) commanded. The absence of the report is noteworthy because, throughout the book, the narrator confirms obedience to Joshua's command by reporting the precise execution of the command.

In an odd twist, the book then finishes with reports of death and
burial (vv. 29-33). The deaths and burials of Joshua and Eleazar bring
closure to the period of conquest and occupation, as does the report
that all Israel served YHWH all the days of the elders who outlived
Joshua. The burial of Joseph's bones at Shechem signals the completion of the larger story, extending back to Genesis, of Israel's journey to
the land. The burial notices promise a conclusion to the story by tying
up loose ends from the past, but even so the reader is left with the
sense that it is not really finished. Confronted with the deaths of faithful leaders and the many suggestions of future apostasy and destruction, the reader is left to ponder a number of unsettling questions. Who
will lead Israel now, since Joshua has not selected a successor? Will Israel remain steadfast in its commitment to serve YHWH, or will it suc-
cumb to the temptation to serve other gods? What will Israel's life in
the land look like? And how long will it last?

Israel's Story and YHWH's Story: 24:1-13

The narrator makes the transition from Joshua's address to the covenant ceremony at Shechem by reporting the participation of the same
group of leaders that had been present on the previous occasion. The
listing of leaders (elders, heads, judges, and officers) also suggests a
link to the ritual of covenant renewal enacted on Mts. Ebal and Gerizim earlier in the book (8:33). On that occasion (and in the same vicinity) Joshua also set alternatives before Israel (through the recitation of
blessings and curses), erected a stone altar (cf. 24:25-27), and wrote a
copy of the book of the law of Moses (cf. 24:26). Allusions to this prior
ceremony highlight the themes of covenant and choosing, projecting
them back throughout all the intervening material. The setting of the episode at Shechem is odd, for nowhere has the reader been informed that
Israel attacked the city. Why has the nation assembled here? Shechem
does not seem to have been taken by force. Is it possible that Israel established some sort of rapprochement with the inhabitants of this city?
The reader knows by this point that there are plenty of precedents for
such a situation, so the possibility that the Shechemites may have
joined the Rahabites, Gibeonites, and others as exempted survivors de-
serves strong consideration.[4] Whatever the case, Shechem serves as the

---

[4] On the previous occasion at Mts. Ebal and Gerizim, in the vicinity of Shechem,
"all Israel" includes "alien as well as citizen" (8:33).

backdrop for the unification of the nation through covenant. References to "all the people" and Shechem occur at the beginning and end of the episode (vv. 1-2, 25, 27), establishing a framework for the task of choosing. This act of choosing is vital for the life of the nation, and the narrative conveys the solemnity of the occasion by referring to its sacral character: "they presented themselves before God."[5]

Joshua begins his address by presenting his words as those of YHWH. The phrase "thus says the LORD," is a common formula in prophetic speech and indicates that what follows is a message from YHWH.[6] In this case the message turns out to be a synopsis of Israel's history, told from YHWH's point of view. A preface depicts the situation of Israel's ancestors on the other side of the Euphrates, before YHWH enters the picture (v. 2b). With the declaration that "I took your ancestor Abraham from beyond the River" YHWH then relates his guidance and formation of the nation during each stage of its existence, from the ancestral period (vv. 3-4) through the Exodus from Egypt and into the wilderness (vv. 5-8) and to the conquest of the Amorites in the Transjordan (vv. 8-10) and Canaan (vv. 11-12). The entire synopsis is presented through succinct reports which move the retrospective along at a rapid tempo, and the heavy concentration of verbs infuses it with energy. Each phase of the story begins with a verb that communicates YHWH's initiative (e.g. "I took," "I brought"), the most prominent being *waʾattēn* ("and I gave"), which is repeated six times (vv. 3, 4 (2x), 8, 11, 13).[7] The density of verbs in the account creates the impression that Israel is a nation swept along by the power of a God who alone has brought it into being through gift and promise and who guides it to fulfillment in a place of its own.

Scholars have long pondered a glaring gap in this recital of the stops on the way to fulfillment. The story of the covenant at Sinai, and the giving of the law through Moses, does not appear in the story, and Moses himself, a towering figure in Israel's history, is markedly diminished here; he shares billing with his brother Aaron, both of whom are identified as emissaries of YHWH to Egypt (v. 5a). Why is there no mention

---

[5] By employing the generic term for the deity, "God" (*haʾĕlōhîm*), rather than the divine name YHWH, the narrator creates a sense of indecision regarding Israel's loyalty. Israel has not yet declared for YHWH, and the reader will learn that it still holds to other gods.

[6] The phrase is often referred to as the Messenger Formula. For more on this formula, see C. Westermann, *Basic Forms of Prophetic Speech* (Louisville: Westminster John Knox, 1991) 98–128.

[7] Most of the verbs are drawn from the Pentateuchal texts to which they refer. See R. Nelson, *Joshua*, OTL (Louisville: Westminster John Knox, 1997) 273–5.

of the covenant at Sinai, particularly in this preamble to the making of a covenant at Shechem? And why does Moses assume such a seemingly incidental role in the story, especially since so much of the book focuses on obedience to his commandments? To explain this lacuna, scholars have generally looked for clues in the circumstances of the book's composition. One prominent hypothesis is that the overview constitutes an early creed. From this perspective, the absence of Sinai may indicate that the traditions associated with the Sinai covenant were originally separate from those associated with the Exodus and the gift of the land.[8] The absence of Sinai, however, may be explained on stylistic grounds. The present episode emphasizes the people's exclusive choice of YHWH rather than a pluralistic devotion which would embrace the many gods surrounding them, and as noted above, covenant in this context signifies a permanent, public testimony to this choice (covenant as response). Mention of the Sinai covenant, which expresses a greater degree of reciprocity, would unnecessarily complicate the picture and diffuse the episode's linking of covenant with response. Furthermore, Sinai is inextricably linked to Moses. In the context of the book of Joshua, Moses has been associated with the theme of "obedience to commandments" (a theme also implicitly connected to the Sinai covenant). But the point of *this* episode is that obedience is a derivative concept, an expression of the act of choosing which constitutes the nation. "Moses" and "Sinai" carry associations that might confuse the rhetorical focus of the episode. Covenant is the choice for YHWH. Obedience to covenant laws is an *expression* of this choice but not at the *core* of what makes Israel who it is. This is the contribution (more in the nature of a reminder) that the episode makes to an understanding of covenant, and it is one of the reasons why Joshua finally moves out from the shadow of Moses.

---

[8] The hypothesis that this retrospective should be viewed as an early creedal recitation was first suggested by G. von Rad, who saw parallels between it and other creedal formulations (Deut 6:2-24; 1 Sam 12:8; Psalm 136). Von Rad observed that Sinai is nowhere mentioned in any of these texts and on this basis concluded that the Sinai traditions must have been associated with a cultic situation different than that surrounding that which affirmed the Exodus and gift of the land (which he viewed as the kernel of the entire Pentateuch). He was impressed by the simplicity of Josh 24:2-13, which he called "a Hexateuch in miniature" in a seminal essay entitled "The Problem of the Hexateuch," *The Problem of the Hexateuch and Other Essays* (London: SCM Press, 1984) 1–78. The hypothesis has generated an enormous volume of literature in response which has been summarized well by W. Koopmans, *Joshua 24 as Poetic Narrative*, JSOTSup 93 (Sheffield: Sheffield Academic Press, 1990) 7–162.

The overview begins with a description of the state of affairs before YHWH enters Israel's story (v. 2). We are given two pieces of information about the ancestors, Terah, Nahor, and Abraham: they lived "beyond the River" *(bĕʿēber hannāhār)* and they served other gods. With these two reports, the narrator links geographical otherness with theological otherness. In the course of the book, *bĕʿēber* ("on the other side") has assumed a symbolic significance. It occurs only with reference to the kings and peoples of the land (2:10; 5:1; 9:1, 10; 12:1, 10) or the Israelite tribes who settle east of the Jordan (1:14, 15; 13:8, 27, 32; 14:3; 17:5; 20:8). Those "on the other side" are marked as "outside," either ethnically or geographically.[9] The phrase thus signals a particular point of view, that of the "Israel" which has settled in the Promised Land west of the Jordan. Within the context of the story "the other side" is what lies beyond "Israel." After identifying those in this "other" place (namely, Terah, Abraham, and Nahor), Joshua/YHWH specifies what made them other: they served other gods *(ʾĕlōhîm ʾăḥērîm)*. "Serving other gods" is, of course, the peril that Joshua warns Israel to avoid during his farewell address (23:16). The repetition of the phrase at the beginning of Joshua's next speech now makes a grammatical link between the ancestors beyond the River and a future that he has just warned the nation to avoid at all costs (23:16). Before YHWH, Israel's ancestors were part of the "many," indistinguishable from those who served other gods.

Israel's story begins in earnest when YHWH takes Abraham "from the other side" *(mēʿēber)* and brings him to Canaan, the land where Israel currently resides (v. 3a). The origins of Israel thus stress the initiative of YHWH, who takes Abram from undifferentiated otherness to a place ordained by YHWH. The rest of the patriarchal story is propelled by this initial change of place and associates the land with YHWH's promise and the nation's formation. The report that YHWH made Abraham's offspring many (v. 3b) confirms the promise to Abraham in Canaan (Gen 12:1-3; 15:1-6), and the subsequent repetition of the verb *wāʾettēn* ("and I gave") not only reminds the reader of YHWH's graciousness but of other gifts: Canaan as "the land YHWH has given to Israel" (1:2-3, 21:43) and YHWH's giving of Israel's enemies into its hands (6:2, 16; 8:1; 10:8; 11:6). The former is affirmed explicitly in the third instance, which reports that YHWH gave Esau the hill country of Seir (v. 4b).

Jacob's descent into Egypt (v. 4c) provides the occasion for YHWH to bring about another change of place. Significantly, Israel's departure

[9] The "outsider" status of those tribes in the Transjordan is at the heart of the conflict that arises from the construction of the altar at the Jordan (22:1-34). The phrase *bĕʿēber* appears three times within the story (vv. 4, 7, 11).

from Canaan does not come at the behest of YHWH, a point emphasized by the text's contrasting remarks about Esau and Jacob, "I gave Esau the hill country of Seir to possess, but Jacob and his children went down to Egypt." In Egypt YHWH engineers the sequence of events that results in Israel's liberation from bondage (vv. 5-7). Once again, a density of verbs communicates YHWH's dynamic involvement in the events: "I sent," "I plagued," "I did," "I brought out." However, the first person forms give way to second and third person verbs in the midst of the account (e.g. "when they cried out to the LORD, he put darkness between you and the Egyptians"), and the audience is suddenly transported into the event by a shift from "your ancestors" to "you" (vv. 6b-7b). The grammatical digression brings the experience of deliverance into the narrative present and complements the representation of divine initiative with a report of divine responsiveness. A concluding declaration, that "your eyes saw what I did to Egypt," looks back to the beginning of Joshua's prior address (23:3) and by this device connects YHWH's defeat of Pharaoh's army at the Red Sea with YHWH's defeat of the kings of the land.

Another period of inertia precipitates another change of place. After recounting the deliverance at the Red Sea, the story moves on to note that Israel "lived in the wilderness a long time" (v. 7c). The verb *yāšab* ("live, sit") is an odd verb to employ for this period of constant wandering but probably occurs because of its thematic resonance. It is the same verb as that employed in v. 2 with reference to the ancestors beyond the Euphrates. Repetition of the verb makes a thematic connection between the two periods and sets the stage for YHWH to move the nation along towards its final destination in Canaan. The review returns to the first person with YHWH's declaration that "I brought you to the land of the Amorites, who lived on the other side of the Jordan" (v. 8).[10] In this case, divine action envelopes a threat from other enemies. Inserted between reports that YHWH delivered the Amorites to Israel (v. 8) and rescued the nation from the curse of Balaam (v. 10) is a terse account of Balak's attempt to destroy Israel. The story of Balak and Balaam injects the theme of blessing and curse into the story, with the emphasis on blessing.

The last phase of YHWH's overview brings the story up to the present moment (vv. 11-13). The battle at Jericho receives a different treatment than it does previously in the book; it is here depicted as a site

---

[10] The description of the Amorites as living "on the other side of the Jordan" links them thematically with Israel's ancestors who lived "on the other side of the River" (v. 2).

where the citizens of Jericho, along with all the peoples of the land, fight against Israel. The report of a pitched battle at Jericho is far different from the account rendered previously in the book (where the citizens of Jericho are sequestered within the city; 6:1). But again thematic and stylistic objectives influence the presentation of the event. The listing of the peoples of the land is a clue that the battle at Jericho, the first of all conflicts in Canaan, represents the entire period of conquest and, on a deeper level, the threat posed both militarily and socially by the peoples of the land. The plurality of the peoples draws our attention to their fundamental difference from unified Israel, and *they* are now portrayed as the aggressors: they "fight against Israel." Consistent with the rest of the overview, YHWH again appears as a rescuer and defender. YHWH engulfed the Egyptians when Israel cried out (v. 7), handed over the Amorites when they fought against Israel (v. 8), and now hands the peoples of the land over when they fight against Israel (v. 11). YHWH's deliverance and guidance are thus woven into the warp and woof of the whole story; YHWH propels the nation from place to place and eliminates all who stand in the way. In this way, the battle at Jericho can be seen as a victory over the aggressive threat of Canaanite multiplicity and as another demonstration of YHWH's supremacy. This is a version of Israel's story that places YHWH at the center and emphasizes that the nation's achievements, and indeed its very identity, are due solely to YHWH. Lest his audience miss this point, YHWH makes it explicit with a few concluding remarks (vv. 12-13). The two kings of the Amorites were defeated by the "hornet" YHWH sent rather than by Israel's military prowess or power.[11] Israel cannot, therefore take pride in its achievements, for it can boast of none. All that Israel now enjoys, YHWH contends, comes as a gift, "I gave you a land on which you had not labored, and towns that you had not built, and you

---

[11] The word translated "hornet" (*ṣirʿâ*) is obscure and occurs here to demonstrate the fulfillment of YHWH's promises in Exod 23:8 and Deut 7:20. The "two kings of the Amorites" have previously been identified as Sihon and Og, the two Amorite kings defeated under the leadership of Moses in the Transjordan (2:10; 9:10). If they are the ones meant by the designation, the report is out of place chronologically. They were defeated before, not after, the battles in Canaan. Are these then two other kings, not mentioned in the reports of battles? If Sihon and Og are meant, why are they mentioned here? This question as well can be answered on stylistic grounds. Like the citizens of Jericho, the two kings of the Amorites represent a first, i.e. the first victories over the powerful kings who oppose Israel. They therefore are employed here as a synecdoche for the all the victories YHWH has brought over the kings of the Amorites. (A synecdoche is a device which represents the whole through one of its parts.)

live in them; you eat the fruit of vineyards and olive yards that you did not plant." The life Israel now enjoys in the land, all that it is and all that it possesses, has been accomplished by YHWH.

The Choice: 24:14-24

YHWH's assertion that Israel now enjoys benefits it has not earned (v. 13) derives from Deut 6:10-15, a passage that addresses Israel at precisely this point in its story:

> When the LORD your God has brought you into the land that he swore to your ancestors, to Abraham, to Isaac, and to Jacob, to give you—a land with fine houses filled with all sorts of goods that you did not fill, hewn cisterns that you did not hew, vineyards and olive groves that you did not plant—and when you have eaten your fill, take care that you do not forget the LORD, who brought you out of the land of Egypt, out of the house of slavery. The LORD your God you shall fear; him you shall serve, and by his name alone you shall swear. Do not follow other gods, any of the gods of the peoples who are all around you, because the LORD your God, who is present with you, is a jealous God. The anger of the LORD your God would be kindled against you and he would destroy you from the face of the earth.

As is the case at many points in Joshua, a Deuteronomic text furnishes the structural and thematic framework for the narration of an event. Joshua's dialogue with the people articulates the issues anticipated by Moses as he spoke to another assembly of Israelites on the plain of Moab. Like the Deuteronomic passage, the present episode is fundamentally concerned with the prospect that Israel may serve other gods after experiencing the gracious gifts of YHWH. YHWH himself makes this point via narrative and commentary, and Joshua follows by using the language of the Deuteronomic text ("fear" and "serve") to call Israel to exclusive devotion to YHWH. He also places the alternative, following other gods, before the people, though he presents it now as a choice rather than an admonition. The dialogue concludes, as does the Deuteronomic passage, by countering the image of a gracious God with that of a jealous God who may also become a destructive presence. Joshua's shift from the indicative (vv. 2-13) to the imperative mode thus echoes the Deuteronomic passage in both form and substance. The charge to fear and serve YHWH defines fidelity in the same terms as the Deuteronomic text, while the focus on other gods takes up the most expansive of the Deuteronomic admonitions.

Only the introductory *wĕ'attâ* ("now therefore") and a shift in verbal forms signals that both the speaker and the mood of the speech have changed. Joshua now speaks with his own voice and calls for a response to YHWH's gracious acts (v. 14). Repetition of the verb "serve" (*'ābad*) renders a thematic coherence to Joshua's challenge and prompts both audience and reader to understand the gravity of the choice before Israel. It is a choice that would seem obvious. If through YHWH the nation was brought into being and receives all that it has, why would it offer its loyalty elsewhere? Joshua thus issues a forceful command to fear and serve YHWH with complete devotion ("in sincerity and in faithfulness") and then calls for Israel to express its devotion tangibly by putting away "the gods that your ancestors served beyond the River, and in Egypt." The two commands communicate the holistic response which the nation is called to make. The positive expression of devotion (serving YHWH) also implies a negative expression (putting away other gods). Disposition will be confirmed by an active response that eliminates all vestiges of otherness. Whatever residue of life "on the other side of the River" still clings to the nation must be rejected. Serving YHWH can become a possibility only when the nation puts away other gods.

Joshua recognizes that such wholehearted fidelity may be unattractive, but he presents only one alternative, namely a return to existence before YHWH, "choose this day whom you will serve, whether the gods your ancestors served in the region beyond the River or the gods of the Amorites in whose land you are living" (v. 15). YHWH has been faithful to Israel, both to fulfill his promises and to side with Israel in its conflicts with other nations. Now Joshua calls Israel to respond in kind. Singular devotion cannot coexist with multiple loyalties. If serving YHWH entails the rejection of other gods, the reverse is true as well. A decision not to serve YHWH is tantamount to a decision to serve other gods. The equation is communicated by the repetition of the particle *'im*, which joins the negative ("*if* you are unwilling to serve to LORD") with the positive ("*whether* the gods your ancestors served in the region beyond the River *or* the gods of the Amorites in whose land you are living"). The challenge to "choose this day whom you will serve" unites both parts of the equation and demonstrates that Israel's identity will henceforth be determined by the choice it makes. Since YHWH has made Israel what it is, serving other gods, whether those of the ancestors or those in the land, effectively means the loss of national identity and expresses a desire to return to the many. Joshua, however, lays claim to Israel's distinctiveness by declaring that he and his house will serve YHWH. By announcing his decision in this way, as a decision made by an ancestral household (the basic unit of Israelite society), Joshua implies that devotion to YHWH must take place from the bottom up. Israel's distinctive identity will be constituted and preserved by the decisions of the myriad households that comprise the nation.

In an extraordinary demonstration of corporate unity, the people immediately respond by proclaiming their decision to serve YHWH and by affirming the YHWH-centered version of their story which they have just heard (vv. 16-18). Their response implies that they have understood the lessons of the monologue and have taken them to heart. The people bracket their reply with the negative and positive expressions that Joshua has called for: they will not serve other gods (v. 16) and they will serve YHWH (v. 18b). The first of these (the negative) is uttered in terms strongly reminiscent of the eastern tribes' vigorous denial of apostasy ("far be it from us!"), as if Joshua's challenge contains an implicit accusation (cf. 22:29), but the second (the positive) corresponds to Joshua's declaration to serve YHWH (v. 15). Both conclude, in the MT, with a confession that unambiguously communicates their choice: "Indeed, YHWH is our God" (*kî yhwh ʾĕlōhēynû hûʾ* [v. 17a]) and "YHWH, indeed he is our God" (*ʾet-yhwh kî-hûʾ ʾĕlōhēynû* [v. 18b]).[12] Between these confessions, the people repeat key elements of the overview (although curiously neglecting to mention anything about Abraham's journey from beyond the River to Canaan). Capturing the spirit of YHWH's version, they also infuse their recital with energy and concentrate on what YHWH has done to bring the nation to its present situation in the land. The whole response thus exemplifies the act of choosing which makes this people distinct from all others: the recognition that YHWH has actively shaped and guided the nation and the requisite decision to serve YHWH and put away other gods.

Because the people's response conveys genuine understanding and devotion, Joshua's rebuttal comes as a complete surprise (vv. 19-20). What has all this been for, if not to bring the nation precisely to this point of decision? Why would Joshua bring YHWH and the nation together only to disavow the relationship? Although we might expect a joyful affirmation of mutual commitment between Israel and YHWH, Joshua instead recreates the ominous ambience of his farewell address (cf. 23:15-16) and predicts disobedience and disaster. He begins by presenting a side of YHWH diametrically opposed to the gracious God who guides and protects the nation (vv. 2-13). Again evoking Deut 6:10-15, Joshua declares that YHWH is a holy and jealous God, who will not for-

---

[12] In both instances the confession is skillfully embedded within other declarations, thus the NRSV "*for it is the* LORD *our God* who brought us and our ancestors up from the land of Egypt" (v. 17a) and "therefore we will serve *the* LORD, *for he is our God*" (v. 18b).

give Israel's transgressions or sins (v. 19; cf. Deut 6:15a). Those assembled at Shechem *cannot* serve YHWH , he avers, for this very reason. The stark pronouncement strongly implies that Israel is incapable of exercising the kind of exclusive devotion that derives from an appreciation of the utter uniqueness of YHWH. Directly challenging the people's claim that they never would forsake YHWH, Joshua intimates that the nation will indeed do so and, as a result, that YHWH will turn on them for serving "foreign gods." The particle *kî*, which introduces v. 20, invests his words with a sense of uncertainty corresponding to that conveyed by the concluding admonitions of the previous address (23:15-16; cf. Deut 6:14-15). Is this a warning ("if you forsake the LORD") or a prediction ("when you forsake the LORD")? In either case, Joshua confronts the nation with a future that portends calamity. The "foreign gods" of which he speaks (*ʾĕlōhēy nēker*, "gods of the foreigner") are specifically the deities of Canaan (Gen 35:2, 4; Deut 31:16; Jer 5:19). By mentioning them, Joshua alludes to another Deuteronomic text, set within the end of a previous phase of the story (Deut 31:16):

> The LORD said to Moses, "Soon you will lie down with your ancestors. Then this people will begin to prostitute themselves to the foreign gods in their midst, the gods of the land into which they are going; they will forsake me, breaking my covenant that I have made with them."

With this prediction in the background, Joshua now intimates that Israel will indeed forsake YHWH and fall prey to the temptations posed by the gods of Canaan. Having experienced the goodness of YHWH *(hēṭîb)*, the nation may one day experience the harm *(hēraʿ)* YHWH can bring. By casting his warning in terms of good and evil, Joshua confirms his dark premonition that YHWH will bring all the evil *(hārāʿ)* he has spoken just as he has brought all the good *(haṭṭôb*; 23:16).

Joshua's rebuttal provides the opportunity for the people to confirm their decision, and they do so with another succinct confession which again joins positive to negative: "No, we will serve the LORD" (v. 21).[13] On the basis of this second confession Joshua acknowledges the choice the people have made, although once again his response is less than enthusiastic: "You are witnesses against yourselves that you have chosen the LORD, to serve him" (v. 22a). Though softer in tone than his response to the people's first declaration, these words are still foreboding.

---

[13] For emphasis, the people employ the same particle *(kî)* that Joshua has just used with good effect to warn (or predict?) the consequences of apostasy (v. 21; cf. v. 17): *lō kî ʾet-yhwh naʿăbōd*.

To be "a witness against" (*ʿēd bĕ*) is a phrase generally associated with an indictment for wrongdoing (Num 5:13; Deut 19:16; Prov 24:28; Mic 1:2). In this context, it now suggests that Joshua is issuing a proleptic indictment of the apostasy. The rejoinder thus confirms the decision that the people have made but implicitly calls them to acknowledge that they will not honor it. Their response ("we are witnesses;" v. 22b) thus assumes an air of self-recrimination even as it confirms a choice for YHWH.[14]

As he does during his initial charge, Joshua demands that the people immediately authenticate their decision by changing their disposition and putting away the other gods in their midst (v. 23, cf. v. 14). The second demand corresponds to the first through the use of an initial *wĕʿattâ* ("now therefore;" v. 14, "then;" v. 23), and the reference to "foreign gods" (i.e. the gods of the land) completes the catalogue of other gods (joining those "beyond the River" and "in Egypt") which Joshua has told the people to put away. By bracketing Israel's repeated confessions with summons to inner devotion to YHWH and outward rejection of all other gods, the text stresses that serving YHWH encompasses both inclination and behavior. Once again the people respond affirmatively with a confession of YHWH as their God and a promise to obey his voice (v. 24).[15] The entire dialogue thus illustrates both Israel's determination to serve YHWH and its potential to fall prey to the allure of the other gods. Moreover, the repeated demand that Israel put away the other gods in its midst reveals a community that has not uniformly embraced the Deuteronomic program of homogeneity and singularity. Even at the conclusion of the story, we discover that the gods of Mesopotamia and Egypt still compete with YHWH for the loyalty of the people. The Israelites have achieved victories and occupied the land given by YHWH, all the while carrying with them the gods of their ancestors (v. 14) and even making room for the gods of Canaan (v. 23). The reader therefore has good reason to believe Joshua's predictions. Israel still seems infatuated by the multiplicity that characterizes all other peoples and the objects of their worship. Other gods are at Shechem even as the people devote themselves to YHWH and no other.

---

[14] Joshua's pronouncement that the people are witness against themselves is uttered with particular emphasis, literally "witnesses are *you* against yourselves because *you* have chosen for yourselves YHWH to serve him." The repetition of the independent pronoun *ʾattem* (italicized in the above translation) sets the people against Joshua and reinforces the sense that Joshua is issuing an indictment. In the MT, the people's final response is even more terse. They simply utter the word "witnesses."

Set In Stone: 24:25-28

Joshua formalizes Israel's decision to serve YHWH by enacting a covenant. The action is somewhat puzzling, since there is no mention that YHWH takes part in the ceremony. This covenant thus does not seem so much a pact enacted between the people and their God as a pact that the people make with themselves. Joshua enacts the covenant to concretize the solemn commitment the nation has just made. Having agreed to be witnesses against themselves, the people now participate in a ritual that places them under obligation to their own confession.[16] No details of the ritual, however, are given. Although of significant import for present and future Israel, the narrator does not devote any attention to it beyond reporting that Joshua made "statutes and ordinances for them at Shechem" (v. 25).[17] For the narrator, it is enough to report that it codified the people's decision to serve YHWH. The thrust of the entire episode has led the reader to view covenant not so much as the execution of commandments and decrees but rather as a freely-chosen and exclusive commitment of heart and life to the God who has brought the community into being.

Joshua reinforces the sense of covenant as self-obligation by writing "these words in the book of the law of God" and setting up a large stone under the oak at the sanctuary of God (v. 26). Within the context of the episode, "these words" are the words of choosing and commitment which the people have repeatedly uttered. The "book of the law of God" is a strange phrase which establishes a continuity with past choices (cf. Deut 31:9, 24) but also carefully distances *this* "law" from that of Moses (cf. 1:7-8; 8:30-35). Within the book of Joshua, Moses and his book of law have been associated with the theme of obedience to commandments. By referring to "the book of the law," the narrator thus forges a strong link with all that was given through Moses.[18] However,

---

[15] The issue of obedience enters the dialogue at this late point, and not earlier, so that the reader will understand that the concept of exclusive devotion to YHWH lies at the very heart of Israel's corporate life.

[16] The form and function of this covenant has been a hotly debated issue within scholarship. For a brief discussion and bibliography see R. Nelson, *Joshua*, OTL (Louisville: Westminster John Knox, 1997) 276–8.

[17] The phrase "statutes and ordinances" is a hendiadys (a device that communicates a single concept by two connected terms) which probably means something like "fixed rule" (Nelson, *Joshua,* 277). The sense conveyed by the note is that Joshua makes the nation's decision official.

[18] The text does not specify whether Joshua is adding to the body of law contained in Moses' book or whether he is writing a completely new book.

by labeling it "the book of the law *of God*" the narrator also prompts the reader to think differently of "the book," to view its quintessence as an act of choosing rather than the execution of diverse commandments. Israel's relationship with YHWH is defined, *at its core,* by the holistic act of choosing rather than by particular expressions of obedience. Joshua undergirds this perspective by installing a large stone and declaring that it has also heard words and stands as a witness (v. 27). The words that the stone has heard, he declares, are those of YHWH, who opened the episode with a summary of his mighty acts on behalf of the nation (vv. 2-13). Having heard all that YHWH has done, the stone also stands ready to indict Israel if it ever responds to YHWH's graciousness with falsehood. As one who has heard these words, Joshua identifies with the people ("the words of the LORD that he spoke to us") but, on the issue of response, he separates himself from recrimination ("it shall be a witness against you"; cf. vv. 19-20). With this final warning, Joshua dismisses the people into their future in the land (v. 28).

Grave Plots: 24:29-33

Reports of death and burial conclude the book of Joshua and bring it to a close on a note of sobering finality. The end of the book tells of the ends of Joshua and Eleazar and, by extension, the end of an era. The scope of ending is expanded even wider by the burial of Joseph's bones, which signifies the completion of the much longer story that extends back to the early chapters of Genesis (cf. Gen 50:22-26). The various ends promise a sense of satisfaction. Joshua now bears the title "the servant of the LORD," an epithet previously reserved only for Moses, and the title has acquired deeper significance through its thematic connection with the ceremony at Shechem. "Serving the LORD" is the leitmotif that binds the words of Joshua and the people. During the ceremony Joshua declares, "as for me and my household, we will serve the LORD" (v. 15). Now he is linked with Moses as the epitome of devotion to YHWH. The whole book is thus bracketed by references to the deaths of YHWH's servants, beginning with the death of Moses the servant of the LORD (1:1-2) and ending with the death of Joshua the servant of the LORD (24:29). In addition, the sequence of reports repeats the language used throughout Joshua to signify legitimate possession and occupation of the land. The story draws to a close with burials in Joshua's "own inheritance" *(naḥălātô),* in the portion of ground *(ḥelqat haśśādeh)* purchased by Jacob, and in the town which had been given *(nittan-lô)* to Eleazar in the hill country of Ephraim. The burials of Israelite dignitaries in the land provide the finishing touches to the program of the entire book, imbuing the possession and occupation of the land with a sense of permanence.

Although they are independent units, the components of this final segment are united by thematic threads. After reporting the burial of Joshua, the narrator picks up the theme of serving YHWH and connects it to all those of Joshua's generation (v. 31), "Israel served the LORD all the days of Joshua, and all the days of the elders who outlived Joshua and had known all the work that the LORD did for Israel." The report allows the narrator to repeat the connection between "serving" and YHWH's acts; knowing what YHWH has done and serving YHWH are closely linked by the language of the report. The next piece, the burial of Joseph's bones, also touches on the death of Joshua by putting the notion of land as "inheritance" into a broader perspective (v. 32). The burials of Joseph in his inheritance and Joshua in his inheritance connect Israel's posterity to its present experience. The purchase of the plot at Shechem, where Israel has just gathered to confess its devotion to YHWH, originally foreshadowed the possession of the entire land. Joseph's burial in that plot, in textual proximity to the burial of Joshua, one of his descendants through Ephraim, signals the realization of the hope which it represented. The final notice, the burial of Eleazar, completes the section by noting that the burial took place in the town given to him, just as Joshua was buried in the town of his inheritance (v. 33). Eleazar has appeared at key points in the narrative (14:1; 17:4; 19:51; 21:1), and his death severs Israel's last link with the era of occupation.

This well-constructed ending, however, does not succeed in closing the story, which overflows the narrative's discrete boundaries. Although the past and present have been put to rest, Joshua's grim admonitions have introduced a future filled with portents of doom. The burial reports convey a sense of finality and completion, but the reader is now aware that the story has not in fact come to an end. Its conclusion has yet to be told, and it does not necessarily lead to a sense of rest and satisfaction, for the future does not look bright for Israel.

Looking Ahead

Just as the burial reports connect Joshua to a larger story, so also does the sense of openness conveyed by the reports of peoples that remain and the portents of failure and doom. The burial reports signal an end and effectively close what has gone before. The ancestral promise of the land has now been fulfilled. YHWH has brought Israel into the land of Canaan and has enabled the nation to occupy it.[19] However, the occupation of the land remains incomplete, pointing to a future under-girded by the faithfulness of YHWH but threatened by the peoples of the land and by Israel's susceptibility to their influence. This sense of in-completeness hints that the larger story does not end here. Joshua thus assumes a Janus-like character, looking into the past and the future at the same time.

Judges, the book which follows Joshua in the canon, picks up the final message of Joshua (that Israel is a people constituted by choices), and makes it the focal point of the continuing story. However, Judges makes the point in the negative, reversing many of the themes of Joshua. The plot of Joshua moves in the direction of solidarity and con-solidation. "All Israel" acts as a unit and wins victories over powerful kings in obedience to the commands of Moses, Joshua, and YHWH. How-ever, Judges moves in the opposite direction. It begins by depicting a piecemeal conquest, in which each of the tribes attempt to subjugate and settle their respective territories (1:1-36). The image which con-fronts the reader is one of a fragmented Israel comprising individual tribes that pursue their own ends and aspirations. Following this overview, the narrator of Judges succinctly reintroduces the theme of choices (and the covenants that signify them) and sets it at the center of Israel's life and aspirations (2:1b-3):

> I brought you up from Egypt, and brought you into the land that I had promised to your ancestors. I said, "I will never break my covenant with you. For your part, do not make a covenant with the inhabitants of this land; tear down their altars." But you have not obeyed my command. See what you have done! So now I say, I will not drive them out before you; but they shall become adversaries to you, and their gods shall be a snare to you.

Significantly, choosing is now expressed in negative terms. YHWH will not break his covenant with Israel, and Israel must not make a cove-nant with the peoples of the land. But Israel has not obeyed YHWH's command, and YHWH will not drive out the remaining peoples.

The remaining plot of Judges takes the shape of a spiral which charts the steady disintegration of the nation. After reporting the death of Joshua (2:6-10), the narrator describes this spiral in a programmatic summary that focuses on Israel's inveterate inclination to choose the

[19] For a survey of the thematic significance of the land promise within the Penta-teuch, see David J. A. Clines, *The Theme of the Pentateuch*, 2nd ed. (Sheffield: Sheffield Academic Press, 1996).

gods of the land and transgress the covenant (2:11-23). Subsequent events reveal what happens when Israel abandons its center. Military operations involve only groups of tribes (4:9-10; 6:35; 11:8), and fundamental bonds of kinship dissolve as petty jealousies and dissensions set tribes against each other. As the book approaches its conclusion, the fabric of Israelite society unravels. Parents kill children (11:34-40), Israelites slaughter their kindred (12:1-6) and deliver their own into the hands of their enemies (15:11-13), children deal deceitfully with their parents (14:1-9; 17:1-13), a tribe is separated irrevocably from its tribal allotment (18:31), and the most basic bond, that between a man and woman, is demolished in a brutal orgy of bloodshed, rape, and kidnaping (20:1–21:25). Judges as a whole confirms that Israel will exist as a coherent nation only as it chooses YHWH. But that is another story.

FOR FURTHER READING

The following comprises a selected list of works for additional study. I have grouped them under headings related to the study of Joshua. The works under each heading encompass a wide range of perspectives and methods and include literature both within biblical studies and outside the discipline.

COMMENTARIES AND MONOGRAPHS ON JOSHUA

Butler, T. C. *Joshua*. WBC 7. Waco: Word, 1983.

Boling, R. G. *Joshua*. AB 6. Garden City: Doubleday, 1982.

Coote, R. B. "The Book of Joshua." Pages 553–719 in *The New Interpreter's Bible*. Vol. 2. Nashville: Abingdon, 1998.

Hawk, L. D. *Every Promise Fulfilled: Contesting Plots in Joshua*. LCBI. Louisville: Westminster John Knox, 1991.

Hess, R. S. *Joshua*. TOTC. Downers Grove: InterVarsity, 1996.

Howard, D. M., Jr. *Joshua*. NAB. Nashville: Broadman & Holman, 1998.

Mitchell, G. *Together in the Land*. JSOTSup 134. Sheffield: Sheffield University, 1993.

Nelson, R. D. *Joshua*. OTL. Louisville: Westminster John Knox, 1997.

ARTICLES AND ESSAYS ON JOSHUA

Begg, C. "The Function of Josh 7:1–8:29 in the Deuteronomistic History." *Bib* 67 (1986) 320–34.

Brekelmans, C. "Joshua 24: Its Place and Function." *Congress Volume Leuven 1989*. VTSup 43. Ed. by J. A. Emerton, 1–9. Leiden: E. J. Brill, 1991.

Campbell, K. M. "Rahab's Covenant." *VT* 22 (1972) 243–4.

Culley, R. "Stories of the Conquest: Joshua 2, 6, 7, and 8." *HAR* 8 (1984) 25–44.

Fensham, C. "The Treaty between Israel and the Gibeonites." *BA* 27 (1964) 96–100.

Grintz, J. M. "The Treaty of Joshua with the Gibeonites." *JAOS* 86 (1966) 113–26.

Gunn, D. M. "Joshua and Judges." *The Literary Guide to the Bible*. Ed. by R. Alter and F. Kermode, 102–21. Cambridge: Harvard/Belknap, 1987.

Hawk, L. D. "Strange Houseguests: Rahab, Lot, and the Dynamics of Deliverance." *Reading Between Texts*. Ed by D. N. Fewell, 89–97. Louisville: Westminster John Knox, 1992.

Kearney, P. "The Role of the Gibeonites in the Deuteronomic History." *CBQ* 35 (1973) 1–19.

Liver, J. "The Literary History of Joshua IX." *JSS* 8 (1963) 227–43.

McCarthy, D. J. "The Theology of Leadership in Joshua 1–9." *Bib* 52 (1971) 165–75.

Weinfeld, M. "The Pattern of the Israelite Settlement in Cannan." *Congress Volume Jerusalem 1986*. VTSup 40, 270–83. Leiden: E. J. Brill, 1988.

_____. "The Extent of the Promised Land—the Status of Transjordan." *Das Land Israel in biblischer Zeit*, GTA 2. Ed. by G. Strecker, 59–75. Göttingen: Vandenhoeck & Ruprecht, 1983.

Wenham, G. J. "The Deuteronomic Theology of the Book of Joshua." *JBL* 90 (1971) 140–8.

Younger, K. L. "The 'Conquest' of the South (Jos 10, 28–30)." *BZ* 39 (1995) 255–64.

SOCIAL IDENTITY

Barth. F. "Introduction." *Ethnic Groups and Boundaries: The Social Organization of Cultural Difference*. Ed. by F. Barth, 9–38. Boston: Little, Brown, 1969.

Beal, T. K. and D. M. Gunn, eds. *Reading Bibles, Writing Bodies: Identity and the Book*. London: Routledge, 1997.

Brett, M. G. "Interpreting Ethnicity: Method, Hermeneutics, Ethics." *Ethnicity and the Bible*. BIS 19. Ed. by M. G. Brett, 3–22. Leiden: E. J. Brill, 1996.

Cohn, R. L. "Before Israel: The Canaanites as Other in Biblical Tradition." *The Other in Jewish Thought and History: Constructions of Jewish Culture and Identity*. Ed. by L. J. Silberstein and R. L. Cohn, 74–90. New York: New York University, 1994.

Edelman, D. "Ethnicity and Early Israel." *Ethnicity and the Bible*. BIS 19. Ed. M. G. Brett, 25–55. Leiden: E. J. Brill, 1996.

Davies, G. F. *Ezra & Nehemiah*. BO. Collegeville: The Liturgical Press, 1999.

Goldenberg, R. *The Nations That Know Thee Not*. New York: New York University, 1998.

Gunn, D. M. "Colonialism and the Vagaries of Scripture: Te Kooti in Canaan (A Story of Bible and Dispossession in Aotearoa/New Zealand)." *God in the Fray: A Tribute to Walter Brueggemann*. Ed. by T. L. Linafelt and T. K. Beal, 127–42. Minneapolis: Augsburg Fortress, 1998.

Habel, N. *The Land Is Mine: Six Biblical Land Ideologies*. OBT. Minneapolis: Augsburg Fortress, 1995.

———."Conquest and Dispossession: Justice, Joshua, and Land Rights." *Pacifica* 4 (1991), 76–92.

Hawk, L. D. "The Problem with Pagans." *Reading Bible, Writing Bodies*. Ed. by T. K. Beal and D. M. Gunn, 153–63. London: Routledge, 1997.

Hoffman, Y. "The Deuteronomistic Concept of the Herem." *ZAW* 111 (1999) 196–210.

Hostetter, E. C. *Nations Mightier and More Numerous*. BDS 4. N. Richland Hills: Bibal, 1995.

Jobling, D. S. "'The Jordan a Boundary': Transjordan in Israel's Ideological Geography." *The Sense of Biblical Narrative II*. JSOTSup 39. Sheffield: JSOT, 1986.

Kaminsky, J. S. *Corporate Responsibility in the Hebrew Bible*, JSOTSup 196. Sheffield: Sheffield University, 1995.

Linafelt, T. and T. K. Beal. *Ruth & Esther*. BO. Collegeville: The Liturgical Press, 1999.

Miller, P. D. "The Gift of God: The Deuteronomic Theology of the Land." *Int* 23 (1969) 451–65.

Mullen, T. J., Jr., *Narrative History and Ethnic Boundaries: The Deuteronomistic Historian and the Creation of Israelite National Identity*. Atlanta: Scholars, 1993.

Nash, M. *Ethnicity and Nationalism*. London: Pluto, 1993.

Nelson, R. D. "*Ḥērem* and the Deuteronomic Social Conscience." *Deuteronomy and Deuteronomistic Literature*, BETL 133. Ed. by M. Vervenne and J. Lust, 39–54. Leuven: Leuven University, 1997.

Rowlett, L. "Inclusion, Exclusion, and Marginality in the Book of Joshua." *JSOT* 55 (1992) 15–23.

Schäfer-Lichtenberger, C. "ЈHWH, Israel und die Völker aus der Perspektive von Dtn 7." *BZ* 40 (1996) 194–218.

_____. "Bedeutung und Funktion von Herem in biblisch-hebräischen Texten." *BZ* 38 (1994) 270–5.

Schwartz, R. M. *The Curse of Cain: The Violent Legacy of Monotheism*. Chicago: University of Chicago, 1997.

Smith, A. D. *The Ethnic Origins of Nations*. Oxford: Basic Blackwell, 1986.

Smith, J. Z. "What a Difference a Difference Makes." *To See Ourselves as Others See Us: Christians, Jews, "Others" in Late Antiquity.* Ed. by J. Neusner and E. S. Frerichs, 3–48. Chico: Scholars, 1995.

Sparks, K. L. *Ethnicity and Identity in Ancient Israel.* Winona Lake: Eisenbrauns, 1998.

Sternberg, M. *Hebrews Between Cultures: Group Portraits and National Literature.* Bloomington: Indiana University, 1998.

Stulman, L. "Encroachment in Deuteronomy: An Analysis of the Social World of the D Code." *JBL* 109 (1990) 613–32.

Thompson, L. L. "The Jordan Crossing: Ṣidqôt Yahweh and World Building," *JBL* 100 (1981) 343–58.

Warrior, R. A. "A Native American Perspective: Canaanites, Cowboys, and Indians." *Voices from the Margin: Interpreting the Bible in the Third World.* 2nd ed. Ed. by R. S. Sugirtharajah, 277–85. Maryknoll: Orbis, 1995.

Composition and Text

Auld, A. G. *Joshua Retold: Synoptic Perspectives.* OTS. Edinburgh: T&T Clark, 1998.

_____. *Joshua, Moses and the Land.* Edinburgh: T & T Clark, 1980.

Kallai, Z. *Historical Geography of the Bible: The Tribal Territories of Israel.* Jerusalem: Magnes, 1986.

Lohfink, N. "Geschichtstypologisch Orientierte Textstrukturen in den Büchern Deuteronomium und Josua." *Deuteronomy and Deuteronomic Literature: Festschrift C. W. Brekelmans.* Ed. by M. Vervenne and J. Lust, 133–60. Leuven: Leuven University, 1997.

Mayes, A. D. H. *The Story of Israel between Settlement and Exile.* London: SCM, 1983.

Noth, M. *The Deuteronomistic History.* JSOTSup 15. Trans. by J. Doull et al. Sheffield: Sheffield University, 1981.

Peckham, B. "The Composition of Joshua 3–4." *CBQ* 46 (1984) 413–31.

Weinfeld, M. *Deuteronomy and the Deuteronomic School.* Oxford: Oxford University, 1972.

Younger, K. L. *Ancient Conquest Accounts: A Study in Ancient Near Eastern and Biblical History Writing.* JSOTSupn 98. Sheffield: Sheffield University, 1990.

Narrative Studies

Alter, R. *The World of Biblical Literature.* New York: Basic, 1992.

_____. *The Art of Biblical Narrative.* New York: Basic, 1981.

Berlin, A. *Poetics and Interpretation of Biblical Narrative*. BLS 9. Sheffield: Almond, 1983.

Chatman, S. *Story and Discourse*. Ithaca: Cornell University, 1978.

Crites, S. "The Narrative Quality of Experience." *JAAR* 39 (1971) 291–311.

Eslinger, L. *Into the Hands of the Living God*. JSOTSup 84. Sheffield: Sheffield University, 1989.

Fewell, D. M. and D. M. Gunn. *Gender, Power & Promise: The Subject of the Bible's First Story*. Nashville: Abingdon, 1993.

Genette, G. *Narrative Discourse*. Ithaca: Cornell University, 1980.

Gunn, D. M. and D. N. Fewell. *Narrative in the Hebrew Bible*. OBS. Oxford: Oxford University, 1993.

Polzin, R. *Moses and the Deuteronomist: A Literary Study of the Deuteronomistic History*. New York: Seabury, 1980.

Ricoeur, P. *Time and Narrative*. Trans. K. McLaughlin and D. Pellauer. 3 vol. Chicago: University of Chicago, 1984–8.

Rimmon-Kenan, S. *Narrative Fiction: Contemporary Poetics*. London: Methuen, 1983.

Sternberg, M. *The Poetics of Biblical Narrative: Ideological Literature and the Drama of Reading*. Bloomington: Indiana University, 1985.

White, H. "The Value of Narrativity in the Representation of Reality." *CI* 7 (1980) 5–27.

SCRIPTURE INDEX

SUBJECT INDEX